Fieldwork
under Fire

Mozambique
(Photo: Joel Chizíane)

Fieldwork under Fire

Contemporary Studies of Violence and Survival

EDITED BY

Carolyn Nordstrom
Antonius C. G. M. Robben

UNIVERSITY OF CALIFORNIA PRESS
Berkeley   Los Angeles   London

University of California Press
Berkeley and Los Angeles, California

University of California Press
London, England

Copyright © 1995 by
The Regents of the University of California

Library of Congress Cataloging-in-Publication Data
Fieldwork under fire: contemporary studies of violence and survival /
    edited by Carolyn Nordstrom, Antonius C. G. M. Robben.
        p.   cm.
    Includes bibliographical references and index.
    ISBN 0–520–08993–6 (cloth: alk. paper).—ISBN 0–520–08994–4
(pbk.: alk. paper)
    1. Ethnology—Field work.   2. Violence—Research.   3. Violence—
Moral and ethical aspects.   4. Ethnologists—Crimes against.
5. Anthropological ethics.   I. Nordstrom, Carolyn, 1953–
II. Robben, Antonius C. G. M.
GN346.F536   1995
303.6'072—dc20   95–6235
                                                                                    CIP

Printed in the United States of America

1 2 3 4 5 6 7 8 9

CONTENTS

The Anthropology and Ethnography of Violence and Sociopolitical Conflict

Antonius C. G. M. Robben and Carolyn Nordstrom

We wondered, while writing this introduction, in which state of mind this book would be read. Which wars will rumble through its words? Which images will provide a visual background to the chapters presented here? As we were editing the contributions, we could not help but think and talk about the war in the Balkans. The term "ethnic cleansing" made us remember other times and other wars and made us realize that the place may be different, and the suffering unique, but that everyday life under war is at any place and any time confusing and full of anguish. This realization is so obvious that it is almost banal, yet why is this perennial chaos of warfare and the incomprehensibility of violence for its victims so seldom addressed in scholarly writings? Why do we find so many intricate studies about war and so few about human suffering? Let us compare two quotations that were written half a century apart.

> I'm writing from the shed. It is half past five in the afternoon, you can hear shots outside and the exploding of mortar shells. Father and Asim are asleep, grandma is playing cards. How idyllic, isn't it? We are already spending our fifth month in this way. Terrible. I do not know where to begin. . . . It is so difficult to write this. There is so much, and I am so confused. Now and then I have a crisis, just like everybody. I'm afraid, depressed. Everything is so hopeless. I don't know if you can understand this at all. Probably not. At the beginning we didn't understand anything either. When they bombed us, this turned out to be nothing compared to everything that happened thereafter.

> Strange are the ways of life in the ghetto, abounding in surprises of every sort. Nothing is logically predictable, and people often wrack their brains over one or another turn of events that had seemed completely clear but underwent a change at the last minute. . . . What is the determining factor here? What influences this situation? Why do omens of improvement so

often end with things becoming worse and vice versa? These are questions that disturb the entire population and for which no answers can be found, answers that may not even be found before the war is over! It could be whim, and it could be necessity!

The first quotation is from a letter written on August 14, 1992, by a woman in Sarajevo and sent to her brother living in exile in the Netherlands (reprinted in *De Volkskrant*, 10 September 1992). The second quotation was written on August 30, 1942, and comes from the hand of an official chronicler of the Lódz ghetto (Dobroszycki 1984:245–246). We begin with these stories from Europe to emphasize that violence is not somewhere else—in a third world country, on a distant battlefield, or in a secret interrogation center—but that it is an inescapable fact of life for every country, nation, and person, whether or not they are personally touched by direct violence.

Such stories as these are all too common: we could as easily have drawn similar ones from Somalia, Guatemala, Sri Lanka, the United States, Mozambique, Ireland, Spain, and China. SIPRI, a Swedish conflict research and documentation center, has identified 32 major wars in 1992 ("major" being defined as producing over one thousand casualties a year). If we consider conflicts with under one thousand killed annually, then the figure rises to 150. And if we expand our definition according to greater anthropological sensibilities to include the pressing conflicts in many people's lives—riots, gang warfare, tribal genocide, and forms of terror warfare such as rape and torture—then we find that the number of people directly affected by violence extends into the hundreds of millions.

The foregoing quotations have another significance that is of central importance to this volume: they evoke everyday experiences of violence in its myriad manifestations, ranging from war to popular protest, from rape to the contestations surrounding rumors of violence, from moral discourses concerning conflict to the tragedies of senseless brutality. We want to focus on the experiential dimension of conflict, on the ways in which people live their lives in contests marred by inescapable violence. We believe that violence is a dimension of people's existence, not something external to society and culture that "happens" to people.

By way of explaining this, we return once again to the example of the Balkans. As one peace plan after another is being rejected, and as one truce after another is being violated, a mood has been growing among many people and politicians in Europe and the United States that there is simply no solution to the war because the combatants "have gone crazy," "are acting like barbarians," or "are drawing on their basest instincts." The war no longer belongs to the realm of political conflict; it has regressed to a level of inhumanity that is outside normal social life, an unreal world where soldiers enjoy killing and rape is a military strategy.

While such sentiments are common, we think they represent a dangerous misconception. For too many people everywhere in the world, violence is an all too human reality. This includes the victims of violence but also the perpetrators who themselves are caught in spiraling conflicts that their actions have set in motion but that they can no longer control. To understand their plight and to try to begin to forge solutions, we must confront violence head on, place it squarely in the center of the lives and cultures of the people who suffer it, precisely where they themselves find it. Violence may not be functional, and it is certainly not tolerable, but it is not outside the realm of human society, or that which defines it as human. As this book shows, violence is not enjoyable, except perhaps for the pathological few. Nor is it a devolution into a seething "proto-" or "precultural" set of behaviors. Like creativity and altruism, violence is culturally constructed. As with all cultural products, it is in essence only a potential—one that gives shape and content to specific people within the context of particular histories. Little can be said about the concrete form of violence or the content of human existence pursued outside the constraints of society and culture. Warfare is, as Margaret Mead (1964) says, "only an invention."

Moreover, these quotations express the confusion of cultures and communities in crisis and how life has to be reinvented each time anew under ever-changing circumstances. Violence is confusing and inconclusive. Wars are emblematic for the extremes that people's existential disorientation may reach. Such life-threatening violence demonstrates the paralysis as well as the creativity of people coping under duress, a duress for which few are prepared. Even soldiers, who have been trained to deal with the risks and uncertainties of action on the battlefield and have been prepared to carry out dangerous and complex tasks under enemy fire, cannot rely on the routines of exercise and command. The everydayness of war is a never-ending stream of worries about the next meal, the next move, and the next assault. This immediacy of action characterizes not only war but any form of violence. There are few social prescriptions on how to cope and survive in violent situations.

This emphasis on how people come to grips with life under siege, on the experience, practice, and everydayness of violence, makes attention to fieldwork conditions necessary. The emotional intensity of the events and people studied, the political stakes that surround research on violence, and the haphazard circumstances under which fieldwork is conducted entwine fieldwork and ethnography. These tensions weave their way through the whole of the anthropological endeavor—coloring the lives and perspectives of the researchers and those they study alike. This introduction therefore focuses on the three principal concerns of this book: the everyday experiences of people who are the victims and perpetrators of violence; the relationship between field-workers and the people studied, including the distinct research problems and experiences of ethnographers who study situations of violence; and the theoretical issues that emerge from studying topics that involve personal danger. These introductory remarks elaborate on the notion implicit in all the chapters in this book, that the ontics of violence—the lived experience of violence—and the epistemology of violence—the ways of knowing and reflecting about violence—are not separate. Experience and interpretation are inseparable for perpetrators, victims, and ethnographers alike. Anthropology on this level involves a number of responsibilities above and beyond those associated with more traditional ethnography: responsibilities to the field-worker's safety, to the safety of his or her informants, and to the theories that help to forge attitudes toward the reality of violence, both expressed and experienced.

THE ETHNOGRAPHY OF VIOLENCE

Sociopolitical violence can be approached in many ways. At some level, however, to be able to discuss violence, one must go to where violence occurs, research it as it takes place. This volume seeks to address these understandings, placing ethnography and the ethnographer in the context of violence.

Firsthand ethnography of violence does not provide us with an uncontested set of explanations for what we have seen. As Michael Taussig (1987) has pointed out, violence is slippery; it escapes easy definitions and enters the most fundamental features of people's lives. Violence is formative; it shapes people's perceptions of who they are and what they are fighting for across space and time—a continual dynamic that forges as well as affects identities (Feldman 1991). The complexity of violence extends to the field-workers and their theories as well. Understandings of violence *should* undergo a process of change and reassessment in the course of fieldwork and writing because it is not only unrealistic but dangerous as well to go to the field with ready-made explanations of violence so as to "find truths" to support our theories. For this reason, we do not attempt to provide any overarching theory. A dynamic approach to violent conflict mitigates against essentialist and singular definitions and against the reification of violence. As Allen Feldman (1991) has noted, theory emerges from experience. The danger lies in making definitions of violence appear too polished and finished—for the reality never will be.

Most of the chapters in this book have not been constructed toward definitive conclusions, but their arguments are developed processually. Very much like the lives of the people they describe, they portray a growing understanding of violent conflict that proceeds as in a hermeneutic circle where fragmentary and aggregate perspectives take turns. This understanding is constructed as much from the many stories ethnographers hear from victims and perpetrators as from their own experiences written down in their field notes.

Researching and writing about violence will never be a simple endeavor. The subject is fraught with assumptions, presuppositions, and contradictions. Like power, violence is essentially contested: everyone knows it exists, but no one agrees on what actually constitutes the phenomenon. Vested interests, personal history, ideological loyalties, propaganda, and a dearth of firsthand information ensure that many "definitions" of violence are powerful fictions and negotiated half-truths.

Violence is also an intricately layered phenomenon. Each participant, each witness to violence, brings his or her own perspective. These testimonies can vary dramatically. There is the political reality: the doctrines, deeds, and behind-the-scenes machinations of power brokers. There is the military reality: the strategies, tactics, and loyalties of commanders; the camaraderie, actions, and briefings of soldiers. There is the intellectual reality, forged in coffee shops and the halls of academia, as well as the journalist's world of gossip and frontline vignettes. There is also the psychological reality: the fear, the anxiety, and the regression and repression among refugees and prisoners of war. And then there is the reality of life on the front lines: the stories and actions of people as disparate as perpetrators and casualties, advisers and arms merchants, mercenaries and doctors, criminals and relief workers.

Ethnography can be conducted at any of these levels of warfare. But for the authors in this book, the most pressing reality is that of sociopolitical violence enacted in the center of civilian populations, social process, and cultural life. It is the noncombatant as well as the combatant, the everyday, the mundane, and the not so mundane spheres of life that are the social field of violence expressed—the targets of terror, the templates on which power contests are carved, the fonts of resistance, and the architects of new social orders and disorders. In peeling back the layers of the many realities that impinge on this question of what violence is, we find that even the most horrific acts of aggression do not stand as isolated exemplars of a "thing" called violence but cast ripples that reconfigure lives in the most dramatic of ways, affecting constructs of identity in the present, the hopes and potentialities of the future, and even the renditions of the past.

Our assertion that violence is a dimension of living does not imply that we regard it as functional. Unlike René Girard (1977), whose understanding of violence as a contention about human existence we acknowledge as valuable, we do not argue that violence serves as a safety valve for intrasocietal tensions. Violence is not functional. Particular forms of violence, such as that exerted by judicial and disciplinary institutions and even certain revolutionary movements, can serve to redress violence, but other instances of violence may raise the levels of disruption.

We prefer to regard violence as a socially and culturally constructed manifestation of a deconstitutive dimension of human existence. Thus there is no fixed form of violence. Its manifestation is as flexible and transformative as the people and cultures who materialize it, employ it, suffer it, and defy it. Violence is not an action, an emotion, a process, a response, a state, or a drive. It may manifest itself as responses, drives, actions, and so on, but attempts to reduce violence to some essential core or concept are counterproductive because they essentialize a dimension of human existence and lead to presenting cultural manifestations of violence as if they were natural and universal. Violence is not reducible to some fundamental principle of human behavior, to a universal base structure of society, or to general cognitive or biological processes. We do not deny that people often construct such general explanations of violence themselves to provide a frame of reference for their troubled lives. These cultural frameworks of understanding are a legitimate object of ethnographic study— even though the research interest of this book lies elsewhere—but these local models should not be confused with theoretical or universal explanations of violence. We want to keep such misguided essentialist approaches in check by remaining closer to the experience of violence and focus on its empirical manifestations.

This focus on the empirical and experiential keeps us from a singular focus on the devastating consequences of violence and guides us to a more inclusive approach to conflict and survival. It is when we try to give empirical content to violence as an issue of human existence that we notice the limitations of a too-restricted preoccupation with death, suffering, power, force, and the infliction of pain and constraint. Most of the time, people are attending to the routine tasks of their lives, to eating, dressing, bathing, working, and conversing. Conceiving of violence as a dimension of living rather than as a domain of death obliges researchers to study violence within the immediacy of its manifestation. War, rebellion, resistance, rape, torture, and defiance, as well as peace, victory, humor, boredom, and ingenuity, will have to be understood together through their expression in the everyday if we are to take the issue of the human construction of existence in earnest. A too-narrow conceptualization of violence prevents us from realizing that what is at stake is not simply destruction but also reconstruction, not just death but also survival.

The political and economic consequences of warfare, the lasting impact on people's futures, and the widespread death, destruction, and suffering are so compelling that they push to the forefront of scholarly and popular attention. However, the lives of those who suffer under violence or are engaged in warfare are not defined exclusively in global political, economic, social, or military terms but also in the small, often creative, acts of the everyday. This is why Erich Maria Remarque's *All Quiet on the Western Front,* a sensitive portrayal of life in the trenches and its lasting emotional legacy to the survivors, is such an intriguing account of World War I.

> We are at rest five miles behind the front. Yesterday we were relieved, and now our bellies are full of beef and haricot beans. We are satisfied and at peace. Each man has another mess-tin full for the evening; and, what is more, there is a double ration of sausage and bread. That puts a man in fine trim. (Remarque 1958:7)

These experiences are not restricted to trenches and battlefields. The fear of a woman who under the threat of quat-chewing teenagers armed by local warlords has to cross the streets of Mogadishu with her daily ration of water, the anguish of a peasant in Cambodia that he might step on a land mine on his way to the rice paddy, or the worry of a family in Guatemala that their son who is active in a labor union will disappear after a counterinsurgency raid on their home—all convey realities of war very different from the United Nations resolutions on Somalia and Cambodia or the annual report on human rights violations published by Amnesty International or Americas Watch.

In dealing with these issues, we must admit that what counts in one society as a tolerable level of violence may be condemned in another as excessive. Julia Kristeva (1993), Barbara Johnson (1993), and Wayne C. Booth (1993) have, as scholars, tackled a question that has plagued Amnesty International since its inception: How can anyone determine what are human rights and wrongs, and how can these be universalized, when in fact we have not even determined what such fundamentals as self, identity, existence, society, and culture are?

The work of Michel Foucault, in particular *Discipline and Punish* (1977), broke new ground for social scientists in showing that violence could be embedded in social and material structures that were taken for granted by Western society as normal, natural, just, humane, reasonable, and even enlightened. The disciplinary education of criminals in an edifying prison regime was considered an advance of civilization over the barbaric torture and vengeance of earlier times. Foucault demonstrates the perfidity of the prison system and reveals the violence masked by an Enlightenment rhetoric. Antonio Gramsci's (1971) notion of hegemony has also had a major impact on our understanding of the violence embedded in complex societies. Violence, force, and power are sublimated in social institutions and cultural conceptions of hierarchy that reflect the ideology of the ruling class and have been taken for granted by the subordinate classes. Pierre Bourdieu's (1977, 1984) concept of habitus can serve a similar purpose of explaining how structures of violence may be reproduced in society. A society may have internalized a habitus of violence—for example, systems of racial segregation and gender-based discrimination—that structures social interaction in coercive ways, which, in turn, reproduce the cultural divisions on which those very same forcible practices are based. We would like to add Elias Canetti (1966), whose "stings of command" demonstrate that social interaction in every society, irrespective of its complexity or size, involves practices of coercion that are experienced as natural but are nevertheless oppressive and therefore evoke resentment and resistance. Commands, orders, instructions, directions, and procedures suffuse much of our lives from childhood through adulthood. The irritation that these stings of command leave behind accumulate to intolerable levels, according to Canetti, until they are finally shed by means of a catharsis that evokes feelings of equality and temporarily neutralizes the subordination suffered.

When we look at sociopolitical violence and its relationships to power in their dynamic forms—in their manifestations and not in their institutional framing—then we realize that focal points multiply and that the center is a constantly changing nexus. Thus violence is not *simply* about power, as is tacitly assumed in many studies. We prefer instead to include power within an all-embracing concept of human existence. "Lived experience," writes Michael Jackson (1989:2), "overflows the boundaries of any one concept, or any one society." We cannot affix violence to any single domain or any one locus of power. This indeterminacy confounds traditional political and military theory that postulates political elites and institutions, military commanders and organizations, as the definitive loci of power and conflict. This allows perpetrators and victims of violence to emerge—wherever they find themselves, on a designated battlefield or on urban streets—as core actors in the drama of violence and its resolutions. Traditional studies often reduced the mass of civilian casualties to precisely a "mass" who were victims of something they might not understand and could not control, while portraying power holders as omnipotent instigators. We are concerned here not to pacify the populations exposed to violence as helpless, undifferentiated masses, or to stereotype the perpetrators as either resistance heroes or brutal power mongers. Neither do we want to become entrapped in a distorting dichotomy of victim versus victimizer as if one is, by definition, passive and the other active. In this book, we find the front lines much more volatile and inchoate, with violence being constructed, negotiated, reshaped, and resolved as perpetrators and victims try to define and control the world they find themselves in. For, through violence, people forge moral understandings about the implications of their actions, stand up in the face of brutality, and develop forms of resistance to what they perceive as insufferable oppression.

As the theoreticians cited above demonstrate, violence is not something alien to human existence—which does not mean that it is just—and does not only occur in the space of death. Violence is a dimension of living. Attempts to apply equations of rationality or irrationality or to adjudicate violent events as meaningful or meaningless are beside the point because they are based on the misguided assumption that violence should be understood in terms of its function or objective. Violence may be carried out with logical precision, which does not make it reasonable, and is imbued with meaning, even though often emotionally senseless. Our search is not for cause or function but for understanding and reflexivity. Let us once more invoke Remarque (1958:5) by quoting the almost apologetic preface to his novel.

> This book is to be neither an accusation nor a confession, and least of all an adventure, for death is not an adventure to those who stand face to face with it. It will try simply to tell of a generation of men who, even though they may have escaped its shells, were destroyed by the war.

Remarque wanted his novel to tell about the practice of war in the trenches and the disillusions of their survivors. The novel was so successful because contemporary historians "failed to find explanations to the war that correspond to the horrendous realities, to the actual experience of the war" (Eksteins 1989:291).

We want to be careful, however, not to reduce considerations of violence to frontline, male, Western, European perspectives (Enloe 1983, 1989). We want to caution not only against the fallacy of reducing conflicts to wars, troops, and male aggression but also against theories that have taken this perspective as their basis. As important as Foucault's contribution to studies of power and violence are, feminist critiques of power and Western epistemology by authors such as Nancy Hartsock (1990) provide a scholarly counterhegemonic. Helene Cixous (1993:35) said in her Oxford Amnesty Lecture about the question of human rights,

> What can you not speak of? What is prohibited on pain of death? Publishing statistics of the fifty years of the Nobel Prize is allowed. You can say that there have been 510 men and 24 women among the winners. But thou shalt not use the word *misogyny* about this, nor anything else.

To raise the question of Nobel Laureates in a study of sociopolitical violence is not as tangential as it might seem. As both Foucault and Hartsock have shown, structures of power are reproduced throughout the sociopolitical enterprise, and it is in this way that power retains its hold. We want to divest people of the notion that violence is separate from the larger social and cultural dynamics that shape our lives. This is perhaps nowhere better demonstrated than in Cynthia Enloe's (1993) discussion of the relationships among war, unequal economic development that disenfranchises women's work, rape, assault, and prostitution, and political representation—all products of the militarization of people's lives in a global context. To sequester these into discrete arenas of analytic concern is to provoke conceptual violence. This is a point we have consciously addressed in collecting the essays for this volume: How can we in good conscience, on the experiential level, separate Cathy Winkler's rape in Georgia from those Maria Olujic documents in Croatia, dissociating them as individual tragedy versus collective war?

These horrendous, contradictory realities that characterize war in particular and violence in general—realities that are both prosaic and chaotic, unadventurous and incomprehensible; realities that befall women and men, young and old alike—are found in the contributions to this book. Our emphasis on the everydayness of violence is not intended to suggest that situations of violent conflict are ever routine or taken for granted. Unlike punishment, coercion, and even power, which may become predictable when embedded in structures of domination, violence adds to these an inordinate degree of uncertainty because it is played out at the experiential level. The uncertainty of violence is invariably related to a summoning of fear, terror, and confusion as well as resistance, survival, hope, and creativity.

These reasonless and orderless qualities of violence need more scholarly attention because they have fallen through the meshwork of the institutional analyses of war. What has remained of the chaos of warfare is a rational and coherent structure of death as manifested in such expressions as "a war machine," "do the job," "a surgical operation," and "an order is an order." An unintended and harmful effect is that these analyses tend to rationalize and domesticate, if not justify, the use of violence. The equation of war with the rationality of military strategy and an army of men with a "war machine" turn war into a teleological phenomenon.

Instead of rationalizing violence, this book gives voice to the puzzling contradictions of lives perturbed by violence—puzzling especially to the rationalist, functionalist, and pragmatist—namely, the contradictions of a simultaneous existence of laughter and suffering, fear and hope, indeterminacy and wont, creativity and discipline, and absurdity and commonplace.

NARRATION AND AUTHENTICITY

What legitimacy do anthropologists have to speak for others, in particular, for the victims of violence? Herein lies, arguably, the most important meaning of the expression, the "absurdity of war." *Absurd* literally means insufferable as well as deafened. The absurdity of war is that those whose fate is being decided are seldom heard because they have little voice in the events that determine their lives. They are the muted injuries of war. Just as anthropologists have traditionally given many cultures an image and, in the last few decades, have even given them a history, so do the contributors to this book want to make the voice of victims and perpetrators audible.

"Writing violence," however, will never be a straightforward matter. Gayatri Spivak (1988) challenges Western anthropologists to question their motives in studying non-Western peoples, their (un)witting location in power relationships when they try to "speak" for those among whom they have worked, and the intended and unforeseen effects that accrue from their work. For Spivak, research and representation are irreducibly intertwined with politics and power. The anthropologist who proclaims to "give voice" to those less able to do so, warns Spivak, is often engaged in little better than postcolonial discourse refashioned for a postmodern world (see also Trinh 1989). For Spivak, Western anthropologists are suspect by the mere fact of being Western anthropologists, as is their ability to give voice to others. Unless they undertake serious self-critique—not only as anthropologists but as Westerners, as historical products, and as a nexus and network of privilege—and incorporate that analysis into their presentations and publications, Spivak admonishes, their sincerity and abilities must be doubted.

Spivak has a point. One need only read V. Y. Mudimbe's *The Invention of Africa* (1988) to come to the embarrassing realization of the extent to which the colonial enterprise resonates within anthropological texts. Perhaps more unsettling is the recognition that this is not restricted to North Atlantic justifications of superiority. The sheer force of Western enculturation blinds even declared egalitarians to the destructive beliefs they carry and impart to those they study. We depart for the field bowing under the weight of our own culture, propped up and propelled by Western assumptions we seldom question, shielded from the blaze of complex cultural diversity by a carefully crafted lens of cultural belief that determines as much as clarifies what we see. When we purport to speak for others, we carry the Western enterprise into the mouths of other people. No matter our dedication, we cannot escape the legacy of our culture.

Yet Taussig (1987) and Nancy Scheper-Hughes (1992) equally have a point when they challenge anthropologists to speak out against the injustices they encounter. To do anything less is tantamount to condoning them. If our position grants us privilege, it can be employed to help those with less. For scholars like Taussig and Scheper-Hughes, this is not an option but a duty.

We have reached a stage of theoretical development wherein we can no longer throw out uncomfortable contradictions. The world is not governed by the positivist's dream of rational coherency, and neither must our theories or research practices be. We share Spivak's apprehension about the murky underbelly of academia, mottled with issues of power and authority that are too often obscured behind cultural habit and scholarly rhetoric. We also share Taussig's conviction that we not only can but must write against repression and injustice. We doubt that either can, or should, supplant the other. Just as unavoidable is the contradiction that privilege will be applied for its own benefit and reproduce itself even at the expense of others, while at the same time it will be applied to protest against the inequities and injuries caused by the scramble for gain. We make no attempt to resolve these contradictions. We do not attempt to quiet Spivak with a more liberal dose of Taussig, or vice versa. This dilemma is part and parcel of anthropology as a research tradition that straddles cultures and hierarchies.

Equally pertinent is the question of the ethnographic style of any account of violence, whether it is through eyewitness reports, photographs, or poems. One can count the dead and measure the destruction of property, but victims can never convey their pain and suffering to us, other than through the distortion of word, image, and sound. Any rendition of the contradictory realities of violence imposes order and reason on what has been experienced as chaotic. "Inasmuch as violence is 'resolved' in narrative, the violent event seems also to lose its particularity—i.e., its facthood—once it is written" (Young 1988:15). Together with its facthood, it loses its absurdity and incomprehensibility; paradoxically, the very qualities that we would like to convey.

The transformation of violent events into narrative accounts raises the issue of veracity and authenticity. Given that a distortive mediation of event and text is inevitable, there is still a difference between contemporary and posterior accounts. The difference lies in the moment and voice of the text. "If the diarists' and memoirists' literary testimony is evidence of anything else, it is of the writing act itself. That is, even if narrative cannot document events, or constitute perfect *fact*uality, it can document the *act*uality of writer and text" (ibid., 37). A contemporary account is more authentic than a posterior account—simply because it was written at the time of the event and not with the hindsight of its outcome. However, it cannot make any claim to greater veracity or insight than posterior documentary, fictional, poetic, or cinematographic expressions. The degree of authenticity says little about the truth value of the discourse. Truths are always historical and cannot be frozen in time or pinned down in particular modes of discourse. The questions and issues raised by a narrator are constricted by the historical context in which they are made (see Gadamer 1985). Richard Rorty (1986:3), cited by Jackson (1989:182), observes, "Let us then accept that there is no ahistorical, absolute, nonfinite reality *either outside or within us* that we can reach by adopting a particular discursive style. The *world* is out there, to be sure, and deep within us too, *but not the truth.*" Truth and understanding are therefore always conditional and situated, even though historical understanding may deepen with the progress of time and the study of new instances of violence.

Notwithstanding the historicity of understanding and the paradox that narration infuses a violent event with an order, meaning, and rationality that it does not have, there are ways to reduce the degree of distortion. The closer one remains to the flow of life, to its often erratic progression, the greater understanding one will evoke among the readership about the daily existence of people under siege. The gathering of local knowledge about events through direct experience—also called participant observation—or at least by talking to the protagonists themselves rather than working through secondhand accounts has been one of the hallmarks of anthropology (see, e.g., Barnett and Njama 1966; Edgerton 1990; Feldman 1991; Kapferer 1988; Lan 1985; Lavie 1990; Manz 1988; Nordstrom and Martin 1992; Ranger 1985; Sluka 1989; Tambiah 1986; Taussig 1987; Zulaika 1988). Here, anthropology can make an important contribution to the study of war and violence. However, before anthropologists will be able to engage in a serious dialogue with other disciplines on areas hitherto reserved to the historical and political sciences, it will be important to clarify how fieldwork, description, and understanding are uniquely interrelated in anthropological research.

FIELD EXPERIENCES

Many ethnographers who study violence have experienced bewilderment on first seeing it. There seems to be no higher ground from which to observe the world of violence with relative detachment. Most of the authors in this book have passed through this stage, a stage that might be misinterpreted as culture shock. The tensions experienced by most of us can be better qualified as existential shock. This shock can be felt as much in our own familiar social circle as in another culture. It is a disorientation about the boundaries between life and death, which appear erratic rather than discrete. It is the paradoxical awareness that human lives can be constituted as much around their destruction as around their reconstruction and that violence becomes a practice of negating the reason of existence of others and accentuating the survival of oneself. It is this confrontation of the ethnographer's own sense of being with lives constructed on haphazard grounds that provokes the bewilderment and sense of alienation experienced by most of us.

Existential shock is a highly personal and context-specific research phenomenon. Manifestations of violence to which many American ethnographers have become accustomed and that often do not even reach the news media, so commonplace they have become, such as street assaults, rape, child abuse, and racketeering, may be shocking to ethnographers from other societies.

Existential shock does not occur only in facing the traumas of the field. It is an equally powerful experience to encounter the creative and the hopeful in conditions of violence. Several authors in this volume have looked at the importance of imagination and celebration in traumatic situations. The tragedies of violence can be counterbalanced by the often remarkable solutions people themselves create while facing violence.

The chapters in this volume have been arranged along a temporal continuum of features that speak most profoundly to the realities of studying dangerous topics in dangerous locales. Each author has selected one term or phrase that critically weaves together three concerns: the pressing realities faced by the people undergoing violence; the experiences of the anthropologist as she or he works with these people under difficult circumstances; and the implications this has for responsible theory. Taken as a whole, this collection of terms illustrates many of the core features of what one is likely to confront in experiencing and studying sociopolitical violence. We hope, as studies of this nature grow, that more terms and a greater understanding of existential shock and creative responses to violence will emerge.

We have organized the sequence of chapters to follow the trajectory of the actual field encounter, starting with the researcher's initial confrontation with violent events, moving through the complexities of actual fieldwork, and ending with his or her return from the field with finished notes in hand, or return to the field for second insights. We hope that this book may help ethnographers of violence and sociopolitical conflict to recognize these existential problems, to solve them, and to turn them to their advantage. A fieldwork crisis, as personal as it is political and theoretical, may deepen the understanding of ethnographers, of the people with whom they associate, and of the violence they study. We also hope that this book will take away some of the anxieties of doing fieldwork on violence and will encourage anthropologists to carry out more research projects on this topic.

We begin with a chapter by Ted Swedenburg, who has a considerable autobiographical involvement with the people among whom he conducts fieldwork. When does empathy turn into identification? When do personal lives and professional interests merge in ethnographic fieldwork? Swedenburg's special relation with the Palestinian people provokes doubts about his own identity, which become inextricably intertwined with his research questions. His student years at the American University of Beirut during the 1970s gave him Palestinian friends with whom he shared moments of hardship that left deep emotional traces. His research on the intifada in the West Bank leads him to a self-reflective exegesis, so well captured in the double entendre *prisoners of love*, of Jean Genet's musings on his years with the Palestinians in the early 1970s. Both Genet and Swedenburg felt a sense of exhilaration at witnessing a dangerous world of revolutionary zeal while tasting some of the bittersweet fruits of resistance and retaliation. Yet they also share an unbridgeable cultural detachment from this political movement with which they can never completely identify. Nevertheless, they empathize with the friends who were tortured and killed, abhor the squalid refugee camps, and share the humor and spirit of the people condemned to live in them. Swedenburg finds himself progressively wandering away from a violent, conflict-ridden Middle East and into the homes of dispossessed Palestinians with their laughter and generosity. This passage marks also a return to his childhood memories of the Palestinian people and the indelible impression they continue to leave on him.

One of the most common and also complicated problems of fieldwork on violence is how to deal with *rumors*. Every field-worker runs across a good deal of gossip, hearsay, slander, rumor, and even character assassination, but they acquire inordinate importance in violent situations in which access to such information can make the difference between life and death, safety and injury. Rumors are often the only source of ethnographic information available to the anthropologist under rapidly changing circumstances. The news media are unable to report satisfactorily on the swirl of events, and life-threatening danger prevents the ethnographer from collecting most field data personally. Anna Simons describes the ominous outburst of street violence in Mogadishu on July 14, 1989. Was this the first rumbling of what was to become one of the most devastating conflicts in Somali history? Can the runaway violence of the ensuing civil war be traced to this particular day? Hindsight tends to reduce the contradictory dynamics of violence to linear paths of historical development and to discard contemporary explanations as inconsistent and misinformed. However, Simons shows that misguidance and incongruity are the very stuff out of which history is written. She describes the conflicting rumors that buzzed around the capital and the social networks that were mobilized to gather and verify them. But how to sift fact from fiction, truth from disinformation? Which rumors have been invented, and which correspond to real events? These questions become compelling for ethnographers of violence who have to decide on the spot where to direct their limited time and research attention. Rumor, as Simons shows, provided people in Somalia with a perspective on an unstable situation. It infused the political confusion with an unending flow of seemingly credible but immediately discredited rationales. These rumors—supplanted, discarded, and forgotten almost at the moment of their appearance—turned out to be the meat of fieldwork, important for the coherent historical narrative constructed in hindsight, and therefore deserve as much ethnographic attention as the events that have remained present in the collective memory.

We have touched repeatedly on the uncertainty of violent events. This uncertainty equally besets the anthropologist who becomes suddenly enveloped in a situation of violence for which he or she was not prepared. What research strategy should be chosen? Some try to carry on with their original project as if nothing has changed. Others prefer to leave to safer areas or even decide to abandon the field and return home. Still others would like to study the new situation but hesitate to do so because they feel they lack sufficient preparation on the topic of violence. The following case describes how one ethnographer solved this dilemma. Several Western scholars working in Beijing were irritated when the protests at Tian'anmen Square in May 1989 kept them from visiting the archives and going about their research projects. Frank Pieke, however, realized that the Chinese People's Movement was of historic importance and was begging to be studied. He decided to incorporate this accidental political development in his ongoing research on the economic reform policies of the 1970s. Pieke urges anthropologists neither to stick to the execution of a predetermined research plan nor to start all over again when they run into unexpected events. *Accidental anthropology* is not about emergencies but rather about understanding contingencies in a wider social and cultural context. In very much the same way as the Chinese people, Pieke tries to make sense of the events through a continued dialogue that reaches back to past events that acquire new meaning in the present. Roaming the streets of Tian'anmen Square, he observes the student demonstrations and asks his informants about the protests. He realizes that such involvement is not without risk when he is asked to act as a human shield to protect the students against the bullets from the forces of repression. Pieke's contribution demonstrates the versatility and creative potential of anthropological fieldwork and the unexpected ethical dilemmas that may arise when our informants turn to us for help and compassion.

How is fieldwork affected when people not only ask ethnographers for compassion but also for collaboration and even complicity? What happens to the dialectic of empathy and detachment when victims and perpetrators of violence engage in a politics of truth and try to make ethnographers accept their accounts as the only correct version? Antonius Robben encountered these problems in his research into the contested historical reconstruction of Argentina's "dirty war" as told by its chief protagonists and survivors. Because of the high political and emotional stakes of this violent conflict, strategies of persuasion and concealment were played on him by generals, bishops, politicians, former guerrilla commanders, and human rights leaders. Robben uses the term "ethnographic seduction" to describe these strategies. He turns a frank and probing eye to the question of how the sophisticated rhetoric of Argentine military officers affected his critical sensibility and how the anguished testimonies of their victims enwrapped him in silence and sorrow. Ethnographic seduction disabled his ethnographic gaze as his interlocutors tried to entice him away from a deeper understanding of the troubled 1970s to a surface of reason and emotion. Tossed between rational justifications of war and appeals to universal human rights, torn between compassion for the victims and a sincere attempt to understand their victimizers, Robben slowly begins to apprehend the analogies between the seduction brought down on him by the architects of repression and the dirty war practices of disappearance, deception, and terror wielded on the Argentine people. This awareness allows him to expose the transparency of dictatorial power, recognize the perfidiousness of its domination, and empathize more fully with the victims of repression.

If seduction manipulates ethnographers, then fear, anxiety, and intimidation may paralyze them. Most of the authors in this book have lived through frightening moments, but Linda Green has explicitly analyzed *fear* in a personal and political context. The culture of fear that has reigned in Guatemala since the 1960s has unraveled the social fabric by infusing distrust into friendships and family ties. Fear has entered the social memory and the social practices. Silence and secrecy are the concomitants ethnographers face when they want to carry out fieldwork in a country that is still under authoritarian control, where counterinsurgency units have a free hand and death squads intimidate and assassinate citizens and foreigners alike. Green sketches the eerie calm yet visceral disquiet of everyday life under repression. The culture of subterranean terror in the town of Chicaj fuses with the routines of fieldwork as Green herself is summoned to the military commander who controls the area. Climbing out of the valley and up the hill to the garrison that surveys the town from high above, she retraces the steps and relives some of the fears so many women before her have faced in the innocence that they, and their disappeared husbands and children, had "done nothing wrong." Sharing her experience with the widows of Guatemala, she learns of the importance of silence as a strategy of survival as well as an instrument of repression. Coming to grips with fear does not mean succumbing to the state of normalcy and routinization on which it thrives but to endure its ambiguity in memory and defiance.

Not only chaos but also creativity accompany war and violence. Many of us have felt unable to respond when asked about the reason and sense of violent situations. The rational explanations of the perpetrators contrast sharply with the painful realities of the victims. Carolyn Nordstrom describes how she has struggled and continues to struggle with the senselessness of the violence inflicted on the population of Mozambique by

Renamo's war. The excessive violence deliberately attacks people's sense of family and community, shattering the foundations of their cultural and human existence. Anthropologists themselves, like those among whom they work, cannot remain removed from the impact of witnessing tragedy but must struggle with the implications of working in a context where violence throws into dramatic relief core questions about human nature and culture. She makes clear that the scholarly reflex to explain violent events and portray these in a coherent narrative impose an order and reason that erase the chaos dirty war is intended to produce. Nordstrom eventually abandons this futile search for explanation because war plays "conceptual havoc" with analytical tools and categories developed in the peace and quiet of our comfortable offices. She rejects apologetic rationalizations of warfare in a radical move by striking out ~~Reason~~ as it applies to war. Instead, she becomes alert to meaning, creativity, and imagination as strategies of survival and reconstruction amid the people of Mozambique. Instead of reasoning away her bewilderment or surrendering to the inevitable distortions and constrictures of reasonable narration, she focuses on the poetics of the cultural discourse of the victims of war who create their worlds anew with the shards of their broken homes and lives.

Cathy Winkler is an ethnographer who had to pick up the shattered pieces of her own life. Anthropologists are not immune from the violence that seems endemic to human society. Anthropologists have been assassinated, at home and in the field. They have been mugged, robbed, and raped. Yet very few turn their personal tragedies into research, and even fewer consciously used their anthropological training during a rape. Winkler describes how she was abused repeatedly by a rapist and then became the victim, survivor, witness, plantiff, investigator, and researcher of her own assault. Ethnographer and ethnography collapsed into one totalitarian whole in which objectivity and subjectivity were jumbled in ambiguity. The research object became subject, and the subject survived by behaving as an object. Winkler's contribution excels in conveying the confusion, irrationality, and bewilderment of the rape attack in particular and of violent conflict as well as research on violence in general. The incongruence of behavior and discourse, which Winkler observed and experienced in the rapist, can also be found in many other violent situations. The person under attack is placed in a disordered world of ambiguity and incongruency. The resulting existential shock—felt by many ethnographers of violence but in a heightened sense by the ethnographer who becomes a victim-survivor—is experienced as the deconstruction, destruction, transformation, traumatization, and, ultimately, assassination of identity and self.

This book ends with chapters by Maria Olujic and Joseba Zulaika, who return to their home countries as expatriate scholars living in the United States. They struggle with the conflict between the violence that tears their compatriots apart and the wistful memories of childhood. Olujic writes about her perturbed departure from California to the war-torn republic of Croatia. It describes a departure for the field that is at the same time a *coming home*. Olujic returns after an absence of two decades to a motherland that no longer corresponds to her childhood memories. The irony of her mother buying her a gas mask epitomizes the ambiguity of returning to a homeland that cannot offer her any security, neither physical nor emotional. Her chapter is more than a description of her life in Zagreb. Filtering through her lines is a continuing despair at the violence in the Balkans as she clutches her ethnographic skills to retain her balance. Attentive to rituals of coping under duress, such as celebrations, public dances, poetry readings, and theater and music performances, she herself learns to cope. Talking as much for herself as for all authors in this book, she emphasizes the ethical dilemmas of the ethnography of violence and sociopolitical conflict by reminding us of its dire consequences. We should be careful, Olujic stresses, in asking victims of violence to tell their story when we are unable to relieve the reliving of their traumas. We may give a voice to the victims of violence, but we can never restore their lives.

Attentiveness to the ethical responsibilities of anthropologists raises the question of where research ends and personal involvement begins. Zulaika starts on an ethnographic research of Euzkadi Ta Azkatasuna (ETA) violence in his native Basque land, but for him it is also an autobiographical search that brings him face-to-face with the ethical dilemma of being both a privileged scholarly outsider and a neighborly cultural insider. His boyhood friends from the town of Itziar have become prominent members of the ETA, and Zulaika wonders how he, like the rest of the community, can reconcile these conflicting images of the political activists as heroes and terrorists, in a drama as replete with irony and farce as it is with pride and courage. However, his ambivalence is not simply provoked by the jagged border between sympathy or revulsion but also by the question of how an ethnographer can enter into a dialogue with and give a public forum to guerrillas-cum-"terrorists." Dialogue is about showing one's face in recognition of each other's existence and humanity, violating exactly the greatest taboo for terrorism experts: giving a *face* and a voice to the "terrorist." This dilemma becomes more complicated as he is asked by his home community to report on the findings of his fieldwork. Like the community as a whole, he grapples with his inability to find a higher moral ground from which to explain and judge ETA violence. The violence that grew within Basque society is narrated in competing modes of emplotment that can only emerge through a dialogue with the community's demonized and effaced terrorist sons and an acknowledgment of a shared personal and political responsibility for their violence.

The chapters in this volume are discussed by Allen Feldman, whose groundbreaking work on political prisoners in Northern Ireland make him an apt critic. We resist the temptation to incorporate—and domesticate—his astute observations in this introduction but will give the reader the final word. Having read about the epistemological, methodological, and theoretical problems of fieldwork under dangerous circumstances, this same reader might still be left with some burning questions about how to cope in situations of violence. We have therefore included a special section on the practice of the ethnography of violence and sociopolitical conflict. We begin with a few letters from the field by the anthropologist Myrna Mack as a tribute to all anthropologists who have been killed while conducting research. Mack died in 1990 at the hands of Guatemalan soldiers in downtown Guatemala City as she left her office to go home. Her crime: working to uncover the stories of Guatemalans living under political repression. The letters are prefaced by Elizabeth Oglesby, who worked with Mack for five years in Guatemala before her murder. Mack's story chronicles both the tragedy and the community that surrounds scholars working on issues of sociopolitical violence. Outrage from scholars around the globe and courageous work by her own family and friends served to bring five Guatemalan soldiers to trial for her murder.

Ricardo Falla, anthropologist and priest, has also dedicated his life to assisting and chronicling the lives of Mayas living under political duress in Guatemala. At considerable risk, Falla has spent over half a decade living with Mayas in the "Communities of Population in Resistance." In an interview conducted by Beatriz Manz—noted for her probing work of Guatemalan violence against civilian populations—Falla weaves together the morality and the practicality of what may more accurately be called a life's passion than ethnography.

In the concluding piece, we move to the day-to-day specificities that make research in dangerous places possible. Jeffrey Sluka gives practical suggestions on how to enhance personal safety. His recommendations are based on his own extensive research on the Irish Republican Army and the Irish National Liberation Army in a Catholic housing project in Belfast, Northern Ireland.

REFERENCES

Barnett, Donald L., and Karari Njama
    1966   *Mau Mau from Within: Autobiography and Analysis of Kenya's Peasant Revolt.* New York: Monthly Review Press.
Booth, Wayne C.
    1993   "Individualism and the Mystery of the Social Self; or Does Amnesty Have a Leg to Stand On?" In *Freedom and Interpretation,* ed. Barbara Johnson, 69–102. New York: Basic Books.

Bourdieu, Pierre
    1977   *Outline of a Theory of Practice.* Cambridge: Cambridge University Press.
    1984   *Distinction: A Social Critique of the Judgement of Taste.* Cambridge: Harvard University Press.
Canetti, Elias
    1966   *Crowds and Power.* New York: Viking.
Cixous, Helene
    1993   "We Who Are Free, Are We Free?" In *Freedom and Interpretation,* ed. Barbara Johnson, 17–44. New York: Basic Books.
Dobroszycki, Lucjan, ed.
    1984   *The Chronicle of the Lódz Ghetto, 1941–1944.* New Haven: Yale University Press.
Edgerton, Robert B.
    1990   *Mau Mau: An African Crucible.* London: I. B. Tauris.
Eksteins, Modris
    1989   *Rites of Spring: The Great War and the Birth of the Modern Age.* Boston: Houghton Mifflin.
Enloe, Cynthia
    1983   *Does Khaki Become You?* London: Pandora.
    1989   *Bananas, Beaches, and Bases: Making Feminist Sense of International Politics.* Berkeley, Los Angeles, and London: University of California Press.
    1993   *The Morning After: Sexual Politics at the End of the Cold War.* Berkeley, Los Angeles, and London: University of California Press.
Feldman, Allen
    1991   *Formations of Violence: The Narrative of the Body and Political Terror in Northern Ireland.* Chicago: University of Chicago Press.
Foucault, Michel
    1977   *Discipline and Punish: The Birth of the Prison.* New York: Pantheon.
Gadamer, Hans-Georg
    1985   *Truth and Method.* New York: Crossroad.
Girard, René
    1977   *Violence and the Sacred.* Baltimore: Johns Hopkins University Press.
Gramsci, Antonio
    1971   *Selections from the Prison Notebooks.* New York: International Publishers.
Hartsock, Nancy
    1990   "Foucault on Power: A Theory for Women?" In *Feminism/Postmodernism,* ed. Linda J. Nicholson, 157–175. New York: Routledge.
Jackson, Michael
    1989   *Paths Toward a Clearing: Radical Empiricism and Ethnographic Inquiry.* Bloomington: Indiana University Press.
Johnson, Barbara
    1993   "Introduction." In *Freedom and Interpretation,* ed. Barbara Johnson, 1–16. New York: Basic Books.
Kapferer, Bruce
    1988   *Legends of People, Myths of State: Violence, Intolerance, and Political Culture in Sri Lanka and Australia.* Washington, D.C.: Smithsonian Institution Press.

Kristeva, Julia
  1993   "The Speaking Subject Is Not Innocent." In *Freedom and Interpretation*,
          ed. Barbara Johnson, 148–174. New York: Basic Books.
Lan, David
  1985   *Guns and Rain: Guerrillas and Spirit Mediums in Zimbabwe.* Berkeley, Los
          Angeles, and London: University of California Press.
Lavie, Smadar
  1990   *The Poetics of Military Occupation: Mzeina Allegories of Bedouin Identity
          under Israeli and Egyptian Rule.* Berkeley, Los Angeles, and Oxford: Uni-
          versity of California Press.
Manz, Beatriz
  1988   *Refugees of a Hidden War: The Aftermath of Counterinsurgency in Guate-
          mala.* Albany: State University of New York Press.
Mead, Margaret
  1964   "Warfare Is Only an Invention—Not a Biological Necessity." In *War,*
          ed. Leon Bramson and George W. Goethals, 269–274. New York: Basic
          Books.
Mudimbe, V. Y.
  1988   *The Invention of Africa: Gnosis, Philosophy, and the Order of Knowledge.*
          Bloomington: Indiana University Press.
Nordstrom, Carolyn, and JoAnn Martin, eds.
  1992   *The Paths of Domination, Resistance, and Terror.* Berkeley, Los Angeles,
          and Oxford: University of California Press.
Ranger, Terence O.
  1985   *Peasant Consciousness and Guerrilla War in Zimbabwe.* Berkeley, Los An-
          geles, and London: University of California Press.
Remarque, Erich Maria
  1958   *All Quiet on the Western Front.* Greenwich, Conn.: Fawcett.
Rorty, Richard
  1986   "The Contingency of Language." *London Review of Books,* 17 April, 3–6.
Scheper-Hughes, Nancy
  1992   *Death Without Weeping: The Violence of Everyday Life in Northeast Brazil.*
          Berkeley, Los Angeles, and Oxford: University of California Press.
Sluka, Jeffrey A.
  1989   *Hearts and Minds, Water and Fish: Support for the IRA and INLA in a
          Northern Irish Ghetto.* Greenwich, Conn.: JAI Press.
Spivak, Gayatri
  1988   "Can the Subaltern Speak?" In *Marxism and the Interpretation of Culture,*
          ed. Carl Nelson and Lawrence Grossberg, 271–313. Urbana: Univer-
          sity of Illinois Press.
Tambiah, Stanley J.
  1986   *Sri Lanka: Ethnic Fratricide and the Dismantling of Democracy.* Chicago:
          University of Chicago Press.
Taussig, Michael
  1987   *Shamanism, Colonialism and the Wild Man: A Study in Terror and Healing.*
          Chicago: University of Chicago Press.

Trinh, T. Minh-ha
  1989   *Woman, Native, Other.* Bloomington: University of Indiana Press.
Young, James E.
  1988   *Writing and Rewriting the Holocaust: Narrative and the Consequences of Interpretation.* Bloomington: Indiana University Press.
Zulaika, Joseba
  1988   *Basque Violence: Metaphor and Sacrament.* Reno: University of Nevada Press.

"Genet"
(Photo: Ted Swedenburg)

With Genet in the Palestinian Field

Ted Swedenburg

Two unavoidable risks confront me when I discuss the dangers of the "field" of Palestine. The first is that a sensational or heroic aura might, without justification, become attached to me because I have worked in treacherous, frontline field sites. I admit that when I agreed to write this piece, I planned to spend the spring and summer of 1992 in the West Bank and thought I would be able to write a firsthand report on the quandaries of fieldwork during the intifada. As it turns out, I was only there during August 1992, a period of relative quiescence. Not that my stay was devoid of stimulating episodes. I witnessed *shabab* (young men) burning tires and throwing stones at Israeli soldiers, I was teargased, and I encountered both *mulaththamin* (the famous "masked men" who soldiers have orders to shoot on sight) patrolling a village and Israeli soldiers senselessly harassing pedestrians and vendors in East Jerusalem. But such incidents have become thoroughly routine and unremarkable. No Palestinian in downtown Ramallah who noticed this unitedstatesian visitor weeping and gagging from CS gas made-in-the-U.S.A. considered the sight uncommon or bothered to console him. Moreover, while Palestinians are loath to characterize the current situation as "postintifada," they will say that the struggle has entered a new stage. Many people were weary, worn down, introspective, pessimistic about the outcome of "peace" negotiations, preoccupied by the dull grind of economic hardships, alarmed by the growing constraints on the activities of women. The heroic days of intifada on the march are over, and the uprising's outcome is more cloudy than in 1988 and 1989. Perhaps—even though the violence has escalated considerably since my visit in August 1992—it is time to speak of the West Bank not just in terms of "danger" and spectacular violence.

The other peril is that a researcher can sometimes be tainted with the dangerous images associated with his or her informants. This hazard seems particularly acute when one chooses to consort with Palestinians and, by some contagious magic, one is contaminated with their "terrorist" or "anti-Semitic" reputation. "To choose to focus your research on a Palestinian subject," a recent report in the *Chronicle of Higher Education* gently put it, "was not always a wise career move" for aspiring academics (Coughlin 1992: A8). I hope that someday someone will document how aspiring graduate students, from various disciplines, were warned by advisers not to do research on Palestinians, how guilt by association with Palestinian "terrorists" affected academic hiring and promotion, how the taboo on this subject severely circumscribed academic discussion of the issues, and so on. Yet the inescapable trap in the context of this discussion is that when a researcher explains how she faced real or imagined difficulties in the academy due to her Palestinian affiliations, *she* will be seen as a victim, and attention will thus be deflected away from her relative privilege and away from the more serious, although certainly related, suffering.

In this regard, we should be pleased that the political atmosphere in the U.S. academy regarding Palestine has entered a postintifada phase. Terrorist images are less hegemonic, and it has become somewhat more "respectable" to work on the question of Palestine. Many anthropologists are now doing so,[1] and the topic appears to be marketable—in the publishing arena at least. If the issue remains contentious, the academic environment at least is less perilous than in the past.

So I would like to take advantage of the changed circumstances and avoid the issues of the ersatz heroism and/or victimization of the ethnographer who ventures into hazardous territory. Instead I want to consider the instructive account of another Western adventurer. It is still not well known in the United States that, while stricken with throat cancer, Jean Genet devoted the last years of his life to completing a book based mainly on his experiences with the Palestinians, with additional material on the Black Panthers, with whom he stayed in spring 1970. This marvelously quirky text from one of the century's greatest writers, *Un Captif amoureux,* appeared in France a little over a month after Genet's death in 1986. Pan Books (a mainstream publisher) brought out an English translation, entitled *Prisoner of Love,* in England in 1989, but the book did not find a U.S. publisher until 1992. The reasons for the delay in U.S. publication are somewhat murky. Grove Press, recently acquired by Hallmark Cards, is the U.S. publisher of all Genet's other work. It declined to pick up the option to *Prisoner of Love,* claiming that the Genet estate demanded an excessive price.[2] But I suspect the work's "controversial" nature also had some bearing on Grove's decision. In any case, we are indeed fortunate that Wesleyan University Press found the means to pay the fees that Grove/Hallmark deemed exorbitant and that *Prisoner of Love* is at last available.[3]

I am personally drawn to this text not merely by its literary merits—although very different from Genet's earlier *oeuvre,* it is fully that works' stylistic equal—but because it represents a kind of ethnography that resonates with my own experience. *Prisoner of Love* recounts, principally, the time Genet spent, between 1970 and 1972, among Palestinian fedayeen in Jordan. Of course, his sojourn did not constitute "professional" ethnography. Genet was, as is well known, a thief, a homosexual, a prisoner, a novelist, and a playwright. When he visited the Palestinians he was over sixty, and his writings of the last decade or so had consisted primarily of the occasional journalistic piece and political statement. He was still a celebrated if somewhat scandalous political figure. But he was not an ethnographer. Genet admits, for instance, that his knowledge of Arabic was rudimentary (how many professional field-workers could afford to make such an admission?); he stayed with the guerrillas at the invitation of the Palestine Liberation Organization (PLO) leadership—hardly a prescription for "objectivity"; and he makes no pretense of writing a scholarly book.[4] Nonetheless—and perhaps precisely *because* of the absence of "academic" constraints—the work contains many astute observations regarding doing ethnography in dangerous fields.

FIELDWORK?

The first issue *Un Captif amoureux* raises for me concerns the very definition of fieldwork. Genet's rendering of his experiences among the fedayeen in the hills of 'Ajlun and of his encounters with Palestinian leaders in Amman and Beirut manifests an acute and sensitive self-awareness about the limits of its own subject position. I will return to these issues below. But, more significant, it brings to mind the time I spent in many of the same spots between 1961 and 1976. Genet's work leads me to wonder whether there is a legitimate(d) way for me to discuss, in an "academic" context, my long prefieldwork experiences in the Arab world, the time I passed, living, studying, working, playing, and traveling there. Is lapsing into this sort of autobiography merely a narcissistic exercise? Do only the fourteen months I spent in the Occupied Territories in 1984–1985, traveling to villages to interview veterans of the 1936–1939 revolt with notebook and tape recorder in hand, sanctified by Ph.D. candidacy and a Social Science Research Council (SSRC) grant, qualify as "fieldwork," as the only database for all my future academic writing on Palestinian memory, identity, and culture?

Perhaps many ethnographers who are similarly motivated to work in "treacherous" sites face similar questions. I have been forced to confront this issue whenever sympathetic colleagues have asked me how I manage to cope with working in and writing about a geographic/academic area that seems so emotionally and politically overcharged and so excessively violent. I can only begin to make sense of how *natural* it feels for me to be involved in this field by referring to personal history. Probably I have been there/here, emotionally, at least since I was twelve. My family first visited the West Bank—during the course of an extended pilgrimage to the "Holy Land"—in the winter of 1961–1962, when it was still ruled by the Hashemite Kingdom of Jordan. One day a U.S. Christian relief worker took us to Twayni, a "border village" in the Hebron district.[5] We made our way from Hebron (al-Khalil) by Land Rover, over a poorly marked and rugged goat track. Twayni's inhabitants, we learned, had lost their farmlands, located in the nearby plains, to the Jewish state when Israel was created in 1948. Since the villagers still retained their dwellings in the highlands, they could not be classified as "refugees" and therefore—although they had no means of livelihood—they were ineligible for assistance from the United Nations Relief and Works Agency (UNRWA). Coming from the Santa Clara Valley, I was astonished and appalled by the stark poverty. My memory (since refreshed by slides my father took) is of a bleak grayish brown atmosphere, the rocky hills, the ground, and the mud-and-stone houses all hewn from the same monotonous color, unrelieved by the greenery of trees or plants. I recall buzzing flies, scrawny animals, urchins in shabby dress, an absence of plumbing, sewage, or electricity. We quickly departed Twayni when we learned that the villagers, ever the hospitable and friendly Arabs despite their destitution, were rounding up the few stringy chickens we had noticed earlier, scrabbling around on the rugged ground, so that they could honor us with dinner.

Perhaps, ever since, I have wanted to repay those generous, desperate villagers who the world had ignored, for their offer of roasted chickens. And maybe I began to comprehend the hazards of sympathizing with such people (even before they were known as "Palestinians") some months later, back in California, shortly before my family's 1964 move to Beirut. My father had fired off a letter to NBC television news anchorman Chet Huntley, taking issue with his newscasts' uninformed, anti-Arab slant. The reply came in the form of a curt postcard that read, "Dear Reverend Swedenburg: Your anti-Semitism is showing. Chet Huntley."

During the time I lived in Beirut, between 1964 and 1976, the significance and stakes of the Palestine question only intensified, especially after Israel occupied the West Bank and Gaza in 1967 and Palestinians took up arms, thereby transforming their global image from one of hapless refugees to, depending on your point of view, terrorists or freedom fighters. Events in Palestine and its diaspora were especially crucial for my life once I enrolled at the American University of Beirut (AUB) in 1969 and made friends and allies with Palestinians who were active in student politics and in various factions of the resistance movement. These relationships made the escalating violence of the 1970s tangible and personal. I will never forget one Palestinian friend, the gentle and unassuming Nabil Sa'd. Nabil was the child of refugees from the Galilee who, after 1948, had taken up residence with their Maronite Christian coreligionists in Ashrafiya (East Beirut). Although active in student politics, Nabil was never a particularly prominent figure; after receiving his B.A., he began teaching in a local secondary school. In fall 1975, early in the Lebanese civil war, right-wing Phalangist militiamen kidnapped Nabil, tortured him with knife blades and glowing cigarettes, shot him through the head, and discarded his body in a vacant lot. The only apparent motive was that Nabil was a Palestinian. Nabil's parents' flat in Ashrafiya was plundered and burned, and the family was left with no photographs of Nabil except for the snapshot taken in the morgue. I will never forget the hours I spent with Nabil's younger brother, trying to lend comfort and to convince him of the folly of attempting revenge.

I could mention two other Palestinian friends from AUB, who were arrested and tortured by Israeli interrogators after they returned home to the Occupied Territories. I could tell of a unitedstatesian friend who suffered similar (perhaps even more brutal) treatment at the hands of Syrian intelligence. But it would be painful, and my aim is neither to horrify nor to elicit sympathy. The point is simply that my Beirut friendships and experiences were crucial for my subsequent fieldwork project in the West Bank—because they ensured support networks and thus enabled my understanding of, and capacity to manage, life under military occupation. Many researchers, I assume, have a similar complex mix of attachments, investments, relations, experiences, emotions, or understandings that connect them to the trouble spots in which they work. Such links usually cannot be defined as "academic," and we have therefore not been encouraged to speak about them. The usual assumption is that the "field" is "virgin territory" for the researcher, and therefore ethnographic accounts are full of fables of "first contact." But others of us may have prior contacts with people in the areas where we work, ties that are crucial to understanding our motivations and capacities for undertaking "dangerous" fieldwork. To speak of such ties is not merely a self-indulgent conceit.

FIELDWORK AS FUN?

The second suggestion that Genet offers is that we admit, moreover, that we might actually be *attracted* to such perilous sites. "It was for *fun* as much as anything," he informs us, "that I'd accepted the invitation to spend a few days with the Palestinians. But I was to stay nearly two years . . . neither

afraid nor surprised, but *amused* to be there" (1989:9; emphasis added).
Genet returns to the theme of enjoyment several times. During a shootout
between fedayeen and King Hussein's army, he informs us, he experienced
a kind of "idiotic delight" crouching against a wall while bullets sprayed
nearby, watching the "happy smiles" and "calm" on the faces of the Palestinian fighters (ibid., 53). Genet also speaks of his great passion for the
guerrillas: "From late 1970 to late 1972, more than anything or anyone
else I loved the fedayeen" (ibid., 373). The Palestinian revolt in the hills
of 'Ajlun, he declares, was a "party that lasted nine months," and he compares it to "the freedom that reigned in Paris in May 1968"—except, he
notes, "the fedayeen were armed" (ibid., 247).

Strange motivations. What could they have to do with ethnography? Is
doing ethnography in a hazardous field really supposed to be a question
of fun, or love? Aren't we supposed to be attracted to intriguing intellectual problems? Isn't it magnanimity that compels us to live with the
wretched of the earth? Yet maybe if we admitted that struggles sometimes
exude a party atmosphere and exert a magnetic pull, the heroism sometimes associated with our dangerous ethnography would be diminished.

I recall my visit to Jordan in spring 1970, partly for the purpose of researching a paper for a sociology course with Samir Khalaf, on the topic,
"Is the Palestinian resistance a force for modernization?"[6] I found Amman's atmosphere, during those days of Palestinian mobilization and gun-
slinging guerrillas in the streets, exhilarating, the promise of radical change
inspiring, the spirit of defiance contagious. I was particularly moved by a
performance I witnessed at Baqa' refugee camp, where young women and
children danced the *dabka* and sang nationalist songs with transcendent
joy and determination. And it was discussions with some astute leaders
and members of the Popular Democratic Front for the Liberation of
Palestine that originally sparked my interest in Marxism.

The ambience at AUB in the late 1960s and early 1970s was equally
electric and frequently scary: strikes, occupations of buildings and demonstrations, bloody fights between rival student groups, endless political arguments and Marxist study groups, militancy, foolish excesses, work camps
in refugee camps, and Stalinist demagogy. Although I also spent a year
and a half in the United States during this period, for me "the sixties" was
primarily a Beirut experience; and armed revolt and brutal repression
were an integral part of that political reality. Like Genet, I was enamored
of the Palestinian revolution, ensnared by its charms and dangerous allure.
So when talking about dangerous ethnography, I must admit the appeal,
the thrills inherent in projects for social change. I feel extraordinarily
lucky to have tasted something of the joys of insurrection, the—if I may *dé-
tourn* Durkheim's phrase—"collective effervescence" of revolt.

NOT A LAUDABLE OCCUPATION

But Genet also cautions that *our* particular brand of fun, in such situations, is linked to our privileged vantage points. While he professes love for the fedayeen, Genet acknowledges "how far away" he was from the Palestinians (1989:90), underscoring that he was "among [*auprès*]—not with [*avec*]" them (ibid., 3; 1986:11). Among, not with. "When I was writing this book," he explains,

> out there among the fedayeen, I was always on the other side of a boundary. I knew I was safe, not because of a Celtic physique or a layer of goose fat, but because of even shinier and stronger armour: I didn't belong to, never really identified with, their nation or their movement. . . . Everything was in it at one time or another; but never my total belief, never the whole of myself. (1989:90)

Genet is also blunt about the unglamorous nature of his task: "There was nothing for me to do but look and listen. Not a very laudable occupation" (ibid., 91). Not laudable, but nonetheless *privileged*: "[I] looked on at the Palestinians' revolt," Genet says, "as if from a window or a box in a theatre, and as if through pearl-handled opera glasses" (ibid., 90; translation modified).[7]

Under such conditions *participant* observation is impossible. And how absurd this paradoxical anthropological conceit seems, when you are among men shouldering Kalashnikovs who are slated for death, prison, torture (ibid., 97). Genet may be full of love, chaste desires, and identification, but ultimately he is simply an outside observer.[8] He even has doubts about what the fedayeen *really* felt about him, what they truly thought his role was (ibid., 302). This is no fable of ethnographic "rapport." Genet always recognizes the difference, the gap separating him from the fighters (ibid., 344). And he actively shuns the notion of any heroism on his part. "My whole life," he asserts, "was made up of unimportant trifles cleverly blown up into acts of daring" (ibid., 148). A rather remarkable statement given the legendary outsider status of the man who asserted in 1974, "It was completely natural for me to be attracted to the people who are not only the most unfortunate but also crystallize to the highest degree the hatred of the West."[9]

Genet admits of other complications in his relationship to the Palestinians. After the 1973 war, his "passionate love" faded and "the typical lover's weariness" set in. "I was still charmed," he writes, "but I wasn't convinced; I was attracted but not blinded. I behaved like a prisoner of love" (ibid., 188). A prisoner of love who continues to exercise great care and caution in depicting the Palestinians because he is well aware of the West's antipathy. He constantly underscores the fedayeen's bravery, the nobility of their cause of liberation. At the same time, he apologizes for his language. "In other days," he affirms,

> I think I'd have avoided words like heroes, martyrs, struggle, revolution, liberation, resistance, courage and suchlike. I probably *have* avoided the words homeland and fraternity, which still repel me. But there's no doubt that the Palestinians caused a kind of collapse in my vocabulary. I accept it in order to put first things first, but I know there's nothing behind such words. (ibid., 272)

The sides are so polarized, the fedayeen so universally maligned, that Genet feels pressured to employ corrupted vocabulary and exercise self-censorship in order to defend them (ibid., 178).

I too have felt caught in such dilemmas, inherent dangers of doing ethnography in a hazardous and highly politicized field. My fieldwork in Palestine during 1984–1985 concerned how elderly Palestinian villagers remembered the 1936–1939 revolt. I was principally interested in "popular" memories of the insurrection and their relationship to official nationalist histories. But I found myself constantly trying to balance between my interest in the subaltern versions of the revolt, on the one hand, and, on the other, the felt necessity to respect and sometimes even defend the nationalist imperatives of a people living under occupation, without their own state, many of whom wished to preserve a memory of the revolt that was untarnished by internal conflicts. When I write I make a constant effort to balance my interest in exposing the seams and cracks in nationalist history with the need to safeguard the nationalist history from vilification by its powerful opponents. Genet's example suggests that such solidarities are necessary, that they have their price, and that they must be undertaken self-consciously.

But he does not advocate cheerleading. His depictions of the PLO leadership, for instance, are scathing. "I found the manners of almost all the ordinary Palestinians, men and women, delightful," he writes. "But their leaders were a pain in the neck" (ibid., 243); many were guilty of corruption. The legs of the guerrilla chiefs "often wilted," he asserts, "at the sight of heaps of gold or the sound of new banknotes" (ibid., 164). His descriptions of the Palestinian bourgeoisie, the "Leading Families," are equally caustic. Nor does Genet shy away from blasting the PLO's illusory military strategy. He labels the poorly defended fedayeen positions in the hills of 'Ajlun, where he stayed in 1971, "Potemkin" bases (ibid., 125). The United States and Israel "were in no danger," he asserts, from such PLO "sham[s]," from "defeats presented as victories, withdrawals as advances—in short, from a shifting dream floating over the Arab world, capable only of such unsubtle acts as killing a plane-load of passengers" (ibid., 149). Fedayeen, Genet maintains, were often sent off on "operations without really know-

ing from start to finish what their objective was" (ibid., 289). Even his be-
loved fighters were not all innocents. Fateh, the organization that welcomed him into its camps, seemed to attract youths "who delighted in
scrapping and looting and guns . . . more hooligans than heroes" (ibid.,
202). Genet witnesses fedayeen lording it over Jordanian peasants (ibid.,
340) and other fighters who were "glad to be able to pilfer cars, cameras,
discs, books and trousers with impunity" and who excused their actions as
revolutionary (ibid., 227). Such biting critiques are unusual for a partisan
account.

LEAPFROGGING OVER CORPSES

But what, you might now object, about the *real* issues? What is all this talk
of love and play? What about the horror and terror, what about all those
people killed, wounded, tortured? Genet does deal with death and suffering, somehow managing to sustain a kind of impassioned coolness of
tone. In particular, he discusses the carnage at the Beirut refugee camp of
Shatila, which he wandered through in September 1982 shortly after the
Phalangist-inflicted massacres there and at Sabra camp.[10] "I've gone down
the main street in Chatila having almost to leapfrog over the corpses block-
ing the streets," he tells us. "The number of obstacles I've had to jump
over in my life. The smell of decomposition was so strong it was almost visible, and insurmountable as a rampart" (ibid., 338). Other horrific images
from Shatila are interspersed throughout. And, he tells us, "when I hear
the word Palestinian, I shudder and have to recall the image of a grave
waiting like a shadow at the feet of every fighter" (ibid., 329).

Strangely, he does not dwell on the bloodbath at Sabra and Shatila, although this experience made a deep impression. His chief means of dealing with bloodshed and oppression is through personalization. The most
important and recurrent image in *Prisoner of Love* is of the fighter Hamza
and his mother, who take care of Genet for a few hours in the midst of a
battle at Irbid in 1971. When Genet later hears that Hamza was captured
and tortured by the Jordanian army, he asserts, "My hatred for [King]
Hussein and his Bedouin and Circassians focused less and less on their
massacring of the Palestinians and the fedayeen [in 1970 and 1971].
Hamza's torture-blackened legs, nothing but two huge wounds, were
enough for me, though I'd never seen them and knew they belonged
more to the Palestinian people than to me" (ibid., 264).

Reading this and other similar passages, I too want to personalize the
violence and oppression. I think of Ahmad Kilani, assassinated by Israel's
"special forces" during the first year of the intifada. I think of my friend
Sam'an Khuri, who spent three and one-half years in jail during the intifada. Although I have never witnessed anything like Sabra and Shatila,

sometimes I feel that involvement in this field has also required me to hop over corpses, with all the pain and privilege attendant on the outsider who inevitably survives the struggle and feels compelled to bear witness.

The first time I sat down to write about the personal effects of experiencing such violence and horror—albeit at second hand—I was paralyzed with pain, nausea, and depression. Whenever I think of this issue, a troubling jumble of images assaults me. I lived through the first months of the Lebanese civil war in Beirut (until January 1976), going to sleep every night to the music of machine guns, bombs, and rocket-propelled grenades in the distance, and losing a number of friends and acquaintances in the process. For years I was virtually unable to talk about Beirut, and I am still beset by violent dreams about the civil war. My fieldwork in 1984–1985, unlike my "sixties" experiences in Beirut and Amman, was mostly not "fun." This was a period when West Bank Palestinians were building grassroots institutions that laid the basis for the intifada, but it was also a period of repression, of the security forces' "Iron Fist," and a time when many friends were rounded up. I was often frightened, depressed, and nervous. After I returned to the United States, I twice came close to mental collapse; both times memories of West Bank violence (plus my mother's death and the breakup of my marriage) played a major part in the breakdown. I remember one delirious moment two weeks after my return—it now seems quite amusing—when I was convinced that a gardener who was trimming the hedges and dressed in camouflage fatigues outside my sister-in-law's home in San Francisco was an Israeli soldier holding an Uzi who would shoot me if I stepped outside. I am glad that, for my own sanity, I returned to the Occupied Territories in summer 1992 and that I experienced the violence of the occupation again, at a time when Palestinians seemed much more fearless than in the past. Somehow a bit of their strength rubbed off on me as well.

In short, while I have had my fun, I have found that moving through dangerous field sites took its toll as well. Perhaps the hardest thing is how impossible it is to convey the everyday *normality* of the violence to anyone living in our safe middle-class U.S. enclaves. It is extremely difficult to convince anyone of Walter Benjamin's insight, that such a "'state of emergency' . . . is not the exception but the rule" (1969:257). So one usually shies away from speaking about the horror, since most people respond with looks of shocked disbelief and exaggerated compassion (both for you and for the Palestinians) but rarely with the realization that the "state of emergency" connects to their own lives.

FABULOUS IMAGES

Perhaps this is why, even though images like corpses, severed digits, and mutilated bodies are scattered throughout the pages of *Un Captif amou-*

reux, they are not Genet's principal focus. His chief concern is to capture the life, the humor, amid the blood and suffering. He recognizes, of course, how tricky this task is. "To depict the Palestinian resistance as a game or a party," Genet maintains, "doesn't mean one is taking it lightly. The Palestinians have been denied houses, land, passports, a country, a nation—everything! But who can deny laughter and a light in the eye?" (ibid., 305).

It is not always regarded as a "laudable occupation" to convey the levity that is an undeniable part of insurrections. In summer 1992, together with the filmmaker Joan Mandell,[11] I began work on a video about the polyvalent uses of the Palestinian *kufiya,* the Palestinian scarf. Our aim was to produce a video that blends politics and culture; memory, history, and fantasy; struggle and humor. We tracked the *kufiya*—a quintessential signifier of Palestinian identity and struggle—through space and time and across national, gender, and class borders. We investigated the *kufiya*'s uses by peasant rebels in the 1936–1939 revolt; its adoption by Israeli soldiers in the 1950s as a sign of bravado; its embrace by the armed fedayeen in the 1960s; its appearance in the United States among Palestine solidarity groups in the 1960s and as an accessory of stylish boho outfits in the early 1980s; how Palestinians as well as foreigners living in the West Bank placed it on their car dashboards to keep from getting stoned by youths; its employment by the masked men of the intifada and its appropriation by Palestinian women activists; how Israeli undercover agents donned it to entrap intifada militants and were sometimes shot by soldiers who mistook them for Palestinian.[12]

Many people with whom we discussed this project were skeptical. They found the topic light and insignificant, an evasion of the *real,* pressing issues. Why not make a film about death squads or torture? Or the crushing taxation that is causing a slow hemorrhage of the Palestinian economy? We met similar responses from funding sources in the United States. Foundations that normally support films with a "cultural" orientation find a Palestinian subject too dangerous or controversial, while those that back "progressive" films regard our approach as frivolous. The Paul Robeson Fund for Independent Media, for instance, rejected Joan's grant application because "a lighthearted and cultural look at the Palestinian issue was not a funding priority." "I guess I should have called it 'heavy-handed,'" she remarked after receiving the rejection letter.

I do not know if Genet would urge us on, given that he left so many projects uncompleted. But witnessing the holocaust at Shatila in September 1982 was what set him to writing *Un Captif amoureux,* which was completed twenty-five years after the publication of his last play, *The Screens* (*Les Paravents*) (see notes to Genet 1991:406). He felt compelled to write, in part, so that the revolt he had witnessed might leave its mark. For the fedayeen, he asserts, knew that "their persons and their ideas [would]

only be brief flashes against a world wrapped up in its own smartness. . . .
[T]he fedayeen . . . are tracer bullets, knowing their traces vanish in the
twinkling of an eye" (1989:179). Genet sees his role as the sender of "fabulous images" of the struggle "into the future, to act in the very long term,
after death," images that might be "starting point[s] for actions" (1989:
262). He does not pretend that he is "giving voice" to the Palestinians or
acting as the relay of *their* messages. Rather, he accepts responsibility for
the fact that the interpretation is all his own.

> The construction, organization and layout of the book, without deliberately
> intending to *betray* the facts, manage the narrative in such a way that I proba-
> bly seem to be a privileged witness or even a manipulator. . . . All these words
> to say, This is *my* Palestinian revolution, told in my own chosen order. As well
> as mine there is the other, probably many others. (1989:308–309)[13]

What image did Genet hope to project as the fedayeen's delegate into
the future? An image of beauty and life, of humanity amid the warfare, revolt, and dying. An image of the affection of a mother and her son, Hamza,
for each other, and a tenderness they also extended to Genet. A son and
mother, both slinging guns, who express their love as the battle rages
against Hussein's army. What sticks with me are not the guns but the fact
that it is Ramadan and that Hamza's mother, on learning that Genet is an
atheist, says with a smile, "Well, if he doesn't believe in God I'd better give
him something to eat" (ibid., 162). Genet returns again and again to the
image of Hamza and his mother, ponders it, mulls it over, examines it
from every conceivable angle. It is not merely a warm, humane image, it is
Genet's strange obsession.

Although he hopes to dispatch such images into the future, and even at
points compares his role to Homer's,[14] Genet equally expresses doubts
about the ultimate utility of his work. "Perhaps what I write is no use to
anyone," he wonders. "'What's the use of talking about this revolution?'
It . . . is like a long-drawn-out funeral, with me occasionally joining in the
procession" (ibid., 190). And again, "Any reality is bound to be outside
me, existing in and for itself. The Palestinian revolution lives and will live
only of itself" (ibid., 374). While hoping to disseminate a certain image of
the revolution, he acknowledges that it may be able to flourish on its own.

With the onset of the intifada, the Palestinian movement indeed seems—
all by itself—to have thrown up a powerful new image of struggle, that of
the stone thrower. But Genet's sensitive portrait of the fedayeen cautions
us against uncritically seizing on this new and relatively pacific image of
the slinger of stones. For his account forces us to recognize that we may be
embracing the stone thrower to deny or displace the troubling image of
the guerrilla under arms, an image so readily associated with terrorism, an
image that might taint the ethnographer who ventures into dangerous ter-

ritory. Even Genet, of all people, had trouble getting published in the era of postintifada.

VITALIZING THE WILL

Perhaps, in trying to avoid getting caught up in either the heroic or the terrorist image associated with the Palestinians, I have neglected my own dangerous ethnography. I have mentioned my own investments and experiences, but I have spoken more of Genet—maybe because Genet's text provides a vehicle for me to address issues that are still difficult for academics. After all, the outlaw Genet did not face all the constraints that professional ethnographers usually encounter. He visits the guerrillas at their invitation, openly declaring his partisanship, fearlessly affiliating with "terrorists." (Our affiliations are usually with the Ford and Rockefeller foundations, the National Endowment for the Humanities, the Social Science Research Council.) Moreover, Genet's overt solidarity permits him the paradoxical freedom to be devastatingly critical. (While we have to be cultural relativists.) He also speaks of investments—desire, pleasure, anger—which the academy avoids. And he is concerned principally not with analysis or interpretation but with producing images, images with hoped-for future political and aesthetic value. Perhaps because he is a brilliant writer, the images will be remembered.

We, of course, are not Genet. Because we operate under quite different constraints—professional, political, generic—we cannot imitate him in any precise way. But I am encouraged to keep looking for affirmative images amid the mounting piles of rubble and skeletons. Knowing that, as Walter Benjamin once remarked, "Only images in the mind vitalize the will."

Here is an image that instances the kind of boundary crossing and transnational popular solidarities that Genet's life epitomized and that seem so necessary for our survival in this postmodern era.[15] It comes from Los Angeles, site of the April 1992 intifada, where the city government is deploying a "West Bank" strategy in its battle with the "terrorists" (gang members) of South Central. Landlords are being sued, tenants are being evicted, and houses suspected of being "drug nuisances" are being bulldozed, in imitation of the former Housing and Urban Development secretary, Jack Kemp's, policy of "expelling *families* of those *arrested* (not necessarily convicted) for drug dealing" (Davis 1990:284). My friend Joan Mandell knows an Egyptian in Los Angeles who works as a journalist, is active in the Palestinian solidarity movement, and is a practicing Muslim. When the uprising broke out, his radio station assigned him to cover South Central. He was apprehensive about going there because of his fair skin, so he consulted his African-American friends at the mosque. They told him, just put a *kufiya* on the dashboard of your car and the brothers will know you're okay!

Perhaps I continue seeking such images in this ethnographic minefield because I hope, somehow, to prove that I am worthy of having been offered a taste of roasted chicken by dispossessed, but generous, peasants.

ACKNOWLEDGMENTS

The first version of this chapter was presented at the session, "Dangerous Ethnographies: Fieldwork, Field Themes and Theory in High Conflict Research," at the annual meeting of the American Anthropological Association, San Francisco, December 4, 1992. Thanks to Donald Moore, Carolyn Nordstrom, Maureen O'Malley, Martina Rieker, and Antonius Robben for helpful comments and criticisms. My father, Romain Swedenburg, helped me "remember" some details of my earlier encounters with the "field." My academic/political trajectory would be unthinkable had not my father and late mother, Bertha, determined back in 1963 that my brother and I would grow up with a limited and distorted view of the world if we stayed in upper-middle-class suburban California (Los Gatos) and therefore decided to move to Beirut.

NOTES

1. For instance, the anthropologists who participated in the session, "Breaking Boundaries: New Voices on Israel/Palestine," at the annual meeting of the American Anthropological Association in San Francisco, December 2, 1992: Nadia Abu El-Haj, Glenn Bowman, Rebecca Torstrick, and Davida Wood. See also recent work by George Bisharat (1989), Smadar Lavie (1992), and Julie Peteet (1991).

2. Thanks to Steven Shaviro for this information.

3. One hopes that a translation of Genet's *L'Ennemi déclaré* (1991), a collection of articles by and interviews with Genet between 1964 and 1985, which includes additional material on the Palestinians, is soon to follow.

4. In fact, an editor with a basic knowledge of Middle East history should have corrected the occasional but nonetheless egregious errors of historical chronology, spellings, and basic fact.

5. For a general account of the phenomenon of "border" or "frontier villages," see Plascov 1982.

6. Layla Shahid, my Palestinian classmate and a member of Fateh, took me around to meet various resistance officials in Amman. By chance, the same Layla (now known by her married name, Layla Shahid Barrada) later befriended Genet. He was staying with her family in Beirut when the Sabra-Shatila massacres occurred (see Genet 1991:405–406; also 269–296). I have not seen Layla since the early 1970s. Layla Shahid is now the PLO ambassador to France.

7. Genet speaks too of "watching revolution from plush and gilt stage boxes." But, he says, "what other place are we to watch from if the revolutions are first and

foremost wars of liberation? From whom are they trying to free themselves?" (1989:264).

8. Abu Omar, Genet's contact in the PLO leadership, tells Genet that his "job" with the fedayeen "will be a difficult one: don't do anything." Genet understands "this to mean I was to be there, listen, but say nothing, look on, agree or seem not to understand" (1989:151).

9. Quoted in Edmund White's introduction to *Prisoner of Love,* in Genet 1989: viii.

10. See his remarkable "Quatre heurs à Chatila," which originally appeared in *Journal d'Etudes Palestiniennes* and is reprinted in Genet 1991:243–267.

11. Her previous films include *Gaza Ghetto* and *Voices in Exile.*

12. Some of these uses are discussed in Swedenburg 1992.

13. See also Genet 1989:205–206, 255.

14. "The fame of heroes owes little to the extent of their conquests and all to the success of the tributes paid to them. The *Iliad* counts for more than Agamemnon's war. . . . But what survives is the evidence" (1989:5).

15. Genet spent his last years living in Morocco, where he is buried (see Muhammed Choukri's *Genet in Tangier*). He was an active supporter of the rights of Arab immigrants in France and an early champion of Maghrebi authors like Tahar Ben Jelloun writing in French (see Genet 1991). He was always actively disloyal to French, and Western, civilization.

REFERENCES

Benjamin, Walter
   1969   "Theses on the Philosophy of History." In *Illuminations,* ed. Hannah Arendt, trans. Harry Zohn, 253–264. New York: Schocken Books.
Bisharat, George
   1989   *Palestinian Lawyers and Israeli Rule.* Austin: University of Texas Press.
Bowman, Glenn
   1994   "'A Country of Words': Conceiving the Palestinian Nation from the Position of Exile." In *The Making of Political Identities,* ed. Ernesto Laclau, 138–170. London: Verso.
Coughlin, Ellen K.
   1992   "As Perceptions of the Palestinian People Change, Study of Their History and Society Grows." *Chronicle of Higher Education* (February 19): A8–9, A12.
Davis, Mike
   1990   *City of Quartz: Excavating the Future in Los Angeles.* London: Verso.
Genet, Jean
   1986   *Un Captif amoureux.* Paris: Gallimard.
   1989   *Prisoner of Love,* trans. Barbara Bray. London: Picador.
   1991   *L'Ennemi déclaré: Textes et entretiens,* ed. Albert Dichy. Paris: Gallimard.
Lavie, Smadar
   1992   "Blow-Ups in the Borderzones: Third World Israeli Authors' Gropings for Home." *New Formations* 18:84–106.

Plascov, Avi
   1982   "The Palestinians of Jordan's Border." In *Studies in the Economic and Social History of Palestine in the Nineteenth and Twentieth Centuries,* ed. Roger Owen, 203–241. Carbondale and Edwardsville: Southern Illinois University Press.
Peteet, Julie
   1991   *Gender in Crisis: Women and the Palestinian Resistance Movement.* New York: Columbia University Press.
Swedenburg, Ted
   1992   "Seeing Double: Palestinian-American Histories of the *Kufiya.*" *Michigan Quarterly Review* 31(4):557–577.

News: Cause or Effect?
(Photo: John T. Jordan, Jr.)

The Beginning of the End

Anna Simons

It was always possible during the first November I was in Mogadishu to pass through a shady but still hot downtown and watch Somali men nonchalantly emerge from the Central Bank with bulging plastic bags full of bundled Somali shillings. No one accosted, confronted, or robbed people of such obvious means. One year later, that scene was inextricably altered: Land Cruisers were being carjacked, and no one blithely walked anywhere anymore with telltale sacks of money.

During the year I happened to be in Mogadishu (1988–1989), I witnessed a transformation that social scientists more often analyze as aftermath than as action. Midway through my stay, Mogadishu erupted with violence that briefly gained it world attention. That was on July 14, 1989, and the violence then (as we shall see) involved government troops and civilians. It was acute violence and did not immediately recur. Nevertheless, by the time I left Mogadishu in November 1989, it was more than apparent that the entire "nation" was on a cusp: the blister of discontent had to either burst or callous over; either Somalis would work out their differences once and for all in what everyone predicted could only be a paroxysm of violence or individuals would become inured and the nation would be able to carry on.

Of course, now, in 1993, hindsight already makes it seem obvious that Somalia slid over the cusp in a horrific way. But hindsight is not yet 20/20; there is still time for people to become irreversibly inured to violence, if they have not already. Indeed, one of the new givens may be that as long as automatic weapons and weapons suppliers exist, Mogadishu may never return to quiescence. Or, alternatively, Mogadishu may have finally entered the arena of world capitals that proclaim control over nations but cannot provide security within their own municipal limits.

In examining the sketchy beginnings of what has led to this end, we face two theoretical issues. One concerns hindsight: Is it a potentially misleading analytical tool? The second ponders the length, breadth, and depth of social memory and its markers. Each of these is critical to anthropology given our current penchant to project back through time in order to contextualize settings. Perhaps the clues we retool for analysis will not stand the test of time. Or perhaps we can already guess at the historical implications of July 14.

What complicates the interpretation of events is the role rumors play. During moments of crisis and, indeed, in general in Somalia on the cusp, rumors composed knowledge. Not only were rumors the only source of information to publicly circulate but the conflicting nature of competing rumors also made plain to people that they *were* relying on rumors for information. Obviously, rumors were manufactured. The questions to be asked, then, were, by whom? why? when?—which themselves generated conjecture and the construction of new logics.

These logics that linked "fact" to "fact" to "fact" may be no less informative now. Outside the press of immediacy and taken together, they reveal that there may have been no privileged view, that the composition of reality *was* situational, person-dependent, and unduplicatable from individual to individual, that facts were often linked up haphazardly depending on what was available but not necessarily "truly" related. As a result, explanations tended to overreach themselves and sought too much complicity, conspiracy, and intentionality in situations for which there had been no previous practice—or forethought.

Nevertheless, based on their own internal consistencies, rumors could seem convincing and could compel people to action, never mind that hindsight would later prove them wrong. At the time, we must remember, no rumor *could* be right. Proof would have canonized it as truth, not supposition, while as supposition, rumor narrowed the possibilities not only for what to think but also for in which direction to look for the future. Ironically, that is precisely where hindsight would be waiting to neaten the passage (and eliminate alternative explanations), after the fact. And narrative?

There are numerous different perspectives from which to consider the visitation of violence on Mogadishu, the bureaucratic center of a country that can be divided differently according to what you believe you are unpeeling: geographic, or linguistic, or socioeconomic, or genealogical segments, each potentially as critical to the dissociation of the "nation" and its capital as the next.

For instance, sometime between 1969 when he declared himself leader of Somalia and 1989 when he was being ridiculed as the "Mayor of Mogadishu," President Mohamed Siad Barre lost his grip. All of Somalia's peripheries began to swing out of control, exposing a center that felt threatened and undermined yet was itself perceived to be acting threateningly and brutally. Again, these peripheries can be described in a number of ways. For instance, by 1988, the north had become an entire region within which the central government was waging war. The regime's opponents were northerners, who tend to belong to the Isaq clan, which comprise most of the membership of the extremely successful opposition Somali National Movement (only one of a number of clan-based oppositions). Hence members of other clans within the army were being forced to take sides in a dispute that could be read either empathetically, as one of opposition to a corrupt regime, or dispassionately, as one of clan rivalries and reconfigurations being worked out over control of state resources— with all of this (on the broadest scale) eerily reassembling the former divide between northern British Somaliland and southern Italian Somalia, which themselves originated as cookie-cutter shapes imposed on nonstate (Somali) peoples by colonial (European) powers. That is one scan of the macro picture.

A second scan might hone in on Siad Barre's dictatorship and blame that for Somalia's demise. In brief, Siad Barre came to power in a military coup in 1969, pledging to stem clannism and corruption, which—initially, and to his great credit—he did. However, his government's involvement in the Ogaden War in 1977–1978 and Somalia's subsequent defeat by a Soviet-backed Ethiopia unraveled his successes. Economically, politically, and even tribally, Siad Barre reacted as if under siege; many suggest that Siad Barre sought to shift blame to others for Somalia's loss in the war. Such blame and his own retrenchment then served to reintroduce clannism, while the return of Western aid and assistance (to counter the Soviet presence in Ethiopia) renewed and fueled corruption. A potent combination, which in the decade to follow steadily lost Siad Barre so much support and control that it becomes increasingly difficult to work backward and fathom, first, why violence did not occur sooner, and second, why (and whether) it was one particular thing *or* nothing in particular that then set it off.

At the microchronological level we find Monsignor Salvatore Colombo, an Italian national and the archbishop of Mogadishu, shot and killed on July 9, 1989, while five days later, on Friday, July 14, government troops opened fire on Muslim worshipers as they were leaving Friday's *juma* (noontime) mosque services. Two days of street fighting followed. Mass arrests, civilian massacres, rapes, and lootings also took place. While Hargeisa, the northern capital, was already unlivable (having been bombed and strafed by government forces the previous summer), this was the first large-scale violence in Mogadishu in fourteen years.[1]

JULY 14

At the time the shooting started, I was in a compound rented for American military advisers by the U.S. government from a Somali general. Only one adviser was home, and two Somali watchmen were on duty at the front gate.

At first I thought Bastille Day had begun early, as the French embassy was planning a gala celebration. However, the embassy was too far away and it was just after noon, too early for fireworks. No, this had to be something else. And by the time I had thought that through, it was increasingly obvious that gunfire was coming from many different directions at once, although Mogadishu's spread made it impossible to know the extent of the shooting until the American walkie-talkie net began to crackle with broadcasts.

All "official" Americans (those working directly for the embassy or for USAID or on contract to a U.S. government agency) were supplied with walkie-talkies, not only with this eventuality in mind but simply for the sake of communications. Mogadishu's telephone system was considered to be abysmal at best.

Because official Americans lived in pockets scattered throughout the city, it was possible to get some sense of what was going on out of direct hearing range as people reported in on the net. However, as most people were located within largely elite neighborhoods, it was never entirely clear what was happening throughout the city. All the embassy officials could confirm over the walkie-talkies was that the Somali army was involved in the fighting. While most people later admitted to assuming this marked the beginning of a revolution or a coup, such conjecture was never broadcast. If anything, the embassy was extremely circumspect in its pronouncements. For instance, when one woman clicked on to ask about reports of an anti-Christian element to the uprising, she was told that it would be better to avoid that topic for the moment.

Meanwhile, my own (ir)rationale at the time was that if this was really a significant confrontation, there would have to be a cataclysmic, massive shootout to prove it. Consequently, I spent the whole day and that first night anticipating a sudden crescendo of gunfire. Instead, I heard only small-arms fire. Still, I was probably more anxious waiting for what did not occur than I was about the bullets that did occasionally zing over our roof.

Throughout the day Americans were advised to stay indoors and to keep their walkie-talkies with them throughout the evening and night. Roll calls were taken regularly. However, very little new information was offered.

As an unofficial American (without my name on the roll or the privilege of my own walkie-talkie but fortunate enough to be in an official house whose inhabitants did count as far as the U.S. embassy was concerned), I had to wonder what the few other unofficial Americans in Mogadishu had to be thinking, with no access to any sort of communications. What would happen to those of us who did not count should an evacuation become necessary? The embassy had proved time and time again just how rigid their socioeconomic hierarchy *and* disinterest in us was. Indeed, I knew from one of the six World Bank-employed but unofficial Americans evacuated from Hargeisa the previous year that when they suddenly arrived in Mogadishu (via UN transport) after a harrowing five days in that besieged northern town, all the consular officers offered were change-of-address cards.

Meanwhile, I was still better protected than, say, the watchmen on duty just inside the compound gates who knew little more than we did; Radio Mogadishu, still in government hands, was not very informative either. However, the watchmen too seemed to think this might be the beginning of the end of the regime, and despite continued shooting in the distance, they headed home before dark—the only way to find out whether their own families were safe.

Early the next morning (Saturday), the shooting had died down. The government announced the imposition of a dusk-to-dawn curfew, although the American embassy continued to warn its employees not to leave their homes. The BBC provided more concrete information than the walkie-talkies did, reporting casualty figures cited by the government as 23 killed (the number was later revised to 32) and 59 injured, as opposed to the opposition's figures, which counted the dead in the thousands. Meanwhile, the Somali government's position was that it had responded to violent demonstrations. The various opposition groups, in contrast, condemned the government for having willfully ordered troops to open fire on worshipers leaving juma prayer.

The curfew felt like citywide house arrest. Although there was still shooting once dark fell Saturday night, despite—or perhaps because of—the curfew, Sunday was quiet. By Monday the embassy was allowing most people to return to work in certain parts of the city, advising everyone to avoid traveling downtown or through other areas where the fighting had been fiercest (and where there were still thought to be pockets of trouble). Still, Monday was not quite normal.

Not surprisingly during those first few days, most of the Somalis I knew were extremely reticent about discussing what they thought had occurred and why they thought violence had finally erupted. All I was told when I asked about the present mood in Mogadishu's neighborhoods was that I should not go downtown and that under no circumstances should I ride the local buses (my normal means of transport). No one was sure that there was anti-European sentiment so much as they were unsure of just what people were feeling and what might set them off.

Within the English-speaking expatriate community, however, there was no dearth of commentary. According to a number of expatriate eyewitnesses and at least one Somali, there *was* an anti-Christian element to some of the "rioting." At least one woman was chased down a residential street by a mob of men yelling "*gaal, gaal*" (infidel) before a Somali family pulled her to safety inside their compound, and several of the houses occupied by nonproselytizing Mennonites were ransacked by Somalis who clearly knew whose homes they were ransacking (no other American homes were violated).

Because these stories began to circulate relatively quickly in the expatriate community, there was a heightened sense of concern that Somalis were turning or would turn anti-Western, and anti-American in particular. The normally besieged mentality of expatriates in Somalia ("a hardship post") was certainly (and perhaps justifiably) heightened as a consequence of the random incidents directed at them on July 14.

Meanwhile, Somalis had altogether different safety concerns. After all, it was Somalis who were being killed by other Somalis. Indeed, the danger for Somalis was on an altogether different plane than it ever was for Americans. For instance, in the days immediately following July 14, it was commonly asserted by a number of Somalis I knew that Siad Barre had armed all members of his (Marehan) clan living within Mogadishu. In response, other groups were apparently arming themselves—for defense, not offense. One person, for example, assured me that people who were unable to purchase firearms were buying bows and poisoned arrows for protection. At the same time, a young woman recounted the arguments taking place within her family about whether or not to flee into "the bush." Already her mother had buried most of the family's gold.

Corollary to this rampant fear, though, was a distinct rise in expectations throughout the first week. People expected and talked about the likelihood of there being more bloodshed on the following Friday, the 21st. For expatriates, the expectation was that if there was more unrest, they would finally be forced to leave the country that none of them particularly cared for and that many of them had assumed, from their very first day, would sink into chaos. Indeed, on my second full day in Somalia eight months previous, a USIS bureaucrat told me that I should not bother to begin any research; she kept one bag always packed, ready for flight; Somalia was going to blow.

However, on that Friday, July 21, government forces were conspicuous throughout town, imposing a de facto curfew, while the embassies imposed a de jure one, and from midmorning until late afternoon at least one small scout plane flew menacingly low over the city's rooftops. In the end, after so much anticipation (of both good and bad), there was no trouble on that day. Instead, people gradually returned to being anxious about the more routine grind of daily living and how to survive.

By the time I and most of the other expatriates ventured downtown again, nothing appeared to be physically out of place. It was as if no shooting had occurred, no massacres or atrocities had been committed. There was nothing beyond the sense of a troubled future shattered. Indeed, beyond the memory of gunfire, the only tangible evidence that anything *had* happened was the government-imposed ban on visiting the beaches—the usual weekend escape for Mogadishu's elite and many expatriates. With most expatriates already feeling that Somalia offered no pleasures, this circumscription (supposedly enforced because prisoners had been taken to, shot, and disposed of on the beaches) only further heightened the sense that the country deserved to be cut adrift.

At the same time, it is significant that I did not hear any expatriates talk about Somalis they knew who had been killed or imprisoned—a small indication of how circumscribed expatriate existence was. Many Somalis did have friends who had been killed or were arrested and dragged away, and certainly most knew of someone in their neighborhood who had disappeared. However, as this was still not a good time to wander freely, it is hard for me to say what effect the violence had within Somali neighborhoods—an admission that itself should indicate the chronic distance between expatriate and Somali existences, which, now that it was acutely visible, also froze me.

Yet, despite new physical limitations and obstacles, speech was suddenly less controlled, and a brief window of honesty opened between fears not realized and expectations not met. Sometime after the first week and into the second, when it became clear that change was not going to occur overnight but that change was still "about" to occur, Somalis began to talk openly—for the first time—about tribalism, the regime, and the horrors it was perpetrating. Up to this point open discussion of tribe or clan, which was illegal, had been virtually nonexistent. People spoke in euphemisms when discussing "family" and lineage, which is why, during this brief hiatus, it was as if a lid on several pots had been lifted at the same time, invigorating the air with a whole new feeling. Indeed, everyone I knew (from the watchmen at the compound gates to World Bank-dependent civil servants) became eager to explain to me just how many wrongs Siad Barre and his fellow clan members, the Marehan, had committed (all Marehan were lumped together in these castigations).

Unfortunately, though, this window of discussion lasted less than two weeks before it closed again, for (I believe) one reason: nothing was happening. There was no further violence aimed *at* the government, only further violence undertaken *by* the government. This violence increasingly took the form of mass arrests, death by firing squad, lootings, and rapes. It was directed by soldiers and thugs against the citizenry when they were most vulnerable—in their own homes and at night. As a consequence, people became uncertain again, of everything and everyone.

As this continued, Black Friday (as July 14 was dubbed) became less and less potent as a catalyst for immediate change. This passing, though, yielded a second effect. People were pausing; theories finally began to emerge and circulate as to what had happened on July 14. Also, it was only in the aftermath of July 14 that the assassination of the bishop became significant.

Most stories I heard from Somalis in Mogadishu linked Black Friday to the date (if not the act) of the bishop's assassination. However, more theories circulated concerning the bishop himself (who was more of a mystery to most Somalis) than July 14. Here are four. One, the bishop was involved in the black market or some other illicit trade and his death was the result of a private quarrel. Two, the bishop was not the actual target; the intended victim was another Catholic who was active in providing information to Western governments and organizations about Somali human rights abuses. Three, Islamic fundamentalists shot the bishop either to make the government look bad or because they disapproved of the bishop's proselytizing or because they were fanatics. Four, the government itself hired a killer to shoot the bishop to make it look as though Islamic fundamentalists had done it. It is this last theory that seemed most credible to Somalis I knew.

Interestingly, the logic directly linking the bishop's death and the attacks on the mosques was never particularly tidy, although people did express wonder about why the government was offering such a large reward for capture of the killer. Apparently it was common knowledge that leading imams and sheikhs had been arrested on the afternoon of July 13 (Thursday). Less clear was whether (a) they had actually been advocating antigovernment demonstrations to follow the Friday noon prayer, as the government claimed (thus leading to their arrest), (b) whether it was the imams who had not been arrested who advocated demonstrations to protest the arrests, (c) whether Siad Barre had gotten wind of rumors of demonstrations and therefore staged his soldiers outside the mosques in anticipation, or (d) whether it was merely disinformation put out by government officials that led people to believe demonstrations were planned, so that potential demonstrators would gather and could be arrested. Additionally, there were conflicting accounts as to what the worshipers *were* planning. It is unclear whether they were shot at as prayers were breaking up or as they were preparing to march. It is hard to imagine the two being distinguishable, since there are only so many doors from which worshipers could exit the mosques and any resultant outpouring *could* have looked suspicious.

Some of the subsequent world media reports did cite worshipers wielding stones, knives, and sticks. However, even this is a dubious provocation since many Somali men always wear daggers and some Somali men (particularly older men and particularly on Fridays) carry "herding" sticks.

Here it must be noted that there were no journalists in Mogadishu, so despite whatever the BBC or Voice of America may have been told by telephone, there is no conceivable way—given the spread of violence and the lack of physical vantage points—for anyone to have known who was provoking violence where. Nevertheless, a number of journals and periodicals in Britain, the United States, and elsewhere (*News from Africa Watch, Africa Confidential,* and *Indian Ocean Newsletter,* among others) did begin to publish accounts offering more detailed reasons for the outbreak of violence on July 14 (although these certainly were never available to most Somalis, and I only saw them after I had left Somalia). Like the rumors in Mogadishu, though, these written narratives were cobbled together representing much the same range of elements (anger and fear over fundamentalism, proselytizing, revelations of human rights abuses, a business venture having gone awry, etc.), but with names, clan affiliations, and other particulars included: the kinds of details that automatically lend an aura of authenticity.[2]

What is most striking when analyses such as these are compared to one another is not the narrow band of information or circumspect logic they contain, or the clear discrepancies among them, so much as the uniformity of narrative construction; they make sense of a situation that most people in Mogadishu at the time could not make such sense of. In short, they stitch together what may well be correct facts but in so doing omit gaps, as if correlations can always eventually be linked by causal arrows, with the strength of detail then proving causality.

Here already, then, we can glean hints of hindsight at work, noting that no two hindsights about July 14 were identical in any of these accounts.[3] Also we can suggest that while the creation of an apparently substantial narrative out of chronological facts may neaten reality enough to make the description of it *seem* factual, its very tidiness should alert us to the dangers of connecting dates rather than confusions: perhaps the difference between "making" sense and conveying *a* sense.

For residents of Mogadishu, then, July 14 and July 21 came and went. Of the two, July 14 made its mark in certain foreign journals. Because nothing newsworthy happened on July 21, that date was left to be remembered only in Mogadishu, where it was increasingly buried beneath new troubles, difficulties, and worries. Nevertheless, the remembrance of violence on July 14 in light of nonviolence on July 21 was still a part of discourse, particularly as October 21 approached.

OCTOBER 21: THREE MONTHS LATER

For two decades, October 21 had been celebrated as a national holiday commemorating Siad Barre's accession to power. Every year this anniversary included a parade in Mogadishu designed to display the state-cum-president's martial power. This particular October 21 marked the twentieth anniversary of Siad Barre's rule.

As October 21, 1989, approached, people again began to expect violence. Since the nonviolence of July 21, this was the only date already fixed as momentous, the only date around which people could spontaneously rally. And the symbolic timing was just too perfect: the twentieth anniversary, the government's increasingly desperate search for international support, and worsening economic conditions. But there was also the underlying hope that all Siad Barre really wanted was to enjoy his anniversary celebration and then voluntarily step down.

Siad Barre did not step down. Indeed, the fact that he attended the parade and sat in the reviewing stand was interpreted by some as a sure sign of his defiance and, more disturbing still, of his renewed or renewing strength.

Like July 21, October 21 came and went—another nonviolent letdown that seemed to postpone the significance of July 14. As for the significance of this October 21, it could only (now) be a marker of Siad Barre's longevity as nothing out of the ordinary occurred to otherwise fix it in people's memories.

Given such inflation/deflation of meaning, we begin to see how social memory itself is constructed, with liberal editing between unknowns and constant alteration as people scan forward with expectation and then past with forgetfulness.

FLOWS OUTSIDE OF TIME

To split apart what otherwise might also seem to be an unrealistically neat, chronological narrative, I will pause to examine what else was going on: the praxis of everyday life, supralocal-level interferences, and the variable construction of knowledge, emphasizing that these were all simultaneously occurring and dialectically interlinked yet could never be perceived as such without distanciation in time (itself a distortion).

First, let us briefly consider constraint at the local level. Daily life for many Mogadishu residents was economically circumscribed in at least three ways. First, there was the constant struggle of daily existence. Second, there were no reliable media in Somalia to report trends or patterns, make predictions, or analyze the local economy for the average citizen. Third, the government, wittingly or not, *was* in control of certain financial levers.

For instance, in the weeks just prior to July 14, cash began to run short in the capital. Clearly, this exacerbated people's frustration with, and anger at, the government. It not only symbolized the regime's corruption and corrosion; such blatant bankruptcy on the part of the government also had to contribute to the sense that it was no longer in control and that even the most basic services were no longer safe from increasing threats of anarchy.

A second wave of cashlessness occurred later in the summer, well after July 14 (although for government employees, there were no salaries for a full eight weeks). This event appeared to have different roots. While a large percentage of Somalia's cash was thought to still be in the hands of nomads (who had been paid massive sums for livestock transshipped to Saudi Arabia for the Hajj in early July),[4] there were also reports that the president was bribing potentially mutinous officers and their troops with large sums of money and that merchants were withholding money from the banks to do their part to bring down the regime. Whether any of these rumors was accurate, or all were accurate in part, there was also evidence that bank officials themselves were partially to blame. In a form of protest over their inadequate pay, clerks and cashiers began demanding 10 percent of any check a client wished to cash or 10 percent of any sum he or she sought to withdraw. However, it also may have been that the government purposely sought to dry up cash reserves to keep people busy searching for money and credit, thereby preventing them from having the time or wherewithal to engage in antigovernment protests.

While this (like so much else) is speculative, there is some indication that the government did occasionally operate in such a manner. For instance, at times there was no electricity in Mogadishu because the generator plant malfunctioned, or because the fuel had been stolen, or because the government ordered the electricity shut off so that people could not congregate at night. There were even rumors that the electricity was deliberately stopped on Wednesday afternoons because this is when the BBC broadcast its Somali report. Alternatively, during prolonged fuel shortages when tensions rose and people who did have fuel found themselves and their vehicles viciously stoned, fuel for the general public would somehow magically rematerialize. It was almost as if the government was playing chicken with the populace; either the regime was exceptionally clever at gauging the local temper and playing the limit or it was continually testing the waters to see how much it could get away with.

Siad Barre's government was best able to achieve such local control and to successfully stage manage an authoritative face by ceaselessly interjecting itself on the international front. This appeared to be done by purposely dealing with countries opposed to each other in quick succession; for example, immediately after Siad Barre would return from Libya his defense minister would visit Kuwait. Such practices were as old as the regime. Similarly, as long as the USSR still supported Ethiopia and the cold war was extant, members of the regime must have felt that they could keep the United States toeing a line of assistance far more often than the United States could successfully coerce them into more than token human rights gestures. At the same time, the more Siad Barre and his government could be seen hosting and being hosted by representatives of other governments on state-controlled television, the more legitimate and powerful the regime (and even Somalia itself) seemed.

Meanwhile, too, there was the conjunction of international finance and finesse at the highest levels—evident in International Monetary Fund, World Bank, and United Nations High Commission for Refugees (UNHCR) policies that dovetailed suspiciously often with U.S. and even Soviet reactions to the Somali government's latest overtures on the diplomatic front. These multinational agencies, although familiar to many Somalis, were also skilled at publicly masking the real messages they were sending the government, and the Somali state-controlled media could further gloss the rationales the agencies publicized to serve the Somali state's purposes. Thus, the interconnectedness of action, response, and countermeasure at the supralocal level would have been as hidden from most people as the "real" reasons cash was absent or the electricity fitful and fuel spotty at the most local levels.

RUMORS

Still, as with the activity on and around July 14, people consistently sought to rub lemon juice on government actions and pronouncements, to search for real reasons and to conflate conjecture with knowledge. Because knowledge could not be substantiated on the streets, information that came in the form of rumor was often treated as knowledge and, in a sense, became knowledge.

Somalis and expatriates ran parallel rumor mills. Some Americans were officially better informed than others. On occasion there was even cross-pollenization among communities. Certainly one way to enhance standing (of a sort) in the expatriate community was to become a source of information about Somalis. One then became a sort of bank: as with gossip, the rule seemed to be that the more one was able to divulge, the more information one was likely to receive to divulge elsewhere. Networks were key, not only for the receipt of information but also for the construction and dissemination of reputation. Essentially, then, there was what amounted to an economy of rumors.

However, expatriate acceptance of rumors was quite different from the way Somalis treated rumors. Among expatriates various tricks were used for couching rumors in such a way that they appeared to have originated from significant and important sources. Quite often arguments arose in defense of rumors brought to the table. At times it seemed as though people forgot that, at best, these were only rumors they were discussing; they acted as if rumors were property. At worst, despite this proprietary behavior, everyone always had a pretty good idea who everyone else's sources could be: essentially either office colleagues, government acquaintances, or *boyessas* (cleaning women). Nonetheless, the facade of unimpeachable sources and information was maintained by the use of the third-person plural, the mysterious (numerous) "they."

As for my own random network of Somalis, who were other people's boyessas, drivers, and watchmen; tailors, street vendors, tea shop workers; restaurateurs, civil servants, and young intellectuals, they had already prepared me for confusion. Well before July 14, I had already heard too many different descriptions from Somalis of courtship and marriage—two seemingly straightforward "cultural" matters that always differed significantly in the details, despite anthropological rules—not to wonder whether the piecemeal nature of what I was being told and what I could be told might not also reflect the piecemeal nature of the field for Somalis, too. Therefore, the one pattern that was discernible across the board—namely, variability—seemed to make sense, for me, of Somali reactions to rumors.

In contrast to the expatriates, the Somalis I knew were usually very precise about couching everything they suspected to be rumor *as* rumor and not as "a" (possible) truth or "the" truth. Rather, information was usually offered as the best possible explanation for making sense of a situation according to whatever a person happened to have heard up until that particular moment. Information was never considered unimpeachable or fixed.

On the contrary, information was suspect for at least two reasons: there was no centralized credible news media in Somalia, and far too often the government engaged in the dissemination of disinformation. It was commonly asserted that false rumors were purposely planted as trial balloons, or fake papers were left lying around so that rumors *would* circulate. This was done (it was said) so that the powers that be could gauge public reaction either to something they were planning to do or to whatever they hoped to spoil for opponents or critics.

For instance, in late June a murky set of rumors circulated. These accused northerners in the capital of being witches who fed on other Somalis. Anyone I asked said that these were government-generated rumors.

Why the government was promulgating such notions, though, was less obvious. I heard three divergent explanations: either the government was trying to keep people inside their homes at night to staunch a slowly increasing crime rate, or the government was trying to keep people inside their homes at night to stem the rising tide of antigovernment graffiti and discontent, or the government was trying to keep people housebound to prevent the spread of AIDS.

The kernel of truth that may have spawned two of these explanations was that earlier in June there had been a wave of antigovernment graffiti writing at night on city walls, only to be erased by government workers in the morning. Reportedly even cows that usually wandered the Ceel Gaab market area had been defaced by graffiti. As for the third explanation (which involved AIDS), this too was a subject for speculation since it was widely acknowledged that prostitutes found to be infected with HIV were taken out into the desert and shot.

Even more significant was that most rumors only increased tension as people increasingly tried to determine the roots of the tension assumed to be spawning the rumors. In other words, the search for causes for rumors produced more rumors.

Also, because of the diverse nature of people's experiences, occupations, and networks, what individuals could observe, glean, and piece together varied considerably. People could be incredibly clever in reading meaning into seemingly unconnected events or occurrences. As no information could be disproved, anything was possible. As long as one's logic was internally consistent, one could render any explanation of events believable. Clearly, too, what people already knew predisposed them in various ways. On the one hand, this made for a proliferation of approaches to the same array of "facts." On the other hand, it meant that all "facts" could be threaded together by singular lines of logic.

Consequently, it was this proliferation of rumors along with a desperate need for knowledge that both directly and indirectly led people to continue thinking along certain lines and not others, channeling their logic and creating expectations that, when they were not realized, often blistered into frustration, despair, impotence, rage, and produced and reproduced danger.

It is this residue from rumors that we now know as history. And this may be problematic. For instance, rumors themselves tend to be too slippery and their half-life too short to leave traces in individual, never mind social, memory. Instead, along with kaleidoscopic changes in mood, their significance as mood enhancers or mood dampeners and vectors for action gets swallowed up in concern over the flurry of their results: "events." In turn, as these events become ordered for narrative, the tendency is to reduce, collapse, and edit out the very terror of not-knowing, which is at the heart and soul of every rumor. Consequently, the critical link—that all events are interpreted by nothing but rumors—gets missed and this terror of not-knowing comes to look hollow and tinny, even peripheral beside the blood, guts, and drama of physical violence.

This is clearly evident the further along the time line we move from July 14, 1989. By late 1992 (a little more than three years later), Black Friday was no longer part of any outsider's explanation for the anarchic unseemliness of Mogadishu.

1992: THREE YEARS LATER

Even at the height of the media blitz, with self-declared experts explaining away the disaster that had become Somalia by December 1992, we find no mention of July 14 as a pivotal date.[5] I suggest this is so for at least three reasons: the immediacy of what needed to be reported, the sources for this reporting—who tended to be journalists new to Somalia (who had not been there in 1989)—and the drowning out of the violence on July 14 in the depths of a broader, more continuous reign of violence.

Also, just as it proved impossible to step outside of July 14 on July 14 in Mogadishu, to analyze it with any dispassion or any sense of context-in-the-making, the constancy of violence since July 14, 1989, has made it virtually impossible to rearrange the local, regional, national, and international flows into a streamlined, sensical narrative. Indeed, the reality itself is such that narrative seems impossible when the beginning is so dependent on an ending that is so unsure.

Having said this, though, it should not be hard to see that for all the same reasons that July 14 did not exist in the foreground of consciousness in 1992 and 1993, it will nonetheless likely reappear and be treated as a historical turning point in the narrative future. This will be so because July 14 has already been documented as a date of importance (by the media immediately after July 14) and consequently has been lent archival stature. Also, when the smoke clears, it will be necessary to search for plausible beginnings to all the violence of 1990, 1991, 1992, 1993. July 14 still stands as the first day of violence in Mogadishu during this period.

In many respects, then, July 14 will reappear correctly, but for potentially wrong reasons. For example, it was not as a date that July 14 had significance on July 14, 15, or even 21. Rather, it held significance as a marker of thresholds and as a moment of confusion that linked all communities in Mogadishu together by threatening to tear all of them apart. Conceivably, the only thing that was clear to everyone about that day on that day is that it was apparent as soon as shots rang out that something momentous and out of the ordinary was happening, so that at the time it *was* felt that this would become The Event that would usher in a series of other, new events—and a new order. In other words, everyone (Somali and non-Somali alike) realized on July 14 that Somalia was finally in the breech. What marked the breech was that there had been a relatively safe before in contrast to a now-violent present and what was already knowable as a bloodstained after.

Ironically, it is precisely this felt knowledge, this experiential, terrifying, time-warping, never-complete sense of what was happening *then* that history will never record and that future contexts will lack. In part, that will be because history will not be interested in the essence of July 14—confusion, anguish, expectation—and how these emotional responses shook, branded, seared, and altered virtually everyone. But in part, too, this loss will reflect a loss of memory in those present who can no longer be sure how this one day did change their lives, when so many other days of confusion, anguish, expectation, exhaustion, and terror have intervened between an unremarkable then and a no longer remarkable now.

It is also likely that the full range of rumors that constituted knowledge at the time will similarly escape recounting, since they, too, are as evanescent, fleeting, yet cumulative and evaporative as emotion. As a result, history will connect dots of chronology to construct narrative and seek narrative with chronologically probing questions. Yet such a production of hindsight will automatically be checkered. Ultimately, this may also be because it is time, not we, that stretches truths and railroads realities.

Nevertheless, if anthropology can offer any antidote at all to the generalizations of social history, the tailored particulars of political economy, or the momentous occasioning of chronology, it may well be to counter all narrative flows with the confusion of participants' emotions and the observed realities of chaos. For instance, in November 1988, Mogadishu was a safe place for most people although people felt safe expecting violence; by November 1989, Mogadishu felt dangerous because people had not yet settled their differences violently enough. In other words, nothing definitive had happened in the space of that year except that Mogadishu had definitely turned a corner. This was felt at the time—in the tension spawned by rumor and reactions to rumor, in crime, in uncertainty, in heightened expectation. Nevertheless, the proofs for such gut-level knowledge have likely already disappeared. Yet in their wake, and as clues continue to be obliterated, the puzzle still remains: What has Mogadishu turned the corner to? This question will likely always taunt us, because time will always stretch our meanings.

POSTSCRIPT

Time continues to stretch meanings as well as significance. And we continue to rely on rumor.

It is now shortly after a second U.S. withdrawal from Somalia (spring 1994), and all I can say today with assurance is that I again know what it feels like not to really know. Not only have I not been able to return to Somalia but so far, in the first few months after Operation Restore Hope, it is still unclear what, if anything, has been resolved there: whether the supposed chaos, or the violence, or the settling of old-turned-into-new or new-recast-as-old scores.

Indeed, Operation Restore Hope itself spawned an entire industry of rumors outside of Somalia; one can only imagine the intensity of these rumors within Somalia. For instance, many of us here (Somali and non-Somali alike) have had to wonder, why *was* the United States leading the charge back into Somalia? Clearly—according to one logic—it had to be because Somalia had something the world still found valuable: oil, geo-strategic significance, something. Otherwise, why help starving Somalis when there were starving Sudanese, Angolans, Mozambicans, and even Americans who could equally have used assistance?

Interestingly, even U.S. soldiers stationed in Somalia agreed: humanitarianism could not be the real reason they had been sent so many time zones away. When I posed this question to 10th Mountain Division infantrymen (during a visit to Fort Drum in July 1993), their response often came close to responses I heard from Somalis living in the United States: the intervention had to be politically motivated. Of course, the political intricacies the soldiers saw were somewhat different from those that Somalis in this country tended to focus on.

While some soldiers cited a newspaper article[6] describing Somalia's potential oil fields, as well as then–President George Bush's close ties to the oil industry, and agreed that this must have been the real reason their units had been sent, others assumed that the United States needed a military base in Somalia, which this intervention would secure. What is significant about this last conjecture is that it reveals the partiality of knowledge about Somalia even when there was a surfeit of sources to indicate otherwise. These soldiers were clearly unaware that the United States *had* been interested in Somalia from the late 1970s onward, in part *because* there was an extant base the United States "purchased" access to (namely, Berbera). Berbera had since become superseded as a jumping-off point for U.S. soldiers bound for the Middle East, and this, too, should have been common knowledge in Somalia—if not through the military itself, then through the now-ubiquitous Western media.

However, that soldiers were not so well informed even about what they could/should have known suggests something else about rumors and conjecture: how easily these can substitute for factual information and then preclude the need to search for actual fact. It also suggests something else, about how often people scan for the future in the present, rather than the past.

For instance, another American musing was that Operation Restore Hope was President Bush's way of leaving incoming President Bill Clinton with a quagmire. Alternatively, there were Americans as well as many Somalis who assumed that Operation Restore Hope had been engaged in to preempt Islamic fundamentalists from gaining a stronghold in Somalia. Indeed, Somali rumors were well elaborated on this score, centering in part around the machinations of UN Secretary-General Boutros Boutros-Ghali, who (it was said) still had strong ties to the Egyptian Foreign Ministry, which, some Somalis believed, had its own (if not just antifundamentalist) interests at stake.

Nor is this at all an exhaustive survey of the rumors that swirled around, resulted from, and perhaps even helped lead to Operation Restore Hope. Rather, it is merely a sampling of how rumor worked to try to fathom the why-fors of a very well publicized yet ultimately very confusing intervention.

Ironically, the confusion may stem in part from the fact that the intervention was advertised as humanitarian. Whether or not we take the declared aims of Operation Restore Hope (to feed the starving) at face value, we still have to recognize that humanitarian ends were sought through a whole array of suspect means: closed-door politics, U.S. soldier–Somali segregation, the use of force. All of which was bound to fracture coherence among Somalis, between Somalis and Americans, and between Somalis and the UN. No wonder suspicion and rumor resulted. Given so much secretiveness, how could there not be hidden agendas?

Meanwhile, once rumor became a substitute for—and suspicion replaced—knowledge, clarity was bound to dissipate. As was certainty. With vengeance.

NOTES

1. Major political demonstrations in Mogadishu had been reported most recently in October 1988 (*Africa Confidential,* 18 November) and August 1987 (*Africa Research Bulletin,* 15 October). However, the most recent violent demonstrations had occurred in 1975, when Muslim leaders led opposition to Siad Barre's declaration of Family Law.

2. In their July 21 issue, *News from Africa Watch* wrote,

The killing [of the bishop] is thought by many in Mogadishu to have been carried out by two members of the President's own clan, the Marehan, leading to resentment about the apparent attempt to implicate Moslem religious figures. According to the reports we have received, when the authorities learned of these rumors, they publicized a six million shilling reward for information leading to the identity of the assas-

sin, both to quash the rumors and to create the impression abroad that the government was determined to apprehend and prosecute the offenders. . . . They also began a
campaign that identified religious elements as the guilty parties on the basis that many
of them are "fanatic fundamentalists" who had openly attacked the government's
offer of a substantial reward for the killing of the Bishop. (6)

Africa Confidential, in contrast, explained in its July 28 issue that the bishop
was shot in his cathedral on 9 July. The government offered a reward of 5 million
Somali Shillings, which led to criticism that it was larger than anything ever offered as
a reward for the arrest of the murderer of any Muslim. Rumors were spread that the
bishop, best known for his help with refugees and for recovering bodies from the NSS
[National Security Service] when families were too frightened, had been trying to
convert unemployed Muslim youth. (7)

The Somali novelist Nruddin Farah added the detail that many Somalis believed the bishop had buried unclaimed corpses without the proper Islamic rites,
in effect "converting" them to Christianity after death (*Manchester Guardian,* 18
August 1989).

Interestingly, six months after Black Friday, there was a completely different
spin on the bishop's assassination in *Africa Events,* which suggested that the murder
was carried out by a member of the NSS at the instigation of one Issa Ugas, the
head of a shoe factory in Mogadishu and a close relative of the president's. Issa
Ugas had allegedly received the shoe factory, confiscated from the Vatican, when
the Somali government nationalized Somalia's industries. Shortly before the bishop's murder, *Africa Events* reports, rumors indicated that the IMF and World Bank
were going to force the privatization of small industries and that the Catholic
Mission had displayed interest in regaining their factory, thus the bishop was shot
(January 1990).

Finally, one and a half years after Black Friday, a Somali writer in *New African* asserted that Siad Barre had long been suspicious of the bishop for being too knowledgeable about human rights abuses and the inner workings of the regime. It was
after Amnesty International's June 1989 visit to Mogadishu that Siad Barre had the
bishop eliminated—shortly after the bishop also protested the president's autho-
rizing of a family member to take over a plot of land belonging to the church
(February 1991).

3. See note 2, above.

4. Prior to the annual Hajj, Somalis usually transshipped millions of head of
stock to Saudi Arabia from Berbera and other northern Somali ports. However,
with civil war raging in the north, much of the Hajj transshipment took place
through Mogadishu and included unprecedented numbers of stock from the central parts of the country.

5. Either in the *Washington Post,* the *New York Times,* the *Los Angeles Times,* or a
variety of news magazine accounts—or for that matter in CNN or network news
commentary or analysis.

6. In fact, a front-page story from the *Los Angeles Times,* 18 January 1993.

ACCIDENTAL ANTHROPOLOGY

The Morning after the Massacre, Beijing, June 4, 1989
(Photo: Collection Chinese People's Movement 1989,
International Institute of Social History, Amsterdam)

Witnessing the 1989
Chinese People's Movement

Frank N. Pieke

On April 18, 1989, about five months into my doctoral fieldwork in Beijing, a student demonstration in commemoration of the recently deceased Communist party leader Hu Yaobang took me completely by surprise. Students from various universities in Beijing staged protests in Tian'anmen Square, using their mourning over Hu's death to make political demands.[1]

> After dinner I go out for a walk in the direction of Tian'anmen Square. At the Monument for Revolutionary Heroes a large crowd is assembled. Most of them are curious bystanders like myself, but several youths are busily copying down poems pasted on the sides of the monument.
>
> Facing the Great Hall of the People there is more activity. The focus of attention is a group of about 300 students sitting on the pavement. Suddenly three of them get up and walk toward the entrance of the hall. I ask the person next to me whose representatives they are. The students', he tells me. What are their demands? He says there are seven, but does not want to say anything more. Obviously, the people here are extremely reluctant to talk to a foreigner. Even a colleague whom I happened to run into treats me like somebody with a contagious disease.
>
> The student representatives leave the hall again, met by loud cheers from their fellows. The representatives raise their hands, and one of them unfolds a large sheet of paper with, I assume, their demands. For a while nothing happens until several men emerge from the hall. They stay on the stairs leading to the entrance, about one hundred yards away, and wave at the crowd. Nobody knows who they are. First I am told that Premier Li Peng is among them, but later this is scaled down to the mayor of Beijing.
>
> After the men have retreated into the hall, a couple of students produce a paper wreath with on both sides a vertical banner attached to it, car-

rying the words "*minzhu hun*" (democratic soul). After parading the wreath all around the square, they proceed to the Monument for Revolutionary Heroes. The wreath is then hauled onto the monument. This is rewarded with loud cheers from the other students on the monument and the crowd gathered in front of it. The students start singing the International, off-key, making the crowd and themselves laugh. Nothing more happens for quite a while, and I decide to return home. (Field notes, April 18, 1989)

Without yet realizing it, I had been witnessing the first stage of the largest political movement in the People's Republic since the Cultural Revolution of the 1960s. Throughout the 1970s and 1980s, the history of the People's Republic had been punctuated by protest movements. All these earlier movements played an important role in the construction and development of the 1989 protests, providing much of the shared knowledge among the participants on the methods, symbols, and goals of efficacious and legitimate political protest. Yet in terms of its scale, duration, and impact on the general population, the 1989 movement eclipsed all its precursors.

The earliest and arguably most famous of these earlier protests was the 1976 Tian'anmen Incident in Beijing and other cities. Although this movement was in many respects very similar to the early stages of 1989 protests, a swift crackdown by the authorities had precluded its development into an acute threat to the Maoist leadership. Other protests, such as the 1979 Democracy Wall and the 1986 student movements, mainly involved small groups of political activists or university students.

The 1989 movement that is the topic of this chapter escalated after the *People's Daily*, the official Communist party newspaper, published a strong-worded denunciation of the movement in its editorial of April 26. Large student marches on April 27 and May 4 ensued, which, for the first time, were tacitly supported by Beijing citizens who watched along the way. Just as important, the students received support from party General Secretary Zhao Ziyang who had been away on an official visit to North Korea at the time of the *People's Daily* condemnation. The escalation of the demonstrations, the support by ordinary citizens, and the split within the party leadership were enough to force the government into negotiation with the students.

These confidential negotiations did not produce quick results, however. In response, about two thousand students decided to go on a hunger strike on Tian'anmen Square. Their only demands were that the government agree to a public dialogue on the basis of equality with the students and acknowledge that the student movement was patriotic. The government was willing to do neither. The suffering of the hunger strikers and the government's harsh attitude unleashed the long-felt sympathy of Beijing's citizens for the students' cause. Mass demonstrations in support of the hunger strikers followed; first by Beijing's intellectuals on May 15 and then by delegations from work units on May 17 and 18.[2]

Alarmed by the escalation of events, a coalition of moderate and conservative party and state leaders, put together by Deng Xiaoping, brushed aside Zhao Ziyang and declared martial law in the Beijing area. However, attempts on May 20 and 21 to enter Beijing with local troops failed because the people of Beijing blocked the entrances to the city and the troops refused to open fire. The failure of the local troops to crush the movement forced the party and state leadership to change course. Negotiations with army leaders from other provinces followed to persuade them to deploy their troops or at least remain neutral while other armies marched on Beijing.

The leadership took two weeks to solve the political and logistical problems of the new strategy. At ten o'clock on the evening of June 3, the army again marched on Beijing. At the cost of many casualties, the columns of tanks and armored personnel carriers broke through the roadblocks that were manned by students and citizens, reaching Tian'anmen Square at two o'clock on the morning of June 4. After sealing off the square, the army allowed the students remaining in the square to leave. Beijing had been captured, and the People's Movement had been broken.

Throughout the five months of my fieldwork, I could not have anticipated a movement of this magnitude. Although I had been interested in social movements and political protest in China for a long time, I had never thought I would be able to witness and study one close at hand. My original fieldwork, therefore, concerned an entirely different set of issues. My aim had been to acquire a grassroots perspective on the dynamics of Chinese state socialist society under the impact of ten years of reform in order to understand the interaction between the fabric of daily life and the course taken by the reform policies initiated since 1978.

After April 18, I did not hesitate long before shifting my attention to the observation and analysis of the People's Movement. Indeed, it was almost impossible not to do so. With more and more people involved, the movement became the only meaningful event, coloring all others. It became impossible to talk about the issues I had been studying without relating them to the People's Movement. Earlier, my informants had already expressed feelings of dissatisfaction or disappointment about the breakdown of morality in society. Now, these same feelings had become much more sharply focused. In the course of the movement, a moral discursive frame had been developed to single out the enemy: corrupt cadres and national leaders. Moreover, a strategy had been developed to stop their digressions.

Rather than constituting a completely separate fieldwork project, my study of the movement shed light on my earlier interviews and observations of the more mundane aspects of life in Beijing. Conversely, because of my earlier fieldwork, I was able to understand the movement much better and, even more important, through the eyes of the participants. Although the outbreak of the movement was an accident, my study of it was definitely not accidental anthropology. It became part of an evolving fieldwork experience. My ideas about the nature of anthropological fieldwork and my experiences during my earlier, "ordinary" fieldwork in Beijing had prepared me to respond to such accidents. My reconstruction of life under the reforms and the story of the People's Movement cannot be divorced from the intensely personal experience of trying to construct a fieldwork project in Beijing. I will therefore begin by briefly narrating this experience.

CONSTRUCTING A FIELDWORK PROJECT IN THE PEOPLE'S REPUBLIC OF CHINA

Generally speaking, after having negotiated his or her way into China, an anthropologist can, in my opinion, embark on one of two alternative strategies. He or she can decide to stay in China for a relatively brief period and try to collect factual data on a limited and concrete set of topics. In this case, the fieldwork can only supplement information gathered in other ways such as library research or refugee interviewing in Hong Kong or elsewhere outside China. Alternatively, the field-worker who wants to stay in China to immerse himself or herself in Chinese life for a much longer period will have to be extremely flexible. Such field-workers have to be prepared to change their research design and even its topics to accommodate the shifts and changes of Chinese daily life and politics. In China, a choice for dialogical and improvisational fieldwork is therefore not merely a matter of theoretical and methodological preference but a strategy for anthropological survival, a point I will return to below.

The problems of anthropological fieldwork in China already begin with the difficulty of obtaining official permission. In general, it is essential to have a Chinese organization that is willing to act as official host. By acting as the field-worker's temporary work unit, this organization can help overcome the many hurdles the Chinese bureaucracy puts in the way of the proposed project. In the case of my fieldwork, the Institute of Sociology at the Chinese Academy of Social Sciences in Beijing agreed to receive me. The academy is a ministry-level organization and therefore fairly independent. Yet since its foundation in 1977 it has been a controversial institution. Its research institutes provide a haven for independent-minded intellectuals, many of them with a personal history of criticism of the regime and ensuing persecution. The academy is a source of constant criticism of the regime, and before June 1989 some of its institutes were undiluted think tanks for radical leaders. With official patronage these intellectuals have thus been able to carve out their own liberalized niche in the bureaucratized social structure, but, as I was soon to find out, at the price of isolation from the other parts of that structure. It has been no coincidence, therefore, that several of the intellectuals who have fled China or have been arrested after the People's Movement, such as Su Shaozhi, Bao Zunxin, and Yan Jiaqi, were associated with the academy.

My position in China was made even more difficult because the Institute of Sociology had been the official host of Stephen Mosher, a Stanford anthropology graduate student denied reentry into China in 1980 after what the authorities considered to be repeated breaches of trust (Pieke 1986). Subsequently, the institute had been pressing the leadership of the academy for several years to grant permission again to invite foreigners to conduct fieldwork, but this had been given only in the summer of 1988. For me, it meant living in a fishbowl. Engaging in behavior that might cause the institute serious political trouble would effectively have closed the door on future foreign anthropologists wanting to get access to China through the institute.

Being fully aware of the problematic nature of fieldwork by foreigners, I arrived in China with a research proposal already strongly adapted to suit Chinese sensitivities. I had chosen as the topic of my research the social structure of a work unit. This, I hoped, would give me the opportunity to interview both ordinary members and cadres of a unit. Moreover, this topic could accommodate a broad range of subjects such as the organizational structure of the work unit and its relationships with other parts of the bureaucracy, the structure of individual families within the unit, or informal processes of decision making.

Unfortunately, things in China turned out to be worse than what I had prepared for. On arrival, I was asked to translate my fieldwork proposal into Chinese. Subsequently, the foreign affairs officer at the institute completely rewrote the proposal, adapting it so as not to offend the bureaucrats who would have to approve it. After she had done her job, my already watered down proposal had become an unrecognizably bland statement.

This started a period of two months during which the institute tried to negotiate permission from various bureaucratic levels in the Beijing municipality. Meanwhile, I was forced to remain largely idle. In the end, the institute's efforts proved unsuccessful and permission was not granted because "the conditions at the basic level are not satisfactory." Fortunately, being considered somewhat of a test case and having spent so much time in Beijing, my hosts felt obliged to come up with an alternative. The four or five researchers at the institute with whom I had become friendly, my hosts suggested, should together have enough friends and acquaintances to act as my interviewees for a while. After all, the municipal authorities had not refused to grant permission but had merely stated that the conditions were not satisfactory. Nothing would stop me from looking for people to talk to and interviewing them informally. This network-centered approach worked, and I succeeded in interviewing about forty-five families, many of them several times, in the three-month period between mid-February and mid-May 1989.

Despite the succcess of the interviews, the research plan had to be adapted once again to the new circumstances. No longer was a community or geographic area the locus of activities; instead people from all over Beijing would be interviewed. More important, I could only do this by shifting the focus of the interviews away from the social structure and the networks in one community to family and individual strategies both at work and in private life. Methodologically, this meant that the subjective reality of my informants in the context of concrete events became my primary concern, instead of a social structure supposedly existing external to and independent from my informants. In other words, the constraints of my situation had forced me to become more of a postmodern anthropologist than I had ever intended to be.

By February 1989, I had finally arrived at a research design that suited the many constraints imposed by Beijing society. The outbreak of the People's Movement in mid-April, however, forced me to change the focus of my research once more. During the interviews many people had talked about their hardship and the inequity caused by the reforms, but there was no indication that these tensions could lead to widespread social unrest in the near future. Yet this was precisely what happened.

During the first stages of the movement, I remained merely an interested bystander. I tried to follow what was happening but felt that the student movement would either quickly be suppressed or else lose its force. I therefore saw no compelling reason to cancel my departure for Xiamen in Southeast China to participate in an academic conference.

During the student demonstrations of April 27 and May 4, however, the movement showed for the first time that it could potentially mobilize large segments of the population. After my return from Xiamen on May 1, I decided to devote more of my time to observing the demonstrations, taping speeches, collecting pamphlets, and asking questions concerning the movement in interviews and informal conversations.

The May 4 demonstration was very interesting to watch from an anthropological point of view, although as a demonstration it ended somewhat inconclusively. The students seemed to lack a clear issue to demonstrate for. The most important point seemed to be *that* the demonstration happened and that the people along the route expressed their support. A colleague at the institute told me that this is part of the students' strategy. The demonstration was meant as "propaganda." It is obvious that the movement is everything but spontaneous. The students—or at least their leaders—seem to have a clear idea of what they want and how to achieve it.

What struck me very much when watching the demonstration was that most people did not participate as individuals but as members of delegations of their school or department. Each delegation carried its own identifying banner and was sealed off from other delegations and from the bystanders by a ring of people walking hand in hand. To me the symbolic effect of this was that the students isolated themselves from the people for whom they demonstrated. The enthusiastic bystander remained a spectator, only able to express his support by applauding, cheering, and donating money, food, or ice cream. At the institute a couple of days ago I was told that the latter was the most important invention of the big demonstration of April 27. By cheering and giving food and money, the people, "including even individual entrepreneurs" (considered by many the parasites of society), had clearly shown their support for the movement. According to this colleague, the rings around the delegations were only meant to keep troublemakers out. Things had to stay peaceful and orderly to avoid giving the authorities a splendid excuse to crack down on the movement. Hearing this I cannot help thinking that although one demonstrates for the people, the people still cannot be trusted.

Another topic everybody discusses is the attitude of the government: when will the repression begin? At the moment, plainclothes policemen are taking pictures of the students, but when will they start arresting people? The students refuse to use violence, but so does the government. They have reached the point at which the one who first resorts to violence will be the loser of a moral and symbolic contest and implicit dialogue. (Field notes, May 5, 1989)

For the students, nonviolence and openly expressed loyalty to party and system were the cornerstones of their strategy. It allowed them to play the role of the representatives of the people seeking a dialogue with the government on terms of equality, a dialogue about the pressing problems facing the nation. This put the authorities in a very difficult position. They could not simply brand the students as counterrevolutionary elements and sweep them off the streets. Conversely, agreeing to an equal dialogue would be interpreted as a major victory for the students and as recognition of them as legitimate representatives of the people. This would have devastating consequences for the ruling ideology and system, which was built on the role of the party as the sole representative of the working class and the leading force in society. In this context, the support from bystanders gave the demonstrations a powerful political impact, transforming the Maoist concept of "the people" from an empty propaganda slogan into an actual and existing political actor. As a worker in a state factory told me during an interview on May 12,

I am very concerned, concerned about that movement, concerned about the disturbances, and even more concerned about the reputation of our country. [About] whether this student disturbance is good or not, I think that still it is good. Although they have created some disturbances, and have made things difficult, at least they have attacked corrupt elements, and especially those within the party. They have sounded the alarm bell on them. They are also [in] the Communist party, which is the leading party, and [the students] have exposed them. Why is it that the students are talking like that? It is because they at least have a solid social basis. No matter what the students want, the workers and the peasants . . . Question: But, apart from the problem of corruption, the students have also raised more abstract issues like freedom and democracy. Answer: These things . . . I nevertheless think they are necessary. They are indispensable in the people's lives. The least you need is freedom and democracy. These must be safeguarded. . . . All those manifestations of corruption, you can see them everywhere. Isn't that so? (Tape 29, interview of May 12, 1989)

The open support of the people during the demonstrations already amounted to an important cultural invention. The next development, however, was even more far-reaching. Under the impact of the student hunger strike that began on May 13, the support for the students changed to active participation. Hesitantly at first but quickly gaining momentum, the movement swept up everybody in its vortex. Because of its tragic conclusion, it is now often forgotten that the movement was an exhilarating experience for all involved. Pent-up frustrations going back many years could suddenly be shouted out to resonate with those of countless others. It was the time when it seemed that the impossible could be achieved and the unthinkable could become true. This development culminated in the mass demonstrations of May 17 and 18 when the people of Beijing dared to defy the government more openly than ever before.

Today the lid really was pulled off the pan. Yesterday, workers already participated in large numbers demanding the resignation of Deng Xiaoping. Today, I estimate at least a million people demonstrated officially (that is, within the delegation of their work unit). From the tenth floor of a hotel as far as I can see the whole of Chang'an Avenue is completely packed. This amounts to a general strike, and indeed people are using this word now, instead of merely talking about support for the hunger strikers.

The delegations come from work units all over Beijing. Because of the distances involved, many delegations come by truck, driving down Chang'an, around the square, and back to the work unit.

The atmosphere is that of a carnival, or rather of liberation. The people are exhilarated, but still disciplined. Many yell at each other, "We have won!" (*Women shengli le!*) It is clear that the act of demonstrating in itself is a potent emancipating experience, regardless of the actual demands or the hoped-for result. Testifying to this are banners with "Afraid?" (*Pa?*) or "Wake Up" (*Xing*) written on them. Some walk around with portraits of Zhou Enlai or

Mao Zedong, others yell "Long Live Chairman Mao!" (*Mao zhuxi wansui!*).[3]
(Field notes, May 18, 1989)

At this juncture, the movement had become the only topic of conversation. It halted the normal flow of life, becoming what I propose to call a *total event*. A total event imposes its interpretive frame on the whole of society. Normally, an event is intricately tied up with the myriad other events that constitute its context. A total event, however, is autonomous. Instead of the normal dialectic between event and context, a total event creates its own context from its environment and determines the meaning and significance of all other events.

The dominance of a total event also entails that there is no escaping from it. Nonparticipation and neutrality have ceased to be a legitimate option. All social actors are forced into the arena, while all fundamental problems and conflicts in society are expressed in terms of the interpretive frame of the total event. The compelling force of a total event even extends to very peripheral social actors such as foreign anthropologists. During the movement, I thus felt that I had no option but to study it.

Once again, therefore, Beijing society was determining the subject and method of my research. But this time it was different. It was not me trying to find ways and means to wring opportunities from an indifferent society and a positively unwilling municipal bureaucracy. The initiative was resolutely pulled out of my hands, and the Chinese themselves started to decide what my fieldwork would be about.

As I had written in my field notes of April 18, the early stages of the movement still saw the apprehension of foreigners normal to Chinese society. Very quickly, however, foreign observers became vitally important to the movement. The Chinese-language radio dispatches of the BBC and the Voice of America allowed the student activists to circumvent the media monopoly of the authorities. Through foreign journalists, they could address a nationwide audience and even mobilize world opinion to their cause.

Similarly, my personal experience with the initial stages of the movement was limited because my hosts at the institute asked me to avoid any involvement. They did not allow me to take pictures in the square, talk to the students, or go to their campuses. Suspicious activities on my part could very well be used as a pretext to crack down on my research and make it much more difficult in the future to arrange fieldwork opportunities for other foreign anthropologists. Having spent the first fifteen weeks of my stay trying to get permission to do fieldwork, I was prepared to listen to that argument.

Fortunately, by the first week of May, my hosts had relaxed their standpoint considerably, which probably had much to do with Zhao Ziyang's reappraisal of the movement on May 3 and 4. Still, they did not want me to talk to, let alone interview, student activists, but at least I could take pictures, collect documents, and tape speeches. Privately, however, my colleagues at the institute had from the beginning been one of my most important sources of information. Those who had received their training at a university in Beijing often still maintained contacts there and were kept informed about what the students were discussing and planning.

In the new context of the People's Movement, my roles as social scientist and student of China were redefined as witness and historiographer. Producing a record of the righteous struggle against unjust rulers is an extremely important item on the political agenda of Chinese remonstrants. All participants in the movement knew this and never stopped me from observing, photographing, or taping any aspect of the movement.

The declaration of martial law on May 20 and the subsequent attempts of the army to gain control of Beijing by force heightened the drama of the movement. Violence, suppression, and martyrdom were felt to be inevitable. Yet the identification with the cause of the movement, exemplified by the student activists who continued to occupy Tian'anmen Square, had become so great that retreat simply ceased to be an option. Under martial law, the frustrated citizens of Beijing had no other recourse but to confront the suppression head on. After work they stood guard at street corners, waiting for the army that would come sooner or later. Others mounted their bikes and headed for the square. Thousands rode up and down Chang'an Avenue late in the evening of May 22, singing this song again and again:

> If Premier Li Peng does not step down
> We will come day after day
> Those who sleep at night will come by day;
> Those who sleep by day will come at night.
> (Field notes, May 22, 1989)

In this way the students at the square were protected by millions of people who were prepared to give their lives.

People soon began to realize that all the rhetoric about righteousness and martyrdom might have very real consequences. On May 21, the invasion of the army seemed imminent. The following comments made by two students during a public speech were characteristic of the mood pervading the city that day.

> Student 1: I am a high school student, and by participating in the movement I am risking my future, my chances to enter a good university and to study abroad, but I think that I will have to sacrifice this when necessary.

> Student 2: I am nineteen years old, have not even reached twenty. Of course, I am afraid of dying, but if it is to happen tonight I know I will not have died in vain. (Field notes, May 22, 1989)

The new atmosphere that pervaded the city also had a very strong impact on me. I was no longer only an observer. The catastrophe that was about to happen changed me into a participant. Although undeniably a foreigner, the threat of violence from a common enemy made me part of the people I had come to understand and respect during my seven months of fieldwork. Nonetheless, my new sense of identification occasionally confronted me with difficulties of its own.

> A woman I meet in Tian'anmen Square tells me "I want you to tell the whole world," after which she bursts out in tears and can speak no more. I put my arm around her, but suddenly I realize again I am in China and look up to see the stupefied expression on the faces of the Chinese around us. Ashamed and confused I hurry away. (Field notes, May 22, 1989)

After an interlude of two weeks, on the evening of June 3, the army finally moved into Beijing.

> Today, June 3, everybody seems to be convinced that tonight will be the showdown. At around 8:00 P.M. I ride my bike to the square. . . . At the southeastern corner of the square I run into a large crowd blocking the road. Several Western cameramen are filming from transport bikes or portable ladders. Their floodlights are reflected in the helmets of a battalion of soldiers about 30 yards from me. The people around me ask if I don't want to go over there, too. The soldiers will never dare to shoot at a foreigner, they say, so my presence will stop them from advancing any farther. I decline the honor. I point out that although the cameramen are getting paid handsomely to become revolutionary martyrs, I am not. After a couple of minutes the crowd moves up toward the soldiers who, apparently not under orders to shoot, retreat in the direction they have come from. . . . At 1:30 A.M. I walk back to the square together with a couple of Dutch friends. . . . People coming from the opposite direction tell us of 30, 60, 200 casualties farther down. When we arrive at the Peking Hotel, about 300 to 400 yards from the square, we hear heavy machine-gun fire very close by. The crowd in front of us runs back in panic. We decide to take shelter in the Peking Hotel. Before climbing the fence of the hotel, we are told by a waitress to hide our cameras because the police are already in the hotel. This proves to be good advice. In the lobby of the hotel I see five plainclothes policemen trying to pull the camera out of the hands of a foreign photographer. When he refuses they throw him to the floor and start beating and kicking him. I run over to help him, but other policemen block my way. After a couple of seconds the photographer gives up and releases his camera. We decide that this isn't the best place to hide and leave again through the driveway at the side of the hotel. Walking through the small alleys off Chang'an Avenue we meet groups of people who still don't know anything about what is happening at the square. When we tell them their reaction is remarkably subdued. After all, this is what everybody knew to be inevitable. (Field notes, June 4, 1989)

Although everybody in Beijing knew that violence was unavoidable, the students and the people of Beijing refused to be the first to resort to it. As I pointed out earlier, nonviolence was one of the prime strategies of the movement. Through it, the participants strengthened their claim that they did not intend to overthrow the government but only sought to address the injustices of the political system. Nonviolence raised the political contest between the leadership and the participants of the movement to the level of a moral discourse concerning the future of China. This left only two options open to the political leadership: It could suppress the movement or agree to enter into the dialogue demanded by the hunger strikers. The parameters of dialogue, however, had been set by the participants in the movement, who would therefore hold a superior position. As it turned out, the leadership refused to negotiate, leaving it only with one option: the use of force.

The strategic value of nonviolence makes it understandable that the people of Beijing refrained from any violent behavior until the army opened fire on the evening of June 3. Harder to understand is why the popular resistance, once begun, was so persistent and gruesome. Yet it is precisely the timing of the use of force by the people that is the key to the explanation of this apparent paradox.

In the context of the People's Movement, the army's march on Beijing entailed a breach of the earlier nonviolent discursive frame and established a new one in which violence suddenly became the dominant means of signification. Simultaneously, the invasion constituted the final rejection by the authorities of the movement's legitimacy and the right of its leaders to represent the popular voice. For the people, violence was not a rational choice made during a life-and-death struggle but the expression of their moral outrage and frustration at not being taken seriously.

The new, violent discursive frame left the people of Beijing only one way to express their feelings. Soldiers were not just disarmed and taken prisoner. They were pulled out of their tanks and beaten to death or, in some cases, hanged from trees or lampposts. Moreover, violence and resistance continued for days after Beijing had been taken by the army, long after they could possibly have had any impact. Again and again people blocked roads by dragging whatever they could find across them or setting fire to abandoned army trucks, actions that made little sense in terms of a direct means-end rationality. The violence was therefore simultaneously excessive and irrational and patterned on a new moral and cognitive order of retribution.

The massive support for the movement was a political factor that even the staunchest Leninist could not ignore. In the propaganda war that commenced immediately after the massacre, the authorities capitalized on the violent resistance the army had met, constructing an account of the popular violence that left the authorities with maximum credibility. First, the authorities played down the bloodshed committed by the army itself and portrayed it as a measured response. Second, some elements of the discursive frame of the movement were hegemonically incorporated into the official accounts of the events.[4] The authorities acknowledged that the student activists and the masses who had supported them were patriots loyal to the party. Simultaneously, they created a fictitious category of counterrevolutionaries and bad elements who had capitalized on the legitimate activities of the students and the masses. The handful of counterrevolutionaries had tried to drive a wedge between the party and the masses and had plotted to overthrow the government. By inventing this category of counterrevolutionaries, the organic bond between party and masses was thus cleverly restored. The movement was included in the party's official "revolutionary" history, allowing the current leadership to reemerge as the infallible guardians of the correct revolutionary line and the vanguard of the revolutionary masses.[5]

However, as far as the participants in the movement themselves are concerned, the truth about the death of so many innocent people confirmed the wickedness of the authorities and the legitimacy of future protest. People therefore made a point of displaying the dead in front of photographers and cameramen. Hiding photographs, tape recordings, and documents made or collected during the movement and narrating to each other what happened or what one had heard from others was another important way of ensuring that the massacre would not be forgotten. Already during the massacre, the construction of an alternative to the official history had thus begun, reinforcing the alienation that had grown between the leadership and the people in whose name they claimed to rule.

> An elderly woman tells me that the ordinary people hate the troops because of what they have done. What happened shows that the leaders are no longer human. Even in April, she continues, the people did not know what democracy was and did not care about it. The only reason they came out in the streets was to support the students. Now that the crackdown has happened, however, they know that China will need democracy, they know that a system in which only a few decide is no longer possible. (Field notes, June 8, 1989)

Suppression had destroyed the faith in the party and its ideology. In my opinion, this breach is the most important result of the movement. It is too early to say whether the landslide caused by the People's Movement will be permanent or whether the authorities will succeed in restoring at least a semblance of discursive dominance. The authorities' ability to exercise continued control over the bureaucratized social structure will surely be important to prevent the organized expression of mass disenchantment.

If a successful career continues to be dependent on ideological correctness, most people will have to keep up at least an outward show of orthodoxy. During a return trip to Beijing in 1991, I became convinced that this is, however, only a matter of temporary necessity for most. The repression of June 4, 1989, has not been forgotten and will return to haunt its perpetrators when an opportunity presents itself. Whatever may happen in the future, for the present leadership, the repression of the movement will prove to be a Pyrrhic victory only.

The People's Movement was so all-absorbing that it left a vacuum after its suppression the night of June 4. After six weeks of exhilarating political activity, returning to one's normal life seemed somehow pointless. The total event had collapsed and life had suddenly become literally meaningless. Still, about ten days after the massacre, the flow of life had superficially returned to normal, although almost all foreign businessmen, students, diplomats, and even journalists had fled the country, and the marks left in the streets by tanks and armored personnel carriers had not yet been repaired.

For the people of Beijing, resuming their daily routines was the only option. I had an alternative, however. I could go home. My involvement in the movement had given me meaningful things to do there. Moreover, it became clear to me that staying behind in Beijing until September, as I had originally planned, would be pointless politically, professionally, and personally. The city was clearly preparing for a prolonged period of vicious repression and rectification. Under these conditions finding people to interview would be almost impossible, and very dangerous to them. Two weeks after the massacre, I boarded a practically empty Boeing 747 and left Beijing for the Netherlands.

But even back home, I was not completely free from the constraints imposed by Chinese society. The Chinese Academy of Social Sciences had played a very active role during the movement. Early on during the movement, my hosts had told me that my writing about the movement would not help them survive the political campaign that would inevitably follow its suppression and, so they added, would make it very difficult to receive me or other field-workers in the future. In the end, it was decided that I had best write under a pseudonym. As a result, Frank Niming, who has since published several articles and a book about the movement (e.g., Niming 1990), was born. The completion in 1992 of the dissertation on which this chapter is based (Pieke 1995), however, seemed to be the appropriate moment to bury Niming. The academy has survived the campaign against "bourgeois liberalization," although not without some scars. The future of foreign fieldwork in China, too, seems no longer to depend on the writings of one anthropologist about his experiences during those hectic weeks in 1989.

Experiencing the People's Movement in the context of a long-term fieldwork project involved me to an unanticipated extent in Beijing society and culture. Moreover, my experiences show that anthropological field-workers can become more than just peripheral actors in the community or events they study. When the stakes are raised, their observations and experiences are not only interesting to themselves or to other anthropologists but can be important to the people they study as well. The anthropologist's writings can be a way for the local people to decontextualize the events making up their lives and invest them with a future relevance for their own society. By helping the anthropologist write the events of their culture, the people studied ensure that their own point of view can survive the forgetfulness of public opinion and the vicissitudes of military suppression and political control.

FIELDWORK AND ACCIDENTS

Before setting out for the field, I had already been steeped in the criticisms leveled by anthropologists against conventional, Malinowskian field-work. Fieldwork, I had come to agree, should indeed be more than harvesting data. Anthropologists should leave their methodological ivory tower and aim at "writing" a culture by engaging in an intersubjective and equal dialogue with the people studied (Clifford and Marcus 1986; Crapanzano 1980; Dwyer 1982; Marcus and Fischer 1986; Rabinow 1977). Yet I had no real image of what this would mean in terms of my daily activities while in the field. The immediate challenge was to be granted, in the first place, an opportunity to talk to a member of that elusive category "the natives." In such a context, the lofty ideas concerning dialogical anthropology seemed of little relevance. Indeed, the time-honored strategy to grab the data and run appeared to make all the sense in the world.

Nonetheless, as I have showed throughout this chapter, I came to appreciate the value of dialogical anthropology even during the difficult field-work I had embarked on. Caught in a situation that made a traditional community study and much initial structuring impossible, I was forced to translate and rethink an abstract epistemological choice into a strategy to become an anthropologist of a society seemingly designed to frustrate field-workers. I came to understand that dialogical anthropology was much more than sitting on a bench in the village square exchanging ideas and information with the natives. Dialogical fieldwork should be a dialogue with the entire social reality encountered, a chain of events heard about, observed, and, above all, experienced.

When they occur, the events making up a fieldwork experience are often perceived as fortunate or unfortunate accidents. Yet they are related because they take place in the same social and cultural setting and may even be causally connected. More important, subsequent anthropological accidents are experienced by the same field-worker. The efforts of the ethnographer to make sense of what seem to be random accidents at first sight are similar to the creative interpretive work native actors engage in to make sense of their world. Earlier events provide (part of) the interpretation of later ones and take on new meaning in the light of later experiences.

Dialogical fieldwork therefore differs from more conventional fieldwork in that it is not shaped by the anthropologist's preoccupations but focuses on reality as it presents itself to an outsider who makes the effort to sensitize himself or herself to it. In the case of my own fieldwork, there were two practical aspects to this. First, during my conversations and interviews, I did not pursue what I thought to be important but tried to let my informants talk about what they themselves thought were meaningful events in their lives. While listening, I developed an understanding of how my informants gave meaning to their daily experiences and how they shaped their own behavior accordingly. Second, considering fieldwork a developing experience rather than the execution of a research plan enabled me to make the best of sudden shifts and changes in the circumstances, negotiating the difficulties and grasping the opportunities the circumstances presented. This attitude paid off most clearly when the unfolding People's Movement began to occupy center stage in Beijing.

In the context of my dialogical fieldwork, the decision to study the movement was only natural, indeed almost inevitable, and I thought of it more as a continuation of my earlier work than as a new project. I set out to study the movement as I had studied the local dynamics of the reforms. I was essentially under the same constraints and used many of the same strategies. During the earlier stages, my exposure to the movement was largely determined by the help provided and the constraints imposed by my host organization. Accordingly, one of the limitations I imposed on myself was never to participate in the demonstrations I was following, because this might do much harm to my project, my hosts, and future field-workers.

As the movement progressed, however, my study developed its own dynamics. This was partially a development similar to my experiences with the interviews. Because I learned increasingly more about what was happening and about the people involved, my work became progressively easier. I had to struggle less and less for things to observe or people to talk to. Events happened and people had progressively less inhibitions to talk to me. For the first time during my stay in Beijing, I could simply apply the skills I had learned in the course of my training as an anthropologist and use the opportunities offered to the best of my ability.

Yet my study of the People's Movement was also different from the earlier interviews. As the movement developed, its impact on Beijing society deepened. By the time of the hunger strike in mid-May, the movement had eclipsed in importance all other events and concerns. Contrary to my earlier interviews, it therefore became impossible to avoid being sucked up by it and to take sides in the unfolding events. In my analysis of the People's Movement, I cannot but write from the perspective of the people with whom I experienced it. I simply do not have the ethnographic experience and empathy to do equal justice to the perspectives of, for instance, the Communist party leadership or the student activists.

The People's Movement offered a unique opportunity to an anthropologist whose focus is on events rather than on the reconstruction of a structure of culture that is assumed to exist external to observable reality. Processes, which have to be teased out with great difficulty when studying more mundane (or past) events, were there for everybody to see. First, the People's Movement, purposely designed as a public event, took place largely—albeit not completely—in the streets. Second, the People's Movement consisted of a clearly demarcated sequence of subevents, which followed more or less logically from one another. The events developed their own internal moral order and history, making it possible to analyze the movement as one macroevent. Third, and most important, the movement was a total event, subjecting all other events in society to its interpretive frame, and could therefore be studied as an autonomous phenomenon. Here I was no longer dealing with ordinary adaptations of the social order with their largely unseen and unintended effects but with the construction of an alternative order that challenged the existing state of affairs. The People's Movement was studying Chinese society and history while it was being made, and for a brief period I was allowed to be a participant in that process. Despite its tragic conclusion, I will therefore always think of the People's Movement as the moment when I was in a full sense what I had hoped for years to become: an anthropologist of the Chinese people.

NOTES

1. Tian'anmen Square, located about a mile from my guest house, is the geographic and symbolic center of Beijing and the focus of many political movements in twentieth-century China. The Monument for Revolutionary Heroes is located at the center of the square, the Great Hall of the People at the western edge.

2. Work units (factories, shops, ministries, schools) are the most important basic-level elements of the bureaucratized social structure of urban China. They fulfill many of the functions catered to by specialized bureaucratic organizations in other state socialist or Western societies.

3. Both Zhou and Mao are simultaneously legendary leaders of the party and symbolic rallying points for remonstrance. For Zhou, this is because of his moderating role during the Cultural Revolution, while Mao is still revered because of his leadership of the Communist revolution and the impact of his personality cult.

4. The most authoritative of these is the report by the mayor of Beijing (Chen 1989).

5. A similar ruse had been used in 1981 when the present leadership rewrote the history of the Cultural Revolution, limiting it to a factional struggle between them and the "Gang of Four." The mass denunciations and persecution of the current leaders were carefully edited out of the official history to obscure the fact that they had been anything but the representatives of the revolutionary masses at that time (Chan 1992).

REFERENCES

Chan, Anita
  1992   "Dispelling Misconceptions about the Red Guard Movement: The Necessity to Re-Examine Cultural Revolution Factionalism and Periodization." *Journal of Contemporary China* 1(1):61–85.
Chen Xitong
  1989   "Report on Checking the Turmoil and Quelling the Counter-Revolutionary Rebellion." *Beijing Review,* July 17–23, 1989, i–xx.
Clifford, James, and George E. Marcus, eds.
  1986   *Writing Culture: The Poetics and Politics of Ethnography.* Berkeley, Los Angeles, and London: University of California Press.
Crapanzano, Vincent
  1980   *Tuhami: Portrait of a Moroccan.* Chicago: University of Chicago Press.
Dwyer, Kevin
  1982   *Moroccan Dialogues.* Baltimore: Johns Hopkins University Press.
Marcus, George, and Michael N. J. Fischer
  1986   *Anthropology as Cultural Critique: An Experimental Moment in the Human Sciences.* Chicago: University of Chicago Press.
Niming, Frank
  1990   "Learning How to Protest." In *The Chinese People's Movement: Perspectives on Spring 1989,* ed. Tony Saich, 83–105. Armonk, N.Y.: Sharpe.
Pieke, Frank N.
  1986   "Social Science Fieldwork in the PRC: Implications of the Mosher Affair." *China Information* 1(3):32–37.
  1995   *The Ordinary and the Extraordinary: An Anthropological Study of Chinese Reform and the 1989 People's Movement in Beijing.* London: Kegan Paul International (forthcoming).
Rabinow, Paul
  1977   *Reflections on Fieldwork in Morocco.* Berkeley, Los Angeles, and London: University of California Press.

Mothers of the Plaza de Mayo Street Protest against Disappearances
(Photo: © ANP Foto)

The Politics of Truth and Emotion among Victims and Perpetrators of Violence

Antonius C. G. M. Robben

"Let me help you," he said, as he held up my coat. "Thank you very much," I said. My arms slipped effortlessly into the sleeves as he gently lifted the coat onto my shoulders. Before I could return the gesture, he had already put on his overcoat.

We passed through the dark corridors of the old palace, walked down the marble stairway, and left the Officers Club through the main entrance. "You know, Dr. Robben," he began, "I am a very religious man. And I know deep down in my heart that my conscience before God is clear." We turned the corner at the Café Petit Paris and continued along Santa Fé Avenue. I looked at him and tried to overstem the noise of the traffic: "Well, general, but there are many Argentines who . . ." "Look out!" he yelled and stretched his right arm in front of me. A taxi nearly hit me as I was about to step on the pavement.

A few months later, on October 7, 1989, the general was released from criminal prosecution by a presidential decree (*indulto*). He had been indicted for ordering the disappearance of Argentine citizens and for carrying the hierarchical responsibility for their rape and torture by the men under his command. The decree did not acquit him of the charges or exonerate his military honor but merely dismissed his court case and those of dozens of other high-ranking officers. The Argentine president, Carlos Menem, hoped that this decree would "close the wounds of the past" and contribute to a "national pacification, reconciliation, and unity" among a people divided by the violence and repression of the 1970s.

Six months earlier I had arrived in Buenos Aires to study whether or not these wounds were closing and how the Argentine people were coping with the tens of thousands of dead and disappeared in what the military had called the "dirty war" against the leftist insurgency.[1] If Argentine society was to be pacified, then the people had to reconcile themselves with each other and their past. Chapters of history cannot be turned by decree. Crucial to national reconciliation was how the Argentine people made sense of the years of intense political repression and violence during the 1976–1983 military dictatorship. At the time, most people had only a vague notion of the incipient civil war that waged during the first half of the 1970s. Many welcomed the coup d'état of March 1976 as necessary to end the country's political and economic chaos. Constitutional rights were suspended, the Congress was sent home, and the unions were placed under military guardianship. People were aware of the censorship of the mass media, the pervasive intelligence network of the security forces, and the many arrests that were made, often under the cover of darkness. They also heard about the worldwide denunciation of human rights violations in Argentina, but the military government was quite successful in convincing the many Argentines who had not been affected personally that these accusations were being orchestrated by the revolutionary Left at home and abroad. It was only after the 1982 defeat of the Argentine armed forces at the Falkland/Malvinas Islands that the public learned of the extent and brutality of the political persecution during the dictatorship. The Argentine people wanted to know and understand what had happened. At the fall of the military regime in 1983, retired generals, former cabinet ministers, human rights activists, union leaders, bishops, and politicians were flooding the news media with their conflicting accounts and analyses. The protagonists of the years of repression had become the nation's historiographers.

The historical reconstruction of the 1970s became intensely contested during the decade following the turn to democracy, not only through conflicting discourse but also through controversial political actions, including one guerrilla attack on an army base, three amnesties, and five military mutinies, the last and most violent of which occurred during my fieldwork. The adversary interpretations came principally from the armed forces, the former guerrilla organizations, the human rights groups, and the Roman Catholic church. The public discourse of the leaders of these four groups became the centerpiece of my research on the contested historical reconstruction of the political violence of the 1970s. I was not interested in writing a history of the so-called dirty war. Instead, I focused on how that history was being remembered, contested, negotiated, and reconstructed in public by its protagonists. I told my interlocutors that I was not in Argentina to establish truth or guilt because that was the prerogative of Argentine society. I made it clear at the start of every interview that I wanted to talk to the principal political actors and understand their explanations of the recent past in a time when opinions and interpretations were still being formed and reformulated. I wanted them to explain their position, just as they had done previously in television and radio programs, newspaper articles, public speeches, and their numerous meetings with local reporters, foreign correspondents, diplomats, and international fact-finding delegations. I chose this approach to the conflicting discourse about the decades of political violence because the historical protagonists refused to enter into face-to-face debates with their former adversaries. Hence I interviewed them about the same principal historical events, contrasted their arguments and interpretations, and compared the opinions imparted to me with their other public pronouncements.

It was in my interviews with the Argentine military that I first realized the importance of seduction as a dimension of fieldwork. My military interlocutors must have known that the image I had received abroad—and which they reckoned was being confirmed in my talks with their political opponents—was one of officers torturing babies and ordering the disappearance of tens of thousands of innocent Argentine civilians. I had, of course, anticipated their denial of these serious accusations, but I did not expect to be meeting with military men who exuded great civility and displayed a considerable knowledge of literature, art, and classical music. The affability and chivalry of the officers clashed with the trial records I had read, affected my critical sensibility, and in the beginning led me astray from my research focus. It was only later that I realized that I had been engrossed in ethnographic seduction. This process of seduction and subsequent awareness repeated itself in my meetings with bishops, human rights activists, and former guerrilla leaders. Each group was seductive in its own way, and it was only after months of interviewing that I succeeded in recognizing the prevalent defenses and strategies and learned to distinguish seduction from good rapport.

I have chosen the word *seduction* to describe those personal defenses and social strategies because it means literally "to be led astray from an intended course."[2] Seduction is used here exclusively in its neutral meaning of being led astray unawares, not in its popular meaning of allurement and entrapment. I prefer seduction to other terms, such as concealment, manipulation, or deception, that carry negative overtones and suggest dishonesty or malintent. Seduction can be intentional but also unconscious and can be compared to the ways in which filmmakers, stage directors, artists, or writers succeed in totally absorbing the attention of their audiences.

I am aware of the risks of using the word *seduction* in the context of violence. The association of the words *victim* and *seduction* makes me vulnerable to the charge that I am implying that somehow the victim brought on himself or herself the pain that was inflicted, while the mere suggestion that victims of violence might mold what they tell us runs the danger that I will be accused of contributing to their victimization. Ultimately, it might make people question my moral standards. How can I place doubt on the horror stories I have been told and distrust their narrators? It is much easier to acknowledge manipulation by victimizers than by victims. We have more sympathy for unmasking abusers of power than doubting the words of their victims. I have the same sympathies. However, I also realize that in the end the victims may be harmed and their testimonies discredited if we report their views naively and uncritically. We need to analyze their accounts and be attentive to our own inhibitions, weaknesses, and biases, all to the benefit of a better understanding of both victim and victimizer. The ethnographic seduction by victims and perpetrators of violence will in this way become a font of instead of an obstruction to insight.[3]

This chapter focuses on the ethnographic encounter because the most common transmission of cultural knowledge in fieldwork takes place through open interviews with key informants. I will argue that seduction is a dimension of fieldwork that is especially prominent in research on violent political conflict because the interlocutors have great personal and political stakes in making the ethnographer adopt their interpretations. The importance of seduction is enhanced by the special circumstances of studying-up conflict. An anthropologist who wishes to understand a major armed conflict from the perspective of its principal protagonists cannot resort to participant observation in its traditional sense but is restricted to account interviews. These interviews may range from a unique half-hour meeting to a series of long conversations. It is during these face-to-face encounters that ethnographic understanding and inquiry are most vulnerable to seduction.

EMPATHY AND DEHUMANIZATION

Ethnographic understanding through empathy and detachment has been generally accepted as a common dialectic in fieldwork. We must establish a good rapport with our interlocutors to grasp the world from their perspective, while a simultaneous reflective detachment as observers must objectify our perceptions and enhance our analytical insight.[4] "One of the most persistent problems we confront is how to so subject ourselves and yet maintain the degree of 'detachment' necessary for us to analyze our observations: in other words, to be anthropologists as well as participants" (Ellen 1984:227). Bronislaw Malinowski conceived of anthropological research in these terms, and it was to remain a canon of our profession until the 1960s when Clifford Geertz began to problematize fieldwork and ethnography with his notion of "thick description."

Geertz calls attention to the many-layered subjective construction of culture and argues for reproducing this complexity in the ethnographic text.[5] He notes that the relation between informant and field-worker is bespeckled with mutual misunderstandings, clientelistic interests, power games, and cultural proselytizing. These problems of cultural interpretation are of central concern to the ethnographer. Geertz (1973:15) proposes, therefore, the "thick description" of culture "cast in terms of the constructions we imagine" our interlocutors "to place upon what they live through, the formulae they use to define what happens to them." A question that arises immediately is whether people's constructions and formulas—not just their content—change under social tension and to what extent violent conflict will therefore affect the thick description of culture. This chapter will show that an examination in the field of the principal methodological and epistemological problems of conducting ethnographic research under violent conflict may yield significant insights about people's interpretation and construction of the conflict under study.

The problem of ethnographic seduction deserves attention because it subverts the *thick conversation* that precedes its description in ethnographic texts. We may become engulfed in seductive strategies or defenses that convince us of the thinness of social discourse. We believe to be seeing the world through our interlocutor's eyes. Yet these eyes are looking away from that which we think they are seeing. We have been led away from the depths of culture to its surface in an opaque intersubjective negotiation of cultural understanding.

This manipulation of appearances touches on the heart of seduction, so Jean Baudrillard (1990) tells us.[6] Appearance rests on a deep faith in the immediacy of our senses and emotions. Sight, sound, and feeling are intimately tied to our subjective experience of authenticity. Seduction wins us over through this pretense of real understanding. However, what is revealed to us is nothing more than a trompe l'oeil, and a surreal one at that. The ethnographic seduction trades our critical stance as observers for an illusion of congeniality with cultural insiders.[7] We no longer seek to grasp the native's point of view, but we believe, at least for the duration of the meeting, that we have become natives ourselves. We have become so enwrapped in the ethnographic encounter that we are led astray from our research objectives, irrespective of the theoretical paradigm we are using and the anthropological understanding we are pursuing.

Problems of representation, intersubjectivity, polyphonic complexity, and the historicity of truth aside—all of which have already been discussed at length in anthropology—I am calling attention to the epistemological pitfalls of ethnographic seduction. Ethnographic seduction subverts our understanding of social and cultural phenomena by dissuading an inquiry beyond their appearance. The difficulty with ethnographic seduction is that we are not aware it is taking place. Unlike ethnographic anxiety, which according to George Devereux (1967:42–45) is produced by our repression of cultural experiences in the field that correspond to unconscious desires and wishes, ethnographic seduction puts the ethnographer often at ease. Repression makes the ethnographer "protect himself against anxiety by the omission, soft-pedalling, non-exploitation, misunderstanding, ambiguous description, over-exploitation or rearrangement of certain parts of his material" (ibid., 44). Seduction, instead, makes us feel that we have accomplished something profound in the encounter, that we have reached a deeper understanding and have somehow penetrated reality. We are in a state of well-being, and have a we-feeling with our informants that we mistakenly interpret as good rapport. It is only when we look back at our meeting and review the information gathered that we realize that we displayed a personal inhibition to break our rapport with critical questions. We realize that we have mistaken seduction for empathy.

If, on the one hand, seduction disarms our critical detachment and thus debilitates the gathering of cultural knowledge, then, on the other, our empathy in research on violent conflict may be hindered by our awareness of the protagonism of our interlocutor. Going one morning from an interview with a mother who had lost two sons during the first year of the dictatorship to a meeting with a general who might have ordered their disappearance, it became hard not to dehumanize them both. How can we engage in constructing an intersubjective understanding with a person who either has violated or transcended the humanity we are trying to understand?

At the early stages of my research I was confounded both by the veil of authenticity that shrouded the personal accounts of my interlocutors and by the public discourse that depicted military officers as beasts or saviors and human rights activists as subversives or saints. We may become so overwhelmed by the presence of political actors who have been dehumanized in society that we may also begin to see them only as saints and sinners or heroes and cowards. As I became more conscious of these public characterizations in Argentine society, I realized that this same process of dehumanization had contributed to the escalation of political violence in the 1970s, when political opponents became enemies and enemies were less than human, only fit for elimination.

Ethnographic seduction sidesteps empathy and detachment. The Socratic dialectic that brings us ever closer to the truth, the positivist model of an oscillation between inductive and deductive steps through which falsification becomes possible, and finally the hermeneutic model of a spiraling ascendance between whole and part that deepens understanding encompass epistemological approaches that become suspended by seduction. Ethnographic seduction reduces communication and knowledge to appearance.

THE MANAGEMENT OF IMPRESSION AND AMBIGUITY

Around the same time that Geertz problematized ethnography, questions were raised about the ethics of covert fieldwork in Latin America and Southeast Asia. In the 1960s, anthropologists began to take a closer look at their research practices. This methodological reflection was greatly influenced by West Coast sociologists such as Herbert Blumer, Harold Garfinkel, Erving Goffman, Aaron V. Cicourel, and Harvey Sacks who inspired ethnographers to focus on the dramaturgical dimension of the relation between field-workers and their informants. Anthropologists could not routinely study the social and cultural conduct of their subjects but had to realize that the actors might deliberately manipulate and obstruct the gathering of ethnographic knowledge. "The impressions that ethnographer and subjects seek to project to one another are . . . those felt to be favorable to the accomplishment of their respective goals: the ethnographer seeks access to back-region information; the subjects seek to protect their secrets since these represent a threat to the public image they wish to maintain. Neither can succeed perfectly" (Berreman 1972:xxxiv).

The work of Goffman (1966, 1969) on impression management remains highly relevant for our understanding of the interactional processes that develop in ethnographic encounters.[8] Nevertheless, impression management encompasses only part of the much more comprehensive and complex dimension of ethnographic seduction. Ethnographer and interlocutor may try to protect their public image and try to gain access to each other's back stage, as Berreman explains, but which boundary should they protect and which region do they wish to enter? The ethnographer's definition of the secret knowledge of the interlocutor may not coincide with the respondent's perception. This misunderstanding provides opportunities not only for dramaturgical impression management but also for unintended and counteractive seduction. For example, victims of repression who assumed that I regarded the torture session as the most personal and therefore most valuable back region, assumed that this appraisal could enhance their credibility as a reliable source of information about the years of political violence. Even though many informants intended to tell about it, they still veiled their experiences to impel the inquisitive ethnographer to urge them to share their stories. The more persuasion that was needed, the more persuasive their accounts would be. A troubling similarity between interrogation and interview appeared which could not have escaped the attention of these victims of torture. But now, they had control over how and which valuable information they would give. Several interviewees were conscious of the manner in which this knowledge was imparted and therefore delayed its disclosure. Others did not try to withhold their revelations, but the effect was the same: I stopped at the threshold of their back region. Why did I refuse to accept the valuable knowledge that was eventually offered?

Baudrillard (1990:83) has written that "to seduce is to appear weak." Certain interviewees did not try to dominate or overpower me but, instead, disarmed me by showing their vulnerabilities. In my interviews with victims of torture, I seldomly asked directly about the abuse they had been subjected to but usually concentrated on their interpretation of the political violence of the 1970s. Being used to journalists who invariably asked them to provide graphic descriptions, several expressed their surprise at my reluctance and volunteered to give me detailed accounts. I generally responded that such painful recollection was not necessary because I had already read their declarations to the courts. Maybe I wanted to spare them, but I probably also wanted to protect myself. Whatever my motives, this voluntary offering of very personal experiences enhanced in my eyes the credibility of the entire interview, whether justified or not. The ethnographic seduction operated through a partial revelation of a dark world that was not further explored but was taken at face value in the belief that such hidden knowledge could always be uncovered.

RHETORIC AND PERSUASION

Persuasion seems to be the counterpole of seduction. Seduction wins us over by appearance, persuasion by argument.[9] It is not appearance and emotion that seem at stake but reason. We are supposed to become persuaded by a clear exposition of hard evidence that moves us to reconsider our poorly informed opinions. But how is the proof presented to us? How is the evidence rhetorically couched? How is the information molded to make its greatest impact on us and divert us from the questions we want to examine in depth? Are the interlocutors always aware of the rhetorical dimension of their conversations?[10]

Plato and Aristotle made a distinction between dialectic reasoning based on logic and rigorous proof, which would lead to truth, and rhetoric reasoning, which tried to persuade people by arousing their emotions. "Rhetoric is that part of any self-consciously calculated piece of communication which fails to meet a philosopher's standards of accuracy, coherence, and consistency, but is still necessary if the communication is to be fully successful" (Cole 1991:13). Our suspicion of rhetoric comes from a distrust of such manipulation of our emotions. We feel somehow robbed of the ability to weigh the pros and cons of an argument. Nevertheless, rhetorical and aesthetic modes of exposition are not only an inextricable part of scientific discourse (see Gilbert and Mulkay 1984; Gross 1990) but "potentially powerful resources for the advancement of the sciences: promotion of hypotheses by appeal to aesthetic criteria; jocular and satirical critique of standard and entrenched practices" (Jardine 1991:236). Rhetoric stirs us discursively with tropes, allegories, and modes of exposition. Like seduction, rhetoric may become a play of appearance that diverts us from our research objectives.

Most of my Argentine interlocutors were public figures with great conversational experience and finesse. I could therefore safely assume that they had become sensitized to the effectiveness of various rhetorical devices. Invariably there was an exchange of social courtesies to create a friendly atmosphere for what we perceived could become a weighty and possibly painful conversation. These courtesies failed to seduce because of their blatant transparency. Seduction does not work through openness but through secrecy and mystification. Hence the common ground that became established at the start of a conversation depended to a great extent on an acquaintance with each other's cultural identity. Many of my interviewees had visited Europe, expressed their love of seventeenth-century Dutch painting, their admiration of the canals and polders, or recalled with glee the title match victory of Argentina over the Dutch team at the 1978 World Championship soccer tournament in Buenos Aires, during the heydays of the military regime. They also interpreted my presentation of self, assessed my class background, and tried to detect my political ideology. My being Dutch yet living in the United States, my status as a university professor, and above all my access to their political adversaries were of great importance. I, in turn, would praise the friendliness of the Argentine people, the beauty of the countryside, and the architecture of the main avenues of Buenos Aires.

Aside from this obvious impression management, there was a seductive dimension to discourse that was much harder to isolate but that first became clear to me in my conversations with former *guerrilleros*. Many of them had been college students. They had perfected a sophisticated political discourse through innumerable discussions in cafés, prisons, hideouts, and foreign hotels. They would speak in the intellectual's tongue. Well versed in the jargon of sociology and political science, their historical interpretations had a truthful ring. It was difficult to distinguish their vocabulary and semantic constructions from my own.

It was tempting to become absorbed in this discourse. It had an emotional pull. It seduced me by an indescribable familiarity, by its allure of going to the heart of historical events together with their architects; all this set in the special atmosphere of the grand cafés of Buenos Aires with their dense cigarette smoke, the buzzing of voices, and the waiters swiftly maneuvering through the maze of wooden tables while carrying trays of small coffee cups. I felt that I could take my guard down in this environment and become absorbed in a close discussion in which I could share intellectual doubts and queries with people of my own generation. I felt that I could not afford such openness with the military, the clergy, or with human rights activists who might become offended by too penetrating questions and deny me another interview. What I did not realize was that by this openness I had also abandoned my critical detachment.

Unlike the pseudoacademic discourse of the revolutionary Left, which allowed me to retain many of my conceptual tools, my interviews with the other three groups obliged me to adapt my vocabulary. For example, human rights groups use the term "concentration camp" (*campo de concentración*) to describe the secret places where disappeared persons were held. This term conjures up images of the Second World War and, by extension, suggests that the Argentine military are Nazis at heart. The use of the term "concentration camp" in conversations with military officers would immediately brand me as a sympathizer of the human rights groups and thus hinder the exchange. I therefore used their own term, "detention center" (*centro de detención*). This neutral term was part of an objectifying vocabulary that gave a semantic rationality to the violent practices of the dirty war.

The discursive strategy of the military consisted of appealing both to my common sense and to the dispassionate logic of reason that is supposed to be the hallmark of any scientist. This discursive technique consisted of an outright dismissal of any major human rights violations without denying that they could have occurred. If this technique failed to have the intended effect on me, then they began to relativize the Argentine abuses by making a comparison with atrocities committed by the so-called civilized Western world. In an interview on June 26, 1989, I asked the general mentioned at the beginning of this article about the relevance of licit and illicit rules of engagement, as defined by international law, to the "dirty war strategy" employed by the Argentine military.

> I say that when we go to war—and in a war I have to be willing to kill my enemy because otherwise there would be no war—when I am willing to kill my enemy I can kill him with an arrow, but if the other has a machine gun then the arrow will be of no use to me. I have to find a cannon. When the other has . . . [when] I have a cannon, the other will look for a larger cannon or an aircraft. When the other has an aircraft, I will have to try, try to take a missile, and so on. That is to say, war by itself is a social phenomenon. . . . What is licit and what is illicit, when war presupposes that I am going to kill my enemy? Now, the philosopher of war par excellence is [Carl von] Clausewitz. And he says that war is evidently a human phenomenon in which I try to impose my will on the enemy and I therefore resort to violence. Now, he talks about the tendency to go to extremes. He then says that he who tries to impose violence without any consideration will have an

advantage over he who has consideration. Well then, what happens? When they talk to me about restrictions in warfare, these are lucubrations made by jurists. The nations have not respected them. For example, when they threw the nuclear bomb on Hiroshima and Nagasaki, this was forbidden according to the Geneva Convention. But who was to say to Mister Truman, "Mister Truman, this is forbidden. Why did you throw it? You come along, we are going to take you to the Nuremberg tribunal." No, because he won the war. Who was going to do it? Now, why did Mister Truman do it? Because he said, "Well, there will die 200,000 persons, but if we do not throw the bomb then 600,000 North Americans will die, or one million. Well then, between 200,000 Japanese and one million North Americans let 200,000 Japanese die," and he threw the bomb. Because the distinction between the licit and the illicit in warfare is absurd to me, because war presupposes from the start the use of violence—as Clausewitz says—and the use of violence without restraint till the objective is attained.

Other Argentine officers also referred frequently to the bombings of Hiroshima, Dresden, and Nagasaki and to the double standard of the "human rights prophets," the French, who collaborated with the Nazis during the Vichy government, tortured Algerian partisans, and in 1985 bombed a Greenpeace ship in New Zealand, yet who convicted in absentia the Argentine navy officer Alfredo Astiz for his alleged role in the disappearance of two French nuns who had collaborated with subversive organizations, so the Argentine military argued. When I objected that two wrongs do not make a right, that the comparisons do not hold, or that many of the offenses by Western nations were backed by written orders, the Argentine military appealed to the vicissitudes and unpredictabilities of warfare.

Such rational discourse may be highly persuasive from a logical point of view—especially when one has not yet found equally powerful counterarguments or succeeds in listening dispassionately to the rationalizations—but produces an uncomfortable tension with one's emotional aversion to the consequences of warfare. Just as it is hard to reconcile our instantaneous repudiation of violent death with a military necessity to fire on people, so it becomes very difficult to stand one's moral ground in the face of these technorational arguments for human suffering. The barrage of sophisticated rationalizations of violence together with the argument that the use of force is the constitutional prerogative of the security forces are very hard to counter. My objections that the violence was disproportional, that more humane counterinsurgency methods could have been used, that the prisoners were not given due process, that these methods violated the very principles of civilization that the military professed to protect, and, finally, that what was justified as mere excesses of war were deliberate and planned violations to paralyze the political expression of the Argentine people were dismissed either as leftist propaganda or as a manifestation of my unfamiliarity with the practice of warfare.

Another discursive tactic was to sketch ominous scenarios of what would have happened if the Argentine military had not destroyed the insurgents root and branch. The grave situation in Peru during the late 1980s, when the Shining Path revolutionaries controlled large areas of the highlands, and had even succeeded in reaching the gates of Lima at the time of my fieldwork, was mentioned as a nightmare that had been prevented in Argentina through the resolute action of the armed forces. Finally, the fall of the Berlin wall and the subsequent disenchantment with communism in Eastern Europe were presented as arguments for the moral righteousness of the repression in Argentina during the 1970s.

The human rights activists and former guerrilleros could have equally made appeals to common sense, but many preferred to make an emotional plea to a moral sense of humanity and justice. How to respond to an indignant rejection of torture, to the kidnapping of babies for the benefit of childless military families, and to the extraction of money from desperate parents with misleading information about the whereabouts of their disappeared son? Rational arguments, such as those given to me by the military, justifying torture as a conventional practice in counterinsurgency warfare, as was the case in Algeria, South Africa, Vietnam, Indonesia, Northern Ireland, Spain, Peru, El Salvador, and many other countries, are impotent against the tears of the parents of a revolutionary who was abducted, tortured, and executed. I became virtually unable to penetrate this emotional shroud with questions that might be easily misperceived as apologetic, uncaring, cold, callous, and hurtful.[11] The more emotional the reaction, the greater my personal inhibition to discuss these issues further.

The following fragment from an interview with the father of a seventeen-year-old member of the outlawed Peronist Youth (Juventud Peronista) who disappeared in April 1976 demonstrates this inhibition, despite the encouragement of the interlocutor to proceed. After his son failed to arrive at a birthday party where he was expected, the father began a desperate search. He contacted an acquaintance who is a police officer, and they began to make inquiries at the precincts and hospitals of Buenos Aires, all to no avail. After several months, the father came into contact with a colonel in active duty through the mediation of a befriended retired first lieutenant. The following dialogue took place.

> And he says, "Tell me what happened." So I told him what happened. And with all virulence, you looked at . . . I looked at this man, but I tell you as I told you before, that I tried to see from all sides if I could find the point of the . . . of the thread of . . . , to, to arrive at the thread or the needle in the haystack [*punta del ovillo*], trying to, to discover anything. After telling him everything, he says, "Good. Look, you have to do the following: you have to pretend as if your son has cancer." I was listening and saying to myself, What is he saying? [The colonel continues.] "Pretend that he has cancer and that

they have . . . that he is in an operating room and that there is a butcher and a doctor; pray that it will be the doctor who will be operating on him." And then I looked at, at the one with whom I had made a certain friendship, and he took hold of his head and covered his, his face. Because he must have said, he himself must have said, What is this sonofabitch saying? Because then he realized that all his venom, his virulence came out of him [the colonel]. This man had stuck a dagger in my wound and had twisted it inside me. I say to him, "Pardon me," I say, "Sir, but do you know something?" I said this because of what he was telling me. "No, no, I am weighing the various possibilities [*hago una composición de lugar*] and I am making a supposition. I don't know anything of what might have ha——." And I say, "But how do you have the gall to . . ." and because of my nerves the words couldn't come out, but I had wanted to say "You are a son of a thousand bitches." You see, tell him whichever barbarity. And then the other saw my condition because he thought that I was going to lose it. . . . I wanted to grab him by the throat and strangle him, but then anyone of those who were there would have taken their gun and killed me. There, for the first time in my life, the desire came over me to murder someone. I had been destroyed. . . .

Something [my wife] didn't know. With the passage of time I have told her. These are unfortunate things that happen to you in life. And there, yes, it crossed my mind that yes, that day I could have ended up killing that man. I don't know what stopped me. Because I was desperate. But you cannot imagine how, with what satisfaction he said what he was telling me. And you should analyze that, that this man was in active service.

But I was unable to analyze. Exactly as he had tried to detect any sign in the face and words of the colonel that betrayed the tiniest bit of information about his son but became paralyzed by the cruel supposition, so I became unable to stand aside and observe. He had incorporated me into his torment, sometimes discursively placing me in his shoes and at other times highlighting the moments of his greatest anguish. I could have asked him about the place of the meeting, the spatial arrangement of the offices, which army regiment had been involved, whether he ever heard of the colonel again, how he knew that the man was a colonel and not an extortionist who would try to wrest money from him, whether he ever saw the first lieutenant again, and so on. But my mind went blank, and I could only share this man's sorrow in silence.

I intuitively hesitate to present this account as an example of rhetorical seduction because the term "seduction" immediately evokes the association of an intentional manipulation of truth for dishonest ends. This is not the case here. I do not have any reason to doubt that this dialogue— whatever the exact words—took place, and I believe even less that the narrative was consciously constructed. Still, I think that the term "rhetorical seduction" is appropriate here because the repeated telling of the same story has led to a formulation that has proven to be the most moving and therefore most persuasive.[12] The account affected my emotional state to such a degree that I was no longer able to see the discourse behind the conversation. I could not ask further questions but allowed my interlocutor to take me along on the incessant search for his son.

Sometimes, I would end an interview here, unable or unwilling to continue. At other times, I would gently relieve the tension by leading the conversation into neutral waters, discussing highly abstract concepts such as war, justice, or political freedom. Only a radical break with my emotions would allow me to regard the conversation once again as analyzable knowledge.

This example has demonstrated the emotional incorporation of the ethnographer in the ethnographic encounter, but this intersubjectivity also has a counterpart in the interlocutor's reactions. An Argentine anthropologist, who knew one of my interviewees, a former guerrillero, recounted to me one day his rendition of my meetings with him. He had told her that during a stirring moment of our conversation in which he was reflecting on the terrible waste of lives in the political struggle of the 1970s, he saw tears in my eyes. This intensified the awareness of his own tragedy and made him break down as well. At these moments of a complete collapse of the critical distance between two interlocutors, we lose all dimensions of the scientific enterprise. Overwhelmed by emotion we do not have the need for any explanation because we feel that all questions have already been answered. What else is there to ask? What else is there to tell? What more do we need to know? What more is there to know?

SECRECY AND TRUTH

Any research on political violence runs into too many skeletons to handle, too many closets to inspect. Aside from deliberate lies, half-truths, and unfounded accusations—many of which are impossible to trace or verify— there is a lot of malicious gossip and character assassination. One way in which interlocutors try to add credibility to their charges is by means of a staged confession introduced by statements such as "Let me tell you a secret," or "I have never told this to anyone," or "I will tell you this, but you may not record it or write it down."

Secrecy seduces. The belief that the interlocutor is hiding a darker side is seductive because it teases the ethnographer to surrender. Only a surrender to the interlocutor's conditions of truth will yield the desired information. The remarks about secrecy made by my interlocutors served as a strategy to overpower my interpretive stance as an observer. It was an invitation to complicity. I do not want to exaggerate the political influence of social scientists, but most of my interlocutors were aware of the potential impact of an authoritative analysis of the last dictatorship. The impartiality of local scholars is called into question by most Argentines. They are accused of writing polemic books (*libros de combate*), polemic in its most literal sense: books for waging war. These books are believed to sacrifice scientific accuracy to political ends. Foreign authors are regarded as more neutral than national scholars, and some of them, such as Robert A. Potash (1969, 1980) and Alain Rouquié (1987*a*, 1987*b*), have become household names.

The political weight of my research became most apparent during my last interview with the general who had saved me from being run over by a taxi. Almost two months after the presidential decree that dismissed the court case against him, I met him again at the Officers Club. After a quarter of an hour I told him that I noticed a change in his demeanor. He was much more relaxed than during our last series of interviews. He laughed and said that four months ago he was in the middle of a political battle (*batalla política*). "Now," he said, "everything is history, and eventually the Argentine people will realize that the military acted in a correct way." Comparing this last interview with our previous conversations, he had become almost aloof and seemed uninterested in persuading me of his rightness. His short answers were delivered in a casual and offhand manner. The political battle had ended. Had I been one of its foot soldiers? Had I been used as a sparring partner for a future crossfire examination by the public prosecutor, or had I been used as a gullible courier of the general's political message?

The question of truth does not receive much attention in the many books on fieldwork that have appeared in the last three decades.[13] In contrast, earlier generations of anthropologists were much more concerned about prying the truth out of their informants (see Rosaldo 1986). For instance, Marcel Griaule (1957) writes in his book on fieldwork: "The role of the person sniffing out social facts is often comparable to that of a detective or examining magistrate. The fact is the crime, the interlocutor the guilty party; all the society's members are accomplices" (quoted in Clifford 1983*b*:138). S. F. Nadel, Griaule's contemporary, favored equally inquisitive methods: "In the case of interviews which bear on secret and forbidden topics, I have found it most profitable to stimulate the emotionality of a few chief informants to the extent of arousing almost violent disputes and controversies. The expression of doubt and disbelief on the part of the interviewer, or the arrangement of interviews with several informants, some of whom, owing to their social position, were certain to produce inaccurate information, easily induced the key informant to disregard his usual reluctance to speak openly, if only to confound his opponents and critics" (1939:323). Finally, a classic field guide recommends: "It is sometimes useful to pretend incredulity to induce further information" (RAI 1951:33).

James Clifford (1983*b*:143–144) has remarked, "By the late sixties the romantic mythology of fieldwork rapport had begun publicly to dissolve. . . . Geertz undermines the myth of ethnographic rapport before reinstating it in an ironic mode. Like Griaule he seems to accept that all parties to the encounter recognize its elements of insincerity, hypocrisy, and self-deception." However, a major difference between the two authors is that Griaule was still hunting for undisputable truth. Geertz, instead, is representative of an entire generation of anthropologists who accompanied the interpretive turn of the 1960s and 1970s. Function and explanation were exchanged for meaning and understanding, and many anthropologists felt more identified with notions such as the definition of the situation and the social construction of reality than with a positivist belief in truth and method.[14]

Even though most anthropologists today feel much closer to Geertz than to Griaule and Nadel, our informants continue to think in terms of truth and falsehood. This issue becomes especially relevant in research on violence because the protagonists of major political conflicts are often accused of undermining the very foundation of society and of being responsible for the ensuing human suffering. The question of historical interpretation is of great political importance to them, and they will do their best to convince us of their rightness and to ignore dissenting views. We can, of course, not expect our interlocutors to incriminate themselves or recount their traumatic experiences with an anesthetized detachment but, instead, we should anticipate that they may consciously or unconsciously try to divert us from our investigative aims by disarming our critical gaze. In response to Geertz: not all Cretans may be liars, but some are, and some of them are seducers as well.

Having become temporarily disillusioned by the subtle strategies of persuasion of my Argentine interlocutors, I turned to the texts they had produced in the 1970s. This led to a search for secret army documents, intelligence reports, human rights pamphlets, and the clandestine publications of the revolutionary Left. I realized, of course, that these written sources were just as much discursive constructions as the spoken word of their authors. Nevertheless, the texts were concurrent with the historical events I was studying, and I could compare the oral accounts I had recorded of those actions, decisions, and events with contemporary clandestine, classified, and official sources. I hoped to puncture the appearances of my interlocutors, disentangle myself from their seduction, and reach back in time to the origin of their talk, the events, ideological articulations, power struggles, and armed confrontations. The anxiety of not being able to rely on oral history made me cling to contemporary inscriptions that at least had an appearance of authenticity.[15] I do not use "authenticity" here in the sense of true or real but rather as genuine to the interlocutor's own sense of truth and reality. "Authenticity relates to the corroborative support given an account . . . by its internal consistency or cross-reference to other sources of information" (Brown and Sime 1981:161; see also Denzin 1970, on triangulation). An analysis of the interviews and a comparison with statements made during the time of repression allowed me to distance myself from the surface account that they tried to make me accept as the only true reality.

Clearly, the ethnographer of violence and political conflict may become encapsulated in the webs of seduction spun by his or her informants and interlocutors. Just as Lenin had inverted von Clausewitz's definition of war by stating that politics is the continuation of war by other means, so seduction became the continuation of Argentine politics after the turn to democracy in 1983.[16] Neither brute force nor coercion but the molding of appearances became the weapon of influential players in the Argentine polity. Ethnographic seduction was my personal experience with a national debate in Argentina among the adversarial protagonists of the decades of political violence.

But why resort to seduction? Those who dispute power and authority are aware of the importance of seduction. They realize that arguments alone do not persuade people, that charisma is the privilege of the gifted few, but that appearances are taken at face value by many. We as ethnographers are also subjects of seduction because our informants have a stake in making us adopt their truths. They perceive us as the harbingers of history. We will retell their stories and through our investiture as scientists provide these with the halo of objectivity that our academic stature entails.

What a weight on our shoulders; the weight to be the arbitrators of an absolute truth in which we have lost faith ourselves. What should we respond? That there is no truth? That truth is always historical? That their truth is not the truth of their opponents? That they have entrusted us with a Rankean authority in which we do not believe and which we do not want? That we cannot verify what they tell us? "But what are you saying?" they asked me. "How can you doubt the tears I have shed with you?" They reassure me. "You will be able to tell the truth about what really happened in Argentina." "We need foreign researchers like you who will be able to tell the truth that we cannot write." "Abroad, they can write a truth that nobody wants to publish here." They made appeals to my responsibility. "We need scientists like you whose books will allow the Argentine people to reach a reconciliation." They even tried to induce guilt. "I have told you my story so that you can write the truth." "Do not use the things I have told you against us." "Make sure that my story can never be used by those who killed my daughter."

SHREDDING SHROUDS OF POWER

He had been on their hit list for more than three decades, old admiral Rojas; this diminutive man with his piercing eyes and hawkish nose. He and general Aramburu had been the strongmen of the revolution against Perón in 1955, and in 1956 he had personally signed the execution order of general Valle after his failed uprising against the military government. Aramburu had been kidnapped in 1970 and was executed by the Montoneros guerrilla organization. Rojas was to be next.

The two petty officers in the hallway asked me to open my briefcase. After examining its contents, one of them opened the elevator door and we stepped inside. We stopped at the fourth floor. He accompanied me to the door. The admiral invited me in with a jovial gesture. I sat down on the couch as he sank away in a large armchair. "I have a great many grandchildren," he began. "They often come to visit me and stay for lunch or dinner." Now I knew why there was a pile of heavy-metal records next to the turntable. The image of an 84-year-old admiral Rojas listening to AC/DC in the company of his teenage grandchildren was disarming. This had been one of the most influential men in Argentine politics in the 1950s, but the stack of heavy-metal records gave him away. These records revealed the transparency of power.

Because isn't power nothing but seduction; a mesmerizing play of brocaded clothes and ermine mantles; an enchanting appearance that obscures the seducer's vulnerability? Seeing the bearers of Argentine authority surrounded by the photographs of their children, smelling the food from their kitchens, and walking on the plush carpets of their apartments disintegrated power into human transience.

But, you may object, power rests on real force, and our ethnographic judgment should not be swayed by outward niceties and runaway emotions. I think you are right. One may become so familiar with the power holders—in the sense of convivial as well as knowledgeable—that it may obstruct one's perception of the authority vested in them. I therefore have to retrace my final steps and erase the imprint they have left. Seduction means after all, in a literal sense, "to be led astray from an intended course."

I went to Argentina to understand the contested historical reconstruction of the violence of the 1970s but soon became entangled in the rhetoric and seduction played upon me by its protagonists. Disillusioned, I sought refuge in the denuded truth of some "hard facts," only to discover that my understanding had run aground in the shallowness of the written word. I had to retrace my steps and stop where seduction, rhetoric, interpretation, and intersubjectivity suffused the ethnographic encounter. I could only subvert seduction by playing along with it and grasp its meaning from the inside. This experience made me sensitive to what many Argentines, especially those who had suffered the disappearance of a relative, had felt during the years of repression. The disappearance was a form of deceit in which all appearances were kept up; the appearance of justice, of innocence, and due process. Where people became surface manifestations. Where lives changed course surreptitiously. And where reappearance depended on a gesture, on a nod of the head. It was in this clearing that I realized that ethnographic seduction crosscuts the interplay of empathy and detachment that sound fieldwork ordains. Standing in this clearing, it became finally possible to realize that the many directions I had been sent to were only intended to entice me away from where I was already standing.

NOTES

1. The research in Buenos Aires, Argentina, from April 1989 until August 1991 was made possible by grants from the National Science Foundation and the Harry Frank Guggenheim Foundation. I thank Adam Kuper, James McAllister, Carolyn Nordstrom, Frank Pieke, and Jan de Wolf for their thoughtful comments.

2. Devereux (1967:44–45) has used the term "seduction" in his discussion of countertransference reactions among anthropologists. However, he defines it not as conscious manipulation but as emotional allurement.

3. An additional danger of using the term "seduction" is that it might result in an unwelcome association with Freud's seduction theory. For all clarity, my use of the term stands clear from Freud's theory about hysteria and distances itself from the implied notions of the repression of sexual desire.

4. Rapport is generally regarded as essential to successful fieldwork, "simply because of the assumption that people talk better in a warm, friendly atmosphere, and the additional assumption that attitudes are somehow complex and hidden and a lot of talking is essential before the attitude is elicited" (Hyman 1954:22). The issue of rapport has been discussed with much greater depth in sociology than in anthropology, possibly because the methodological emphasis on participant observation makes anthropologists downplay the actual importance of interview situations for acquiring local knowledge. See, e.g., the discussion of rapport by Hyman (1954:153–170) and Turner and Martin (1984:262–278) and the critique by Cicourel (1964:82–86).

5. Despite this call for attention to the native tongue, Clifford (1983a, 1988: 38–41) has argued that Geertz has always remained the authoritarian voice that arbitrated the interpretational disputes among his informants. Clifford has emphasized the dialogic intersubjectivity of the ethnographic encounter with its polyphonic variations and discursive conflicts, as exemplified by Dwyer (1982) and Crapanzano (1980).

6. This chapter has drawn inspiration from Baudrillard's general statements about seduction but should not be taken as an application of his ideas (for a feminist critique, see Hunter 1989).

7. The opposite of the illusion of the cultural insider is the illusion of the objective investigator. "Methodological objectivism is a denial of the intersubjective or dialogical nature of fieldwork through which ethnographic understanding develops" (Obeyesekere 1990:227).

8. The account interview is not a context-free exchange of information but in the first place a social relationship with all its concomitant complexities (Brenner 1978, 1981). The impression management during my research in Argentina involved an array of stratagems. The location of the interview was chosen with the aim of exuding authority or familiarity. Some preferred their homes, while others invited me to the stately buildings of the church and the armed forces or the personalized offices of the human rights and former guerrilla organizations. Impression management also involved a manipulation of the senses. Dress, physical gestures, facial expressions, and ways of making eye contact and shaking hands are all part of a presentation of self that influences the social interaction between ethnographer and interlocutor (Agar 1980:54–62). For an analysis of the unique problems of female researchers who study the military, see Daniels 1967.

9. Simons (1976:134–138) distinguishes between co-active, combative, and expressive forms of persuasion. The co-active form attempts to bridge the psychological differences among interlocutors by stimulating the identification between speaker and audience. The combative form tries to persuade through coercion and intimidation. Combative approaches are most effective in situations of social conflict. Finally, there is an expressive approach that deliberately rejects the conscious manipulation of the audience but that hopes to raise people's consciousness through self-criticism and by openly sharing experiences. The co-active form of persuasion is the most versatile strategy because it can incorporate aspects of the other two forms.

10. Roloff (1980) analyzes aspects of rhetorical persuasion that remain hidden to both speaker and audience.

11. A scene from *Shoah* comes to mind in which Claude Lanzmann virtually coerces Abraham Bomba, a survivor of Treblinka, to recall his experiences: "AB: A friend of mine worked as a barber—he was a good barber in my hometown—when his wife and his sister came into the gas chamber. . . . I can't. It's too horrible. Please. CL: We have to do it. You know it. AB: I won't be able to do it. CL: You have to do it. I know it's very hard. I know and I apologize. AB: Don't make me go on please. CL: Please. We must go on" (Lanzmann 1985:117).

12. Part of the dialogue quoted here can be found in almost the exact same words in Cohen Salama (1992:230).

13. Historians and sociologists have paid more attention to deliberate distortion; see Dean and Whyte 1970; Ginzburg 1991; Gorden 1975:445–460; Henige 1982:58–59.

14. During the same period, there was also considerable interest in action research and Marxist and feminist analyses. These three approaches are at the opposite end of seduction because the ethnographer tries to seduce people into accepting his or her interpretation of social reality as the most objective and correct analysis. The language of oppression and exploitation is used as a powerful rhetoric of persuasion.

15. Devereux (1967:46) explains this "anxious clinging to 'hard' facts" as an expression of the ethnographer's fear that he or she is not properly understanding or communicating with the informants.

16. War, according to von Clausewitz (1984:87), is "a continuation of political activity by other means."

REFERENCES

Agar, Michael H.
1980   *The Professional Stranger: An Informal Introduction to Ethnography.* New York: Academic Press.
Baudrillard, Jean
1990   *Seduction.* New York: St. Martin's Press.
Berreman, Gerald D.
1972   "Prologue: Behind Many Masks, Ethnography and Impression Management." In *Hindus of the Himalayas: Ethnography and Change,* ed. Gerald Berreman, xvii-lvii. Berkeley, Los Angeles, and London: University of California Press.
Brenner, Michael
1978   "Interviewing: The Social Phenomenology of a Research Instrument." In *The Social Contexts of Method,* ed. Michael Brenner, Peter Marsh, and Marylin Brenner, 122–139. London: Croom Helm.
1981   "Patterns of Social Structure in the Research Interview." In *Social Method and Social Life,* ed. Michael Brenner, 115–158. New York: Academic Press.
Brown, Jennifer, and Jonathan Sime
1981   "A Methodology for Accounts." In *Social Method and Social Life,* ed. Michael Brenner, 159–188. New York: Academic Press.
Cicourel, Aaron V.
1964   *Method and Measurement in Sociology.* New York: Free Press.
Clausewitz, Carl von
[1832] 1984   *On War.* Princeton: Princeton University Press.
Clifford, James
1983*a*   "On Ethnographic Authority." *Representations* 1(2):118–146.
1983*b*   "Power and Dialogue in Ethnography: Marcel Griaule's Initiation." In *Observers Observed: Essays on Ethnographic Fieldwork,* ed. George W. Stocking, 121–156. Madison: University of Wisconsin Press.
1988   *The Predicament of Culture: Twentieth-Century Ethnography, Literature, and Art.* Cambridge: Harvard University Press.
Cohen Salama, Mauricio
1992   *Tumbas anónimas: Informe sobre la identificación de restos de víctimas de la represión ilegal.* Buenos Aires: Catálogos Editora.
Cole, Thomas
1991   *The Origins of Rhetoric in Ancient Greece.* Baltimore: Johns Hopkins University Press.

Crapanzano, Vincent
   1980   *Tuhami: Portrait of a Moroccan.* Chicago: University of Chicago Press.
Daniels, Arlene Kaplan
   1967   "The Low-Caste Stranger in Social Research." In *Ethics, Politics, and Social Research,* ed. Gideon Sjoberg, 267–296. Cambridge: Schenkman.
Dean, John P., and William Foote Whyte
   1970   "How Do You Know If the Informant Is Telling the Truth?" In *Elite and Specialized Interviewing,* ed. Lewis Anthony Dexter, 119–131. Evanston: Northwestern University Press.
Denzin, Norman K., ed.
   1970   *Sociological Methods: A Sourcebook.* Chicago: Aldine.
Devereux, George
   1967   *From Anxiety to Method in the Behavioral Sciences.* The Hague: Mouton.
Dwyer, Kevin
   1982   *Moroccan Dialogues: Anthropology in Question.* Baltimore: Johns Hopkins University Press.
Ellen, R. F., ed.
   1984   *Ethnographic Research: A Guide to General Conduct.* London: Academic Press.
Geertz, Clifford
   1973   *The Interpretation of Cultures.* New York: Basic Books.
Gilbert, G. Nigel, and Michael Mulkay
   1984   *Opening Pandora's Box: A Sociological Analysis of Scientists' Discourse.* Cambridge: Cambridge University Press.
Ginzburg, Carlo
   1991   "Checking the Evidence: The Judge and the Historian." *Critical Inquiry* 18(1):79–92.
Goffman, Erving
   1966   *Behavior in Public Places: Notes on the Social Organization of Gatherings.* New York: Free Press.
   1969   *The Presentation of Self in Everyday Life.* London: Allen Lane.
Gorden, Raymond L.
   1975   *Interviewing: Strategy, Techniques, and Tactics.* Homewood, Ill.: Dorsey Press.
Griaule, Marcel
   1957   *Méthode de l'Ethnographie.* Paris: Presses Universitaires de France.
Gross, Alan G.
   1990   *The Rhetoric of Science.* Cambridge: Harvard University Press.
Henige, David
   1982   *Oral Historiography.* London: Longman.
Hunter, Dianne, ed.
   1989   *Seduction and Theory: Readings of Gender, Representation, and Rhetoric.* Urbana: University of Illinois Press.
Hyman, Herbert H., et al.
   1954   *Interviewing in Social Research.* Chicago: University of Chicago Press.

Jardine, Nicholas
   1991   *The Scenes of Inquiry: On the Reality of Questions in the Sciences.* Oxford: Clarendon Press.
Lanzmann, Claude
   1985   *Shoah: An Oral History of the Holocaust.* New York: Pantheon Books.
Nadel, S. F.
   1939   "The Interview Technique in Social Anthropology." In *The Study of Society: Methods and Problems,* ed. F. C. Bartlett et al., 317–327. London: Kegan Paul, Trench, Trubner.
Obeyesekere, Gananath
   1990   *The Work of Culture: Symbolic Transformation in Psychoanalysis and Anthropology.* Chicago: University of Chicago Press.
Potash, Robert A.
   1969   *The Army and Politics in Argentina, 1928–1945: Yrigoyen to Perón.* Stanford: Stanford University Press.
   1980   *The Army and Politics in Argentina, 1945–1962: Perón to Frondizi.* Stanford: Stanford University Press.
RAI (Royal Anthropological Institute)
   1951   *Notes and Queries on Anthropology.* 6th ed. London: Routledge and Kegan Paul.
Roloff, Michael E.
   1980   "Self-Awareness and the Persuasion Process: Do We Really Know What We're Doing?" In *Persuasion: New Directions in Theory and Research,* ed. Michael E. Roloff and Derald R. Miller, 29–66. Beverly Hills, Calif.: Sage Publications.
Rosaldo, Renato
   1986   "From the Door of His Tent: The Fieldworker and the Inquisitor." In *Writing Culture: The Poetics and Politics of Ethnography,* ed. James Clifford and George E. Marcus, 77–97. Berkeley, Los Angeles, and London: University of California Press.
Rouquié, Alain
   1987a   *Poder Militar y Sociedad Política en la Argentina I—hasta 1943.* Buenos Aires: Emecé Editores.
   1987b   *Poder Militar y Sociedad Política en la Argentina II: 1943–1973.* Buenos Aires: Emecé Editores.
Simons, Herbert W.
   1976   *Persuasion: Understanding, Practice, and Analysis.* Reading, Mass.: Addison-Wesley.
Turner, Charles F., and Elizabeth Martin, eds.
   1984   *Surveying Subjective Phenomena.* Vol. 1. New York: Russell Sage Foundation.

"Weaving Justice," by Sebastian Quinac

Living in a State of Fear

Linda Green

Fear is a response to danger. But in Guatemala, rather than being solely a subjective personal experience, it has penetrated the social memory.[1] And, rather than being an acute reaction, it is a chronic condition. The effects of fear are pervasive and insidious in Guatemala. Fear destabilizes social relations by driving a wedge of distrust between members of families, between neighbors, among friends. Fear divides communities through suspicion and apprehension, not only of strangers, but of each other.[2] Fear thrives on ambiguities. Rumors of death lists and denunciations, gossip, and innuendos create a climate of suspicion. No one can be sure who is who. The spectacle of torture and death, of massacres and disappearances of the recent past have become deeply inscribed in individuals and in the collective imagination through a constant sense of threat. In the *altiplano* fear has become a way of life. Fear is the arbiter of power—invisible, indeterminant, and silent.

What is the nature of the fear and terror that pervade Guatemalan society? How do people understand it and experience it? And what is at stake for people who live in a chronic state of fear? Might survival itself depend on a panoply of responses to a seemingly intractable situation?

In this chapter I examine the invisible violence of fear and intimidation through the quotidian experiences of the people of Xe'caj.[3] In doing so, I try to capture a sense of the insecurity that permeates individual women's lives wracked by worries of physical and emotional survival, of grotesque memories, of ongoing militarization, of chronic fear. The stories I relate below are the individual experiences of the women with whom I worked, yet they are also social and collective accounts by virtue of their omnipresence (see Lira and Castillo 1991; Martín-Baró 1990). Although the focus of my work with Mayan women was not explicitly on the topic of violence, an understanding of its usages, its manifestations, and its effects is essential to comprehending the context in which the women of Xe'caj are struggling to survive.

Fear became the metanarrative of my research and experiences among the people of Xe'caj. Fear is the reality in which people live, the hidden "state of (individual and social) emergency" that is factored into the choices women and men make. Although this state of emergency in which Guatemalans have been living for over a decade may be the norm, it is an abnormal state of affairs indeed. Albert Camus (1955) wrote that from an examination of the shifts between the normal and the emergency, between the tragic and the everyday, emerges the paradoxes and contradictions that bring into sharp relief how the absurd (in this case, terror) works.

Writing this chapter has been problematic. And it has to do with the nature of the topic itself, the difficulty of fixing fear and terror in words.[4] I have chosen to include some of my own experiences of fear during my field research rather than stand apart as an outsider, an observer. First, because it was and is impossible to stand apart. It soon became apparent that any understanding of the women's lives would include a journey into a state of fear in which terror reigned, and this would shape the nature of my interactions and relationships in Xe'caj. And second, from these shared experiences we forged common grounds of understanding and respect.

Fear is elusive as a concept, yet you know it when it has you in its grip. Fear, like pain, is "overwhelmingly present" to the person experiencing it, but it may be barely perceptible to anyone else and almost defies objectification.[5] Subjectively the mundane experience of chronic fear wears down one's sensibility to it. The "routinization of fear" undermines one's confidence in interpreting the world. My own experiences of fear and those of the women I know are much as Michael Taussig (1992*a*:11) aptly describes it: a state of "stringing out the nervous system one way toward hysteria, the other way numbing and apparent acceptance."

ANTHROPOLOGY AND VIOLENCE

Given anthropology's empirical bent and the fact that anthropologists are well positioned to speak out on behalf of the "people who provide us with our livelihood" (in Taussig's [1978] words), it seems curious that so few have chosen to do so. Jeffrey Sluka (1992) has suggested that the practice of sociocultural anthropology, with its emphasis on a "cross-cultural and comparative perspective, holistic approach, reliance on participant observation, concentration on local level analysis and 'emic' point of view," is particularly well suited to understanding the subjective, experiential, meaningful dimension of social conflict. Anthropologists, however, have traditionally approached the study of conflict, war, and human aggression from a distance, ignoring the harsh realities of people's lives.

Although the dominant theoretical paradigms utilized in anthropological inquiry over the past century—evolutionism, structural-functionalism, acculturation studies, and Marxism—have examined societal manifestations of violence, the lived experiences of their research subjects have often been muted. When social conflict and warfare have been problematized, it has been in abstract terms, divorced from the historical realities of the colonial or capitalist encounter. Throughout the twentieth century, most studies by political anthropologists have emphasized taxonomy over process; for example, the classification of simple or indigenous political systems, political leadership, law, domination, and intertribal relations (Vincent 1990).[6] Overwhelming empirical evidence demonstrates that state violence has been standard operating procedure in numerous contemporary societies where anthropologists have conducted fieldwork for the past three decades.[7] Despite an alarming rise in the most blatant forms of transgression, repression and state terrorism, the topic has not captured the anthropological imagination (see Downing and Kushner 1988).

In a stinging commentary on anthropology's claim to authority on the subject of Native Americans, Paul Doughty (1988:43) has questioned why monographs have not addressed systematically "the most vital issues that unequivocally affected all Native Americans relentlessly since European conquest," death, discrimination, displacement, dispossession, racism, rampant disease, hunger, impoverishment, physical and psychological abuse. Nancy Scheper-Hughes is insightful in this regard. She writes in her eloquent ethnography (1992:170) of everyday violence in Northeast Brazil that "a critical practice of social science implies not so much a practical as an epistemological struggle." Perhaps this is what lies at the heart of anthropology's diverted gaze. What is at stake, it seems, are the struggles between the powerful and the powerless and what is at issue for anthropologists is with whom to cast their lot.

A number of practitioners today who work in "dangerous field situations" have begun to deconstruct the insidious and pervasive effects and mechanisms of violence and terror, underscoring how it operates on the level of lived experience (Feldman 1991; Lancaster 1992; Nordstrom and Martin 1992; Scheper-Hughes 1992; Suarez-Orozco 1990, 1992; Taussig 1987, 1992*b*). Among anthropologists, it is Taussig who has captured so well the complexities and nuances of terror, giving terror sentience. What is consistently compelling about Taussig's work, despite its sometimes recondite tendencies, is his ability to portray terror viscerally, in effect to take a moral stance against power played out in its more grotesque forms. Recent works by Robert Carmack (1988), Beatriz Manz (1988), AVANCSO

(1992), Ricardo Falla (1983, 1992), and Richard Wilson (1991) have begun to document in Guatemala the testimonies of individual and collective experiences during the most recent reign of terror. In his haunting account of the massacres of the Ixcan in Guatemala between 1975 and 1982, Falla (1992) asks the chilling question of why one ought to write about massacres (and terror). His answer is simple yet provocative: intellectuals can act as intermediaries, can lend their voices on behalf of those who have witnessed and lived through the macabre. Anthropologist as scribe, who faithfully documents what the people themselves narrate as their own histories, that which they have seen, smelled, touched, felt, interpreted, and thought. Not to do so, as Nancy Scheper-Hughes (1992) contends, is an "act of indifference," a hostile act. Monographs can become "sites of resistance," "acts of solidarity," a way to "write against terror." Anthropology itself is employed as an agent of social change.

THE ROUTINIZATION OF TERROR

While thinking and writing about fear and terror, I was inclined to discuss what I was doing with colleagues knowledgeable about "*la situacíon*" in Central America. I would describe to them the eerie calm I felt most days, an unease that lies just below the surface of everyday life. Most of the time it was more a visceral than a visual experience, and I tried laboriously to suppress it.

One day I was relating to a friend what it felt like to pretend not to be disturbed by the intermittent threats that were commonplace throughout 1989 and 1990 in Xe'caj. Some weeks the market plaza would be surrounded by five or six tanks while painted-faced soldiers with M-16s in hand perched above us, watching. My friend's response made me nervous all over again. He said that he had initially been upset by the ubiquitous military presence in Central America. He, too, he assured me, had assumed that the local people felt the same. But lately he had been rethinking his position since he had witnessed a number of young women flirting with soldiers, or small groups of local men leaning casually on tanks. Perhaps we North Americans, he continued, were misrepresenting what was going on, reading our own fears into the meaning it had for Central Americans. I went home wondering if perhaps I was being "hysterical," stringing out the nervous (social) system. Had I been too caught up in terror's talk? Gradually I came to realize that terror's power, its matter-of-factness, is exactly about doubting one's own perceptions of reality. The routinization of terror is what fuels its power. Routinization allows people to live in a chronic state of fear with a facade of normalcy at the same time that terror permeates and shreds the social fabric. A sensitive and experienced Guatemalan economist noted that a major problem for social scientists working in Guatemala is that to survive they have become inured to the violence, training themselves at first not to react, then later not to feel (see) it. They miss the context in which people live, including themselves. Self-censorship becomes second nature. Bentham's panopticon internalized.

How does one become socialized to terror? Does it imply conformity or acquiescence to the status quo, as my friend suggested? While it is true that with repetitiveness and familiarity people learn to accommodate themselves to terror and fear, low-intensity panic remains in the shadow of waking consciousness. One cannot live in a constant state of alertness, and so the chaos one feels becomes infused throughout the body. It surfaces frequently in dreams and chronic illness. Sometimes in the mornings my neighbors and friends would speak of their fears during the night, of being unable to sleep or being awakened by footsteps or voices, of nightmares of recurring death and violence. After six months of living in Xe'caj, I, too, started to experience nighttime hysteria, dreams of death, disappearances, and torture. Whisperings, innuendos, rumors of death lists circulating put everyone on edge. One day a friend from Xe'caj, Nacho, came to my house very anxious. He explained, holding back his tears, that he had heard his name was on the newest death list at the military encampment. As Scheper-Hughes (1992:233) has noted, "the intolerableness of the situation is increased by its ambiguity." A month later two soldiers were killed one Sunday afternoon in a surprise guerrilla attack a kilometer from my house. That evening several women from the village came to visit, emotionally distraught. They worried that la violencia, which had been stalking them, had at last returned. Doña Maria said that violence is like fire, it can flare up suddenly and burn you.

The people of Xe'caj live under constant surveillance. The *destacamento* (military encampment) looms large in the *pueblo*, situated on a nearby hillside above town, from where everyone's movements come under close scrutiny. The town is laid out spatially in the colonial quadrangle pattern common throughout the altiplano. The town square as well as all the roads leading to the surrounding countryside is visible from above. The encampment is not obvious from below to an untrained eye. The camouflaged buildings fade into the hillside, but once one has looked down from there it is impossible to forget that those who live below do so in a fishbowl. *Orejas* (literally, ears; also, spies), military commissioners, and civil patrollers provide the backbone of military scrutiny.

Military commissioners are local men, many of whom have been in the army. In the villages they serve as local recruiters and spies for the army. The program was instituted nationwide in the 1960s and was one of the initial steps in the militarization of the rural areas. The civil patrol system was created in 1982 and by 1985 constituted a rural militia of over one million men, over half the highland male population over fifteen years of age. The PACs, as they are known, function to augment military strength and intelligence in areas of conflict and, more important, to provide vigilance and control over the local population. Although the Guatemalan constitution states explicitly that the PACs are voluntary, failure to participate or opposition to their formation marks one as a subversive in conflictive zones in the altiplano (see Americas Watch 1986).

The impact of the civil patrols at the local level has been profound. One of the structural effects of the PACs in Xe'caj has been the subordination of traditional village political authority to the local army commander. When I arrived in Xe'caj, I first went to the mayor to introduce myself. I asked for his permission to work in the township and surrounding villages, but midway through my explanation he cut me off abruptly, explaining impatiently that if I hoped to work here, what I really needed was the explicit permission of the *comandante* at the army garrison. The civil patrols guard the entrances and exits to the villages in Xe'caj, he said. Without permission from the army the civil patrols would not allow me to enter the villages. My presence as a stranger and foreigner produced suspicions. Why do you want to live and work here with us? Why do you want to talk with the widows? For whom do you work? the alcalde asked. It was the local army officers who told me it was a free country and that I could do as I pleased, providing I had their permission.

One of the ways terror becomes defused is through subtle messages. Much as Carol Cohn (1987) describes in her unsettling account of the use of language by nuclear scientists to sanitize their involvement in nuclear weaponry, the great effrontery of the modern era, in Guatemala language and symbols are utilized to normalize a continual army presence. From time to time army troops would arrive in aldeas, obliging the villagers to assemble for a community meeting. The message was more or less the same each time I witnessed these gatherings. The comandante would begin by telling the people that the army is their friend, that the soldiers are here to protect them against subversion, against the Communists hiding out in the mountains. At the same time he would admonish them that if they did not cooperate, Guatemala could become like Nicaragua, El Salvador, or Cuba. Subteniente Rodriquez explained to me during one such meeting that the army is fulfilling its role of preserving peace and democracy in Guatemala through military control of the entire country. Ignacio Martín-Baró (1989), one of the six Jesuit priests murdered in San Salvador in 1989, has characterized social perceptions reduced to rigid and simplistic schemes as "official lies," where social knowledge is cast in dichotomous terms, black or white, good or bad, friend or enemy, without the nuances and complexities of lived experience.

I was with a group of widows and young orphan girls one afternoon watching a television soap opera. It was mid-June a week or so before Army Day. During one of the commercial breaks a series of images of Kaibiles[8] appeared on the screen dressed for combat with painted faces, clenching their rifles as they ran through the mountains. Each time a new frame appeared there was an audible gasp in the room. The last image was of soldiers emerging from behind cornstalks while the narrator said, "The army is ready to do whatever is necessary to defend the country." One young girl turned to me and said, "Si pues, siempre están lista que se matan la gente" [*sic*] (they are always ready to kill the people).

The use of camouflage cloth for clothing and small items sold at the market is a subtle, insidious form of militarization of daily life. Wallets, key chains, belts, caps, and toy helicopters made in Taiwan are disconcerting in this context. As these seemingly mundane objects circulate, they normalize the extent to which civilian and military life have commingled in the altiplano. Young men who have returned to villages from military service often wear army boots, T-shirts that denote in which military zone they had been stationed, and their dogtags. The boots themselves are significant. The women would say they knew who had kidnapped or killed their family members, because even if dressed in civilian clothes, the men wore army boots. When my neighbor's cousin on leave from the army came for a visit, the young boys brought him over to my house so they could show me with pride his photo album. As the young soldier stood shyly in the background, Juanito and Reginaldo pointed enthusiastically to a photograph of their cousin leaning on a tank with his automatic rifle in hand and a bandolier of bullets slung over his shoulder and another in which he was throwing a hand grenade. Yet these same boys told me many months later after I had moved into my house and we had become friends that when I first arrived, they were afraid I might kill them. And doña Juana, Reginaldo's mother, was shocked to learn that I did not carry a gun.

In El Salvador, Martín-Baró (1990) analyzed the subjective internalization of war and militarization among a group of 203 children in an effort to understand to what extent they had assimilated the efficacy of violence in solving personal and social problems. While generalizations cannot be drawn from such a limited study, what Martín-Baró found to be significant was that the majority of the children interviewed stated that the best way to end the war and attain peace was to eliminate the enemy (whether that was understood as the army or the guerrillas) through violent means. This tendency to internalize violence is what Martín-Baró has referred to as the "militarization of the mind."

The presence of soldiers and former soldiers in communities is illustrative of the lived contradictions in the altiplano and provides another example of how the routinization of terror functions. The foot soldiers of the army are almost exclusively young rural Mayas, many still boys of four-teen and fifteen years old, rounded up on army "sweeps" through rural towns. The "recruiters" arrive in two-ton trucks and grab all young men in sight, usually on festival or market days when large numbers of people have gathered together in the center of the pueblo. One morning at dawn I witnessed four such loaded trucks driving out from one of the towns of Xe'caj, soldiers standing in each corner of the truck with rifles pointed outward, the soon-to-be-foot soldiers packed in like cattle. Little is known about the training these young soldiers receive, but anecdotal data from some who are willing to talk suggest that the "training" is designed to break down one's personal dignity and respect for other human beings (see Forester 1992). As one young man described it to me, "Soldiers are trained to kill and nothing more." Another said he learned (in the army) to hate everyone, including himself. The soldiers who pass through the vil-lages on recognizance and take up sentry duty in the pueblos are Mayas, while the majority of the officers are ladinos, from other regions of the country, who cannot speak the local language. Army policy directs that the foot soldiers and the commanders of the local garrisons change every three months, to prevent soldiers from getting to know the people, a sec-ond lieutenant explained. A small but significant number of men in Xe'caj have been in the army. Many young men return home to their natal vil-lages after they are released from military duty. Yet their reintegration into the community is often difficult and problematic. As one villager noted, "They [the men/boys] leave as Indians, but they don't come back Indian."

During their time in the army some of the soldiers are forced to kill and maim. These young men, often set adrift, go on to become the lo-cal military commissioners, heads of the civil patrol, or paid informers for the army. Many are demoralized, frequently drinking and turning vio-lent. Others marry and settle in their villages to resume their lives as best they can.

I met several women whose sons had been in the military when their husbands had been killed by the army. In one disturbing situation, I inter-viewed a widow who described the particularly gruesome death of her hus-band at the hands of the army, while behind her on the wall prominently displayed was a photograph of her son in his Kaibil uniform. When I asked about him, she acknowledged his occasional presence in the house-hold and said nothing more. I was first at a loss to explain the situation and her silence; later I came to understand it as part of the rational incon-sistencies that are built into the logic of her fractured life. On a purely ob-jective level it is dangerous to talk about such things with strangers. Per-haps she felt her son's photograph might provide protection in the future. Although I ran into this situation several times, I never felt free to ask more about it. I would give the women the opportunity to say something, but I felt morally unable to pursue the topic. The women would talk freely, although with great pain, about the brutal past but maintained a stoic silence about the present. Perhaps the women's inability to talk about the fragments of their tragic experiences within the context of larger processes is in itself a survival strategy. How is it that a mother might be able to imagine that her son (the soldier) would perform the same brutish acts as those used against her and her family? To maintain a fragile integrity, must she block the association in much the same way women speak of the past atrocities as individual acts but remain silent about the ongoing process of repression in which they live? Dividing families' loyalties becomes instrumental in perpetuating fear and terror.

LIVING IN A STATE OF FEAR

During the first weeks we lived in Xe'caj, Elena, my capable field assistant, and I drove to several villages in the region talking with women and widows in small groups, asking them if they might be willing to meet with us weekly over the next year or so. At first many people thought we might be representing a development project and therefore distributing material aid. When this proved not to be the case, some women lost interest; others agreed to participate. During the second week we drove out to Ri bey, a small village that sits in a wide U-shaped valley several thousand meters lower in altitude than Xe'caj and most of the other surrounding hamlets. The one-lane dirt road that leads to the village is a series of switchbacks that cut across several ridges, before beginning the long, slow descent into the valley. Fortunately for me, there is little traffic on these back roads. Bus service had been suspended during the height of the violence in the early 1980s and a decade later is still virtually nonexistent, although a few buses do provide transport to villagers on market day. The biggest obstacle to driving is meeting logging trucks head on carrying rounds of oak and cedar for export. With their heavy loads it is impossible for them to maneuver, and so I would invariably have to back up- or downhill until I found a turnout wide enough for the truck to pass. Yet the most frightening experience was rounding a curve and suddenly encountering a military patrol.

On this day in February 1989, it was foggy and misty and a cold wind was blowing. Although the air temperature was 50 degrees Fahrenheit, the chill penetrated to the bone—"*el expreso de Alaska,*" Elena explained. Heading north we caught glimpses of the dark ridges of the Sierra de Cuchumatan brooding in the distance. The scenery was breathtaking: pine, cedar, ash, oak, the wide lush leaves of banana trees, and bromeliads mingled with the brilliant purple bougainvillea in bloom; ivory calla lilies lined the roadway. These hills, the softness of the sky, and the outline of trees created an unforgettable image. This was the Guatemala of eternal spring, of eternal hope. The *milpas* lay fallow after the harvest in late January; only the dried stalks were left half-standing, leaning this way and that. On each side of the road houses were perched on the slopes surrounded by the milpas. In the altiplano several houses made from a mix of cane- or cornstalks, adobe, and wood are usually clustered together. The red tile roofs seen farther west have all but disappeared from Xe'caj. Most people now use tin roofs (lamina), even though they retain more heat in the hot dry season and more cold when it is damp and raining. The Department of Chimaltenango was one of the hardest hit by the 1976 earthquake in which more than 75,000 people died and one million people were left homeless. Many were crushed under the weight of the tiles as roofs caved in on them. Today, half-burned houses stand as testimony to the scorched-earth campaign while civil patrollers take up their posts nearby with rifles in hand. Although Elena and I frequently saw a number of people on foot, most women and children ran to hide when they saw us coming. Months passed before women and children walking on the road would accept a ride with me. And even then, many did so reluctantly, and most would ask Elena in Kakchiquel if it was true that I wanted to steal their children and if *gringos* ate children.[9]

On this particular day Elena and I drove as far as we could and then left my pickup at the top of the hill at the point where the road became impassable. We walked the last four miles down to the village. Along the way we met local men repairing the large ruts in the road where soil had washed away with heavy September rains. Soil in this area is sandy and unstable. Most of the trees on the ridge above the road have been clearcut, and the erosion is quite pronounced. The men were putting in culverts and filling in the deep crevices that dissect the road; their only tools are shovels and pickaxes. The men are paid U.S. $1.50 per day. This is desirable work, however, because it is one of the few opportunities to earn cash close to home (most work is found on coastal plantations).

As we descended into lower elevations, Elena and I mused over the fact that there are only seven widows in Ri bey, a village of 300 people. In the several other villages where we had visited women, there were thirty to forty widows, or 15 to 20 percent of the population. Perhaps there had not been much violence in Ri bey, I suggested. One of the notable features of the military campaign known as "scorched earth" is that neighboring villages fared quite differently: one might be destroyed while another was left untouched, depending on the army's perceived understanding of guerrilla support.

Elena and I found Petrona and Tomasa and a third woman sitting in front of the school where we had agreed to meet. We greeted the women and sat down in the sun that was just breaking through the clouds. They had brought several bottles of Pepsi for us to share. I asked doña Petrona, a small thin woman with an intelligent face, why there are so few widows in Ri bey, holding my breath as I awaited the hoped-for answer—that the violence there had been much less. She replied that it was because so many people were killed, not just men but whole families, old people, children, women. The village was deserted for several years as people fled to the mountains, the pueblo, or the city. Many people never returned. Dead or displaced, no one knows for sure.

This was the third village we had visited, and each time it was the same. The women, without prompting, one by one took turns recounting their stories of horror. They would tell the events surrounding the deaths or disappearances of their husbands, fathers, sons, brothers, in vivid detail as if it had happened last week or last month rather than six or eight years ago. And the women, Petrona, Tomasa, Ana, Juana, Martina, Isabel, continued to tell me their stories over and over during the time I lived among them. But why? At first as a stranger and then later as a friend, why were these women repeatedly recounting their Kafkaesque tales to me? What was in the telling? What was the relationship between silence and testimony? As Suarez-Orozco (1992:367) has noted, "testimony [is] a ritual of both healing and a condemnation of injustice—the concept of testimony contains both connotations of something subjective and private and something objective, judicial, and political." The public spaces that we were compelled to use to thwart surveillance were transformed into a liminal space that was both private and public in the recounting.

In each of the villages where I met with women, it was always the same in the beginning. We would meet in groups of three or four in front of the village health post, the school, or the church, always in a public space. It was three months or more before anyone invited me into their home or spoke with me privately and individually. Above all else they had not wanted the *gringa* to be seen coming to their house. Under the scrutiny of surveillance the women were afraid of what others in the village might say about them and me. And when I did start going to people's homes, rumors did spread about Elena and me. The rumors themselves seemed innocuous to me, that I was helping widows or that I was writing a book about women, yet they had potentially dangerous repercussions.

During one particularly tense period, my visits caused an uproar. One day when I arrived to visit Marta and Alejandra, I found them both very anxious and agitated. When I asked what was going on they said that the military commissioner was looking for me, that people were saying I was helping the widows and talking against others in the community. "There are deep divisions within the community. People don't trust one another," explained Marta. "Families are divided and not everyone thinks alike," Alejandra added.

When I said that I would go look for don Martín, the military commissioner, they became very upset. "He said that he would take you to the garrison. Please don't go, Linda. We know people who went into the garrison and were never seen again." "But I have done nothing wrong," I said. "I must talk with them, find out what is wrong." I worried that my presence might reflect negatively on the women. So I went, Elena insisting on accompanying me, dismissing my concerns for her well-being by saying, "Si nos matan es el problema de ellos" (If they kill us it will be their problem). Fortunately for us, the commissioner was not at home, so I left a message with his wife.

The next day I decided to go to the destacamento alone. The trek to the garrison was a grueling uphill walk, or so it seemed. The last one hundred yards were the most demanding emotionally. As I rounded the bend I saw several soldiers sitting in a small guardhouse with a machine gun perched on a three-foot stanchion pointed downward and directly at me. The plight of Joseph K. in Kafka's *Trial* flashed through my mind, he accused of a crime for which he must defend himself but about which he could get no information. I didn't do anything wrong, I must not look guilty, I repeated to myself, like a mantra. I must calm myself, as my stomach churned, my nerves frayed. I arrived breathless and terrified. Ultimately, I knew I was guilty because I was against the system of violence and terror that surrounded me. I asked to speak to the comandante, who received me outside the gates. This struck me as unusual and increased my agitation, since I had been to the garrison several times before to greet each new comandante and to renew my permission papers to continue my work. On the other occasions I had been invited into the compound. The comandante said he knew nothing about why I was being harassed by the military commissioner and the civil patrol in Be'cal and assured me that I could continue with my work and that he personally would look into the situation. A few days later the comandante and several soldiers arrived in the aldea, called a communitywide meeting, and instructed everyone to cooperate with the gringa who was doing a study.

Later when the matter had been settled, some of the women explained their concerns to me. They told me stories of how widows from outlying aldeas, who had fled to the relative safety of Xe'caj after their husbands had been killed or kidnapped, had been forced to bring food and firewood for the soldiers at the garrison and were raped and humiliated at gunpoint. One brave woman carrying a baby on her back, the story goes, went to the garrison demanding to see her husband. The soldiers claimed he was not there, but she knew they were lying because his dog was standing outside the gates, and she insisted that the dog never left his side. Either they still had him or they had already killed him. She demanded to know and told them to go ahead and kill her and the baby because she had nothing more to lose. Today she is a widow.

It was the hour before dawn on a March day in 1981. Doña Petrona had arisen early to warm tortillas for her husband's breakfast before he left to work in the milpa. He was going to burn and clean it in preparation for planting soon after the first rains in early May. He had been gone only an hour when neighbors came running to tell her that her husband had been shot and was lying in the road. When Petrona reached him, he was already dead. With the help of neighbors she took his body home to prepare for burial. Petrona considers herself lucky because she says that at least she was able to bury him herself, unlike so many women whose husbands were disappeared. These are among those whom Robert Hertz (1960) has called the "unquiet dead," referring to those who have died a violent or "unnatural" death. Hertz has argued that funeral rituals are a way of strengthening the social bond. Without a proper burial these souls linger in the liminal space between earth and the afterlife, condemned in time between death and the final obsequies. And yet these wandering "unquiet souls," according to Taussig (1984), may act as intermediaries between nature and the living, buffeting as well as enhancing memories through imagery of a violent history.

The young woman sitting next to Petrona is her daughter, Ana, who is also a widow. Ana took Petrona's nod as a sign to begin. In a quiet voice she said that she was seventeen when her husband was killed on the patio of her house while her two children, Petrona, and her sister stood by helpless and in horror. It was August 1981, five months after her father had been killed. Soldiers came before dawn, pulled him out of bed, dragged him outside, and punched and kicked him until he was unconscious and then hacked him to death with machetes.

Tomasa was just beginning to recall the night her husband was kidnapped when a man carrying a load of wood with a thumpline stopped on the path about fifty feet away to ask who I was and why I was in the aldea. Don Pedro was the military commissioner in the community. I introduced myself and showed him my permission papers from the comandante of the local garrison. After looking at my papers, don Pedro told me I was free to visit the community but advised me to introduce myself to the head of the civil patrol. Tomasa anxiously resumed her story. Her husband was disappeared by soldiers one night in early 1982. She said that several days later she went to the *municipio* to register his death, and the authorities told her that if he was disappeared he was not considered dead. She did find his mutilated body some weeks later; however, she did not return to register his death until several years later. She was told that she now owed a fine of 100 *quetzales* (approximately U.S. $25) because of the lateness of her report. Tomasa planned to leave in a few weeks to pick coffee on a piedmont plantation to earn the money to acquire legal title to her small parcel of land and her house.

SILENCE AND SECRECY

It was the dual lesson of silence and secrecy that was the most enlightening and disturbing. Silence about the present situation when talking with strangers is a survival strategy that Mayas have long utilized. Their overstated politeness toward ladino society, their seeming obliviousness to the jeers and insults hurled at them, their servility in the face of overt racism, may make it seem as though Mayas have accepted their subservient role in Guatemalan society. Their apparent obsequiousness has served as a shield to provide distance and has also been a powerful shaper of Mayan practice. When Elena disclosed to a journalist friend of mine from El Salvador her thoughts about guerrilla incursions today, her family castigated her roundly for speaking, warning her that what she said could be twisted and used against her and her family. Allen Feldman (1991:11), in writing about Northern Ireland, notes that secrecy is "an assertion of identity and symbolic capital pushed to the margins. Subaltern groups construct their own margins as fragile insulators from the center."

When asked about the present situation, the usual response from most everyone was "*pues, tranquila*"—but it was a fragile calm. Later as I got to know people, when something visible would break through the facade of order, forced propaganda speeches, or in my own town when a soldier was killed and another seriously injured in an ambush, people would whisper fears of a return to la violencia. In fact, the unspoken but implied second part of "pues, tranquila" is "ahorita, pero mañana saber" (it's calm now, but who knows about tomorrow). When I asked a local fellow who is head of a small (self-sufficient) development project that is organizing locally if he is bothered by the army, he said no. They (the army) come by every couple of months, and search houses or look at his records, but he considered this "tranquila."

Silence can operate as a survival strategy, yet silencing is a powerful mechanism of control enforced through fear. At times when talking with a group of women, our attention would be distracted momentarily by a military plane or helicopter flying close and low. Each of us would lift our heads, watching until it passed out of sight, without comment. Sometimes if we were inside a house, we might all step out onto the patio to look skyward. Silence. Only once was the silence broken. On that day doña Tomasa asked rhetorically, after the helicopters had passed overhead, why my government sent bombs to kill people. At Christmas Eve Mass in 1989, twenty-five soldiers entered the church suddenly, soon after the service had begun. They occupied three middle pews on the men's side, never taking their hands off their rifles, only to leave abruptly after the sermon. Silence. The silences in these cases do not erase individual memories of terror but create more fear and uncertainty by driving a wedge of paranoia between people. Terror's effects are not only psychological and individual but social and collective as well.

Despite the fear and terror engendered by relentless human rights violations and deeply entrenched impunity in Guatemala, hope exists. Refugees, widows, the internally displaced, Mayan groups, and human rights groups have organized in response to the repression.

One of the collective responses to the silence imposed through terror began in 1984 when two dozen people, mostly women, formed the human rights organization called the GAM (Grupo de Apoyo Mutuo). Its members are relatives of some of the estimated 42,000 people disappeared in Guatemala over the past three decades. Modeled after Las Madres de Plaza de Mayo in Argentina, a small group of courageous women and men decided to break the silence. They went to government offices to demand that authorities investigate the crimes against their families. They also turned their bodies into "weapons" to speak out against the violence. As they marched in silence every Friday in front of the national palace with placards bearing the photos of those who had disappeared, they ruptured the official silence, bearing testimony with their own bodies about those who have vanished.

In 1990, Roberto Lemus, a judge in the district court of Santa Cruz del Quiche, began accepting petitions from local people to exhume sites in the villages where people claimed there were clandestine graves. Family members said they knew where their loved ones had been buried after being killed by security forces. While other judges in the area had previously allowed the exhumations, this was the first time that a scientific team had been assembled under the auspices of the eminent forensic anthropologist Dr. Clyde Snow. The intent of the exhumations was to gather evidence to corroborate verbal testimonies of survivors so as to arrest those responsible. Because of repeated death threats, Lemus was forced into political exile in July 1991. Snow has assembled another team sponsored by the American Association for the Advancement of Science that continues the work in Guatemala at the behest of human rights groups. There are estimated to be hundreds, perhaps thousands, of such sites throughout the altiplano. The clandestine cemeteries and mass graves are the *secreto a voces*—or what Taussig (1992a) has referred to in another context as the "public secrets," what everyone knows about but does not dare to speak of publicly.

In Xe'caj, people would point out such sites to me. On several occasions when I would be walking with them in the mountains, women would

take me to the places where they knew their husbands were buried and
say, "Mira, el está allí" (Look, he is over there). Others claimed that there
were at least three mass graves in Xe'caj itself. The act of unearthing the
bones of family members allows individuals to acknowledge and reconcile
the past openly, to at last acknowledge the culpability for the death of
their loved ones, and to lay them to rest. At the same time it is one of the
most powerful statements against impunity because it reveals the magnitude of the political repression that has taken place. These were not solely
individual acts with individual consequences; they are public crimes that
have deeply penetrated the social body and contest the legitimacy of the
body politic.

Thus the dual issues of impunity and accountability stand between peace
and social justice in Guatemala, as has been the case in Uruguay, Argentina, Brazil, and El Salvador (see Wechsler 1990). Amnesty therefore becomes both a political and an ethical problem with not only individual but
social dimensions as well. "To forgive and forget" the Guatemalan human
rights ombudsman (and as of 1993, president of Guatemala) suggested is
the only way democracy will be achieved in Guatemala. In a newspaper interview in 1991, Ramiro de León Carpio said, "The ideal would be that we
uncover the truth, to make public and to punish those responsible, but I
believe it is impossible. . . . [W]e have to be realistic." Certainly the idea
of political expediency has a measure of validity. The problem, however,
turns on "whether that pardon and renunciation are going to be established on a foundation of truth and justice or on lies and continued injustice" (Martín-Baró 1990:7). Hannah Arendt (1973:241) has argued against
forgiveness without accountability because it undermines the formation of
democracy by obviating any hope of justice, making its pursuit pointless.
While recognizing that forgiveness is an essential element for freedom,
Arendt contends that "the alternative to forgiveness, but by no means its
opposite [which she argues is vengeance], is punishment, and both have in
common that they attempt to put an end to something that without inter-
ference could go on endlessly." Self-imposed amnesty by the military, which
has come into vogue throughout Latin America in recent years, forecloses
the possibility of forgiveness. Without a settling of accounts, democratic
rule will remain elusive in Guatemala as has been the case elsewhere in
Latin America. Social reparation is a necessary requisite to healing the body
politic in Latin America.[10]

NOTES

1. Connerton (1989:12) has defined social memory as "images of the past that
commonly legitimate a present social order." In Guatemala, fear inculcated into
the social memory has engendered a forced acquiescence on the part of many

Mayas to the status quo. At the same time, a distinctly Mayan (counter)social memory exists and is expressed through indigenous dances, especially the dance of the Conquista, oral narratives, the relationship with ancestors maintained through the planting of corn, the weaving of cloth, and religious rituals and ceremonies.

2. Fear of strangers is not a new phenomenon in Guatemala. In the late 1940s, Oakes (1951), in her study of Todos Santos, reported that local people were reticent to talk with the few strangers who came to the community, and she, too, was treated with suspicion at the beginning of her fieldwork. And with some, Oakes never developed a rapport of trust, a common experience for most field-workers. Since the last wave of violence, however, community loyalties have been divided and a level of distrust previously unknown has permeated social life. A climate of suspicion prevails in many villages. Carrescia's two ethnographic films made a decade apart (1982, 1989; before and after the violence) in Todos Santos document some of the profound changes wrought by systematic state terror.

3. The field research on which this chapter is based was conducted in three geographically contiguous *municipios* in the Department of Chimaltenango, Guatemala. I use the fictitious name of Xe'caj to refer to all three municipios and Be'cal and Ri bey as pseudonyms for the aldeas where I worked. My intention is to provide a modicum of protection for the people with whom I worked. In 1993, the situation in Xe'caj remained politically charged.

4. Taussig's (1992a) powerful treatise on the nervous system draws the analogy between the anatomical nervous system and the chaos and panic engendered by the tenuous social system. He notes that across the fibers of this fragile network, terror passes at times almost unnoticed, and at others it is fetishized as a thing unto itself. In this essay, Taussig is preoccupied with the "mode of presentation" of terror in social analysis. He concludes, "This puts writing on a completely different plane than hitherto conceived. It calls for an understanding of the representation as contiguous with that being represented and not as suspended above or distant from the represented, . . . that knowing is giving oneself over to a phenomenon rather than thinking about it from above" (10).

5. See Scarry's (1985) discussion on the inexpressibility of physical pain. While she contends that it is only physical pain that can be characterized with no "referential content," "it is not of or for anything," I would argue differently. The power of terror of the sort that is endemic in Guatemala and in much of Latin America lies precisely in its subjectification and silence.

6. There were exceptions, of course. Lesser (1933), Hunter (1936), and Kuper (1947), for example, were producing politically and socially relevant ethnography during the same period. These studies concerned with the impact on colonialization on marginalized people were marginalized, however.

7. A partial list of countries where state terror has proliferated since the 1960s would include Indonesia, Chile, Guatemala, Kampuchea, East Timor, Uganda, Argentina, the Central African Republic, South Africa, El Salvador, the Philippines, Haiti, Burundi, Bangladesh, Brazil, and Uruguay.

8. Kaibiles are the elite special force troops of the Guatemalan army trained in counterinsurgency tactics. An excerpt from an address by general Juan José Marroquín Siliezar to a graduating class of Kaibiles on 6 December 1989 is revealing. "Kaibil officers are trained to forget all humanitarian principles and to become

war machines, capable of enduring whatever sacrifices, because from now on, they will be called Masters of War and Messengers of Death." As reported in *El Grafico,* 7 December 1989.

9. Rumors of foreigners and strangers eating children are not limited to the women of Xe'caj. Anecdotal data from other parts of Guatemala have reported similar rumors. Scheper-Hughes found some of the same concerns among the people of Northeast Brazil. She also notes the prevalence of Pishtaco myths among Andean Indians (1992:236–237), who believed that Indian fat, in particular Indian children's fat, was used to grease the machinery of the sugar mills. And in the 1980s, a biological anthropologist working among Andean people found his research stymied because of rumors that the measurement of fat folds was actually a selecting process designed to choose "the fattest for their nefarious cannibalistic purposes."

10. On June 23, 1994, the Guatemalan government and the URNG (Guatemalan National Revolutionary Unity) rebel alliance reached an agreement on the establishment of a truth commission to investigate past human rights abuses. The document calls for the formation of a three-member panel to study violations of human rights related to the armed conflict beginning in 1966 to the present. The stated goal of the commission is to "clarify with objectivity, equity and impartiality the violation of human rights, linked with the armed confrontation." The investigations will take place over a six-month period, with an option to extend for another year. The biggest obstacle to justice in the accord, however, is the prohibition of the commission to name the specific perpetrators of human rights abuses. It is this point in particular that has been widely criticized by the civilian sector and popular organizations in Guatemala because it undermines the possibilities of dismantling the structures of impunity.

REFERENCES

Adams, Richard
  1970   *Crucifixion by Power: Essays on Guatemalan National Social Structure, 1944–1966.* Austin: University of Texas Press.
Agoson, Marjorie
  1987   "A Visit to the Mothers of the Plaza de Mayo." *Human Rights Quarterly* 9:426–435.
Aguayo, Sergio
  1983   "Los posibilidades de fascismo guatemalteco." *Uno sumo* (21 marzo): 11.
Alavi, Haniza
  1973   "Peasants and Revolution." In *Imperialism and Revolution in South Asia,* ed. K. Gough and H. Sharma, 291–337. New York: Monthly Review Press.
Americas Watch
  1986   *Civil Patrols in Guatemala.* August. New York: Americas Watch Report.
  1990   *Messengers of Death: Human Rights in Guatemala.* November 1988–February 1990. New York: Americas Watch Report.

Amnesty International
  1981   "Guatemala: A Government Program of Political Murder." *New York Review of Books*, March 19, 1981, 38–40.
  1982   "Guatemala: Massive Extrajudicial Executions in Rural Area under the Government of General Efrain Rios Montt." Special Briefing. July.
  1987   *Guatemala: The Human Rights Record.* New York: Amnesty International.
Anderson, Kenneth, and Jean-Marie Simon
  1987   "Permanent Counterinsurgency in Guatemala." *Telos* 73 (Fall):9–45.
Arendt, Hannah
  1958   *The Human Condition.* Chicago: University of Chicago Press.
  1973   *Origins of Totalitarianism.* New York: Harvest.
Association for the Advancement of the Social Sciences (AVANCSO)
  1988   *La política de desarrollo del estado guatemalteco, 1986–1987.* Cuaderno no. 7. Ciudad de Guatemala: Inforpress.
  1992   *Donde está el futuro? Procesos de reintegración en comunidades de retornados.* Cuaderno no. 8. Ciudad de Guatemala: Inforpress.
Barry, Tom
  1986   *Guatemala: The Politics of Counterinsurgency.* Albuquerque: Resource Center.
Bolton, R.
  1981   "Susto, Hostility, and Hypoglycemia." *Ethnology* 20(4):261–276.
Brecht, Bertolt
  1976   "The Anxieties of the Regime." In *Bertolt Brecht Poems, 1913–1945,* ed. R. Manheim and J. Willet, 296–297. London: Methuen.
Burleigh, Elizabeth
  1986   "Patterns of Childhood Malnutrition in San José Poaquil, Guatemala." Ph.D. dissertation, University of California, Los Angeles.
Camus, Albert
  1955   *The Myth of Sisyphus and Other Essays.* New York: Vintage.
Carmack, Robert, ed.
  1988   *Harvest of Violence: The Mayan Indians and the Guatemalan Crisis.* Norman: University of Oklahoma Press.
Carrescia, Olivia
  1982   *Todos Santos Cuchumatán: Report from a Guatemalan Village.* New York: First Run/ICARUS films.
  1989   *Todos Santos: The Survivors.* New York: First Run/ICARUS films.
Cohn, Carol
  1987   "Sex and Death in the Rational World of Defense Intellectuals." *Signs* 12(4):687–718.
Connerton, Paul
  1989   *How Societies Remember.* Cambridge: Cambridge University Press.
Coronil, Fernando, and Julie Skurski
  1991   "Dismembering and Remembering the Nation: The Semantics of Political Violence in Venezuela." *Comparative Studies in Society and History* 33(2):288–337.
Doughty, Paul
  1988   "Crossroad for Anthropology: Human Rights in Latin America." In

Human Rights and Anthropology, ed. T. E. Downing and G. Kushner, 43–72. Human Rights and Anthropology. Report 24. Cambridge: Cultural Survival.

Downing, Theodore E., and Gilbert Kushner, eds.
1988 *Human Rights and Anthropology.* Report 24. Cambridge: Cultural Survival.

Environmental Project on Central America (EPOCA)
1990 *Guatemala: A Political Ecology.* Green Paper 5. San Francisco: Earth Island Institute.

Falla, Ricardo
1983 "The Massacre at the Rural Estate of San Francisco, July 1982." *Cultural Survival Quarterly* 7(1):43–45.
1992 *Masacres de la Selva: Ixcan, Guatemala, 1975–1982.* Guatemala: Universidad de San Carlos de Guatemala.

Feldman, Allen
1991 *Formations of Violence: The Narrative of the Body and Political Terror in Northern Ireland.* Chicago: University of Chicago Press.

Forester, Cindy
1992 "A Conscript's Testimony: Inside the Guatemalan Army." *Report on Guatemala* 13(2):6, 14.

Franco, Jean
1986 "Death Camp Confession and Resistance to Violence in Latin America." *Socialism and Democracy* (Spring/Summer):5–17.

Fried, Morton H.
1967 *The Evolution of Political Society: An Essay in Political Anthropology.* New York: Random House.

Gough, Kathleen
1968 "New Proposals for Anthropologists." In *Social Responsibility Symposium. Current Anthropology* 9:403–407.

Hertz, Robert
1960 "Contribution to the Study of the Collective Representation of Death." In Hertz, *Death and the Right Hand,* 29–88. London: Cohen and West.

Hooks, Margaret
1991 *Guatemalan Women Speak.* London: Catholic Institute for International Relations.

Hunter, Monica
1936 *Reaction to Conquest: Effects of Contact with Europeans on the Pondo of South Africa.* London: Oxford.

Hymes, Dell, ed.
1969 *Reinventing Anthropology.* New York: Pantheon.

Jonas, Susanne
1991 *The Battle for Guatemala: Rebels, Death Squads, and U.S. Power.* Boulder: Westview.

Jordahl, Mikkel
1987 *Counterinsurgency and Development in the Altiplano: The Role of Model Villages and the Poles of Development in the Pacification of Guatemala's Indigenous Highlands.* Washington, D.C.: Guatemalan Human Rights Commission.

Kafka, Franz
    1937   *The Trial.* New York: Alfred A. Knopf.
Kuper, Hilda Beemer
    1947   *An African Aristocracy: Rank among the Swazi of Bechwanaland.* London: Oxford University Press.
Lancaster, Roger N.
    1992   *Life Is Hard: Machismo, Danger and the Intimacy of Power in Nicaragua.* Berkeley, Los Angeles, and Oxford: University of California Press.
Lesser, Alexander
    1933   *The Pawnee Ghost Dance Hand Game: A Study of Cultural Change. Columbia University Contributions to Anthropology* 16. New York: Columbia University Press.
Lira, Elizabeth, and Maria Isabel Castillo
    1991   *Psicología de la amenaza política y del miedo.* Santiago: Ediciones Chile America, CESOC.
Lovell, George
    1992   *Conquest and Survival in Colonial Guatemala.* Kingston, Ontario: Queens University Press.
Manz, Beatriz
    1988   *Refugees of a Hidden War: The Aftermath of Counterinsurgency in Guatemala.* Albany: State University of New York Press.
Martín-Baró, Ignacio
    1989   "La institucionalización de la guerra." Conferencia prenunciada en el XXII Congreso International Psicología. Buenos Aires, 25 al 30 de junio.
    1990   "La Violencia en Centroamerica: Una vision psicosocial." *Revista de Psicología de El Salvador* 9, no. 35:123–146.
Mason, J. W.
    1973   "A Historical View of the Stress Field." *Journal of Stress Research* (June): 22–36.
Mersky, Marcie
    1989   "Empresarios y transición política en Guatemala." Unpublished manuscript.
Montejo, Victor
    1987   *Testimony: Death of a Guatemalan Village.* Willimantic, Conn.: Curbstone Press.
Nordstrom, Carolyn, and JoAnn Martin, eds.
    1992   *The Paths to Domination, Resistance, and Terror.* Berkeley, Los Angeles, and Oxford: University of California Press.
Oakes, Maude
    1951   *Two Crosses of Todos Santos.* Princeton: Princeton University Press.
Pages Larraya, F.
    1967   *La Esquizofrenia en Tierra Ayamaras y Quechuas.* Buenos Aires: Ediciones Drusa.
Parsons, Talcott
    1972   "Definition of Health and Illness in the Light of American Values and Social Structure." In *Patients, Physicians and Illness,* ed. E. Gartly, 107–127. Glencoe, Ill.: Free Press.

Paul, Benjamin, and William Demarest
    1988   "The Operation of a Death Squad in San Pedro La Laguna." In *Harvest of Violence*, ed. R. Carmack, 119–154. Norman: University of Oklahoma Press.
Peteet, Julie
    1991   *Gender in Crisis: Women and the Palestinian Resistance Movement.* New York: Columbia University Press.
Recinos, Adain, and Delia Goetz, trans.
    1953   *Annals of the Cakchiquels.* Norman: University of Oklahoma Press.
Redfield, Robert
    1930   *Tepoztlán: A Mexican Village.* Chicago: University of Chicago Press.
Rosset, Peter
    1991   "Non-traditional Export Agriculture in Central America: Impact on Peasant Farmers." Working Paper 20. University of California, Santa Cruz.
Rubel, Arthur J., Carl W. O'Nell, and Rolando Collando-Ardon
    1991   *Susto: A Folk Illness.* Berkeley, Los Angeles, and Oxford: University of California Press.
Sahlins, Marshall, and Elman Service, eds.
    1960   *Evolution and Culture.* Ann Arbor: University of Michigan Press.
Scarry, Elaine
    1985   *The Body in Pain: The Making and Unmaking of the World.* Oxford: Oxford University Press.
Scheper-Hughes, Nancy
    1992   *Death without Weeping: The Violence of Everyday Life in Brazil.* Berkeley, Los Angeles, and Oxford: University of California Press.
Scheper-Hughes, Nancy, and Margaret Lock
    1987   "The Mindful Body: A Prolegomenon to Future Work in Medical Anthropology." *Medical Anthropology Quarterly* 1(1):6–41.
Sluka, Jeffrey
    1992   "The Anthropology of Conflict." In *The Paths to Domination, Resistance, and Terror,* ed. Carolyn Nordstrom and JoAnn Martin, 190–218. Berkeley, Los Angeles, and Oxford: University of California Press.
Smith, Carol A.
    1990   "The Militarization of Civil Society in Guatemala: Economic Reorganization as a Continuation of War." *Latin America Perspectives* 67(4):8–41.
Sontag, Susan
    1977   *Illness as Metaphor.* New York: Vintage.
Stohl, Michael
    1984   "International Dimensions of State Terrorism." In *The State as Terrorist: The Dynamics of Governmental Violence and Repression,* ed. M. Stohl and G. A. Lopez, 43–58. Westport, Conn.: Greenwood.
Stoll, David
    1992   "Between Two Fires: Dual Violence and the Reassertion of Civil Society in Nebaj, Guatemala." Ph.D. dissertation, Department of Anthropology, Stanford University.

Suarez-Orozco, Marcelo

1990 "Speaking of the Unspeakable: Toward a Psycho-Social Understanding of Responses to Terror." *Ethos* 18(3):353–383.

1992 "A Grammar of Terror: Psychological Responses to State Terrorism in the Dirty War and Post-Dirty Argentina." In *The Paths to Domination, Resistance, and Terror,* ed. Carolyn Nordstrom and JoAnn Martin, 219–259. Berkeley, Los Angeles, and Oxford: University of California Press.

Taussig, Michael

1978 "Nutrition, Development, and Foreign Aid." *International Journal of Health Services* 8(11):101–121.

1984 "History as Sorcery." *Representations* 7 (Summer): 87–109.

1987 *Colonialism, Shamanism, and the Wild Man: A Study in Terror and Healing.* Chicago: University of Chicago Press.

1992a "Why the Nervous System." In Taussig, *The Nervous System,* 1–10. London: Routledge.

1992b "Terror as Usual: Walter Benjamin's Theory of History as a State of Siege." In Taussig, *The Nervous System,* 11–36. London: Routledge.

1992c Public Secrets. Invited lecture before the Department of Geography, University of California, Berkeley, 13 February.

Turton, Andrew

1986 "Patrolling the Middle Ground: Methodological Perspectives on Everyday Peasant Resistance." *Journal of Peasant Studies* 13:36–48.

Uzzell, D.

1974 "Susto Revisited: Illness as Strategic Role." *American Ethnologist* 1:369–378.

Vincent, Joan

1990 *Anthropology and Politics.* Tucson: University of Arizona Press.

Wechsler, Lawrence

1990 *A Miracle, A Universe: Settling Accounts with Torturers.* New York: Penguin.

Wickham-Crowley, Timothy

1990 "Terror and Guerrilla Warfare in Latin America." *Journal of Comparative Studies in Society and History* 32(2):201–216.

Wilson, Richard

1991 "Machine Guns and Mountain Spirits: The Cultural Effects of State Repression among the Q'eqchi of Guatemala." *Critique of Anthropology* 11(1):33–61.

Wolf, Eric

1966 *Peasants.* Englewood Cliffs, N.J.: Prentice-Hall.

1969 *Peasant Wars of the Twentieth Century.* New York: Harper and Row.

Renamo Graffiti
(Photo: Carolyn Nordstrom)

War on the Front Lines

Carolyn Nordstrom

War is perhaps impossible: it continues nonetheless everywhere you look.
SYLVERE LOTRINGER (1987)

MUNAPEO

As I wandered up into the town of Munapeo[1] from the dirt strip that served as a runway, I noticed the voids in the landscape of village life: the lack of houses and fields—razed, burned, or destroyed. The lack of social flow—well-worn paths empty of men returning from farm plots, women carrying water home, children running in endless games.

It was my first visit to Munapeo, but in the year I had just spent in Mozambique, I had seen a number of towns in similar straits. Munapeo had been held by the rebel group Renamo—responsible for the instigation of the war and the majority of terror-warfare practices and human rights abuses[2]—for some years. The Frelimo (government) forces had recently retaken the town. And the war was not far: gunshots and shouts from Renamo forces could be heard less than a kilometer away.

The sense of eerie abandonment gave way in the town center to an all too common scenario in war-torn Mozambique. Hundreds of people sat, slept, and worked in a clump of humanity, eschewing the few remaining bombed-out buildings in favor of makeshift tents. A limited supply of emergency foodstuffs, flown in on the cargo plane I had hopped a ride with, were being distributed to a surprisingly orderly line. The plane brought food but not cooking pots or fuel, and the ingenious tried to figure out ways to cook their grains in a town long since plundered for its goods and wood.

The battle-wise and violence-weary knew that food did not bring peace: a concentration of troops brought a concentration of (starving) civilians, which prompted the delivery of emergency resources, which then provoked renewed Renamo attacks seeking to loot the supplies. The war rolls over the town again.

Behind these scenes—the hungry and starving sprawled in the dust and the sun, the bombed-out buildings sporting military graffiti, the wild eyes and careless ranting of someone who "has just seen too much war"—are a host of further tragic realities. Some stories I never got used to: I sat listening incredulously as a soldier explained to me a typical fact of life:

> Renamo comes into town and some soldiers enter a hut and grab the woman and begin to rape her. Another soldier forces her husband to stand close by and look on. Usually these husbands do—they are so afraid for their families that they think they should stay and help in any way they can, and besides, Renamo has threatened them all with their lives if they do not do as they are told. Then we [Frelimo forces] come into town, and if we find out about such rapes, we round up these men. I mean, they must be collaborators (with Renamo), for what kind of man would sit and watch his wife being raped?[3]

A mother comes up to me at this point and asks me to accompany her. She takes me to a shade tree where her son of about four years old is quietly sitting, and she draws back a dirty piece of cloth draped over one shoulder and falling to his lap. He has been shot in the groin, and the bullet is clearly still inside the child. Is there anything I can do? she wants to know. I look around at the town—no clinic, no medicines, no nurses, no running water. Even the indigenous healers cannot get outside of town to collect the herbs they need to treat. Other than passing out some antibiotics and some empty words of hope, there is nothing I can do. I sit down next to the child and realize he already knows.

These and a hundred other stories fill my head as I walk to the dirt airstrip to catch a ride out with a cargo plane that has come. But most of all, I think about the tragic fact that I can leave. The inhabitants of Munapeo cannot. In the contest for towns and the quest for security, both sides use the civilian population "strategically." When the control of a town shifts hands from one set of troops to another, and when the ability of the troops to hold that area is questionable, civilians are often gathered together around a troop base. Theoretically, this is for security: "unprotected" civilians provide easy labor sources or targets for vindictive enemy troops convinced they are supporters of the "other side." But, in fact, forced relocation provided troops with easily guarded populations who provided not only supplies and labor for the troops but also a buffer zone between the troops and the enemy. In case of an attack, it is the civilians who provide a wall of security. Because they were often forbidden to leave the immediate area, this meant that many were unable to attend their farms, and starvation often set in at an alarming rate. Entire communities were known to die off in this way.

It is less than a kilometer to the dirt runway, but no civilians are this far from the town center. I am reminded how close the war is for them when Renamo soldiers in the bush shoot at the plane as the pilot tries to land, something he is completely unaware of because he is landing to a rousing chorus of Aerosmith in his earphones. I think wryly back to the security clearance report I got before leaving for Munapeo: "No problem, safe and secure for travel."

When we touch down at the provincial capital, I glance to see if the two Russian twin turbine combat helicopters stationed there are in. One has "In God We Trust" painted on the side over a picture of an American dollar bill, and the other is emblazoned with the wings emblem from Paul McCartney's first album with his band, Wings.

After more than a year in Mozambique, I was used to days such as this. The layers of conceptual havoc that surround the war had become, in a curious way, a fact of life—almost comfortable in an off-balanced manner. It was not always that way. When I first arrived, I was frequently assailed by what appeared to be sheer chaos. Uninitiated into reading between the lines, I could not figure out why security reports did not match security realities. I was philosophically stalled by listening to a man sympathize with a person for having to watch his wife being raped by enemy soldiers and then targeting him as an enemy for having let this occur. I had no framework with which to deal with a culturally constructed image of war (soldiers on a battlefield) that in reality turned out to be a four-year-old sitting silently under a tree knowing with an uncanny wisdom that he would probably die from a gunshot wound in his groin.

In this chapter I explore the three interrelated themes of chaos, ~~reason~~ (or what Feldman has said may effectively be called a crisis of reason), and creativity. Chaos abounds in war and in fact may be called one of its defining characteristics. It exists as both strategy and effect and permeates the entire war enterprise from perpetrators to victims. War, expanding on Elaine Scarry (1985), "unmakes" worlds, both real and conceptual. Both studying and writing about war call into question some of our enduring notions of reason. But what may be the most powerful aspect of studying war is not merely the deconstructive violence that attends to it but the creativity the people on the front lines employ to reconstruct their shattered worlds.

CHAOS AND CAMUS'S ABSURDITY

A world that can be explained even with bad reasons is a familiar world. But, on the other hand, in a universe suddenly divested of illusions and lights, man feels an alien, a stranger. His exile is without remedy since he is deprived of the memory of a lost home or the hope of a promised land. This divorce between man and his life, the actor and his setting, is properly the feeling of absurdity. (Camus 1955:5)[4]

In considering the many towns like Munapeo I observed during my year and a half of fieldwork in Mozambique, I found that understanding the war does not rest on the fact that the war begins to make any more sense as time goes on but that, as Mozambicans showed me, we begin to accept the existence of senselessness. As a Mozambican explained to me, reminiscent of Camus:

> *Do you know why, when you meet a phantom on the road, you do not pass it by and look at it? Do you know what is so dangerously bewitching, so lethal, about looking? It is because if you turn around and look behind the phantom, you will discover him to be hollow. This war, it is a lot like that phantom.*

For the vast majority of Mozambicans, war is about existing in a world suddenly divested of lights. It is about a type of violence that spills out across the country and into the daily lives of people to undermine the world as they know it. A violence that, in severing people from their traditions and their futures, severs them from their lives. It hits at the heart of perception and existence. And that is, of course, the goal of terror warfare: to cripple political will by attempting to cripple all will, all sense.

To understand the war in Mozambique is to multiply the small vignette of Munapeo a thousandfold. But to understand Munapeo is not to understand the war. For each person's experience of the war is unique, and the characteristics of the war—the form the conflict takes—varies from village to village, district to province. I could as easily have begun this chapter with the story of the town I saw that was completely burned to the ground, all its inhabitants gone, no one knew where. No one knew where, because no one officially knew the town was destroyed. When I returned to the provincial capital and later to the country's capital, I inquired about the fate of this town. No one had even heard it had been burned out. With a war that has affected one-half of the entire country's population, it is hard to keep track of every casualty, including entire towns.

I could also have started this chapter with the story of any of the hundreds of thousands who have been maimed, displaced, or kidnapped. Stories such as the following are legion in Mozambique. These were the words of a person I spoke with the day after he emerged from the bush after having escaped from Renamo:

> *We were under Renamo control for several years. They came in and took everything, including us. We were forced to move around a lot, carrying heavy loads for Renamo here, being pushed there for no apparent reason. People died, people were killed, people were hurt, cut, assaulted, beaten . . . there was no medicine, no doctors, no food to help them. My family is gone, all of them. Only I am here. But the violence and the killing is not necessarily the worst of it. Worst of all is the endless hunger, the forced marches, the homelessness . . . day in and day out a meager, hurting existence that seems to stretch on forever.*

The level of violence in this man's story is considered "normal" in the war. True horror is reserved for stories that combine unbelievable brutality with sheer senselessness.

The Bandidos Armados [Armed Bandits: Renamo] came into our town. They rounded all of us up who had not been killed in the initial attack and brought us to the center of the village. They took my son, and they cut him up, they killed him, and they put pieces of him in a large pot and cooked him. Then they forced me to eat some of this. I did it, I did not know what else to do.

The formation of Renamo and the war helps to explain the inordinate amount of terror warfare that has characterized this war. Mozambique's "internal" war was developed and guided externally. The war began when Frelimo (Frente de Libertaçao de Moçambique) came to power in Mozambique after the country achieved independence from Portugal in 1975. Proapartheid governments, first Rhodesia and then South Africa, formed and led the rebel group Renamo (Resistência Nacíonal Moçambicana) in an attempt to undermine the model and assistance that a successful black-majority Marxist-Leninist country offered to the resistance fighters of their countries. While pro-Renamo supporters and opportunists do exist within Mozambique, essentially the rebel soldiers functioned with little popular support. Because destabilization, not coherent political ideology, was the defining factor in Renamo's formation, dirty war tactics—those using terror tactics in the targeting of civilian populations—predominate. The human rights violations have been recognized as being among the worst in the world.[5]

The extent of the violence in Mozambique can be captured in a few statistics. Over one million people, the vast majority noncombatants, have lost their lives to the war. Over two hundred thousand children have been orphaned by the war (some estimates are much higher). Adequate assistance is more hope than reality in a country where one-third of all schools and hospitals were closed or destroyed by Renamo and where a single orphanage operates. Nearly one-fourth of the entire population of 15 million people has been displaced from their homes by the war, and an additional one-fourth of the population has been directly affected by the war. In a country where 90 percent of the population lives in poverty and 60 percent in extreme poverty, the toll has been devastating.

These stories of war, individually and collectively, are distinctly Mozambican. It is their lives, their suffering, their courage, that is on the line. But the war itself is not uniquely Mozambican. In addition to the founding role played by Rhodesia and then South Africa, disaffected Portuguese former colonialists have played a critical role in Renamo's war. As well, Renamo has been aided by numerous Western right-wing organizations and religious groups and assisted by Western military advisers, arms merchants, and mercenaries—placing the war, and its defining strategies, squarely in an international political, economic, and military network. The strategies used in Mozambique have been applied in scores of other wars around the globe, carried through the same international network by the same international cast in search of power and gain (Nordstrom 1994*a*, 1994*b*).

This international entanglement of alliances, antipathies, and mercenaries allows the transfer of fundamental strategic orientations and specific tactical practices from group to group across international and political boundaries. Transferred with these are the cultural belief systems: beliefs about what are deemed acceptable, and necessary, processes of war, violence, and control in the quest for power. These wars, which have taken place primarily in non-Western countries, have focused on the use of terror tactics and the targeting of civilians and social infrastructure. They carry the legacy of a cold war that has itself been given over to history.

To understand what is attacked in a dehumanizing war necessitates an understanding of what it is to be human. For Mozambicans, this includes, but is certainly not limited to, the following. Mozambicans are nurtured in the bosom of family, and this is grounded in the skills and behaviors that sustain life—in working, in cultivating, in harvesting, in consuming. As family members, they illuminate the nexus of a time/place continuum: the fecundity of the ancestors has been instilled in them and comes to fruition in the familiar landscapes of home, hearth, and the land they were born to. They thrive as part of a community, and a pattern of friendships, obligations, and shared goals gives tangible substance to their sense of world. Mythological space landscapes geographic space: ritual, ceremony, and belief bring the universal home. The eternal, the social, and the collective are made apparent through the individual and the particular. Cultural process brings "home" the nature of reality through the physical form of the participant's everyday world. They sit in a gathering place in their community, just outside their homes, surrounded by their fields and animals and belongings, supported by their family and acquaintances, and they peer through ceremony's door into the mysteries of the universe until they have made sense of it and it of them. Their community, mythical and physical, takes shape in relation to a landscape of cultivated and wild spaces, within a network of other communities that together follow patterns of exchange, of everything from people and goods to aggressions and innovations.

The words of a Mozambican woman friend of mine poignantly demonstrate the destruction that the war has brought to millions of her compatriots:

> *Epah, Carolyn, this war. My youngest son came of age not too long ago, and I felt obliged to take him back to the land of my people to perform the ceremonies that would ensure that he grows into a strong and healthy member of our family. The journey was a heart-stopping one—as you know the roads are so unsafe, and we had to walk a*

majority of the way to avoid land mines and rogue soldiers. I was so frightened I would lose my son before he could even come of age properly. But when we arrived in my birth home, it was so very disappointing. I remember a house filled with the happy shouts of children, lush farmlands flowing out from its doors, vegetables to pick for food, and our animals dotting the hillsides. Always a fire with food cooking, always a story being told.

It is so awful to see it now. My mother is the only one there now: my father, as you know, was killed by Bandidos [Renamo], my grandparents just died of the war: not enough food, medicines, hope. My mother, she will never be the same after all the attacks she has lived through, after seeing her husband slaughtered. The horror of the violence is etched on her face and her soul. The house is dark, decrepit and empty. The Bandidos have carried off everything they could in the innumerable times they have come through. The fields are destroyed, and my mother refuses to replant them, for every time she does, the Bandidos come and raid and then burn the fields. The animals are long gone, killed by the soldiers. The neighbors are few and far between, killed off, run off, starved off. No more laughter, no more stories, no more children. No more home. Even worse, when we arrived there, I found it was going to be really difficult to hold the ceremonies we wanted to for our son. The noise and music of the ceremonies attracts the Bandidos. They hear it and come to attack. We cannot even perform the ceremonies that make us human. We did a ceremony, yes, but a mere skeleton of that which tradition calls for. Skeleton, yes, that is a good word—we are living skeletons of the war.

With the onslaught of excessive violence, the boundaries defining family, community, and cosmos slip, grow indistinct, reconfigure in new and painful ways. And through the breached boundaries, the substance of each spills out across the landscapes of life in a way that is unstructured, highly charged, and immediate. Family has been shattered, not only by death and displacement but by the impossibility of unresolvables: Is a missing relative alive? Can I protect those still with me? How do we live like a family when that which defines family life no longer exists? In its most fundamental sense, family is a historical continuum, and home the place where it unfolds. When these are disrupted, the grounding of self in time, place, and space is upended. Left to a here and now unmoored in time, people lose the guidance of tradition, the comfort of tomorrow. What then becomes of the person severed from time and place? Not the flesh and bones body but the intangible and subjective effervescence animating personal identity and bringing the self to life—that which, all told, makes humans human. The world, as many Mozambicans sadly said to me, is no longer human.[6]

When violence reaches this level of severity, identity itself suffers, as evinced in the words of a *dislocado* (dislocated: internal refugee) in southern Mozambique. As we talked, he stood, handmade hoe in hand, surveying the dry and barren fields where he and many other dislocados had

recently arrived to try and eke out food and a fragile home. I thought at
the time I had never seen a face so sculpted by resignation and determination at one and the same time.

> *We have arrived here from all over, scattered victims of Renamo violence. Everyone has
> lost everything they had. Their homes were burned, their goods stolen, their crops de-
> stroyed, their family members slaughtered. Even those that managed to flee often ran
> different directions from the rest of their families, and today do not know if the rest are
> alive or dead. Many have been through this cycle more than once, having fled to a
> "safe area" only to be attacked again. Me, this is my third relocation. I do not know
> where most of my family is. Maybe we will be attacked yet again—we hear Renamo
> passing by here at night. It is difficult to find the will to plant crops and tend children
> when it may all be taken from us tonight, and maybe we will not survive this time. . . .
> The worst of it is the way this attacks our spirits, our very selves. Everyone here thinks:
> Before this I knew who I was, I farmed the land that my father farmed, and his ances-
> tors before him, and this long line nurtured the living. I had my family that I fathered,
> and I had my house that I built, and the goods that I had worked for. I knew who I
> was because I had all this round me. But now I have nothing, I have lost what makes
> me who I am. I am nothing here.*

If people are defined by the world they inhabit, and the world is culturally constructed by the people who consider themselves a part of it, people
ultimately control the production of reality and their place in it. They produce themselves. But they are dependent on these productions (Taussig
1993). Should one wish to destroy, to control, or to subjugate a people,
what more powerful "target" could be found than that of personhood and
reality? To destroy the world, encapsulated in the nexus of place and person described above, is to destroy the self.

It is my opinion that self, identity, and the experience of the world are
mutually dependent for all people, as contemporary existential, phenomenological, and postmodernist theory are demonstrating. But this view has
long permeated African thought. Without trying to overgeneralize African
epistemology, I found many Mozambicans hold a similar view to the scholars E. A. Ruch and K. C. Anyanwa (1984:86–87).[7]

> The African culture makes no sharp distinction between the ego and the
> world, African culture makes the self the centre of the world. . . . The world
> which is centered on the self is personal and alive. Self-experience is not sep-
> arated from the experiencing self. The self vivifies or animates the world so
> that the soul, spirit or mind of the self is also that of the world. . . . What
> happens to the world happens to the self. Self disorder is a *metaphysical con-
> tagion* [italics in original] affecting the whole world.

It would appear to be equally valid to conclude that world disorder is a
metaphysical contagion affecting the whole self. Yet if the world makes the

self, the self equally makes the world, and this is why terror warfare is ultimately doomed to fail. As we will see in the section on creativity, people have the creative wherewithal to re-create the worlds war has destroyed.

<del>REASON</del>

> *It is worth noting that the language peculiar to totalitarian doctrines is always an academic and administrative language.*
>
> ALBERT CAMUS

Western epistemologies generally try to find "The Reason" (universal and specific) for war—to fix it in time and understanding. If only we could just bring to light the specific structural, mythological, interpersonal acts of domination and resistances, war would make sense. But these are sweeping analyses, ones that all too often leave out the individuals—living, suffering, dying—who *are* the war. Individuals do not make up a generic group of "combatants," "civilians," and "casualties" but an endlessly complex set of people and personalities, each of whom has a unique relationship to the war and a unique story to tell.

Based on my field experiences at the front lines of wars, I hope to challenge—to draw a line through—the epistemologies of Reason, with a capital R, as it applies to War. When war actually becomes a matter of life and death, Reason is replaced with a cacophony of realities. One cannot peel back the layers of the onion to find the core phenomenon; for, as we all know, the onion, like reality, is composed only of layers.

I am reminded of a conversation I had with a young teenage soldier in the bush of north-central Mozambique. I asked him why he was fighting, and he looked at me and in all seriousness replied, "*I forgot.*" For this person, the tattered clothing he was wearing, the gun he carried, the fear and hunger he constantly felt, the "endless days and nights of living in the remote bush on the run without food, shelter, or comfort" were realities. The "why" of it all was far less intelligible; unimportant even.

Behind the political ideologies, the military strategies, the international arms and ally networks that support the war effort, and the commanders that channel this down to the front lines, "I forgot" can exist, the core of the phenomena.

The problems that surround reason do not pertain exclusively to war. The whole notion of reason as it has been defined in Enlightenment philosophy is in crisis. Epistemology can no longer conveniently be separated from ontology, word from act and concept, subject from object, reality from construction. This crisis extends to the heart of theory. For, ultimately, we as theoreticians live our reason. We cannot step outside of it to assess it in any final sense. We are, as Allen Feldman (1991) points out, inescapably implicated in our reasoning about reason. This is nowhere more evident than when we begin to try to "make sense" of the cacophonous flow of our field observations—to wrench word from experience.

Terror warfare, such as that defining Renamo's in Mozambique, seeks to sever all relationships grounding personhood to enforce complete political acquiescence. But, too, our theories are all too often abstracted—and sever personhood from narrative and text. In Western epistemology, we have a legacy of thinking about violence as a concept, a phenomenon, a "thing." We reify it, we "thing-ify" it, as Michael Taussig (1987) cautions, rather than recognize it as experiential and rendering it real. This approach stands in sharp contrast to the Mozambican's view of violence—a view that sees violence as fluid, as something that people can both make and unmake.

A concern with the reasons of war comes dangerously close to a concern with making war reasonable—which, of course, is a goal of the Enlightenment process. Maybe this search for reason has allowed us to "explain war away": concretized in theory, set in fact, distanced to a comfortable vantage point. I suggest we consider the fact that this search for the "reason" for war actually silences the reality of war.

In her study of torture, Scarry (1985) has noted that pain unmakes the world of the victim. Expanding on Scarry, I (1992a, 1992b) have suggested that war's violence unmakes the world at large both for those who experience it and for those who witness it. Violence deconstructs reason. The question then arises, Does writing and reading about violence unmake the world? Is this why so many of our theories on violence are modernist, clear concrete categories distanced from the raw experiences they purport to explain?

Another paradox may lie at the core of this question about "writing" violence in theory. How can we write about the "unmaking" and "creating" of the world in a "made" world of academic prose? No matter how representative we try to be, theory and literature have a structure and an order that they impose in and of themselves, always once removed from experience, intolerant of chaos. As Jean Baudrillard (1987:133) succinctly points out, "Theory is simulation."

Theories about violence will always struggle with these issues of representation. Violence is an unsettling topic. It raises piercing questions of human nature, social in/justice and cultural viability—and about our personal accountability and responsibility in the face of these. It challenges cherished notions of a just world and throws into stark relief the sheer daunting complexities of human and cultural reality. It utters the unutterable.

AND THE ANTHROPOLOGIST?

Lived experience overflows the boundaries of any one concept, any one person, or any one society.

MICHAEL JACKSON (1989)

On entering the field, we enter the domain of lived experience. What is "safe" is a study in smoke and mirrors. Everyone has a story, complete with vested interests, and all the stories collide into contentious assemblages of partial truths, political fictions, personal foibles, military propaganda, and cultural lore. The louder the story, especially when it comes to violence and war, the less representative of the lived experience it is likely to be. In the midst of wars of propaganda and justification, the most silenced stories at war's epicenters are generally the most authentic.

To understand a war is not the same thing as understanding a war in the town of X and among the people who populate it. In the same way that a body cannot be understood by a finger, a war cannot be understood by a single locale. It was the war in Mozambique, and the Mozambicans' experience of it, that formed the core concern of my research. Because this research question demanded different field techniques than those normally associated with anthropological studies set in a specific locale, I followed an approach I call the "ethnography of a warzone" (Nordstrom 1994*b*). Here, the theme of war, rather than a specific locality, situates the study. Process and people supplant place as an ethnographic "site." My reticence to situate this study in a given locale extends to the urban centers and the institutions of power brokers (the "site" of traditional political science research)—the places where war is formally defined, debated, and directed. These sites add to the study, they do not define it.

I selected Zambezia Province, in north-central Mozambique, as my home base for the majority of my stay in the country as it was the province most seriously affected by the war, and one that offered rich cultural diversity. But in the year and a half I worked in Mozambique, I traveled not only throughout the province but also through six of Mozambique's ten provinces. In each location, I followed the ebb and flow of the war from urban centers to rural outposts, visiting locations on the peripheries of the war, locales that had recently been attacked, and villages and towns that had changed hands from the government to the rebel forces a number of times. Roads were heavily land mined and subject to frequent attacks and seldom, if ever, traveled outside of sporadic military convoys confined to a few main transitways. Like virtually everyone else who did not have the skills to walk across provinces, I depended on air travel. Unlike many, my major mode of travel was cargo planes taking emergency supplies to war-devastated areas lucky enough to have a flat dirt runway relatively free of mines. In what I found to be one of the war's many ironies, my ethnography, like emergency supplies and government officials, was confined to locations where a landing strip and a security clearance could be eked out. I dubbed this "runway anthropology."

The nature of this ethnography thus reflects in many ways the nature of the reality of many Mozambican lives: conflict, starvation, deprivation, and the demands of work, family, and health have produced an extremely fluid population. As I noted before, nearly one-third of the population has experienced some form of dislocation.[8] These Mozambicans can no longer, at present, ground their "selves"—their lives, their livelihoods, their dreams—in a single place. In responding to an external threat, they carry reworked notions of home, family, community, and survival with them. Repositioning has come to define a major sociocultural current.

In each place I visited, I made a concerted effort to collect the stories of average people, many of whom found themselves on the front lines of a war they neither started nor supported. Eschewing the popular notion that battlefields are comprised of male adult soldiers—especially since the vast majority of casualties in Mozambique were noncombatants—I turned my attention to both sexes and all ages, equally. Given the circumstances of the war, I worked in areas where the rebels were in close proximity, but I never elected to work in rebel-occupied areas.

The logistics of conducting an ethnographic study in a warzone are not as complicated as the fact that we begin to care about the world we have entered. We can sympathize with the trauma of a person looking over the charred landscapes that used to be called home; feel the gut-wrenching horror they feel wondering if the rest of their family made it to safety or not. We can understand the overwhelming grief of people who had to leave a family member where she or he fell, unburied, as they fled an attack, knowing they have condemned a loved one to roam the earth as a sorrowful rogue spirit with no resting place.

Everyone grapples with violence in his or her own way. What is traumatic, difficult, hopeful is in all likelihood different for every person in the field. It is impossible to escape the impact of the sheer violence: I will carry with me images of violence for the rest of my life which are variously poignant and unsettling, absurd and tragic. Some resonate with examples in the general literature and media on warfare, and these constitute the acceptable, and in many ways privileged, discourses on violence. The maimed and the dead—victims of political torture, heroes and martyrs of causes, innocent victims of repression—fill this category.

Yet it is not the raw violence per se that most captures the essence of war for me. Curiously, the images that have done so for me seldom appear in formal discussions of warfare. To give one example: one of the things that struck me the first time I saw the massacre of innocent civilians was that, in the physical trauma of death, many of the dead men's pants had fallen down. This example may appear frivolous to people who have not witnessed such scenes. But to those living daily with the specter of large-scale political violence, death scenes of familials—not only butchered but exposed—present a powerful statement on death, (in)dignity, and the nature of human existence.

It is misleading, however, to focus exclusively on the physicality of bodies as the repository of violence. When I am among people who have not been near the brute force of war, I am often asked, "What was it like? Did you see many dead bodies?" The question rankles. Even if I were to answer the question, which I never do, it would not be the ruined bodies themselves I have seen that summarizes the agonizing truths of war for me but the stories behind the bodies. In considering the question of what war is like, I might, for example, think of the color pink and the trails it has left on the landscape of war in my mind. Two stories, related only by color, help to explain this.

Early in my years of studying war, I was visiting a village I did not know well, several hours travel from my in-field home. I was sleeping in the house of "a relative of a friend of a friend" I had never met. Quite early in the morning, I was roused unexpectedly from bed and asked to get dressed. No explanation, no food or coffee. There was something people wanted me to see. A group of men were waiting outside the door, most of whom I did not know, and we set off on foot through the fields and finally into the forest. We walked for quite a while it seemed. Finally we came into a small clearing, and in front of us a dead man hung from a tree—suspended on a pink bedsheet. The man in charge turned to me in concern and said, "We need to find out if this is murder or suicide." Had this man chosen to escape insurmountable personal troubles, impossible war demands? Or had the war found him? Had someone killed him?

I am never sure why I am included in or excluded from certain things in the field. I had no idea why I was brought to witness this poor man hanging forlornly in the early morning sun. Did people think because of my interest in traditional medicine I was a medical specialist? Did they want someone to witness the inescapable violence people had to live with, someone who could carry the story back to the urban centers? I never did find out. They asked me to help examine the body to try to determine if the man had been murdered or not, and I did. But mostly I remember watching that body swing on the pink bedsheet in the slight breeze as I wondered about war, tragedy, absurdity, and the insurmountable.

The second story begins in the same time period. I had a friend in the community in which I lived who eased the tragedies of war for me. He was a fun and life-affirming man who loved ceremonies, parties, a good joke, and his fellow human beings. I could always talk to him about the war, and he listened with a sympathetic ear. He hated the conflict tearing at his country.

The next time I visited the country, I looked forward to reuniting with my friend. The war continued, and deprivation and terror had touched everyone's lives. When I reached my friend's house, I was surprised to see an assault rifle leaning in the entryway, a revolver on the living room table. I settled into a chair to catch up on the news. An armed man materialized in the shadows of the porch and had a hurried whispered conversation with my host. I looked quizzically at my friend when he returned, and he sighed and handed me a photo album. The album itself was the kind you could find at any department store: the cover depicted the common scene of a young couple walking hand in hand in some romantic locale at sunset—all colored in bright pinks and images of serenity. Inside, however, were pages of photographs of maimed, mutilated, and murdered youths from the area. My friend shrugged his shoulders and explained the war had reached an intolerable level, something had to be done to save the country. He had decided to join the "security forces" to combat the "terrorists." The pictures were of his work, the "solutions" he and those he worked with employed. The victims, mostly youths, looked to me to have died alone and unarmed: in a search for information; as a warning delivered in a message of terror; in a fearful and retributive rage, anything but as soldiers on a battlefield. I have never gotten over the shock of this. How could I be friends with a man capable of such torture? How could I have *been* friends with such a man? My friendship with this person is over. I have not kept in touch with him. But the impossible quandary of the situation stays with me: it represents the harsh realities of war that many live with on a day-to-day basis. And it is not so much the gruesome pictures of bodies that distresses me; it is the hopeless incongruity of their being in that photo album with the serene pink cover.

These are not the only scenes that define the heart of war for me, nor the only colors, sights, smells, tragedies, and fears I have experienced through other's experiences of war. Each one gives a depth and a complexity to violent conflict that goes well beyond the shallow depictions of war that are offered in the traditional texts and media sound bites that "describe" war.

CREATIVITY

[The world is] created out of human experience.
E. A. RUCH AND K. C. ANYANWA (1984)

Renamo, with its tactics of severing the noses, lips, and ears of civilians, seems to reclaim the original sense of the absurd: "The absurd, from the

Latin, *absurdus,* is literally the deaf, the voiceless, and hence the irrational"
(Ruf 1991:65)

But if war, especially terror warfare, strives to destroy meaning and
sense, people strive to create it. This, ultimately, is why dirty war is doomed
to fail. No matter how brute the force applied to subjugate a people, local-
level behaviors arise to subvert the hold violence exerts on a population.
This, of course, is a highly contested process. The situation at the local
level is complex and contradictory. There are people working within the
political, military, and economic spheres who seek to benefit from the frac-
tures caused by war. Others work equally hard to solve the inequalities, injustices, and abuses caused by war and those who exploit violence for their
own gain. It is the latter that interests me here.

Traditional Western approaches to violent conflict do not often recognize the creative strategies people on the front lines employ to survive the
war. I was little prepared for the way in which people tried to reconfigure
the destructive violence that marked their lives and to rebuild worlds so
wrenchingly taken away from them by violence. It was only when I was
in the middle of Mozambique (both literally and in terms of my research)
that I began to appreciate the creativity of the average people caught in
the traumatic contingencies of warfare. While this creativity does not extend to all people and all parts of the war, I am always encouraged by how
much exists in day-to-day life. To give an idea of the range and richness of
these world-building actions, I will give three different examples that can
be introduced as the creating of symbols (the three monkeys), of society
(the transport of fish), and of culture (the work of healers).

The first example involves three little carved wooden monkeys. When I
first went to the country in 1988, the war economy was such that few market goods of any kind were available. I was always interested in the fact that
one of the things you could find with regularity was a set of three little
carved monkeys: see no evil, hear no evil, speak no evil. For me, this was
especially telling considering the regularity with which one heard stories
of Renamo severing the ears and lips of civilians to silence resistance and
control political will. One day I was sitting on the curb talking with a street
vendor acquaintance of mine with whom I frequently sat and discussed
the war (it had taken his legs, his family, and his home) and better days.
During a lull in the conversation, with a sly twinkle in his eye, he pulled
out a set of three monkeys to show me. The first monkey had one hand
over his mouth and the other over one eye, but the second eye peered out
wide open and both ears were uncovered and listening. The second monkey had one hand over one eye and the other hand over one ear; this time
the mouth was uncovered and twisted into a grimace or a cry, but still one
eye was watching and one ear was listening. The last monkey sat with a

cynical grin on its face: eyes, ears, and mouth open and cognizant. This monkey sat with its hands covering its groin. The symbolism is not lost on Mozambicans: the numbers of women who have been raped in the war are legion, and a significant number of men have been emasculated both physically and figuratively.

I have returned to Mozambique twice since my first trip and have traveled from the plush offices of power brokers to the crumbling embers of villages in the far reaches of the country. And in the places where force became violence, the subversive message of the monkeys—that we will cover our ears when you cut off our lips and still look with one eye; that we will watch, listen, and speak, but we will "cover our tails" in doing so—was reflected time and again, in village after village after town. The first part of the message conveys resistance; the second laces it with wry humor. The two together have given many a hope and a will to survive a very dirty war.

The three monkeys stand as popular symbologues (dialogues based on symbolic representations) that speak both to the war and through the war: statements constructed by the victims themselves to convey the complex way violence is lived, learned, subverted, and survived. Symbologues abound during war. "Violent concentrated action," writes Antonin Artaud (1974: 62), "is like lyricism; it calls forth supernatural imagery, a bloodshed of images." To speak directly about the war is to court danger. So songs, myths, parables, jokes, and stories circulate—each a palimpsest of meaning wherein "mythical" villains, heroes, murderers, and traitors implicate contemporary actors in the war drama. Everyone in the know "knows" what is being conveyed about whom: who to trust, fear, avoid. For those not in the know (one hopes, those who have the power to kill), these are "simply stories." The "reason" Mozambicans apply in such situations extends well beyond that ascribed by Enlightenment philosophies focusing on discursive consciousness. It is a form of creative reasoning that combines symbolic, emotional, representational, discursive, and existential realities. Generally speaking, the split between epistemology, ontology, and life is an artificial one for Mozambicans.

> In African culture . . . experience does not address itself to reason alone, imagination alone, feeling and intuition alone, but to the totality of a person's faculty. The truth of this experience is lived and felt, not merely thought of. (Ruch and Anyanwa 1984:86–87)

There are many other ways people work to subvert terror and destruction and to reconstruct a purposeful social universe. In Mozambique, these are not just part of the war response; they are critical to survival. The second example I cite here became apparent to me when I was in an inland town that had recently been attacked a number of times. Crops and animals decimated and goods stolen, the markets had little to offer. I was therefore taken aback to find for sale some fish that had seen better days. This is particularly noteworthy, for it entailed several men walking with baskets of ocean fish on their heads for seven days from the coast through several language and ethnic communities and a number of dangerous war zones. This is a trip no formal trader would brave: the dangers were too great and the profit negligible. So why make such a trip? The men's answers to me—"Because that's how life goes on"—did not make a lot of sense at first. But as I listened to them talk, I realized that through their journey they performed an invaluable function. They carried messages for families and friends separated by the fighting; conveyed details on troop deployments and dangers; and transmitted critical economic, crop, trade, and political news, not to mention gossip and irreverent stories, between communities severed from one another by the war. They linked different ethnic and language groups in a statement that the war was not about local rivalries and could not be, if they were to survive. They forged trade and social networks through the disordered landscapes of violence. And by walking for seven days with baskets of fish on their heads through lethal front lines, they simply defied the war in a way that everyone they passed could enjoy and draw strength from. They were, literally, constructing social order out of chaos.

These traders created outgoing linkages in the country. In a complementary process, people also work to create a valid community and a stable social universe wherever they find themselves. Curandeiros[9] are a locus of creativity in solving the problems of war. Encoded in their traditions are idea(1)s that mitigate the harmful effects of abusive power, violence, and warfare. While African medicine has long assisted in warfare (Lan 1985; Ranger 1982, 1985), in Mozambique it has largely condemned Renamo's ruthlessness. I spoke with well over a hundred curandeiros throughout the country, and most had developed "treatments" aimed at protecting civilians and ameliorating the violence unleashed on society.

In refugee camps, in informal dislocation centers, in burned-out villages trying to rebuild, I found curandeiros performing treatments to take the war out of the community, the violence out of the people, and the instability and terror out of the culture. As one curandeiro explained,

People have just seen too much war, too much violence—they have gotten the war in them. We treat this, we have to. If we don't take the war out of the people, it will just continue on and on, past Renamo, past the end of the war, into the communities, into the families, to ruin us.

Scholars such as Pierre Bourdieu (1977) and Jean Comaroff and John Comaroff (1991) brought to academic attention what the curandeiros have long known, that hegemonic ideals and cultures of violence can be dangerously, and unwittingly, reproduced throughout a society and can even undermine resistance and resolution.

Hundreds of conversations I had with Mozambicans reflected their preoccupation with defusing the culture of violence the war had wrought. It is a violence, they stress, that can last far beyond formal military cease-fires. People constantly reminded themselves and others about the insidious nature of violence, which allows it to reproduce itself and to destroy worlds and lives in the process. It is as if, fearful of the tendency toward *habitus*— toward what Bourdieu (1977:191) calls "unrecognizable, socially recognized violence"—Mozambicans have set into motion a cultural dynamic that continually challenges the entrenchment of a culture of violence. The following quote is from my field notes. I was sitting with several older women in a village that had seen a great deal of the war. The bombed-out and uninhabited husks of buildings stood outlined behind us in the afternoon sun, behind the sea of small thatch and mud huts that had sprung up to house the many people displaced by the war. We were sitting on the ground chewing on the stalk of a weed (I was chewing on the weed because the women had handed it to me; the women did so out of a habit they had developed to appease their appetites when food was scarce). We were talking about the war's impact on people's lives.

> *When people come back to our community after having been kidnapped and spending time with the Bandidos [Renamo], or arrive here after their community has been destroyed by the war, there are a lot of things they need. They require food and clothing, they need a place to live, they need medical attention. But one of the most important things they need is calm—to have the violence taken out of them. We ask that everyone who arrives here be taken to a curandeiro for treatment. The importance of the curandeiro lies not only in his or her ability to treat the diseases and physical ravages of war but in the ability to take the violence out of a person and to reintegrate them back into a healthy lifestyle. You see, people who have been exposed to the war, well, some of this violence can affect them, stick with them, like a rash on the soul. They carry this violence with them back to their communities and their homes and their lives, and they begin to act in ways they have never acted before. They bring the war back home with them—they become more confused, more violent, more dangerous, and so too does the whole community. We need to protect against this. The curandeiro makes consultations and patiently talks to the person, he gives medicinal treatments, he performs ceremonies, he works with the whole family, he includes the community. He cuts the person off from any holds the war has on him or her, he scrapes off the violence from their spirit, he makes them forget what they have seen and felt and experienced in the war, he makes them alive again, alive and part of the community. He does this with Bandido [Renamo] soldiers too. If someone finds a soldier wandering alone, we take him and bring him to the curandeiro. Most people do not really want to fight. These soldiers have done terrible things, but many of them were kidnapped and forced to*

fight. They dream of their home and family and machambas [farms], of being far away from any war. The curandeiro takes the war out of them, he uneducates their war education. He reminds them how to be a part of their family, to work their machamba, to get along, to be a part of the community. He cures the violence that others have taught.

In the midst of war, the treatments the curandeiros provide are not set prescriptions faithfully reproduced. They are creative acts in the true sense of the word. Worlds are destroyed in war; they must be re-created. Not just worlds of home, family, community, and economy but worlds of definition, both personal and cultural. As people look out over a ruined landscape that was once home—now shorn of life and livelihood, humanity and hope—they cannot simply "reconstruct society as it was before." For in the violence and upheaval, it cannot be, may never be, the same as "it was before."

In the face of the monkey's creation of symbologues, the fish vendor's forging of social order, and the curandeiro's production of culture, I find the theories on the cultural construction of reality relevant but inadequate.[10] They start from the basis of an operating culture that imparts knowledge through interpersonal interaction. What happens when very little is operating and what has operated is of little immediate use? What shards of cultural relevance do the vendors and healers have to build on? Worlds cannot simply be created; they must be created anew. How do the poetics and practices of the people in these three examples interweave in the creation of cultures of survival and resistance?

The dilemma is clear: between the world as it was, the world as it should be, and the now of a world destroyed lies an abyss, a discontinuity, a need to define the one by the other, and the impossibility of doing so. The solution, Mozambicans taught me, lies, in part, with the imagination. I have come to think that this is a trait people have specifically nurtured to counteract destructive violence. When people look out over a land that should resonate with meaning and life, but that now stares blankly back with incomprehensible images of barren fields, broken communities, tortured bodies, and shattered realities, they are left with the choice of accepting a deadened world or creating a livable one. It is the imagination—creativity—that bridges the abyss, if not to reconstruct the past, to make the present livable.

Scarry (1985:163) has argued that pain unmakes the world and imagining makes it. Together "pain and imagining are the 'framing events' within whose boundaries all other perceptual, somatic, and emotional events occur; thus, between the two extremes can be mapped the whole terrain of the human psyche." She invokes Sartre in exploring the idea that absence provokes an imagining of a special sort.

> Sartre, for example, draws conclusions from the fact that his imagined Pierre is so impoverished by comparison with his real friend Pierre, that his imagined Annie has none of the vibrancy, spontaneity, and limitless depth of presence of the real Annie. But, of course, had he compared his imagined friends not to his real-friends-when present but to his wholly absent friends, his conclusions would have been supplemented by other, very different conclusions. That is, the imagined Pierre is shadowy, dry, and barely present compared to the real Pierre, but is much more vibrantly present than the absent Pierre. (Ibid)

In like fashion, it is the destruction of the world that prompts such vivid powers of imagining in victims of war and violence.

But unlike Scarry's view, some Mozambicans are able to imagine their real friend, their real home, their real society and culture as vibrantly as the "real thing." We can afford to leave underdeveloped our ability to imagine our real friend Pierre in a reasonably stable world. But when Pierre is dead, disappeared, or maimed, and when the world that held him is so hopelessly destroyed that left unattended it can only ring a death toll for the society affected, people must create, and to do so, they must first imagine what it is they are going to create. For Pierre will never be the same, and the world is still at war.

For Scarry (1992), imagining is grounded in perceptual mimesis. For the Mozambicans, contemplating their ruined villages and contentious political imbroglios, there is little to mime—and imagining becomes an act of pure creativity.

Not all Mozambicans have such developed powers of creative imagining. Not unusually, the creative members of the culture—healers, visionaries, performers—have developed these skills to a fine art. Their talents lie not only with their abilities to imagine but also with their abilities to convey these images to others so that they, too, may share in the reconstruction of their symbolic and social universes. I have visited a number of communities that had been recently decimated by the war. One of the most powerful experiences I had at these times was sitting with people amid the fragments of what was once their home and community and listening, watching, the imagining—the creation of identity, home, and resistance afresh. I choose the word *watching* as well as *listening* purposefully: as the Mozambicans talk about what has happened and what will happen, and as they discuss this in the context of human nature and the meaning of life, I found I could not only understand but "see" the world they were creating. Apparently so did the others present. New identities of suffering and resistance were forged, home was reinvented, the world was relandscaped with significance, people survived.

NOTES

1. Munapeo is a fictitious name and, in fact, is the name of an illness whose primary symptoms are that one "hurts all over—everything feels bad."

2. Gersony's (1988) interviews with Mozambican refugees who have fled the war recorded that 90% of the severe human rights abuses in the war were attributed to Renamo.

3. All of the conversations with Mozambicans in this article were conducted in Portuguese, Mozambique's national language. The translations are my own.

4. At first glance, it might appear strange to apply a concept like "the absurd" that was formulated as an alienated response to Western techno-urban-industrial society to a bush war in Africa. The application holds for three reasons. First, contemporary dirty war is a product of modern state institutional society. Second, I resist the tendency to differentiate postmodern technological society from non-Western nonindustrialized, and by implication, (pre)modern, society. Mozambicans have long been embroiled in a transnational political economy: centuries ago no remote bush village was safe from the incursions of merchants, slavers, colonialists, and profiteers. Many Africans I know can speak eloquently on the ramifications of living in a postmodern reality and did so well before Western intellectuals gave the perspective a word. Finally, the absurd applies to the experience of human existence, something we all share. The term "absurd" was honed by philosophers and writers who had been affected by wars they themselves had lived through and whose primary focus was on the lived experience of self as it confronts violence and senselessness. An irony of violence, one that gives it an existentially absurd quality, is that it "exists" as an experiential negation of existence.

I concur with Hanna (1969:191) in his use of the term *absurdity*:

> In declaring my own understanding of the term "absurd," I want to insist that it not be taken as some exclusive philosophical concept which stands sovereignly aloof from certain obviously similar terms in the existentialists' vocabulary. With only slight qualifications in each case, I would be quite content to use Nietzsche's "pathos of distance," Sartre's "nausea," Camus' "revolt," Heidegger's "dread," and even the journalistically popular word "meaninglessness" as just as useful as the word "absurd." This extends equally to Kierkegaard's "despair."

5. Excellent comprehensive books on Mozambique include Casimiro, Loforte, and Pessoa 1990; Finnegan 1992; Geffray 1990; Hanlon 1984, 1991; Issacman and Issacman 1983; Jeichande 1990; Legum 1988; Magaia 1988, 1989; Ministerio da Saude/UNICEF 1988; Munslow 1983; Urdang 1989; UNICEF 1989, 1990; UNICEF/Ministry of Cooperation 1990; Vail and White 1980; Vines 1991; World Health Organization 1990.

6. To existential philosophers, angst of this realization provides the pivot where death, negation, and the slippages of reality can confront being and existence. This process, initiated only by individual choice, is viewed by the theorists as the font for creative change and redefinition—for the realization of being and self. In painful comparison, death, negation, and slippages of reality are not lurking possibilities on a cognitive horizon but brutally inescapable facts in the center of Mozambican life. They inhabit being and existence. Far from the self-actualizing function the philosophers impart to the reunion of being/negation, their unbridled penetrations are fundamentally destructive.

7. See Masolo 1983; Oruka 1983; Jackson 1989; p'Bitek 1983 for similar analyses of African epistemology.

8. I choose the word *dislocation* here as in Mozambique, displaced peoples are referred to as *deslocados*—or dislocated by the war and its effects.

9. I use the Portuguese word for healer here. This is intended to cover the range of healers available, including herbalists, diviners, trance performers, and spirit mediums. There are a dozen major languages in Mozambique, each with its own terms for healers, and, as I studied with people from many of these languages, I will use the national language of Portuguese rather than one of the African language groups.

10. For the early definitive works on the social construction of reality, see James (1976, 1978); Schutz (1962, 1964); Berger and Luckman (1966).

REFERENCES

Artaud, Antonin
    1974   *Collected Works.* Vol. 4. London: Calder and Boyars.
Baudrillard, Jean
    1987   *Forget Foucault.* New York: Semiotext(e).
Berger, Peter, and Thomas Luckman
    1966   *The Social Construction of Reality.* Garden City: Doubleday.
Bourdieu, Pierre
    1977   *Outline of a Theory of Practice.* Cambridge: Cambridge University Press.
    1989   "Social Space and Symbolic Power." *Sociological Theory* 7(1):14–25.
Camus, Albert
    1955   *The Myth of Sisyphus and Other Essays.* New York: Vintage.
    1978   *The Rebel: An Essay on Man in Revolt.* New York: Alfred A. Knopf.
Casimiro, Isabel, Ana Loforte, and Ana Pessoa
    1990   *A Mulher em Moçambique.* Maputo: CEA/NORAD.
Comaroff, Jean
    1985   *Body of Power, Spirit of Resistance.* Chicago: University of Chicago Press.
Comaroff, Jean, and John Comaroff
    1991   *Of Revelation and Revolution: Christianity, Colonialism, and Consciousness in South Africa.* Vol. 1. Chicago: University of Chicago Press.
Feldman, Allen
    1991   *Formations of Violence: The Narrative of the Body and Political Terror in Northern Ireland.* Chicago: University of Chicago Press.
Finnegan, William
    1992   *A Complicated War: The Harrowing of Mozambique.* Berkeley, Los Angeles, and Oxford: University of California Press.
Geffray, Christian
    1990   *La Cause des armes au Mozambique: Antropologie d'une guerre civile.* Paris: Editions Karthala.
Gersony, Robert
    1988   *Summary of Mozambican Refugee Accounts of Principally Conflict-related Experience in Mozambique.* Report submitted to Ambassador Jonathon

Moore, Director, Bureau for Refugees Program, and Dr. Chester Crocker, Assistant Secretary of African Affairs. Washington, D.C.

Hanlon, Joseph

1984   *Mozambique: The Revolution Under Fire.* London: Zed Books.

1991   *Mozambique: Who Calls the Shots?* Bloomington: Indiana University Press.

Hanna, Thomas

1969   "Experience and the Absurd." In *New Essays in Phenomenology,* ed. J. Edie, 190–198. Chicago: Quadrangle Books.

Issacman, Allen, and Barbara Issacman

1983   *Mozambique: From Colonialism to Revolution, 1900–1982.* Hampshire, England: Gower.

Jackson, Michael

1989   *Paths Toward a Clearing.* Bloomington: Indiana University Press.

James, William

1976   *Essays in Radical Empiricism.* Cambridge: Harvard University Press.

1978   *Essays in Philosophy: The Work of William James.* Edited by F. Burkhardt, F. Bowers, and I. Skrupskelis. Cambridge: Harvard University Press.

Jeichande, Ivette Illas

1990   *Mulheres Deslocadas em Maputo, Zambezia e Inhambane (Mulher em Situação Difícil).* Maputo: OMM/UNICEF.

Lan, David

1985   *Guns and Rain: Guerrillas and Spirit Mediums in Zimbabwe.* Harare: Zimbabwe Publishing House.

Legum, Colim, ed.

1988   "Mozambique: Facing up to Desperate Hardships in the Post-Machel Era." In *Africa Contemporary Record,* 19:1986–1987, B681–B701. New York: Africana Publishing Co.

Magaia, Lina

1988   *Dumba Nengue: Run for Your Life. Peasant Tales of Tragedy in Mozambique.* Trenton: Africa World Press.

1989   *Duplo massacre em Moçambique: Histórias tragicas do banditismo.* II. Maputo: Coleccao Depoimentos—5.

Masolo, D. A.

1983   "Philosophy and Culture: A Critique." In *Philosophy and Cultures,* ed. H. O. Oruka and D. A. Masolo. Nairobi: Bookwise.

Ministerio da Saude/UNICEF

1988   *Analise da situação da saude.* Maputo, Septembro 1988.

Minter, William

1989   "The Mozambique National Resistance (Renamo) as Described by Ex-Participants." Research report submitted to Ford Foundation and Swedish International Development Agency. African-European Institute, Amsterdam, March 1989.

Munslow, Barry

1983   *Mozambique: The Revolution and Its Origins.* London: Longman.

Nordstrom, Carolyn

1992*a*   "The Backyard Front." In *The Paths to Domination, Resistance and Terror,* ed. Carolyn Nordstrom and JoAnn Martin, 260–274. Berkeley, Los Angeles, and Oxford: University of California Press.

1992*b*   "The Dirty War: Cultures of Violence in Mozambique and Sri Lanka."
           In *Internal Conflict and Governance,* ed. Kumar Rupesinghe, 27–43. New
           York: St. Martin's Press.

1994*a*   "Contested Identities/Essentially Contested Powers." In *War and Peace-
           making,* ed. Ed Garcia, 55–69. Quezon City, Philippines: Claretian Pub-
           lications. Reprinted in Kumar Rupesinghe, ed., *Conflict Transformation.*
           London: Macmillan.

1994*b*   "Warzones: Cultures of Violence, Militarization and Peace." Working
           Paper no. 145. Canberra: Peace Research Centre, Australian National
           University.

Oruka, H. Odera

1983   "Ideology and Culture (The African Experience)." In *Philosophy and
           Cultures,* ed. H. Odera Oruka and D. A. Masolo. Nairobi: Bookwise.

p'Bitek, Okot

1983   "On Culture, Man and Freedom." In *Philosophy and Cultures,* ed. H. O.
           Oruka and D. A. Masolo. Nairobi: Bookwise Limited.

Ranger, Terrance

1982   "The Death of Chaminuka: Spirit Mediums, Nationalism, and the
           Guerrilla War in Zimbabwe." *African Affairs* 81 (324):349–369.

1985   *Peasant Consciousness and Guerrilla War in Zimbabwe.* London: James
           Currey.

Ruch, E. A., and K. C. Anyanwa

1984   *African Philosophy.* Rome: Officium Libri Catholici.

Ruf, Frederick J.

1991   *The Creation of Chaos: William James and the Stylistic Making of a Disorderly
           World.* Albany: State University of New York Press.

Scarry, Elaine

1985   *The Body in Pain: The Making and Unmaking of the World.* Oxford: Ox-
           ford University Press.

1992   "The Problem of Vivacity." Avenali Lecture, University of California,
           Berkeley, November 9, 1992.

Schutz, Alfred

1962   *Collected Papers.* I. *The Problem of Social Reality.* The Hague: Martinus
           Nijhoff.

1964   *Collected Papers.* II. *Studies in Social Theory.* The Hague: Martinus Nijhoff.

Taussig, Michael

1987   *Shamanism, Colonialism, and the Wild Man: A Study in Terror and Healing.*
           Chicago: University of Chicago Press.

1993   *Mimesis and Alterity.* New York: Routledge.

UNICEF

1989   *Children on the Frontline: 1989 Update.* Geneva: UNICEF.

1990   "Annual Report, Mozambique."

UNICEF/Ministry of Cooperation

1990   *The Situation of Women and Children in Mozambique.* Maputo: UNICEF/
           Ministry of Cooperation.

Urdang, Stephanie

1989   *And Still They Dance.* London: Earthscan.

Vail, L., and L. White
    1980   *Capitalism and Colonialism in Mozambique.* London: Heinemann.
Vines, Alex
    1991   *Renamo: Terrorism in Mozambique.* Bloomington: Indiana University Press.
World Health Organization
    1990   *WHO/Mozambique Cooperation.* Organização Mundial da Saude Repre-
            sentação em Moçambique, Maputo, March 1990.

"Author-Artist Self-Portrait," by Cathy Winkler

Ethnography of the Ethnographer

Cathy Winkler, with Penelope J. Hanke

THE PLAN

Most researchers begin with a plan, a focus, a research project. For anthropologists, the research preparation includes visas, proposals, government approval, grants, hypotheses, literature review, and other organizational procedures. The plan allows one to decide when and where to do the research. Researchers can ensure some comfort and security in their own cultural identity by maintaining personal and cultural symbols of meaning in their research program. What a luxury to do research that way.

Yet my research began without my request or planning, or any precautions to protect my identity.

> In the middle of the night, a man, standing over me, kicked me awake. I asked, "What are you doing here?" His response: "You know."

And the data collection period ended when

> I put the pedal to the floor, drove sixty miles per hour through the streets, and sped through every stoplight and sign, slowing but not stopping, intentionally breaking all laws in hopes that I would find sanity: either a police officer or a rape crisis center. One point was central: I felt like I was hanging from the edge of a steep cliff that represented "sanity," peering down into the canyon of insanity. As I clung to the cliff that the rapist had pushed me onto, gravity or this period of time without people who understood added to the forces pushing against me. While I knew the details of the attack, I still wondered how the rapist had been able to torture me into a cliff-hanging position in which I desperately fought for my sanity.[1]

After the hospital staff examined me at the Rape Crisis Center, the police detectives questioned me for evidence. One quickly realizes that for the medical staff and the police, and in fact for most people in our culture, "this knowledge becomes static and mono-dimensional, a 'body' to be observed, analyzed, described, and accounted for. One cannot but wonder, however, as to the reality of these limitations" (Panourgia 1992:6). The police are part of this culture, as are the U.S. researchers: they want objective, quantitative data. Just the facts!

On September 29, 1987, the rapist selected me to be his next victim. I became a victim-survivor (V-S),[2] a part of that culture of violence, an informant in that ethnographic attack setting, and an ethnographer of that torture. The questions I address in this chapter are, What happens when the ethnographer and the ethnography are one and the same? How does one sort out objectivity, subjectivity, and, I add, ambiguity?

In investigating the answers, as an anthropologist I wanted to decipher additional questions: What is rape? What is the meaning behind those violent actions? What is the impact of the torture of the rapist on V-Ss? In pursuing these questions, one must realize that the answers are written on the body of the V-S by the rapist during the attack. In other words, I am the ethnography, and I am the ethnographer. While trauma afterward is a major part of the definition of rape (see Winkler 1994*a*, 1994*b*, n.d.), this chapter dwells on the actions of violence during the attack to analyze the meaning of rape.

Just as physical murder, without just cause, is a heinous crime, would not the murder of one's identity also be a heinous crime? If a person was terrorized into nonexistence, would we not be outraged? That is rape. In the United States, one-third of young girls are raped; it is estimated that one-third of all teenage women are the victims of date rape; the FBI notes that one-third of all adult women are raped; marital rape is still not reported or even considered a crime in some states; and one-third of all boys are raped. If only one out of one thousand rapists are convicted of that crime, do we not live with government and political leaders such as district attorneys and scientific experts who support rapists through legislation and practices and espousing "theories" that support rapists' crimes? Rape occurs once every six minutes: Isn't this everyday violence an ever-present, always-occurring form of repression whose socially murderous attack is attempted genocide on the people raped? If we can now estimate that three-fourths of all women and one-third of all men are raped in their lifetimes, are these not the statistics of a state of war?

WHO HAS THE EVIDENCE OF A RAPE ATTACK?

A rape attack is usually, as defined and ensured by the rapist, a witnessless assault. Two people can describe the crime: V-Ss and rapists. It is acceptable to say that rapists do not recount these secret crimes and do not brag, except perhaps in gang rape contexts, about their "successes."[3] Comprehension and evidence of the crime then fall on V-Ss. While videocameras, tape recorders, or one-way mirrors would make it possible to objectively interpret and record the interactive process between a rapist and a V-S, alas the only method available is one-way mirrors in police lineups. In other words, there is but one source for the collection of data from an attack: the V-S who has survived the tortures. Whether one agrees or not, a subjective perspective of rape attacks is a necessity and perhaps the only way of comprehending the meaning of the acts of rapists.

The focus of collection of data from V-Ss' perspective is a situation of aggravation. The evidence is on her or his body.[4] Exposure of the evidence means that "the personal and private become political and public" (Panourgia 1992:4). The research data on a rape attack then involve bodily investigation, public exposure, and political scrutiny of V-Ss' genitals. To retell these data is to relive the experience of the rape attack, to feel again the torturous moments, and to suffer once more the dissection of one's body.

Few people have placed in writing the hideous description of a rape attack.[5] To write these words is to relive the pain—in full. My intention in writing the unimaginable is, first, to convince the unexperienced in this area that there are reasons that we V-Ss are "fanatic" in our efforts to convict rapists and change this culture; second, to allow other V-Ss to give these words to friends and family to prevent them from having to relive the rape attack through the telling and retelling of the events; and third, to demonstrate to others that the unimaginable is real, that an attack did occur.

But there is a quandary: Will rapists or rape-supportive people use these words for enjoyment? Will they dwell on these words as ideas to excite them? Will they use these words as instigators for future attacks? I hope our efforts to educate will overcome their efforts to abuse. "Embedded in Amnesty's work . . . is the assumption that the act of verbally expressing pain is a necessary prelude to the collective task of diminishing pain. . . . [T]he human voice must aspire to become a precise reflection of material reality" (Scarry 1985:9).

CULTURAL TRANSLATIONS: THE SOA (SUBJECTIVITY, OBJECTIVITY, AND AMBIGUITY) APPROACH

Researchers have defined rape from the culture of the rapist, emphasizing his methods, instead of from the culture and subjective perspective of V-Ss by delineating the impact of the crime.[6] Kathleen Barry (1979:266) notes the issue of sexual identity: "Where there is any attempt to *separate* the *sexual* experience from the total person, the first act of objectification is perversion" (emphases added).

Kurt Weis and Sandra S. Borges's (1973:72) definition extends beyond Barry's perspective: "Rape is a total attack against the whole person affecting the victim's physical, psychological and social *identity*" (emphasis added). These researchers define rape by stressing the intent of the rapists and the impact of the rapists' actions on V-Ss.

Ethnographers translate practices and ideas from another culture into our own. More frequently than not, the translation is into the medium of objectivity, an objectivity that distances us from the culture described, that dissociates us from obligation and feeling, and that places a division between us and them. The translation of the research is a translation without risk, without responsibility emotionally, and without obligation. We may ask: Are we as translators inaccurate in our objective verbal descriptions, or are we presenting ideas to a culture that has only learned to understand ideas when they are objectified interpretations? Quantitative, depersonalized, and dehumanized data are, unfortunately and wrongfully, the coup de grâce in research which convinces and persuades many readers.

U.S. culture's depersonalized perspective results in our dehumanization and objectification of the people we research. Once I heard an anthropologist state that his social and cultural research in a Brazilian town did not contain people. While I gasped at such a statement, I now realize that whether he put people into his research or not, his ethnographic results—objectifying the town—were no different from many ethnographers' cultural translations that depersonalize people.

Likewise, most researchers who have produced studies in the research area of rape, that is, sociologists and psychologists, differ little from their counterparts in the field of anthropology. They are translators, like anthropologists, redefining rape for a culture that lacks understanding of the patterning of violence or the violators. The researchers' objective methods for studying people who have been raped stress controls in life rather than the uncontrollable experience of a rape.

One cannot discard these data or the results. These methods have legitimized terms such as "rape trauma syndrome" (Burgess and Holmstrom 1974), "rape myths" (Burt 1980), "second assault" or "community rape" (Holmes and Williams 1981), and "institutional rape" (Holmstrom and Burgess 1978). This information is important.

Let us extend our perspective on objectivity and subjectivity. To begin, what did you do yesterday? Could you please repeat the details of yesterday's events? I suspect that you will recount meticulously a conversation, project, or activity; you will know more or less how time passed and be able to describe your general living pattern; and then, for some part of the day, you will be unsure of what you did, maybe even vague, perhaps doubt-ful, even to the point of not caring to remember at all. In other words, our daily remembered activities vary from meticulous detail to generalized pat-tern to unsure and unclear, perhaps ambiguous, recounting. Our desires and memory determine what we do or do not record, what actions and exchanges we recall. Ambiguity thus joins objectivity and subjectivity as a relevant part of our pattern of interaction and therefore is also a part of our methodology and our results.

ETHNOGRAPHY OF RAPE

To understand rape, let us first peruse some everyday conversational exchanges.

> *Man*: I'm hungry. What have you got?
> *Woman*: There's a casserole in the refrigerator that I could heat up.

> *Woman*: I'm going to have to move.
> *Man*: You can stay in the neighborhood. I'll take care of that.

> *Man*: I've got five girlfriends that I can see anytime I want.
> *Woman*: Those women must like you a lot and enjoy having you in bed.

These represent daily exchanges between heterosexual women and men. In most cases, we would probably disregard them as forgettable. But let us ex-amine them in context.

Rapist's Plan

Just because the ethnographer-victim in a case of rape did not format a research plan, we should not assume that a plan did not exist. Rapists plan their attacks, and this one was no different. A multitude of evidence veri-fies this. Three days before the attack, I had noticed that some washed socks that I had placed outside the night before were strewn around the yard. Without any other visible evidence, I had assumed that it was one of those laundry calamities: an unknown event had caused those socks to be displaced. But the socks were evidence that the rapist had prepared the basement window for entrance that night. He had loosened two dozen nails from a hard wire mesh screen attached to the house wall, removed the wedge that locked the window, and then replaced everything in its usual "untouched" state.

During the week prior to the attack, I remember receiving a late-night telephone call from a friend, during which I had heard noises. While I re-mained on the telephone, I walked down the stairs, telling my friend I was checking out the sounds. Not finding anything, I returned upstairs and rationalized the noises as endemic to the house. How natural! Unfortunately, after the attack, I could not remember if the telephone call took place the same night the window was prepared. In other words, had the rapist attempted entry earlier but was thwarted by the telephone call and my awakened state? I don't know, and he is not a source of information.

More specific evidence of his plan became apparent during the attack. When the rapist entered, my dog made no noise, not even a movement. She only acted like this when she knew the person. During her days outside, he had made friends with her, a step in his plan. Further, he had said during the attack, "That's a pussy dog." A statement of familiarity.

Time and shock might prevent a V-S from detective work, but in this case, the rapist had given me a few minutes to wake up and to realize the terror of the reality and thus to get my bearings. Moreover, he raped me for three and a half hours, not the usual fifteen to twenty minutes. While some might argue or think that the length of time increases the intensity of the rape, I question that perspective. What is crucial is that the amount of time and my background as a cultural anthropologist helped me collect data against the rapist.[7] Collection of data then became a method to help grasp at sanity. That was *my* impromptu plan.

There was additional evidence of preparation. He had on a worn pair of jean cutoffs with a washed-out T-shirt—clothes that fail to mark an identity—and new shoes without a worn-in smell and without frayed parts to handicap his movements. He carried no wallet or other form of identification that could fall out of his pocket. His hair was close-cropped to hide an identifiable hairstyle. And he had no smell that would expose his work or hobbies. His presentation was an attempt to hide his identity. The most explicit evidence was his statement, "I've been watching you for three weeks." He had surveyed the house and my movements over a period of time to ensure his safety and his success. How like a researcher were his preparations! Like most rapists, he too planned his attack by his selection of a "safe" victim: living alone, new to the neighborhood.

When the police asked me about his education, my thoughts centered on the rapist's ability to execute his plan. Yes, he was educated about rape as evidenced by his research preparations and their execution.

Physical Attack: Authority over the Body

Let me begin with a brief, objective description of the attack before analyzing the details.

> On September 29, 1987, a man broke into my home, woke me, beat me, raped me, robbed me, and raped me again. This lasted three and a half hours.

These are the facts. The following will be an analysis of the interaction—detail by detail. One should be aware that the police frequently asked me, How do you know he was telling the truth? How do you know he was lying? The readers can be the judge. My point is, Why do we even doubt the veracity of V-Ss?

The context of rape is not questionable. The rapist establishes that context and its meaning. After I was first awakened, I asked the question that legal experts imagine a rapist would answer: "What are you doing here?" Explanation, of course, is irrelevant, for the rapist and the V-S, and the rapist demonstrated that: "You know." He was right. I and every other V-S knew immediately the reasons for his presence. Words were unnecessary. We knew. His body standing over my bed in its Rambo-like stance left no doubts as to his intentions. Robbers do not wake up their victims. In the case of this rapist, it was important for me to be awake, because it was my reactions to the terror that provided his enjoyment.

The rapist began by cornering me and physically restricting my movements. The first sight I saw was a slightly muscular male body with arms held straight out as if prepared for a wrestling match. He stood erect over my bed, a mattress resting on the floor. His body then and throughout the ordeal blocked the only exit. During the rapes, he either held my hair—hair that was barely two to three inches long—or like an octopus intertwining its prey, cemented his body on top of mine with his arms restraining my upper arms. As he searched the house, he grabbed my shoulders with his hands. Later the bruises on my upper arms and my quick painful reaction to a shoulder caress from a friend were evidence of his body on my body. He had used his hands and body to control me and my body throughout that period of time and later.

His physical threats were matched by verbal threats. "I have a knife in my pocket." A knife could end my life, it could scar my body, and it could disfigure me in a way plastic surgery could not mask. The way his pants limply fell onto the floor without a noise, the visual clue that his pockets lacked a bulge, his failure to pick up a knife in the kitchen he had passed through on his way to my bedroom—all this made it clear that the physical presence of a knife was not the issue or the basis for the threat. The threat and his intentions were enunciated by the force of his words: "I can break in any place. No house can keep me out." Besides, he did carry another weapon: his body. His body was the instrument of force and the weapon of power for his crimes.

Rapists desire the victim's subjugation. After he undressed, he grabbed my nightshirt to tear it off. I quickly responded: "It's unnecessary. I'll take it off." Ripping and tearing clothes to shreds were just a step, not a goal, in his research plan of rape. Torn clothes were not his issue: his intention to stop any impediment to his desires to rape was. When I complied, I had demonstrated my subordination to his desires, and *that* was his goal.

His fist was a weapon. As he laid down on the bed, he pulled me to his side, saying, "Suck my dick." No one doubts that repulsion grows inside the V-S at that moment. Fear temporarily paralyzed me: I refused to respond, or could not. Aggressively, he pulled my head over his groin. He placed my mouth above his erect penis, but my eyes fell on his left groin. The scar there ignited a force inside me: here was an identifiable fact for the police and the lawyers. The scar would be proof of my accusations against this man as a rapist; it was a believable ID. That information energized me: I raised my fist and struck him at the base of the penis.

In a millisecond, he was on his feet battering my head. His fist initially swung wide, hitting the lamp before it battered my face. I grabbed for his penis, pulling and yanking it. This action further infuriated him, and he swung again, now with increased force. With his left hand, he grabbed my right arm to hold me in position as he continued to place the strength of his body behind his boxerlike fist. He transferred the force of his body onto my face. The force of his battering to my face threw my body against the wall. When I said, "OK, I'll do it," he quit *that* method of force. His blows left my back cracked open, as I learned later at the hospital.

Initially thwarted by the inability to recall the rapist's face, I had but one option: to comply and, through compliance, to try and escape. An escape would have to be timed for the right moment. In the meantime, I was his victim. Later I learned that I had described in the police report a gunshot wound scar. How many people have gunshot wound scars, located in exactly the same place as this one?

Throughout that night of rapes, the rapist gave away several hints of his familiarity with the neighborhood. Besides his explicit comment, "I've been watching you for three weeks," another incident demonstrated his knowledge of the neighbors. At one point when he was conversing with me, after the first rape and the robbery, my dog began to bark. I made the comment, "You'd better leave because the last time this happened the Hopes called the police." There were two windows in my room that faced houses, and he went to the window that faced the Hopes' house. His action was evidence.

With some knowledge of the type of evidence preferred by lawyers, I immediately tried to memorize the rapist's face. Within minutes, I knew that this was an impossibility. I looked at his face, closed my eyes, and could not record it. This is surprising: visual memory had always been one of my best abilities. My hate for the rapist, my shock, and my terror at his presence prevented me from memorizing a face that represented the one idea—rape—that I knew now should not exist. My memory would not let me recall his face then, or even now, because to recall that face is to recall the full impact of the rape. I was not ready then, and now I have had six years of legal battles to further prevent me from resolving this trauma.

The artist's composite, drawn from the details of the features I memorized, is an exact portrait of the rapist. As a matter of fact, the chief assistant district attorney has asked me more than a dozen times, "Why can't you identify him?" With the artist's composite, the police detective selected him during street surveillance and the private investigator I hired found him immediately.[8] As a matter of fact, there are five representations of the rapist's face in my memory:

1. the face of the rapist;
2. the face from the police photo;
3. the face on the artist's composite;
4. the face on street surveillance; and
5. the face in the courtroom.[9]

While these are all the face of the same rapist in different contexts, for me none of them matched.

To supersede my trauma, I argued with myself to calm my feelings of terror and insanity and memorize the features of his face. Between rapes, when he was sitting next to me on the bed and looked away, I noted each detail of his face, from the shape of his forehead, eyebrows, eyes, nose, lips, and chin to the relationship of each of these. The intensity of my concentration on the details of his face prevented me from remembering his conversation at this point.

Throughout the ordeal, one is placed in a situation of unpreparedness, in a situation in which survival is threatened. Rape is a situation of unpredictability and ambiguity. I felt like the rapist had ordered me to climb Mount Everest, and he knew that I had no experience in mountain climbing, that the walls were precipices to death, and that oxygen as one climbs higher becomes scarce, making it difficult to breathe. Each moment demands a life-and-death strategy. While life-and-death strategizing was an ongoing process throughout the ordeal, there was one moment that stood out. The conversation went like this:

"Don't look at me. You're a smart one. You'll go to the police."

"Do the police know you?"

"The police know me." And he added in a cocky tone, "Well, you can't do anything about it."

"Do you have friends in the police?"

"No, it's not that."

"Have you got connections with the police?"

"No, but they know me alright." And he added, "I'm not going back in there again. I'm not going to get caught for this. I know what they'll do to me for raping a woman."

The issue of the police was a crucial one now. I knew that I would go to the police; that was clear in my mind. How could I hide my feelings from him? I had not learned to act psychopathologically, like the rapist. My only solution was to tell the truth.

"What could I do if I did go to the police? I'd have to absolutely ID you, and I can't see without my contacts or glasses. Besides, how many men in the neighborhood have mustaches? You look like every other man around here."

With an agreeable smirk, he laughed and responded, "That's true."

His and my (I will not use the word "our") knowledge of the effectiveness of the legal system in prosecuting rapists was the same. With that information, I was stating what every rapist and every district attorney knows: rape is a crime infrequently prosecuted and rarely resulting in conviction.

Later, the issue of evidence came up. In an ongoing conversation, I brought up the point constantly on my mind:

"Are you going to leave soon? My face and head hurt."

"These [bruises] will show. People will know [that you were attacked]."

"Don't worry. I can hide the bruises on my forehead with bangs, and the rest I can easily cover up with makeup. It's amazing what you can do with makeup." I added, "I can call in sick if necessary. If I did go to work and someone noticed, I could say I ran into a door."

He laughed. His laughter indicated one more moment of survival for me and indicated to him that I could lie for him, or so I wanted him to think. What I did not realize at that time, and he did not point out, was that my battered head had become enlarged and distorted. For my friends who took care of me the following week, the bruises were tolerable, but my deformed head was not. Didn't he notice that?

The rapist always defined the movements of my body. During the hours of the rapes, he decided in which positions he wanted my body. His first act of rape was with his body lounging on the bed and my body in a kneeling position on his right side. His right hand held onto my left shoulder. His left hand grabbed my head, placing it above his penis. With these actions came the repeated demands: "Suck my dick."

In another movement, he laid on his back with his head near the door, his open knees facing the wall. Holding my hair, he placed me between his knees and then he arched his back. More words flowed from his lips: "Lick my ass." Hesitancy and comments only aggravated him. With my body in a kneeling position and my hands on the mattress, an animallike stance, I obeyed. After a few brief licks, I asked him if that was what he wanted. The act, not the length, was his pleasure.

Time depended on his directions and for me, became unmeasurable. During the first and second rape periods, he varied his movements and orders between forcing me to put my mouth on his penis and penile penetration of my vagina. The multiple periods of oral penile interaction, the licking—"Lick it like a lollipop." "Suck on it like a lollipop."—lasted until he wanted to alter positions. That method of torture left my mouth without saliva, and my sandpaperlike tongue had to follow his absolute and impossible orders. I do not know the exact number of times he forced me to place his penis inside my mouth. Here I wanted ambiguity to reign. To count would result in a number, and the number was unbearable knowledge of the licking, sucking, salivating process of unwanted and forced sodomy. The qualitative experience had emotionally crushed me; to know the number of times and the duration of these repeated acts would have been an additional shock. I was not willing to endure knowing that number to satisfy any objective-oriented lawyer in this country. Like the penis licking and sucking periods, the rapist frequently plunged his penis inside of my vagina, inside of me—in any direction, with any force, as often as he desired. How many times did he thrust his penis inside of me? Again, terror is not a quantitative experience: it is inhuman, and it is subjugation. Objective numbers are subjectively irrelevant.

The speed and rate of performance were also elements of time that he controlled. During forced sodomy, he clearly stated, "I want it slowly," and "Don't use your hands." To defer his desires on rate and speed of this sexually disgusting performance was unacceptable to him, and noncompliance was a reason for more fist force.

The rapist defined the organization of his "research project." He noted when something would happen, how it would happen, and the length of time it would last. He orchestrated the movements. He was the master over his victims' bodies and their actions. He dictated the interactions between the victim and himself. Some examples of his dictatorial regime were comments like "I'm here and I'm going to get what I came for," "Open your lips," "Move your tongue," or "Move," referring to his preference that my groin and thighs should be involved in his "sexual play."

Rapists' actions concentrate on the most sensitive areas of the victims' bodies where the greatest number of nerve endings are located: the genital area and the breasts. In the genital area, his penis punched vigorously and rapidly, his lips slobbered over my clitoris, and his hands twisted and contorted the labia and clitoris. In the chest area, he pinched and squeezed my nipples and breasts. His contortions with my body were his forms of "pleasure." Paining me pleasured him.

Not only did he implant his body on mine in order to try to write and define my body as his but he also drenched my body with his fluids. He slobbered saliva over my mouth and facial cheeks. He pushed open my mouth and licked the insides of it. His tongue plunged down into my throat. When his mouth was not slobbering on my lips, his tongue was salivating on my genital area: he sucked and licked as he liked. During the second period of raping, he sweated. When his body was plastered on top of my body, the drips of sweat from his forehead methodically fell over my face, into my eyes, rolling onto my nose and then following the age lines into my mouth. His sweat invaded the tastes in my mouth: swallowing his sweat was like swallowing him. As in the forced sodomy, I could again taste his body fluids. His sperm and saliva were in my mouth; his sperm and saliva were in my vagina; and his sweat ran over my body.

He also wrote his body and activities on my place of residence. Besides his sweat and sperm on my sheets, he ground cigarette butts into the wood floors, and he touched everything—on both levels. He went through the drawers of my desk and bureau. Angrily and with gusto, he threw all the items onto the floor and kicked them out of his way. Later, the police blackened the areas that he had touched to reveal his fingerprints and then left those blackened areas—a method that highlighted the rapist's definition of my home.

After his departure, control of the context was still his. To ensure my isolation, his threats were not sufficient. He ripped out the telephones both upstairs and downstairs, and he took my car keys. While these actions aided his getaway, they were in addition an attempt to keep me in that rape state through isolation from other people and temporary imprisonment in a place marked by his definitions of himself. Without a telephone or a car, how would one find help at 4:30 in the morning? Who would be awake? What cars would be on the roads? Where would one find safety? Of course, my extra set of car keys was never found by the rapist, nor did I mention their existence to him.

The rapist could not leave without the coup de grâce. As he stood in the doorway to the bedroom, he demanded, "Stand up." And of course I asked, "What for?" He replied, "I want to look." He did not even end the sentence with the common phrase "at you." He wanted to look at me like a centerfold picture, not a person centered in his life. With my hands across my body to cover myself, with my shoulders slouched and my back arched forward, I tried to hide the exposure of my body from his view. Standing there, he stared. Then he commented, "You're fine. You have a fine pussy." His last remark and last physical act further underlined my humiliation and subjugation. Those last looks and that last act were another method he used to rape me again.

Emotional Attack: Authority over Feelings

His definitions of my body movements, the context, the time and space were not the end to his intentions; he also defined my feelings, my emotions, my reactions. He orchestrates the body movements of his victims, juxtaposing his comments of how his victims should feel. Taking over his victims' feelings is part of his methodology.

The rapist decreed my emotional reasons for the "sexual responses" of my body. Regarding the rapes, he announced, "You like it." He had even interpreted my body reactions as favorable. In a state of panic and shock, I had closed my body off to him, and my blood pressure had dropped to a low level, resulting in my feeling cold on that hot night. Yet, he had decided differently: "You like it [the rape] because your nipples are hard." I did not like it, and my low blood pressure and the closing down of my body was evidence that he refused to accept.

His misinterpretations to reinforce his desires continued by defining other bodily reactions as favorable. He asked my age. I refused to answer by asking him what age he thought I was. "You must be eighteen because you're tight." Disgustingly, "tight" was how he referred to my vaginal opening. One wonders how much people actually know about sexual intercourse, about the body's reactions during the act of sex! There was no doubt why my body was not open to him, and age was not the factor.

He wanted me to have the same feelings he did: "I'm your boyfriend. I'm your first great boyfriend." With that definition of a supposed emotional relationship, he added, "You liked it." My complete lack of response, lack of participation, lack of interest were verification to him of his ideas. This was not an exchange between two people. This was a context in which one person and only one person—the rapist—had the right to state feelings, whether false or not.

Noncompliance is a method employed by V-Ss when possible. Questioning him was one of my methods of noncompliance. A question I frequently asked was, "What do you want?" Questioning as a method of stalling also occurred: "Is this OK?" "Is this what you want?" In reference to his command "Move," I asked, "What does that mean?" When he asked for my money, I asked, "Is that why you're here?" "Is that why you broke into my house?" In regard to his questioning of previous boyfriends, I asked, "Why do you want to know?" Whenever he tried to define a situation—my age, his definition of the rape as a "pleasure" for me—I would ask, "Why do you think that?" Comprehension of his rape interests was an issue, and for that reason, I asked him questions: "Why did you break in?" "Why didn't you try to talk to me?" "Why didn't you at least try to come in through the front door?" "Why did you do this?" To end the ordeal, I said, "Are you going to leave?" "Why don't you leave that way [through the front door]?"

Feigning ignorance as a delaying tactic was another method of noncompliance. In response to his statement, "You know what I want," I said, "No, I don't." And later, "I don't understand." I beseeched him to explain his interests: "Please just tell me what you want. I'll do it. But you have to explain it to me." Forcing me to lick his anus, I said, "I don't know what you mean. Tell me and I'll do it. But I don't know." If forced anal licking was his desire, then ignorance was my method.

Ignorance of sexual intercourse was also another method of noncompliance. After he ignored my stated fears of VD and AIDS, I used my Catholic background as an excuse. Emphatically he stated, "Don't talk. Do it." That's when I said, "Look, I used to be a nun and I just left the convent. Of course, I've read about sexual intercourse, but I don't know how. You'll have to tell me what to do." When the forced penile penetration began, I feared that the nonexistence of my hymen would expose the lies in my nun story. For that reason, I said, "I wear tampons." Yet all he knew about were Methodist nuns.

Truth is an important issue to us: perhaps we alter the truth diplomatically for friends or family. But honesty is a trait of a respectable person. In this case, I became a liar, assuming the same method as the rapist. Throughout, the rapist had lied to me: sometimes I knew it, and other times I discovered it after the attack. To prevent the rapist from a greater expansion of his power into my life, I lied. He asked me, "Where's your teller card?" And I lied: "I haven't got one. I just opened my bank account." After the first rape, he said, "I'm hungry. What have you got?" And I answered, "There's a casserole in the refrigerator that I could heat up." He knew the refrigerator light made the kitchen off-limits, and I knew but did not state that the refrigerator light had burned out. After his search of my room, he took my camera and then sat on the bed. I asked, "Could you take the film out of the camera? Those pictures mean something to me." To this day, I have no idea what pictures were in the camera or whether I ever had that film developed. Neither point was relevant to me. What was crucial was his attempts to take my identity, and those pictures held a part of my identity—my identity with friends and family. He asked me for my jewelry, and I responded that I only had worthless, costume jewelry. My few pieces of valued jewelry—such as the pair of diamond earrings that my father had given my mother, who then gave them to me after his death—would not become the property of the rapist. For the rapist, lying was a method of attack; for me, lying was a method of self-defense.

I also used lies as a method of self-defense, to avoid future attacks. He thought I was eighteen. I lied and said twenty-one, when in fact I was thirty-eight years old. Thirty-eight would be a threat to him. Women of twenty-one are considered young and naive, an age at which one can manipulate their thinking and their identity. But a thirty-eight-year-old woman has lived two decades beyond that, and her identity and confidence could hamper his escape from this crime. When he asked what subway station I took, I answered first with the truth—"East Lake"—and then followed with the lie—"Sometimes Inman Park." When he asked me what time I went to work, I gave a vague answer: "Seven or eight o'clock. It varies." All rapists are serial, but whether or not this rapist would attack me again is unpredictable. I had to strategize against future attacks.

His emotional bulldozing of my feelings continued with his penetrating gunshots of guilt. Ironically, researchers discuss guilt as an issue of V-Ss[10] or as an issue imposed on V-Ss by supporters. Guilt is not fabricated by V-Ss. Rather, and more important, guilt begins with the rapist, and that is crucial. It is a part of the rape attack(s) via the rapist's words and actions. Numerous times, the rapist made this clear to me. In regard to his beating of me, he said, "You made me do it. It's your fault. I didn't want to hurt you." He wanted to make me believe that I was guilty and that guilt was his retribution against the defense of my self. In regard to the forced sexual intercourse, his words made me feel like a prostitute: "You know how to do it." These words indicated to me that he considered me a professional in the pleasures of male sexual performance, that sex was a physical, not an emotional or mental, action, and that therefore giving sexual pleasure was part of my job in this world.

Guilt for the acts was not sufficient for him; he also wanted to make me feel guilty about future acts. He wanted to control my imminent and forth-coming actions with blame. He wanted my decisions in the future to be based on his current wishes and desires. "Don't go to the police. I'll come back and get you. I won't just hit you a few times." But saying this once was not sufficient. Repetition underlines the guilt feelings he wanted to im-plant in my mind: "Don't go to the police. I'm warning you. I have friends and we'll come back." Threats of pain and disfigurement were words to control my actions now and later.

The rapist wanted to police me, to be "my" protector. Worried about my living situation after the attack, I said to the rapist, "I'm going to have to move." But he had what he thought was the answer: "You can stay in the neighborhood. I'll take care of that." His protection even included advice on choices of locks for windows: Pointing to a lock on the hall window as he was leaving, he said, "Use these locks to protect yourself." Not believing his words, I commented, "How can I stay here?" His controlled response was, "It's OK. I've had you." The implication was that a woman had a right to this neighborhood only after initiation by him, the rapist. From his per-spective, I now had the right to residency, and with that residency came "his" protection.

Mental Attack: Authority over Ideas

People's perceptions of rapists are one-dimensional: rapists commit horrifying physical and emotional attacks by imposing negative interpreta-tions on victims.[11] If that was all that rapists did, one might still ask why rape equals terror. If the rapist presents himself in a one-dimensional, neg-ative, and abusive manner, then couldn't victims just mentally reject his words and actions to preserve their sanity? By entering a state of negation, a victim should not be feeling like she or he is clutching to sanity. The question still remains: Why do the actions and words of the rapist push the victims onto that cliff?

The answer is the juxtaposition of terror and kindness, of lying and truth, of consideration and battering. "Terror's talk . . . fluctuates [on the one hand] between the firmly sensed and usually quite dogmatic certainties that there indeed exists in reason, and a center, on the other hand, on the uncertainties of a diffuse, decentered randomness on the other" (Taussig 1992:18). These uncertainties and the juxtapositioning of contradictory actions and words are "logical" characteristics of psychopathological people, some people in authority, and all rapists. Rapists are addicts of dictatorial power. Their needles are their victims, who are seen as valued commodities. Without us, rapists cannot feel drugged or exuberant. A rapist's statements and actions combine oppositional ideas to create his reality: he is socially diseased. His own words contradict his own words and the context of rape. The rapist's mind games were constant throughout those three and a half hours.

Contradictions between words and actions started at the beginning of the attack. He beat me. Yet his words shortly thereafter were, "You made me beat you up." Moreover, he made it appear that the victim could actually be a determinant over his tyrannical and absolute control of decisions.

Behaviors that were incongruent with his statements were also commonplace. When I asked how he got into the house, he said, "I broke in the window on the first floor." The unnailed screen and the window ajar in the basement was sufficient evidence to refute his statement later. What is not clear is why he would lie. Since he was raping me on the second floor, and since he pointed out that he could even break into a house on the second floor, he clearly used the same designations of first and second floor that I did. But why implant that false idea? The falseness of an idea was not an issue to him. To create the belief that he broke into a first-floor window—ten feet above the ground—would show (or at least he would like to think it showed) his conquering strength. The basement window on ground level was clearly much easier. He wanted to define his reality as one of superpower, to force me to believe him, and to force my reality into nonexistence.

His approach varied from cruelty to kindness. Without remorse and with unbounded strength, he tried to disfigure me. Yet later he said, with kindness, consideration, and intent, "Do you want me to take you to the hospital?" He had never apologized for his actions, and he had never shown any indication that beating me up was inappropriate. Rather, his interest was in the results: an enlarged head, bruised eyes, bleeding lips, a bulging swollen left cheek. Further, if he took me to a hospital, he would be placing himself in jeopardy. Hospital personnel would identify him and evidence of the crime on my body. A rapist who has planned his attack by surveillance, entrance, preparation of his attack clothes, and persistent attention to the forced sexual acts for hours asked a senseless question of care! His behavior was incongruent with acceptable practices. While he forced me onto my hands and knees to do what most people would consider a vile act—licking his ass—he smiled euphorically, satisfied and content at his ability to disgust and degrade me. Likewise, through the acts of forced penile licking and his penile bludgeoning of my vagina, his face portrayed ecstasy. The lack of caring and lack of communicating between us were not issues to him. His Disneyland was a world of pleasure created by the thrill of paining women.

From the rapist's perspective, a victim should feel disgust as pleasure. At one point, he began to put his penis into my anus. I responded in a gentle and submissive way: "Please don't do that." For some reason, which I cannot explain, the rapist said, "Oh, you like that!" With his words, he pulled his penis back and thrust it into my vagina. His interpretation was that I would enjoy or receive pleasure from anal intercourse, so he would not allow it. His "logical" interpretation of my words left me in a state of confusion, unable to determine reality: while I was glad he altered his actions, his statement implied a practice and enjoyment in that form of sexual play. What was the source of his meaning? Not me?

The economics of rape are startling. After the first rape, he put on his clothes and then said, "Where's your money?" While I tried to remain complacent throughout most of the night, I was adamant about not paying him to rape me. But I still spoke submissively: "I don't have any." With his hands controlling my hair and shoulder, he searched the house and on the first floor found two dollar bills in my wallet that he put in his pocket. In the other room were some subway tokens, but he left those: "That's no good. I need money." Later, after the final rape, he left me upstairs and went downstairs where he grabbed the tokens as he left the house. He did want those tokens, but he did not want me to see him take them. Of course, he should have realized that I would discover the tokens were missing. Then again, why would a rapist care whether or not I saw him take a few tokens? The robbery of money had many meanings. First, this is how he makes his living. He had said, "I'm a robber." Second, my cash payment to him for the rapes was another mechanism of his power. He enjoyed my subjugation, and he enjoyed the fact that the victim had paid for her own humiliation.

Compliments and disgust are woven together by the rapist. Earlier in the rapes, he announced, "I've got five girlfriends that I can see anytime I want." Later he referred to those five girlfriends as "holes." One might wonder if the context of our conversation did not influence alteration of his interpretation. In the former, the conversation took place after the first

rape and his search for money. He was sitting on the bed, and he began
the topic of his numerous girlfriends. My desire to avoid greater pain from
him led me to say, "These women must like you a lot and enjoy having you
in bed." He grinned. After the second rape, he was lounging on the bed,
almost reflective as to his next moves. He began with, "You like it [refer-
ring to the rapes]." I changed the conversation: "Why did you break into
my house?" His reply:

> I'm a rapist. I know that I raped you. I know people don't like what I do. I
> am a rapist and a robber. That's what I do for a living. I watched you for
> three weeks. I was going to get you.

I raised the issue: "What about your five girlfriends?" That is when he said,
"They're just five holes." What made him suddenly confess and, in addition, describe "girlfriends" as "holes," I don't know. He juxtaposes himself
as "my boyfriend" next to himself as the rapist. Similarly, his earlier statement about his "girlfriends" later became a statement about "holes" when
he admitted his crime. The answer lies not in an explanation of the patterned interweavings of meaning, context, and other variables but rather
in the fact that some people in our culture demand to control the context.
They will lie, distort the truth, alter the facts to demonstrate their control,
their authority over the context. The answer rests in his "rational" responses
that are criminal behaviors.

Psychopathologically, rapists attack their victims: they thrive off author-
ing the victims' reality. They juxtapose kindness with cruelty. Their words
are in contrast to their own statements. They measure the victim's pleasure by her disgust. They interweave compliments with offensive behavior.
These, I believe, are the ingredients for the trauma that V-Ss experience
later. Also, this explains why date or acquaintance rape is rape. It is a rape
of confidence:[12] Rapists gain victims' confidence and then attack. That is
psychopathological behavior.

Transformation into Victim

The rapist had choreographed my reactions during the rape. In some
instances, he invaded my mind to fabricate false images, and in all instances, he forced me to react in ways that were against my will, values,
and beliefs. Within the constraints imposed by the rapist, choice exists, but
all forms of choice are those of self-defense. Our options as victims all involve how we cater to rapists' methods of disgust, and these options are
limited. To diverge from *his* ideas could result in abuse. Here I analyze
the methods of "choice" that I attempted and follow this with an analysis of my trauma reactions to the rapist's methods in which *no choice* was
involved.

Methods of "choice" fall into two general categories: to fight or to comply. At the beginning, I fought back, but my attempts were unsuccessful and left me battered. My next option was to comply. Compliance is a strategy of self-defense; it is not an attempt to give in or to accept the rape. It is, in addition, a method of detective work.

Realizing that the rapist needed me as his "needle" and in a state of ambiguity as to his malintentions, I wanted him to "like" me. When I said to him, "These women [his five girlfriends] must like you a lot and enjoy having you in bed," truth was irrelevant and flattery became a method of survival.

Realizing that conversation might be a vehicle to safety and increase my "needle" value to him and that any conversational topics that would refer to his identity were off-limits, I told an anecdote from class that day that had centered on anthropologists' interpretation of racism cross-culturally. The anecdote demonstrated that there are a plethora of meanings that people can assign to any given situation.

> You know, when I was six years old, I learned my colors. I learned that brown and black were two distinct colors. The white people had told me to stay away from black people. For a long time, I had wanted to see a black person because the only people I had seen in the States had the skin color of white or brown. Since no one said anything against brown people, I thought that they must be good people too.

Few topics of conversation come to mind during a rape, but I wanted to get him to talk. Instead, the rapist laughed. So my impromptu plan included humor. If humor ensured my life, then it was a valuable method of self-defense. Humor was also a method of safety. The rapist, preparing to leave, ripped the telephone out of the wall and then checked around the room once more. When he came back to the foot of the mattress bed on the floor, he inadvertently kicked something.

"What's that?" he said.

"Probably my iron."

"You know, you could have hit me with that."

"*Now* you tell me." And he laughed.

From the beginning of the attack when I first realized that my nightmare was reality, self-counseling began. My initial responses were to prevent feelings of guilt or denial. I told myself that I was not to blame for what was about to happen and that what was about to happen was rape. As a teacher of rape in Women's Studies courses, as an informed person about the literature on rape, and as a past volunteer in a rape crisis center, I knew the issues. Preventing guilt was difficult given the rapist's attempt to define me in terms of it: "You made me beat you up."

At times self-counseling was unintentional. When the rapist had his body plastered on top of mine the first time and had begun his battering of my genitals, I began to step outside of myself. My self was pulling away from my body. My essence wanted to get away from the body of mine that the rapist was torturing. Confused, I pulled my self back into my physical body. This "stepping outside of one's self" is called dissociation (Warshaw 1988). When I initially wrote the police report, and a year later when I wrote the chapter on the rape attack for the district attorney, I did not mention this. I felt that dissociation was a sign of insanity, and I did not want the police or lawyers to consider me as anything but a "good victim." Such evidence then remained muted. Dissociation, to me at that time, was not criminal evidence, and in fact legal experts in most states today do not accept rape trauma as evidence. But dissociation is evidence; it is evidence of the trauma suffered during the attack.

Other body reactions were comprehensible. These reactions were unintentional and inadvertent. The next morning when I was waiting with the police detectives to reenter the house, they asked me how long the rapist was with me. Except for my vague response of a few hours, I had no precise answer. After the rapist left, I did look at the clock-telephone when I tried to reconnect it. I discovered that it was 4:30 A.M. The detectives had interviewed my neighbors, who had heard a scream at 1:00 A.M. While I had no memory of that scream, I knew that it must have been me screaming during the beating. Ironically, if the police detectives had asked me if I had screamed, I would have answered "No." My voice had loudly expressed my horror, unbeknown to me.

My mind fabricated smells during the rape. As the rapist started pelting my vagina with his penis, I smelled urine and excrement. At first, because the smells were dynamic and forceful, I thought that I must have evacuated myself. But I did not feel anything. My next thought was that the rapist had evacuated himself in the bed. His movements indicated he had not. The obvious next choice was the dog. Dogs will do that sometimes. In the police statement, I noted that my dog had evacuated herself. At the end of the day, when I returned to my bedroom with the police detective, I immediately looked in the corner where the dog had been to clean up the "mess." There was nothing. The detective congenially responded that nothing had been cleaned up. My mind had matched the horror of the rape with the worse smell: being raped was like wallowing in a vat of urine and excrement.

The rapist's beating left marks on my face and body unfelt. In the following weeks, I watched the changes in the colors on my face from dull yellows, light browns, and passive blues and purples to vibrant and distinctive reds, deep purples, and bold blues. I saw the fluid that puffed up my face slowly drain down, creating new forms of facial distortions. What I saw was not felt. I told people about the rape, not the painless beating. My friends and colleagues were shocked when they first saw me because they had knowledge of the rape, not of the facial bruising.

Lack of physical pain during the rape attack was another ingredient of the trauma. When the rapist had initially swung wide in his first attempts to batter me, he had hit the lamp and broken the bulb. The splattered particles of the bulb fell over the bed, and the rapist had pushed my back for hours into those bits of splintered glass that had fallen onto the bed covers. No pain existed for me. After arriving at the hospital, I still had no idea of the condition of my back. During the examination, the doctor noted that she would have to remove the glass particles before sewing up my back. I asked, "Why?" Shock and trauma superseded the pain.

Social Murder = Identity Attack

I began the ethnography of rape with these commonplace exchanges:

Man: I'm hungry. What have you got?
Woman: There's a casserole in the refrigerator that I could heat up.

Woman: I'm going to have to move.
Man: You can stay in the neighborhood. I'll take care of that.

Man: I've got five girlfriends that I can see anytime I want.
Woman: Those women must like you a lot and enjoy having you in bed.

These comments have now taken on their actual meaning in the context of rape. These apparently meaningless exchanges encapsulate the rapists' violence. Perhaps on a lesser scale, these are statements of everyday violence. Each demonstrates the man's attempt to have authority *over* the woman: (1) she should serve him; (2) she should accept him as her protector; and (3) she should accept his sexual "rights" to any woman.

We can now perceive how these supposedly casual comments ignite the trauma in V-Ss. Everyday statements of abuse are the same statements rapists' use. In other words, and I mean this literally, we could decrease the trauma of V-Ss if we altered the interwoven violence of day-to-day conversation. We need to speak without abuse.

The ethnography of rape is the study of the culture of rapists from the V-Ss' perspective. What then is the definition of rape?

Rapists are social murderers (C. Winkler 1991). Physically, rapists bludgeon V-Ss' bodies: marking, scarring, battering, penetrating, devouring, liquidating, salivating on us. Emotionally, rapists stab our feelings: defining, dictating, demanding, manipulating, infiltrating us. Mentally, rapists take authority over our actions and words: distorting, contradicting, deforming, falsifying, contorting us. These are terror mechanisms. Rape is an attack on the identity of V-Ss. Rapists attempt to distort and to sever ourselves from our own identity. He implanted his body, his touches, his ideas, his emotions, his sweat on me, and then he exploded his words and movements into a mangled mixture of chaos. The rapists' chaos becomes V-Ss' reality. If V-Ss suffer such incredible torture, then how valid, either objectively or subjectively, is her or his account? Let us review the attack in these terms.

Objective validation must result from outsiders' corroboration of the data. Conversation is not covered here directly. To begin, the artist's composite is a photograph of the rapist, further verified by DNA fingerprinting (Lewis 1988). The exact match with the defendant caused the chief assistant district attorney to ask me more than a dozen times, "Why can't you identify him?" Police detectives had noted that 80 percent of the details I had provided about the rapist matched the defendant. My responses—dissociation, emotional numbness, and rape trauma—are also evidence, and they are experienced by other V-Ss. Evidence of the house being broken into, the screams heard by the neighbors, and my bruises are details of a physical assault.

Subjective validation is my interpretation of the rapist and his acts of terror. Within this perspective is intertwined my ability to convey my feelings of trauma. In other words, how well do I describe the horror to outsiders? While some readers might respond with the statement "Now, I understand," V-Ss know that this account represents only 1 percent or less of the horror of rape. My brother Jack's comment on the nonfictional quality of the subjective experience was that writers cannot fathom a plot in which glass is crushed into a person's back unfelt and unnoticed.

Ambiguity is evidence of the crime of rape and occurs, in part, when the rape trauma either impedes or prevents our ability to recall the torturous moments of the attack.[13] A survey of rape accounts in the literature points out the extensive detail V-Ss can provide on all aspects of the attack except the rape itself. On that latter point, V-Ss give brief responses: "He [they] raped me." Since a rape takes many forms, the V-Ss' ambiguity with regard to the details of the rape becomes the outsiders' ambiguity. "Intense pain is . . . language-destroying: as the content of one's world disintegrates, so the content of one's language disintegrates; as the self disintegrates, so that which would express and project the self is robbed of its source and its subject" (Scarry 1985:35). Similarly, I had no desire to count the number of times the rapist bludgeoned me with his penis. In rape attacks, V-Ss suffer ambiguity to intentionally protect themselves from the intensity of the torture or as a result of the impact of the rape trauma. Legal experts want V-Ss to be absolutely accurate yet fail to understand that lack of accuracy is proof that a rape has occurred. Ambiguity exists and is evidence, evidence of a rape attack.

Unfortunately, an analysis such as mine eliminates much of the ambiguity. Readers now have a framework by which to conceptualize the attack.

Different people's different perspectives foster ambiguity, and more important, these perspectives have an impact on V-Ss. Let us first consider the rapist. Clearly, ambiguity minimally exists for him because he dictates the situation. He may at times experience uncertainty about his next move, but he is the decision maker. In contrast, the unpatterned and unpredictable, or more to the point, the psychopathological behavior of the rapist, leaves V-Ss in an almost constant state of ambiguity without any perceivable right in the decision-making process. Rapists have forced V-Ss into a state of ambiguity, a chaos of insanity. As a result, the aftermath of trauma involves unexpected jolts of volcanolike eruptions of pain that unexpectedly and unpredictably surface, resurface, and keep resurfacing. Moreover, because the rapist has stabbed the identity of V-Ss multiple times, the impact leaves V-Ss, like myself, to experience lengthy periods of intense crying in which we mourn the loss of part of ourselves. To consider suicide, and in some cases to commit it, is not unusual for us. Suicide, only superficially and fleetingly, has crossed my mind too many times to count; it still does. The rapist dictates a state of ambiguity for V-Ss, and that state survives in us for months, years, even decades.

We must also consider ambiguity in regard to the people in the legal system. First and foremost, they are familiar with the account of the rape attack. In the legal case that I am involved in, I not only gave a five-page single-spaced account at the police station within hours after the attack but I also wrote a thirty-page account for the trial, the trial that has never taken place. The lawyers know the state of ambiguity that I live with, and they know detail by detail the facts of the attack that lives in my memory. Nevertheless, they have spent six years telling me that there will be a trial; in other words, they have spent six years telling me to remember and to be able to recall meticulously every moment of that terror. The lawyers have ignited that terror on a monthly basis, which further magnifies the insecure and doubtful state of my existence. The lawyers' actions reinforce the state of ambiguity by emphasizing one's lack of existence.

Let us not forget the readers. Now that you have read this far, can you state in a few sentences the emotional impact of this account? Yes, it is very difficult. How do you put into words the trauma or anger you may be feeling? Are you perhaps feeling slightly ambiguous about your reactions? How would you express that ambiguity to me, and how then would V-Ss feel about their own imprecise emotional responses?

In another regard, you have learned the details of that attack, but you have no idea of the chronology of events. You have an idea of what happened at certain times, such as at the beginning or at the end, but the ordering of events is a puzzle.

Readers, there are still more reactions to note. You may wish to blame or deny. You may have read this account trying to find a way that I could have escaped. There must have been a moment when I could have fled.

Those readers would have found it, and they blame me for not taking advantage of that imagined possibility. Some readers will accept that a rape attack occurred and that *I* suffered it, but their perspective is that the attack happened to *me*, not *them*. They are invulnerable people: some believe that rape could never happen to a man; others believe that rape is outside the realm of possibility for them. Those of you who hold either of those perspectives, blame or denial, have not accepted the fact that the rape took place. Your lack of support reinforces V-Ss' life of insecurity, an insecurity based on a foundation of ambiguity. Who believes us? Unbelieved, we are silenced, and "silence serves . . . to preserve memory as nightmare within the fastness of the individual" (Taussig 1992:27).

I began this discussion of ambiguity by noting how V-Ss cannot verbalize the rape. We are speechless to explain the fire and brimstone of pain. There are few words for emotions in English, and even a thesaurus contains little help in finding synonyms for torturous and terrorizing emotional destruction. "Whatever pain [or terror] achieves, it achieves in part through its unsharibility, and it ensures this unsharibility through its resistance to language" (Scarry 1985:4). It is no wonder that descriptions of rape attacks are brief. Ambiguity reigns in our utter inability to describe the horror. While this chapter may be one of the most detailed accounts of a rape attack to date, it cannot fully express what a V-S suffers during an attack. I do not know how to express more precisely that terror, that unimaginable torturous terror. In my writings, my first drafts overuse certain words: it was a horror, a real horror, truly horrific, horribly horrible; it was hell, a living hell, an unbearable hell, an unimaginable hell; it was an attack of hate, disgusting hate, malicious hate, unimaginable hate. This is a result of the ambiguity in explaining what rape is.

Despite my precise police statement, ambiguity still exists and affects my memory, as it does every V-Ss' memory. Within the first year, I could not recall exactly why tampons were a part of the conversation. In writing this, six years later, I remembered why. When our memory fails us in our day-to-day lives, we have clues or crutches to help us. We can use these—for example, friends and written material—to remind ourselves and to verify points we are unsure of. Yet in the case of rape, there are always points that remain unexplained and unverifiable: Did the rapist and I talk on the subway a month and a half before the attack? I remember the rapist putting on his baseball cap the same way a stranger who spoke to me on the subway did, and they were both people who use drugs. What conversation kept the rapist occupied while I memorized his face? What did he say that distracted him as I etched his features onto my memory? Did he try to break into my home earlier but gave it up because I received a late-night telephone call? Why couldn't I remember the day of that telephone call and who made it? The most difficult and unverifiable question is, Why did he rape me? "Terror dissolve[s] certainty every bit as it prey[s] on one's heartfelt desire to find its secret order. Yet, the more one look[s] for the order, the more one [is] caught in its sticky web of evasions, bluffs, and hall of mirrors" (Taussig 1992:9). The unavailability of details that have dramatically affected our lives leaves us with more issues of ambiguity.

Ambiguity, then, is a state without rights to knowledge or decision making. Moments of ambiguity are embedded in our everyday lives, but we can live with these because they are relatively unimportant. Yet states of existence in which we are without knowledge and without the ability to make decisions undermine our security and our identity. These states become interwoven into our minds and our existence after an attack, and these states are sources of trauma. How could I meticulously look at and study the face of the rapist for three and a half hours, provide the details for a picture-perfect artist's composite, and *not* recognize him? Chaos is the reign of ambiguity, and ambiguity in V-Ss' lives is the result of rapists' attempts to annihilate our social identity, our security, and our sense of self. An understanding of rape then should include all three perspectives—the SOA (Subjectivity, Objectivity, and Ambiguity) approach—and in my perspective, this approach demonstrates that the rapist confronts the victim with social death. V-Ss are physically functional, but we have had an experience that threatens our social identity and our belief and trust in ourselves and others. Without these social ingredients, there is no life. Luckily, in most cases, these are *attempts* by rapists to commit social murder, and luckily, V-Ss have the strength to reach the top of Mount Everest. Some day, maybe the people in this culture will help us.

Are we at war? This account stresses the torture of rape, the torture known by two-thirds to three-fourths of women and at least one-third of men. This account does not include the millions of cases of battered spouses/lovers and sexually harassed people. Nor does it mention the number of attempted rape victims or the fear of rape that all women accept on a daily basis. The rapist's response to my question, "Why are you here?" is evidence of a state of war: "You know." Yes, we are at war.

Although this chapter has ended, it is not the end of the readers' feelings. It is an author's responsibility not to leave his or her readers traumatized or angry. In the United States, most people tend to fall into one of two categories: abusers or abused. For the former, this chapter could instigate further violence; for the latter, this chapter could fuel past unresolved trauma. If this chapter contributes further to the trauma and abuse in our culture, it has not been successful. For that reason, I have included a postscript and anecdotes: the former to answer some questions; the latter, to relieve tension.

Postscript: It has been a six-year ordeal to find the rapist, overcome legal shenanigans ("loopholes"), counter the legal experts' view of error as always inadmissible in criminal proceedings, and confront scientific experts who support rapists through their "theories." As I finish these words, I am only weeks from testifying against the rapist. I have had to live with the memory of the rape attack: it was first emblazoned in my mind in neon lights by the rapist, and it has been turned on again and again by the people in the legal system who want me to remember each excruciating detail so that I can give an accurate description of my terror to the jurors. In addition, CBS's "48 Hours" has decided to film my legal roller-coaster ride. The filming has involved one to two days a month for one year. I have answered their questions, and my actions during pretrial hearings (and maybe the trial) have been recorded.

Anecdote: When I have previously written articles about horrors such as those presented here, most readers do not give me any response. This is probably because they do not know what to say. Therefore, I have provided below a number of possible responses: the first group includes comments to be avoided; the second group includes comments I and other writers would appreciate.

Unacceptable responses:

- Great article on *your rape*.[14]
- I loved reading about how horrifying it was.
- Now I know what rape is.
- How did you get that information?

Preferred responses:

- This is a heroic piece of writing.
- Your writing is insightful, clear, and appreciated.
- Thank you for having the courage to educate us.
- We all need to learn to take risks like you have, and I am willing now to speak up.

Best response:

- This is great, fantastic, outstanding. You must be equally great, fantastic, outstanding.

ACKNOWLEDGMENTS

I want to thank Carolyn Nordstrom for suggesting the title and for her very helpful editorial comments. I owe her a special debt of gratitude for her enthusiasm, understanding, and humor in supporting me through the writing and pretrial period. I want to thank Neni Panourgia for her comments and constant bibliographical references. Linda Ronald helped me clarify the craziness of rapists. Thank you.

NOTES

1. These quotes are from chapter 1 of my book in progress, *Raped Once, Raped Twice, and Raped a Third Time.*

2. I will use "V-S" for victim-survivor. "V" is for the victory that will happen for us someday; "S" is a pluralistic reminder of the multitude of people raped.

Most researchers and counselors argue that the person raped must be elevated from the status of victim to the status of survivor (Koss and Harvey 1991). While not disputing the victimization by the rapist, I suggest that victims are survivors during the attack. If treated as such, V-Ss would not have to overcome the stigma placed on them by those "supporting" them. In the discussion of the attack by the rapist, I use the term "victim" to emphasize the crime state of the person being raped.

3. Sanday (1990) notes how the fraternity brothers bragged about their actions against a victim during a fraternity party.

4. Sexual role and gender preference or orientation are not deterministic variables of people raped. Both men and women, more the latter, are attacked by rapists. Also, it is important that we choose our phrases carefully, and for that reason, the phrase "people raped" is important. It accentuates that we are persons first; rape is a horror that happened to us, but the attack does not define us.

5. Some personal accounts of rape are Katz 1984, Savage 1990, and Ziegenmeyer 1992.

6. Definitions stress lack of consent and use of force. MacKinnon (1982:532) underlines the point "without consent" for the definition of rape. The concept of violence is critical in the definitions of rape by Burgess and Holmstrom (1974) and Millett (1971). Sheffield (1987) likewise stresses the method of rapists, i.e., terror, as the crux of the definition of rape.

7. My three years of research in Olinalá, Guerrero, Mexico, on the influence of gender in the acquisition and expression of authority also included a study of a rape attack (C. Winkler 1987). This research demonstrated that this community leans toward the rape-free side, a concept suggested by Sanday (1981). After the attack, the people in the community immediately support the V-S and offered the rapist one option: murder. Instead, he exiled himself for life from the community and his family. Someone who had helped a rapist, now exiled, attempted to return in the middle of the night to see his dying parents. He escaped with several gunshot wounds and without seeing his parents. While it had been almost a decade since the rape, the people in the community still felt that he should have been killed for what he did.

8. The police knew, but did not tell me immediately, that I would not be able to identify the rapist, and identification is critical legal evidence. The private investigator's job was not to convict but to locate the rapist. DNA fingerprinting became legally available in the course of my long struggle to pursue the case with the

police (Lewis 1988). I want to thank Marvin Dickson and Louis Ferguson, private investigators, for finding the rapist.

9. After a heated confrontation with the district attorney and the chief assistant district attorney in March 1991 regarding dismissal of the case, part of my memory became available. The defendant and artist's composite are now identical to me. Connection of the multiple faces of the rapist in my memory to the night of the attack is still not available.

10. See research on psychological studies of rape trauma: Ellis 1983; Frank, Turner, and Duffy 1979; Holmes and St. Lawrence 1983.

11. See research on rape myths: Burt 1980; Feild 1978; Schwendinger and Schwendinger 1974; C. Winkler 1989.

12. My student Lisa Cole suggested this term and has given me permission to use it in my work.

13. I want to thank Tony Robben for his help in developing this discussion of ambiguity.

14. Note the wording in this phrase. I prefer that people do not say "my" case; it is *his,* the rapist's, case. It is not "my" rape; it is "*his*" rape.

REFERENCES

American Psychiatric Association
  1987   *Diagnostic and Statistical Manual of Mental Disorders.* 3d ed. rev. Washington, D.C.: American Psychiatric Association.
Barry, Kathleen
  1979   *Female Sexual Slavery.* New York: New York University Press.
Burgess, Ann Woldert, and Lynda L. Holmstrom
  1974   *Rape: Victims of Crisis.* Bowie, Md.: Prentice-Hall.
Burt, Martha R.
  1980   "Cultural Myths and Support for Rape." *Journal of Personality and Social Psychology* 38:217–230.
Ellis, Elizabeth M.
  1983   "A Review of Empirical Rape Research: Victim Reactions and Response to Treatment." *Clinical Psychology Review* 3:473–490.
Feild, Hubert S.
  1978   "Attitudes Toward Rape: A Comparative Analysis of Police, Rapists, Crisis Counselors, and Citizens." *Journal of Personality and Social Psychology* 36:156–179.
Frank, E., S. M. Turner, and F. Duffy
  1979   "Depressive Symptoms in Rape Victims." *Journal of Affective Disorders* 1:269–277.
Holmes, Martha, and J. S. St. Lawrence
  1983   "Treatment of Rape-induced Trauma." *Clinical Psychological Review* 3: 417–433.
Holmes, Karen A., and Joyce Williams
  1981   *Second Assault.* Westport, Conn.: Greenwood Press.

Holmstrom, Lynda L., and Ann W. Burgess
1978   *The Victim of Rape: Institutional Reactions.* New York: Wiley.
Katz, Judy H.
1984   *No Fairy Godmothers, No Magic Wands: The Healing Process After Rape.* Saratoga, Calif.: R and E Publishers.
Koss, Mary P., and Mary R. Harvey
1991   *The Rape Victim: Clinical and Community Interventions.* Newbury Park: Sage.
Lewis, Richi
1988   "DNA Fingerprints: Witness for the Prosecution." *Discover* (June):42–51.
MacKinnon, Catharine A.
1982   "Feminism, Marxism, Method, and the State: An Agenda for Theory." *Signs* 7(3):515–544.
Millett, Kate
1971   *The Prostitution Papers: A Candid Dialogue.* New York: Basic Books.
Panourgia, Neni
1992   "A Native Narrative." Paper presented at the 91st American Anthropological Association Meeting, San Francisco, California.
Sanday, Peggy R.
1981   "The Socio-Cultural Context of Rape." *Journal of Social Issues* 37(4):15–27.
1990   *Fraternity Gang Rape.* New York: New York University Press.
Savage, Audrey
1990   *Twice Raped.* Indianapolis: Book Weaver Co.
Scarry, Elaine
1985   *The Body in Pain: The Making and Unmaking of the World.* New York: Oxford University Press.
Schwendinger, J., and H. Schwendinger
1974   "Rape Myths: In Legal, Theoretical, and Everyday Practice." *Crime and Social Issues* 1:18–26.
Sheffield, Caroline J.
1987   "Sexual Terrorism: The Social Control of Women." In *Analyzing Gender: A Handbook of Social Science Research,* ed. B. B. Hess and M. M. Ferree, 171–189. Newbury Park: Sage.
Silverman, Martin G.
1972   "Ambiguation and Disambiguation in Field Work." In *Crossing Cultural Boundaries: The Anthropological Experience,* ed. Solon T. Kimball and James B. Watson. San Francisco: Chandler.
Taussig, Michael
1987   *Shamanism, Colonialism, and the Wild Man: A Study in Terror and Healing.* Chicago: University of Chicago Press.
1992   *The Nervous System.* New York: Routledge.
Warshaw, Robin
1988   *I Never Called It Rape.* New York: Harper and Row.

Weis, Kurt, and Sandra S. Borges

  1973   "Victimology and Rape: The Case of the Legitimate Victim." *Issues in Criminology* 8:71–115.

Winkler, Cathy

  1987   "Changing Power and Authority in Gender Roles." Ph.D. dissertation, Indiana University and Ann Arbor: University Microfilms.

  1989   "Myths about Rape or Prejudices about Rape: Defamiliarizing the Familiar." Paper presented at the 89th American Anthropological Association Meeting, Washington, D.C.

  1991   "Rape as Social Murder." *Anthropology Today* 1(3):12–14.

  1994*a*   "Rape Trauma: Contexts of Meaning." In *Embodiment of Knowledge,* ed. T. Csordas, 248–268. Cambridge: Cambridge University Press.

  1994*b*   "The Meaning Behind Rape Trauma: Rape Survivors' Personal Experiences." In *Many Mirrors: Body Image and Social Relations,* ed. Nicole Sault, 266–291. New Brunswick: Rutgers University Press.

  n.d.   *Raped Once, Raped Twice, and Raped a Third Time.* Newbury Park: Sage. Forthcoming.

Winkler, John J.

  1990   *Constraints of Desire.* New York: Routledge.

Ziegenmeyer, Nancy, with Larkin Warren

  1992   *Taking Back My Life.* New York: Summit Books.

Childhood's End: Bosnian Refugee in Croatia
(Photo: Maria Olujic)

The Croatian War Experience

Maria B. Olujic

In fall 1991, news reports stated that the Yugoslav [Serbian] navy had ships positioned up and down the Adriatic Sea, their warhead missiles pointing toward the coast. The cities of Zadar, Šibenik, Split, and Dubrovnik were being shelled. This is impossible, I thought at the time, while frantically trying to get in touch with relatives in Split to see if they were still alive. I found it incredible that anyone would want to destroy one of the most beautiful coasts in the world. It simply could not be true. Nobody expected this to happen. But it was true, and it is still happening. The shelling of Dubrovnik is an attack not just on Croatia but on the history of humankind. The old town of Split, enclosed by the walls of the Diocletian Palace, was built by Emperor Diocletianus in 33 B.C. as a summer residence. It survived the Roman, Venetian, and Turkish occupations. Various invaders wanted to own it, but they did not destroy it.

Soon the war was raging, and the daily news reports gave accounts of shelling, fighting, massacres, and the plight of the civilian populations, especially women, children, and the elderly. The damage reports were increasingly getting worse. All the international accounts said that the Yugoslav army was preventing a breakup of Yugoslavia. Neither Slovenes, nor Croats, nor Bosnians had thought that the Yugoslav army would use such force. The fighting had initially broken out when the Yugoslav army attacked Slovenia after its declaration of independence in June 1991. This war lasted less than one month. Immediately afterward, the Yugoslav army attacked different regions of Croatia. The level of violence was impossible to comprehend, even for those who had survived World War II. Yet many Croatians remained optimistic, believing the fighting would ease and the Serbs would stop their attacks. Croatians saw themselves as defending their own territory, their own homes.

Among Croatian-Americans, there was optimism that no matter how bad the current situation, the future would be brighter, because Yugoslavia would no longer exist and the Serbs would no longer have control. The Croats believed they were on their way to full independence, for Croatia was not only at war but in the process of transformation from a totalitarian Communist system into a democratic, market-oriented system. But it desperately needed help and know-how from the West. I was asked to organize and head the International Department in the Ministry of Science because of my training in the United States. As both an anthropologist and a Croatian-American, I was curious, and I also wanted to be a part of the historical process that was occurring. I saw this as an opportunity to be a participant observer in a high-conflict situation. However, I also wondered if I wanted this experience, which carried with it the risk of physical danger. Was my desire to help my people and my curiosity as an anthropologist strong enough to draw me to a war zone? My husband said, "If I were asked to go because of my job, I would not hesitate. I would go." I regarded this comment as a final blessing, and my decision to go was firm. My parents and friends could not talk me into postponing the departure until "things were safe." Once the date was set, my father, his face ashen, told me, "I know what you are doing, but I am not comfortable." My mother, however, tried to be practical. She insisted that I take with me a bullet-proof vest, a gas mask, and even a gun. She expected me to carry the gas mask with me and to wear the bullet-proof vest at all times, even while I slept.

I shrank away from both the gun and the bullet-proof vest, but then I thought she might be right; perhaps I ought to have the protective garment. So I stopped at an army surplus store and asked if they had a bullet-proof vest. The man behind the counter said, "You mean a flak jacket?" I replied, "I don't really know the difference . . . " He cut in and said, "A flak jacket is used to prevent a knife wound, and no, we don't deal with those because only two kinds of people buy them, the bad guys and the police." "Well, I'm neither of those," I muttered half to myself. He heard me and said, "Then what do you want it for?"

I could not tell him that I was an anthropologist who was going to war and that I was afraid, so I simply said, "I am going to Eastern Europe." He looked at me in disbelief and said, "Is it dangerous there? Do they have a lot of crime there?" "Yes," I said. He told me of another store that might carry the jackets. I went there, only to be directed to a third store. The area around the third store did not look safe, and the store had iron bars on its doors and windows. I passed by and sighed with relief when I saw a Closed sign posted on the door.

While driving home, I decided that taking anything with me for safety would be ridiculous. If I was going to get killed, a flak jacket was not going to help me. I have never touched a gun and am repulsed by the thought of handling one, not to mention using one. How could I convince my mother that all I really needed or wanted was a shortwave radio, a flashlight, and a waterproof sleeping bag in case I had to spend time in bomb shelters? I asked her to help me shop for these items, and she was finally convinced. However, the day before my departure, my mother gave me a going-away present, a gas mask. I could not refuse her this indulgence, even if I threw the thing into the garbage once I arrived in Zagreb, Croatia. As I packed my suitcase, I thought there must be a surplus of masks left over from the Gulf War, and I also remembered those Israelis in the bomb shelters during Saddam's SCUD attacks. Would I experience anything like that? What would it be like to be in such a situation?

TWO TRIPS, TWO REALITIES

On my way to war-torn Croatia, I thought of my first return there after several years in the United States. That trip was in the midseventies when I took a short summer vacation during a school break. In the warm glow of the sunset on a scorching summer day, I was picking blackberries by a dusty road adjacent to my father's house. From a distance, I could see a white car piled high with suitcases on its roof. Moving at a snail's pace, the car pulled up and stopped next to me. An elderly passenger, clearly a returning emigrant, stepped out of the car, a suit jacket thrown over his forearm. Without speaking, he approached and wrenched a foot-long branch from the blackberry bush and began chewing on it, including thorns and unripe berries. I looked at him in bewilderment, thinking that he would choke on the sharp thorns. In a quick sweeping glance, I looked at the other three people in the car. No one said anything. The man slowly walked back to the car and got in. As the car left, all I could see was the cloud of dust particles shimmering in the afternoon sun.

At that moment I understood what it meant to return home. I have asked other Croatians to interpret the meaning of what I had observed. The blackberry symbolized the sweet return, the reuniting, and the thorns conveyed the feeling of suffering, the anguish of a foreign place—of not belonging to one's own, of being apart. Pushing the metaphor further, the bush may have represented the meager livelihood of this desolate place and what life is about: identity and belonging.

Now, on my way to Croatia, fifteen years later, I could not help but compare my earlier experience with the one on which I was about to embark.

BRIEF HISTORY AND POLITICAL INTRODUCTION

To fully understand the current situation, it is necessary to step back and look at the historical context. Anyone who visited the former Yugoslavia would have been intrigued by the blend of traditional and modern—themes that affect the question of power and dominance. The nation-state called Yugoslavia was at the same time backward and progressive. The main reason for this dichotomy may be geographic. The former nation-state was located on the Balkan Peninsula, a crossroads between the West and the East. There were always several neighbors claiming the peninsula, and every occupying power had to fight rivals. Yet the fights seldom brought decisive victors, and the frontiers between great powers and spheres of influence ran across the middle of the peninsula. This fault line is exactly where today's war, which has been termed the worst conflict since World War II, is occurring. Croatia, Slovenia, Bosnia-Hercegovina, and the region of Vojvodina belonged to the Austro-Hungarian monarchy, whereas Serbia, Montenegro, and Macedonia were in the Ottoman Empire.

With the creation of the "first Yugoslavia" in 1918, after World War I, East and West were combined in the same state. The South Slavs, with their Austrian imprint, were markedly different from those who had been under Turkish domination. They were also different from the Dinaric freedom fighters (known as *hajduci* and *uskoci*) situated along the Dinaric mountain range, which stretches along the Adriatic Coast. The uniting of these elements after centuries of estrangement made life difficult in the "first Yugoslavia." Cultural differences influenced political realities. According to Vera Stein Erlich (1966:18), "the divisive tendencies seemed to grow stronger than the unifying ones, and the regional peculiarities, developed under Eastern and Western influences, seemed to become even more extreme than before."

The "first Yugoslavia" was referred to by non-Serbs as the "prison of nations" (*tamnica naroda*) because a rigid system of centralism established in Belgrade made possible the hegemony of Serbian ruling groups, who regarded Yugoslavia as an expansion of Serbia. Bitter fighting among the various peoples who made up the "first Yugoslavia" occurred during World War II. However, the regions were once again reunited at the end of World War II (1945), and the "second Yugoslavia" was resurrected under the Communist leadership of Marshal Tito.

The "second Yugoslavia" was based on "fraternity and unity" (*bratstvo i jedinstvo*), and the Communists in power referred to World War II as a "fratricidal war." Post–World War II Yugoslavia was famous for various social experiments. The best known were "self-managing socialism," "worker's self-management," and the "nonalignment" (nonaligned nation movement led by Tito), by which Tito creatively manipulated both the East and the West. All of these contained and maintained the nation-state called Yugoslavia. (In both of these Yugoslavias, the rule of Belgrade was forced on the non-Serbian peoples and nations. On the eve of war in 1991, Serbs comprised more than 70 percent of the officer corps of the "Yugoslav People's Army.")

After Tito's death in 1980, the economy of the country worsened and the foreign debt increased exponentially. This culminated in the rise of the Serbian leader Slobodan Milošević in 1988. Under his direction, Serbia annexed two autonomous regions of Kosovo and Vojvodina and ousted the government of Montenegro by means of a so-called antibureaucratic revolution. It became clear to all the republics that Serbia intended to seize control of non-Serbian territories under the pretext of building a "third Yugoslavia," or as non-Serbians referred to it, "Serboslavia." It was at this point that the Communists in both Croatia and Slovenia allowed multiparty elections because they were afraid of losing their own power to the Serbs.

Thus it is not surprising that at the end of 1990 and at the beginning of 1991, the *New York Times* published several CIA reports stating that the Yugoslav territories were going to experience a major conflict that would spill over their borders. (This was the first warning.) However, only two months earlier (in September 1990), a small Croatian delegation headed by Croatian President Franjo Tudjman had visited with several U.S. officials, including President George Bush. According to one member of the Croatian delegation, this was the first missed opportunity for preventing the current tragic war in the Balkans.

> Our purpose was to present draft documents on a proposed alliance of Yugo-slav states, aimed at establishing a peaceful, nonviolent transformation from the old, Bolshevik-style Yugoslav federation to a new confederation of sovereign states. However, Scowcroft [National Security Adviser] and other U.S. administration members would not support our peaceful aims. They wanted to preserve the unity of federal Yugoslavia seemingly at any cost. In fact, [President Franjo] Tudjman pleaded with Scowcroft for his support in order to avert certain war. He refused and his refusal was logically consistent not only with Secretary of State James Baker's subsequent visit to Belgrade [in June 1991] but also with the U.S. government's slow movement toward recognition of the independence of Slovenia, Croatia and Bosnia and Herzegovina. (Letica 1992:5)

BLURRING OF DIFFERENCES

After all attempts to create a confederation failed, two former republics, Slovenia and Croatia, declared independence based on referendums in both republics overwhelmingly favoring independence (more than 94 percent voted in favor of independence in Croatia). Before the two republics seceded (on June 25, 1991), U.S. Secretary of State James Baker visited Belgrade and assured the Communist government that the United States would support them in keeping Yugoslavia together. In fact, when the war was well under way in Croatia, Baker, addressing the UN General

Assembly in fall 1991, "thanked" Serbia and said that he "appreciated Serbia's efforts in trying to maintain Yugoslavia intact."

Did or did not Yugoslavia exist at that time? Opposing views or definitions of Yugoslavia emerged in the domestic and international communities. In the minds of most of the international community, Yugoslavia did indeed continue to exist until the beginning of 1992. In the minds of Croats and Slovenes, who had voted in free elections to secede, Yugoslavia had ceased to exist in June 1991. In any case, both Slovenia and Croatia were referred to in the U.S. press at the time as "rebel" or "breakaway republics."

While the West continued to oppose the breakup of Yugoslavia, the following issues remained blurred: Was this an "ethnic war"/"civil war" or a "war of aggression"? Calling the conflict the "Yugoslav crisis," the "powder keg of the Balkans," the "Balkan quagmire," and the result of "centuries-old hatreds" promoted the idea of an ethnic war. The jargon used in both the media and the political arenas not only led to further confusion but also encouraged noninvolvement and nonrecognition of the national differences by both the United States and Europe.

Another problem was that the distinction between the aggressor and the victim was unclear to the international community. In the early stages of the war, the U.S. and European media distorted the reality of the war—first by ignoring it, then by downplaying it as a primitive, tribal conflict. Stories that might have educated people about this conflict early on did not get media space, and according to one previously pro-Serbian journalist, Carrol Williams, the East European bureau chief for the *Los Angeles Times,* "If the world had gotten the picture earlier that what happened in Croatia was a one-sided war of aggression, action might have been taken to prevent the spread into Bosnia" (cited by Ricchiardi 1992:21).

George Kenney, who in August 1992 resigned from the State Department to protest the Bush administration's failure to address the genocide in Croatia and Bosnia-Hercegovina, had this to say on the aggressor/victim issue:

> Denying the overwhelming preponderance of evidence that Serbia was responsible for the conflict, senior officers (at the State Department) took every opportunity to find fault with Croatian and Bosnian efforts to defend themselves. (Kenney 1992:35)

To identify who was the aggressor and who the victim, European Community observers, dressed in neutral white jumpsuits and blue armbands with a circle of twelve golden stars, were sent in as referees. Because of their uniforms, these observers were referred to by the Croatian children as "ice cream men." The connotation of the name might have suggested that better days were ahead, but with the rupture of each cease-fire, the war escalated and the number of civilian casualties increased exponentially. Since the beginning of war in Croatia, there had been on the average one peace conference every twelve days. During the peak of Serbian aggression, the following message was sent to a Croatian-American by an American journalist who was in Croatia at the end of September 1991:

> I haven't gotten my ass blown off yet, though not through any lack of effort on the part of the Serbians and the Yugoslav Army! The cease-fire that is reported to be holding despite some "minor skirmishes" has resulted in the biggest jet bombing of the war, damaging or destroying most of central Vinkovci and sending civilians to the hospital or morgue. Serbian snipers are even firing into hospitals.[1]

THE ETHNOGRAPHER IN THE WAR SITUATION

Soon after this message, realizing that I could not wait until the situation improved, in December 1991, during the peak of war, I left for Croatia. I had a standing invitation from the Croatian Ministry of Science to be the deputy minister in order to help them organize and head an International Department. As an anthropologist and as a Croatian-American, I saw this as an opportunity not just to witness but to be a part of history in the making: the formation of new nations in the post–cold war era.

Once I accepted the fact that I was going into a war zone, I accepted that reality to be my living situation. When I first arrived, there were no flights into Zagreb so I had to be picked up in Graz, Austria. It was after midnight and I had to drive across several borders to enter into Croatia. As I approached the Croatian border, the sky was pitch black and the air was very cold and still. I could see the dark outlines of the trees against the sky, and for a moment I thought, I could be attacked from anywhere. Yet at this point, I lost my fear.

In retrospect, I think surrendering my fear was a coping mechanism, because it is impossible to live with fear on a daily basis and continue to function. Even during the air raids or general emergency alerts in gloomy basements and semidark cellars, I tried to record my reality and the reality of the people around me (i.e., talked with people, took notes, shared my shortwave radio). The first time that Zagreb, the capital of Croatia, sounded the general emergency alert, I was in a cellar with fellow residents of Zagreb. They told me, "This is much worse than an air raid because the general alert means that they [Serbs] are using ground-to-ground missiles." And sure enough, a few minutes later on my shortwave radio I heard that Frog 7 missiles had been launched and some of them had hit the outskirts of Zagreb.

Is this the end? I thought. I happened to be in a cellar across from the famous Zagreb cathedral, which was high on the target list. As I looked around, people were sitting quietly without apparent distress; no one was crying or shouting. One man was rocking his six-month-old baby on his knee and telling her, "My little girl, you are growing up like a mushroom in this subterranean cellar." It was during such scenes that I began to ask questions not as a Croatian-American or an anthropologist but as a human being: "Why is this happening?" "How does a person cope with this?"

WAR RITUALS/RITUALS OF COPING

I witnessed strategies of coping with the fear through collective rituals on different levels (e.g., public gatherings in town squares as well as funerals of children and soldiers). Croatian ethnologists have written extensively on coping strategies in a war situation (Povrzanović 1992, 1993). The clearest affirmation of collective ritual on the national level occurred on January 15, 1992, when Croatia was internationally recognized. There was an all-night collective celebration in Zagreb during which traditional hierarchical boundaries dissolved. For the first time since his election, President Tudjman mingled with the people milling about in the main square. Later that night, a great "celebration" highlighting the struggle for independence occurred in the Croatian National Theater in Zagreb. During the event various cultural and national dramatic pieces were performed on stage. These offerings ranged from poetry readings and ethnic dancing to music by rock groups and new music groups formed by soldiers fighting on the front lines. One performance that stood out for me and the people sitting around me was a poem recited by its author, Stjepo Mijović-Kočan. The poem illustrates how the experience and meaning of war affects not just the soldiers, the wounded, and the refugees but the entire culture.

Even I
who shied away from every violence
who withdrew from medical school
because I could not cut into human flesh
even if it was dead
I who offended my mother
because I refused to kill one of her chickens
that she was fattening up for me
the only riches she possessed
when I returned for a visit from distant Zagreb
I who was writing my useless verses
yearning for tenderness, love, fraternity and reconciliation
for every human being and for flowers and for the animals
in front of the television tonight I sincerely rejoiced
when I saw that my brave Dalmatians
struck down those airplanes of the yugo-serbo-occupying enemy

above the gentle Adriatic near Šibenik
who like hundreds of others have showered with bombs
cities, villages, children, and even funerals
of my humiliated, wounded, worn-out, and tortured homeland Croatia
my heart stopped short in my throat
"both are shot, both are down" ["oba, oba"]
I applauded and jumped
not even thinking about the person who perished in the airplane.[2]

Even before I heard this poem, I had heard children and adults in private and public places yell "*oba, oba*" (both, both). When two Serbian airplanes were struck down in fall 1991, the entire event was filmed on video and shown on local and international news. The two airplanes were flying close to each other, and one of them was struck with a stinger. Sounds of rejoicing and "we got one" could be heard. Then the second airplane was struck and a Croatian soldier yelled, "*oba, oba*" (meaning that both were hit). The expression "both, both" has come to mean unbelievable good luck or good fortune and has entered into the daily discourse of the people.

The planes, among the first to be shot down, were the same ones that had been showering bombs for days before. War and the effects of war run deep through the culture. In such circumstances, even the person who detests violence, like the speaker in Kočan's poem, finds it impossible to remain neutral.

Perhaps it is because of this tolerance to violence that the world has stood silently by watching the atrocities labeled the "worst since World War II." It is not surprising then that the violence has become so virulent. We begin to accept what initially was "brutal" as "normal."

Communal experience of war and fear occurred during my first air raid, only a couple of days after my return to Zagreb. Along with the director of personnel from the Ministry of Science, I was waiting in a long line at the Ministry of Interior (Police Station) to obtain an identification card. Suddenly and without much commotion the enormous room emptied almost completely. I looked at my colleague and uttered, "What did we do to deserve no lines?" Her eyes opened wide and she said, "We have an air raid." I replied, "Are you sure? I did not hear a siren. Are you sure?" She said, "Yes, let's go across the street to the Ministry of Science because it will be less crowded in our bomb shelter."

After a couple of minutes in the basement of the Ministry of Science, I assessed my surroundings as well as the people whom I barely had a chance to meet. After several minutes the minister walked through the door of the bomb shelter and said, "Oh, here you are, I am looking for you." I thought, he must be crazy, he can't possibly ask me now to do anything because I am not budging outside of this shelter until this is over, if it is ever over.

He walked up to me, shook my hand, and said, "Congratulations, now you are one of us!" Thinking of that exchange, I cannot help but see it as a ritual of initiation—into the group and into the war context. Croatian friends and colleagues have told me, "My stomach was tied in a knot during the first air raid; then once the bombs began to fall, I was less afraid than when I was waiting for them." I am sorry to say that to this day, I am not as brave as they are. Nevertheless, the group cohesiveness during the peak of the war gave cultural coherence and provided yet another coping strategy in everyday life in wartime (Povrzanović 1993).

THE PERSONAL EXPERIENCE OF ATROCITY

In one of the coastal hotels, women from the so-called temporarily occupied villages of the Dalmatian hinterland were gathered. Outside it was cold, and dusk was approaching. In the darkened room, the women were sitting on chairs that had been nailed against the wall, talking quietly and knitting.[3] Most of them were dressed in black, even the younger ones (women who were widowed in World War II wear black to this day).

The topic of their conversation, it did not matter. Over two years had passed since these women's homes had been "temporarily" occupied, and they had no new place of belonging. The space in which they had known how to live and survive had been taken away from them. For them, the present was just a wait. The loneliness and the fear of returning to their ruined (devastated) homes and their broken lives was their primary concern. "If we die, what will happen to our bodies?" one woman asked me. (It is the custom in the Dalmatian hinterland, as in other parts of the Mediterranean, to have one's funeral clothes all picked out, neatly folded, and stored in a hope chest.) As they waited in the semidark hotel hall, sitting on chairs and knitting the pieces of their broken lives, they were uneasy and uncertain about their road to death. They will remain there despite the Council of Security and Cooperation in Geneva, the United Nations, and all the bilateral and multilateral negotiations. The importance of home to them cannot be underestimated: one woman told me that they had to "touch the threshold once again" to be sane.

Throughout Croatia, loss of home and land is synonymous with the loss of identity. Once the land is lost, identity and self-esteem are also lost. The psychological relationship to the land is a fundamental trait in the whole conscious and subconscious behavior of the Croatian peasant. Land is considered sacred; its importance is seen in the plethora of linguistic terms that differentiate land by use, size of the field, how the soil is cultivated, and overall quality (Olujic 1991). During the war, parts of eastern Croatia, called Slavonia, have fallen to the Serbs. After the fall of Vukovar (a city in Slavonia), a song called "Do Not Touch My Fields Because I Will

Return" became so popular that it is now played during all social occasions, family gatherings, and weddings. The fertile fields of Slavonia, although occupied, are a symbol of identity for the people who are displaced. The following verse is an excerpt from a poem written by Ankica Petričević-Kozarac, a refugee woman from Vukovar.

> We have no soil and no grain
> No one is concerned about our pain
> We have no longer our beautiful costumes
> That our grandmothers have woven
> There are no more young tamburitza men
> There are no more daughters-in-law.[4]

Although the Western media refer to the war criminals as "Mr. Milošević," or "Mr. Karadžić," the victims, homeless old refugee women like those described in Kozarac's poem, remain a nameless, faceless group with no identity. Although they have lost their self-esteem, each one knows herself, her own story, her own personal experience. If they had been perceived as individuals from the beginning, one of them told me, perhaps the West would have been moved to intervene at that time: "If they had seen who we really are in pictures of the war, if they had valued us as people, the world would have much less of a headache with us now."

According to the latest reporting trend, a family's story is complete only when a child is wounded and the woman raped and pregnant. But this is not a suitable completion to survivors. How can a man react to the rape of his wife in a culture in which female honor depends on chastity? If he believes that she had sex with another, whether by force or not, a man must reject his wife to salvage his male pride. To whom will the woman be able to tell her story? To no one. If she was lucky and did not get pregnant, she will bury her story inside herself to spare her family the dishonor. Anything that forces her to be public will be her further tragedy. The fact that some women have committed suicide after giving their stories to Western journalists attests to this shocking situation. Being public further stigmatizes and traumatizes the victim. A woman's silence is her way of protecting her family, no matter what the emotional cost to herself. As researchers or reporters, we will go on to other types of stories as fads change, but the women will live their lives branded by the stigma of rape.

A woman activist in an informal women's group, speaking on the Zagreb radio, stated that women who are victims of rape have to be recognized as heroes by the culture so they can be free to tell everything. Unfortunately, this is not the case. In fact, husbands have killed or abandoned their wives when they learned the truth, and young unmarried women have been disowned by their families. Women of all ages are kept from suicide only by sedatives, and others have been driven crazy by their experiences and the pressure on them to keep silent.

Stories of rape have come predominantly from women who were forced by their experience to choose isolation. Almost all have come from divorced women, widows, or unmarried women who do not have to contend with outraged husbands or other family members. The following testimony from such an unmarried woman reflects the pain of these family reactions.

> A few days after my release from a concentration camp I received an affidavit of support from Germany, so I came to Zagreb. I stayed in Zagreb and underwent one medical examination. That was a gynecological exam because only a friend knew all that has happened to me, and she gave me a telephone number I could call. The lesions on my thighs were getting worse. They had become infected, and I had to see a doctor because of that as well. Because of all the fear I did not tell the doctor what was really the matter with me. After one and a half months the lesions on my leg had healed, but even now I have two scars. After a couple of days in Zagreb my uncle came to pick me up. Immediately after greeting me, he told me that he would prefer to kill me now. Because of his rudeness I did not tell my family about anything that happened to me. Even so, after twenty days they kicked me out.

Today this woman is on welfare, has psychiatric problems, and is looking for a job, but she is afraid of contacts with people. She was brought up in a culture in which rape is so shameful that she could not even tell a physician the real cause of her condition. She could talk about her problems only with friends who had experienced the same aggression. Her life and her suffering are more than just a transient experience.

Reporters put great pressure on the women not only to tell their stories but to identify themselves publicly. They offer to pay them DM 200 for their stories alone and up to DM 5,000 or more if they consent to be identified. For refugee women, homeless, unable to work, and rejected by their families, these are unbearable temptations.

By consenting to participate in the currently popular war coverage, these women are raped again. Their shocking tales of survival thrill readers and television viewers, and we use them for our own purposes. For the reporters, this is just another war, in a series of wars, but the life these women describe is the only life they have. A woman who survived the concentration camp said, "Once again I feel like an object, but now in different hands. They are stirring up the wounds in my soul. Our tragedies are their stepping-stones [ladders] in their careers."

I share these stories because there is a level of human understanding that transcends national boundaries and because the stories are "truths" or "partial truths" of the war mosaic (Clifford and Marcus 1986).

Nevertheless, the question remains, how does one depict war without objectifying the people?

Ironically, the systematic way in which sexual atrocities are committed against victims attests to the fact of the objectifying of people as political tools. There is evidence that Serbian soldiers are coerced into committing sexual atrocities (*New York Times,* 9 January 1993 and 27 November 1992; European Community Investigation Mission 1992; *Die Welt,* 1 October 1992). Women victims range in age from six to eighty. Attempts to rape women in front of male family members point to rape as a means of humiliating men. In addition, there is a deliberate attempt to impregnate women and hold them as prisoners until it is too late to abort. The raped women and their children become constant reminders of suppression and domination of violence. The strongest evidence that rapes are committed for political reasons comes from the victims themselves. Numerous testimonies from raped women reveal that they were told by the aggressors, "You are going to have a *chetnik* [Serbian extremist] baby, and we will wipe out the Muslim blood." Occupying a woman's uterus is synonymous with occupying territory. Rape is used to pollute and dilute the bloodline. In the Balkans, *soil* and *blood* are metaphors for male honor. If a man cannot control them, he has no honor. Through the use of rape in war, armies can violate not only the territory (soil) but the bloodlines of their enemies, exacerbating the humiliation of loss.

The political uses of rape have changed as the war progresses. Although the first rapes occurred during 1991 in Croatia, the Croatian government kept very quiet about the whole matter. In spring 1992, I was told by a gynecologist at a teaching hospital in Croatia that an *ethics committee* in Croatia was discussing the cases of Croatian women who were pregnant and could not abort their fetuses because they were "too far into the pregnancy." This information was kept a *private secret,* away from the press. When the same atrocities occurred in Bosnia-Hercegovina, albeit on a greater scale, the matter became a *public secret.* Why the difference of treatment? Is it because the atrocities occurred on a much larger scale in Bosnia-Hercegovina than in Croatia? Or is it that Muslim women are more valued in Bosnia than Christian women in Croatia? The answers are not as simple as they may first appear.

During the war in Croatia, the rape of Croatian women symbolized the castration of Croatian men by the Serb forces. There is an expression in the Croatian language that means that the men were feminized, made weaker (*napraviti pizdu od muškarca*—"to make a pussy out of a man"). In fact, when the Serb forces burned and pillaged the villages around Dubrovnik, they left signs all over the ruined houses which read, "*Gdje ste sada Ustaške pičke?*" (Where are you now Ustasha pussies? Ustasha were Croatian extremists during World War II.) Thus keeping quiet about the rapes of

Croatian women meant that the Croatian men saved their honor and their face, for public admission would be an admission of weakness.

Although both Croatian and Muslim women were raped in Bosnia, the majority of the victims were Muslim. The sheer scale of the violence against women made it impossible to hide the atrocities. In fact, the Bosnian government has tried to benefit politically from the aggression. Women who have been victims of mass rapes in Bosnian *rape camps* have become bargaining tools of the Bosnian government: they have been used to entice or persuade the West to intervene militarily.

THE REACTION OF THE WEST: WAR AS FAD

There is often a delay and distance between the time an atrocity occurs and the time it is reported in the Western media. Selective reporting and the distance from events shape the image of and reaction to atrocities of war. Reporting is itself shaped by fads or fashions as reporters respond to market pressures such as television ratings and newspaper sales. Viewers and readers in the West follow the same hierarchy and learn to accept this process of *normalization* as violence escalates in sync with routinization.

The *progression of violence* can be described as follows: first there were massacres and expulsion of people; after that churches and cultural monuments were bombed and destroyed; then domestic animals were slaughtered; and then the children, first Croatian, then Bosnian children. I was told about cows whose living skin was carved with Serbian logos, also of domestic pigs eating the bodies of killed children in burned villages. Then came the floods of refugee stories, followed by accounts of life in concentration camps, starvation, and tortures, all in the name of "ethnic cleansing." And now, stories of mass rapes of women are in fashion. As violence escalates, events that initially appeared to be brutal become normal. The raped women were victims before attention from the West, and they will continue to be victims even after war rapes become unfashionable in the foreign press. While on the one hand, media attention helps to pressure politicians into taking action, on the other, women are further victimized by their objectification under scrutiny. Several journalists visited a group of thirty-eight women who were located in one refugee center near Zagreb. After the journalists took their pictures and recorded their stories, seven of the women who had survived the worst aggression and violence committed suicide. The women became "cases." The Western journalists were helping the women to relive their stories but did not prepare the women for the trauma that often accompanies the telling.

Recorders of human suffering should keep several issues in mind when collecting such stories. The first is the traumatic nature of the experiences and the pain of repeating the stories. Can a man easily talk about his life in the concentration camp, about his mother who was raped and killed, about the same fate of his baby sister, about a burned house or abandoned animals, or about pigs eating dead human flesh?

Second, social scientists, going into high-conflict areas, need to be concerned not just with objectivity but with respondents' reliability and thus with the reliability of collected data. The relationship between the interviewer and the victim-informant is crucial. For example, will the victim give every detail of his or her testimony to the Red Cross official, or to any other agency if the interviewer is known to be or might be a Serb?

The reliability of the collected data is closely related to the issue of confidentiality and personal safety when so many are still missing or held prisoner. Informants worry that their relatives will be harmed if their witness to the atrocities they have experienced is broadcast. In addition, how much will the victims' stories be shaped by researchers' and reporters' response to what is currently in fashion, and how much will come out of the victims' need to communicate? If they agree to give testimony, what will they talk about? Will that also be decided by what is in fashion?

Media and journalists are not the only ones who are influenced by fashion. We, the social scientists, the gatherers and recorders of human affliction, are also influenced. We may not be concerned about whether our story will be published on the front pages of leading newspapers, but we care about status and academic position. According to Michel Foucault (1977), all institutions "normalize" or allow for individual differences on a preestablished continuum. Thus they recognize the differences so as to "homogenize" them. Are these institutions (i.e., media, academia) establishing the hierarchy and normalization of violence in the same way? Are individuals who are affected by war only important inasmuch as their "story" or "case" is concerned? By "observing" and "recording" as if in a panopticon, researchers and reporters become a one-way mirror through which the power and domination are visible, yet unverifiable.

MAKING SENSE OF CHAOS: INTERPRETATION OF VIOLENCE

As a Western-trained anthropologist and also a native Croatian, I see conflicting perspectives on the violence. A partial explanation for the unimaginable atrocities lies in the Serbian war victory. According to Carrol Williams, the government-controlled Serbian media was setting the stage even before the fighting started.

> There has been a brainwashing in Serbia for the last three to five years. The
> Serbian media, in particular, have demonized their ethnic enemies the same

way Joseph Goebbels, the Nazi propaganda chief, demonized the Jews in World War II. The propaganda lowered the victims, the Muslims and Croats, to something subhuman so it was no longer a crime to rub them out. (Ricchiardi 1992:21)

Another explanation for such intense violence lies in the specific emic meaning of aggression and dominance. This point is best illustrated by the war rapes. As noted earlier, the experience and the meaning of sexual coercion is played out and manipulated for political gain on both sides. Women are the primary victims of rape, but their tragedy is manipulated by men on both sides. The enemy uses women as a weapon against their own men, who must simultaneously try to protect them while guarding themselves against the shame that rape brings. Thus beneath the discourse about the immoral and destructive behavior toward women lies a repressed realization of the political and moral significance to their men. When both warring parties share the same cultural meanings, rape affects not only the individual but the entire family, community, and nation.

The experience and the meaning of war can be viewed and summarized on three levels: individual, sociocultural, and historical. The individual level is represented by the people who are the targets of the war—soldiers, civilians, families, and kin groups. The sociocultural level comprises the practice of urbanocide, environmental destruction (ecocide), and the destruction of entire peoples (genocide) through "ethnic cleansing" and mass rapes. The historical level consists not only of the actual events but also of the complicating interpretations of events used as propaganda by the various sides. Finally, the experiences of war can be seen through rituals that pervade not only individual lives but also the entire culture. The writing and reciting of war poetry, the "independence ritual," and the initiation ritual during air raids are examples of this phenomenon.

The following story illustrates my conflict as both insider and outsider. I went to a little fast-food restaurant that is known for excellent *ćevapčići* (rolled ground meat in the shape of small sausages), which is eaten with pita bread. The place was packed and there was nowhere to sit. I looked around and saw three young Croatian men in camouflage uniform and black army boots. I went to their table and asked, "Would you mind if I share your table?" From the start our conversation was strained. When I asked if they were in the army, they thought I was being sarcastic. As I heard snippets of their conversation, I almost choked on my food. "He was sent out with only 200 bullets." "I select with whom I go out on the front line." Hearing such remarks, I felt inadequate and almost guilty about my earlier question, which was not meant as an insult or as a sarcastic comment but was perceived as such. I had to hold back tears as I thought of their sacrifices. Pictures of refugee children whom I met on several occasions in a camp outside of Zagreb flashed in front of my eyes. At the same time I thought of my family left behind in California and the Croatians outside of Croatia. I thought of my return to war-torn Croatia a few days before Christmas. When I apologized to them for my earlier remark, explaining that I had just arrived from California, they realized I was in fact no longer a native and they began to warm up to me.

They said that they had come to the fast-food place before the war. The little house was a memory of lost peace, a symbol of carefree life. I asked them, "What will happen to the lost Croatian territory? Are we going to get it back? Why don't we go on the offensive?" One of them replied, "We cannot attack because we would be like them [Serbs]. We value human life. It means something to us."

During this brief exchange, I was struck by the realization that these young men were here for only a few minutes, after which they would return to the front. Why? I kept asking myself silently. Why are they going, why did I come here? I knew that my situation and theirs were not the same. And exactly because of that I could not hold back the tears any longer. The tears rolled down my face in front of these strangers with whom I felt a sense of belonging and separation. As my tears fell, all three men became quiet. One of them said, "Do not worry, you will see your family soon. We will all be okay and we will all return [alive]." I could not explain my dilemma because of the gulf between us. The young men left for the front, and I went to a wake for the European Community observers in the cathedral.

Four coffins draped with blue flags with a ring of golden stars were lined up in the center of the cathedral (One is missing, I thought. Which one? Probably the French officer's body was returned to his homeland; the four Italians were here). On either side of the coffins, four men dressed all in white, a blue band with the same golden ring of stars tied below their left shoulders, stood facing the altar. I moved closer to look at their faces. They were solemn, full of emotion. What were they thinking? Were they asking themselves the same questions I contemplated? Outside the cathedral a priest friend told me, "The deaths of these five observers will mean more to Europe and the whole world, more than all of the deaths of the thousands of Croatians thus far."

In closing, I find myself responding to the violence in three ways. First, as a Croatian, I am expected, because of my ancestry and my history, to have a particular allegiance in this conflict, and in many ways, I do. Second, as a human being, I cannot justify or simply observe and record atrocities on both sides. I realize that war naturally implies that two or more parties are involved. I think we all have an aversion to human suffering, and I am horrified by the lack of international concern about the genocide and the "ethnic cleansing" that is occurring on the ground. Third, and most important for my purpose here, I must examine my role as an anthropologist who is ostensibly trained to have an objective stand—to record what is happening, to observe. However, our method in ethnography is participant observation, but in a high-conflict situation, how does one participate in human suffering and violence?

We need to see these people in all of their humanity. We need to search our own motives in collecting and reporting their reality. A poster of a Vukovar survivor with the statement "*Nikog ne bole Vaše rane*" (Your pain is felt by no one) reminds us that our task is a never-ending struggle with no easy answers. When we are dealing with violence and human suffering, this struggle is even more intensified.

ACKNOWLEDGMENTS

I am greatly indebted to the editors, Carolyn Nordstrom and Tony Robben, for their comments and their stimulating discussions of this chapter. I am particularly grateful for the encouragement and support warmly extended to me by Carolyn Nordstrom. In addition, I sincerely appreciate the support from Andrea Wiley, Linda-Anne Rebhun, and my wonderful mentor and colleague, Gene Hammel. Finally, I am indebted to the Harry Frank Guggenheim Foundation for the generous grant without which much of this chapter would not have been possible. But I do not hold any of these individuals or institutions responsible for the views expressed here.

NOTES

1. An excerpt from a letter sent to me by an American journalist.

2. "*Oba, Oba,*" by Stjepo Mijović-Kočan, a prominent Croatian writer, in 1991. My translation.

3. It was the practice during the Communist regime to nail chairs to walls. This was a means of enforcing order: people were unable to sit in a circle.

4. Excerpt from the poem "Refugees" (*Prognanici*), by Ankica Petričević-Kozarac. My translation.

REFERENCES

Clifford, James, and George Marcus
    1986   *Writing Culture: The Poetics and Politics of Ethnography*. Berkeley, Los Angeles, and London: University of California Press.

Die Welt
    1992   "Serbs Rape on Order of Commanders." Translation. 1 October, front page.

European Community Investigation Mission into the Treatment of Muslim Women
in the Former Yugoslavia

1992   Report issued by European Community Investigation Mission into
         the Treatment of Muslim Women in the Former Yugoslavia, 18–24
         December.

Foucault, Michel

1977   *Discipline and Punish: The Birth of the Prison.* New York: Pantheon.

Kenney, George

1992   "See No Evil, Make No Policy." *Washington Monthly* (November): 33–35.

Letica, Slaven

1992   "Missed Opportunity." *Newsweek,* 30 November 1992, 5.

New York Times

1992   "A Killer's Tale: One Serbian Fighter Leaves Trail of Brutality." 27 No-
         vember, front page.

1993   "European Inquiry Says Serbs' Forces Have Raped 20,000." 9 January,
         front page.

Olujic, Maria B.

1991   "People on the Move: Migration History of a Peasant Croatian Com-
         munity." Ph.D. dissertation, University of California, Berkeley.

Povrzanović, Maja

1992   "Etnologija rata: Pisanje bez suza?" (Ethnology of War: Writing With-
         out Tears?) *Etnološka Tribina* 15:61–79.

1993   "Culture and Fear: Everyday Life in Wartime." In *Fear, Death and Re-
         sistance: An Ethnography of War, Croatia 1991–1992,* ed. Lada Èale
         Feldman, Ines Prica, and Reana Senjković, 119–150. Zagreb: Matrix
         Croatica.

Ricchiardi, Sherry

1992   "Covering Carnage in the Balkans." *Washington Journalism Review*
         (November): 18–23.

Stein Erlich, Vera

1966   *Family in Transition: A Study of Three Hundred Yugoslav Families.* Prince-
         ton: Princeton University Press.

The Face of Joseba Zulaika
(Photo: Iñak Insausti)

The Anthropologist as Terrorist

Joseba Zulaika

During the early 1980s, I did fieldwork on Basque political violence in my natal village of Itziar. Initially, I tried to study the phenomenon in the town of Gernika, that Picassoesque symbol of military terror, but I soon found out that staying at home with my parents was the most sensible thing to do. I had to avoid various kinds of susceptibilities concerning the armed group ETA (Euskadi and Freedom), and the village had its own history of involvement with which I was very familiar. When I went into anthropology I had dreamed of something more exotic than working on my own community and had not anticipated selecting Basque political violence as my dissertation topic, yet my mentor and my past conspired to drive me toward both. As Max Weber wrote of a poet friend of his, it might as well be that I was the object of the gods' malice when I decided to write about subjects who were at once "priests and murderers," to borrow James Frazer's ritual oxymoron.

I found myself in the not unusual fieldwork predicament of being utterly unsure of how I was to go about studying the ubiquitous yet almost unmentionable, the glorified yet heavily tabooed, political violence. I knew personally some of the young boys who had accepted the call to patriotic martyrdom and ended up killing innocent people. They were simply my neighbors. I knew the social and psychological contexts in which they made the decision to embrace military activism and how this very activity, labeled "terrorism" by the world at large, was glorified by the village youth. How fieldwork could bridge the abyss between heroism and terrorism was but the initial antinomy.

To say that the same actions were interpreted simultaneously as heroic duty and as criminal murder is simply to state the obvious concerning the audience contemplating the drama. Yet for the ethnographer, there is no less compelling disparity that concerns the frame of discourse in which to couch ethnographic description. One such possible frame is provided by the discourse of terrorism; that is, a single universal phenomenon that emerges here and there as if by contagion and that requires a well-orchestrated international strategy of containment. Another option is the discourse of universal ethics and moral indignation that condemns any ethnographic approach as the obtuse child of cultural relativism. Yet I was intent on doing ethnography, a discipline that trades in "looking into dragons, not domesticating or abominating them" (Geertz 1984:275), and I am still plagued by the problematics of the venture.

Indeed, as if to underscore the incompatibility of the two approaches, while I was completing my ethnography for publication an international committee of terrorism experts examined the same troubling issues of Basque violence and provided, amid much media fanfare, diagnoses and recommendations informed strictly and exclusively by terrorism discourse. Far from the ethnographer's perspectivism, they espoused a technical, scientific, international, and legal discourse that forcefully advocated social engineering. From police training to intelligence gathering, from the organization of political parties to the role of the social sciences, from primary school to university curricula, the experts had a grand antiterrorist design to eradicate autochthonous terrorism in order, by means of general consciousness raising, to supplant it with a democratic and noncriminal culture.

The ironies of such experts, reminiscent of medieval witches' inquisitors, are too glaring to review in any detail here (see Zulaika 1991). Yet what about the dilemmas and ironies of an ethnographer working among terrorists while being a member of a community that advocates their cause? This chapter addresses some of the perplexities.

Perhaps this is the place to add a note about my own past relationship with ETA. In the middle of Franco's darkest repression, I was informally asked in London, where I was living for a year, to join the armed organization. The invitation came from two ETA members on a hunger strike in Trafalgar Square protesting the death penalties issued against six Basque activists. There were at the time massive demonstrations in Europe's capitals against Franco's military trial. I was not up to the call then, nor was I later, when, back in the Basque country, the same youths requested again my services and my loyalty. By then my only real interest was anthropology. In 1979, after several years of study in Canada and the United States, I returned to my village to do fieldwork on the very thing I had dodged. It was then that I began to realize the incongruities of my role as ethnographer. They became truly alarming when I visited an old friend who was one of ETA's leaders. Through him I met several members of the group in their hideouts in France. Against all common sense, but conscious of the fieldwork rhetoric of initiation, I expressed willingness to join them so as to gain insight into their lives and organizational circumstances. I made clear to them that I was not interested in any nationalist agenda but only in writing a good ethnography. I did not wish to imitate their thirst for martyrdom, yet unexpectedly I too had fallen under the spell that "the truths we respect are those born of affliction. We measure truth in terms of the cost to the writer in suffering" (Sontag 1978:49–50). One of the activists pointed out that for me fieldwork and writing seemed to be something similar to what patriotic martyrdom was for them. They could understand a willingness to sacrifice oneself for political truth, but they were baffled by my disposition for analysis and writing. They did not know what to do and were embarrassed to have to tell me they did not want me around. My time for initiation, with all its distortions, was fortunately over.

A TOWN MEETING AND A COMMUNITY OF FACES

Itziar, a village of one thousand people, had been shaken by six political murders between 1975 and 1980. ETA was responsible for the killings of two police informers, one civil guard, one industrialist, and a worker mistakenly taken to be an informer; the civil guards killed an ETA operative. Against the background of such violent acts, I attempted to reconstruct, as if in a Homeric tragedy, the conditions under which the actors and their audience created each other and ultimately became each other's dilemma.

Yet what sort of dialogue can a field-worker establish with groups who practice or support such violence? What kind of "authenticity" can a writer stage for such an encounter? In my ethnographic work, while deriving various types of models and metaphors from the culture, still I dwelled on the sense of tragedy produced by the phenomenon of violence. The ethnographer is like a poet, I concluded, in his attempts to turn into a song what is incomprehensible in human experience. I could not overcome my essential ambivalence toward the violent subjects, nor could I present a firm moral ground from which to judge the entire historical narrative. If I was nowhere close to discovering any exemplary realm of intact heroism, neither could I finalize the political options of my informants as vicious criminality.

At the end of the fieldwork, I was asked by the villagers to give them a lecture expounding my "findings." I welcomed the exceptional occasion of that town meeting, but the ironies of my role as ethnographer became disturbingly embarrassing for me. At the outset I had to point out that I had no answer of any sort to our deeply perplexing political and moral dilemmas. Nor did I have any startling new factual information that was of true concern to them—except, perhaps, that I found some of our collective assumptions about the village's police informer, killed by ETA, to be false. My ironic predicament—a specialist who knew nothing special about the violence and who was frequently asking his neighbors simple social and political questions about which they had better understanding than he— did not pass unnoticed by my "informants," who, half-jokingly, would even chide me at times about my alleged knowledge. What had I really been doing during all those months of fieldwork? What was the purpose of my writing?

Still, confronted with the town meeting, I was determined to use the very precariousness of the ethnographer's position as my greatest asset when asked to validate my knowledge. Standing in front of my small but unique audience of people tormented by two decades of local political violence, all I had was a parable taken from our recent history: a priest who became secularized and who then attempted to explain to his former parishioners his sacramental status change. After having possessed the indelible sacerdotal character, he had become an ordinary layman. Yet he continued to be the very same person, and he wanted his former parishioners to treat him as such. I was as helpless as the former priest, I told them, if they wanted me to "explain" what makes people choose violent martyrdom or decide that it is no longer necessary. There were no objective grounds to compare the life of the same man when he was a priest and when he was not, no ultimate rule with which to judge the movement back and forth from sacrament to metaphor, from ritual to theater. Indeed, we were hardly able to *say* what we knew about the violence. My audience, who knows and admires that man, understood at once. The historical analogy between the local former priest and the local former "terrorist" seemed to capture a crucial dimension of the violence for all of us. It prompted a dialogue among the competing political and moral identities within the village. For a moment it appeared that local experience, framed as exemplary parable, could be turned into a powerful source of communal solidarity and tolerance.

Irony was, in fact, the master trope in that village meeting: former members of ETA opposed violence, while their sympathizers, who had never undergone the baptism by fire of belonging to the underground organization, continued to support it. The exchanges were of this sort: "I remember I was opposed to your entering ETA," said the brother of one jailed ETA activist to a former ETA member. "I thought it was nothing but activism and volunteerism; we argued and argued about it; my position was that we should organize the working classes, not leave the struggle in the hands of an armed elite. And what about now? Now you are opposed to violence and you are telling me, who was always against it, that the armed struggle is worthless. I am now the violent one because I don't think like you. If it was right for you to do it, why not for others?" To which the former ETA activist replied, "It was all right then when Franco was still alive. Now things have changed a lot. We did the fighting and I am proud of it.

But now we are in a far different world. If I hadn't taken up arms when it was the proper time, I wouldn't be as opposed to it as I am now. Violence makes no sense whatsoever now. It has become our major problem as a people. We can go nowhere with violence." This was, indeed, a face-to-face debate, on questions that were most vital for the community and reflective of one's intimate personal thoughts and experiences.

This was certainly not what the terrorism experts had urged us to do: avoid at all costs anything having to do with the terrorists. The community debate was not about a reified and tabooed abstraction but a face-to-face encounter with the pronouns "I" and "you" on the line, exploring questions and responsibilities over events that had taken place in our own village. We could not find an argument we could all share to soothe the excessive incongruity of the "But how can that be?" prompted by politically motivated killing. But ethnographic perspectivism was at least able to carve out a communal space in which people with irreconcilable conceptions could talk to each other without turning one another into monsters. We as neighbors preferred not to depend on the representations that others—politicians, journalists, experts, social scientists—had made of our lives. But the meeting was even more revelatory in that we realized we could not trust even our own collective representations, as illustrated by our views of the death of the alleged police informer Carlos, well deserved for some, tragically unjust for others (including his political antagonist, Martin).

In that meeting we were worried about something prior to criminality: we wanted to reassure ourselves we were a community, and we looked for the ethical basis supporting our sense of justice. We were not interested in further texts or laws but in the intersubjectivity that had orchestrated the killings. The call not to dehumanize ourselves could be summed up in a commanding duty we were performing: confronting the faces of neighbors to understand the meaning in their silent expressions as well as their words. The daily routine of having to face a neighbor can be evaded in various ways, at times even totally avoided. Yet, at other times, when it radically exposes personal destitution or communal dependency, facing a stark face is the prime burden of solidarity. The message of our meeting was that "the solution" to the problem would not come from further tabooing the faces of the violent subjects but from personally confronting them as revelatory mirrors that can reflect the dilemmas of ethics and politics.

NEIGHBORS VERSUS EXPERTS:
THE TASK OF ETHNOGRAPHIC WRITING

My invitation to speak to the community thus provided an occasion for openly debating such ultimate political-cum-religious constructions of violent resistance. The nature of the violent action itself, as well as the political antagonisms generated by it, depended on the community's definitions. A plurality of views needed to be negotiated. The facts could be described and legitimated in various ways: we were dealing with interpretations that were our own life stories. If there was no correct interpretation even within the community of actors, how could a cultural interpreter impose one?

What the community needed most was a dialogue between the incommensurable perspectives of politics as sacrament—uncompromising, life-giving and life-taking, the unconscious communion with the community's values—and a notion of politics as metaphor—consciousness of the mythology of one's own origins, the relativity of all heroism, the art of the possible. It was the exchange between experience and irony, ethnography and conviviality, that we were attempting to achieve.

That such debate occurred at all, I believe, vindicates the ethnographer's task. By not imposing one's own privileged position, the writer may prompt the community itself to effect a sort of ethnographic distancing from its own modes of believing and acting. The starker the presentation of one authenticity, the more it was contested. The lesson we all learned in that meeting is that such authenticities can be construed in diametrically opposed terms within the limits of a community of several hundred people. It was clear to me that there was more wisdom about "the terrorist other" within that disconcerting internal dialogue than in anything recommended by terrorism experts or ethnographers.

Such inconclusive, halting dialogue among neighbors, grounded in the questioning of the validity of ultimate political commitment, made apparent the ironies of my quest for authenticity and my efforts at cultural interpretation. In those moral and political areas of concern to the entire community, I could not claim any privileged knowledge as an ethnographer. We were all essentially neighbors, members of specific families, each with its own history of political involvement, traumatic experiences, united and divided allegiances. As author, I had no intellectual authority over them; my only powers of persuasion resided in the arguments of the importance of the common good and the use of common sense, positions accessible to any neighbor and made credible only by my lifelong participation in the community's fate. This partly alleviated for me the paradoxes of the fieldwork situation.

In particular, I was relieved from the dilemma of asserting either responsibility or innocence concerning my community's actions. Am I my brother's keeper? I could not be detached from my natal community of family and childhood friends, and at times I was compelled to oppose certain local events and positions. Yet precisely because of the unceasing dialogue inherent in a moral community, I could also feel free from having to judge every action and everyone's consciousness. Vital dialogue requires diversity of intellectual and ethical positions: plurality, polysemy, and dissonance are not a denial of community but rather the essence of communication and creativity (Rorty 1989). We could not ignore the ambiguities and repugnant contradictions that arise from a political engagement, but nobody claimed a position of moral superiority from which to condemn the lives of neighbors.

As ethnographer, I could not taboo as vicious murderers the neighbors I was debating. I want to make this point clear because this is exactly what the terrorism experts demand of Basque society. Not only did they never speak to or see the "terrorists" regarding whom they claim expertise (as they admitted themselves) but one of their key recommendations was that the public as well should never have any contact with them. Personal appearances on television, for example, should be avoided because they "facilitate a personal and direct rapprochement with the masses . . . for people can see as well as hear the person being interviewed" (Rose et al. 1986: 140). Seeing a terrorist's face, even on a television set, or hearing a terrorist's voice, even on a radio, can be a most harmful experience for the public! Thus, in the name of scientific expertise, specific instructions for stigmatizing key members of the society were championed, when in fact any native is likely to have known more than one such loathsome terrorist, probably to have lionized them, and for hundreds of families the existence of a member in prison or exile is an ongoing tragedy.

The social strategy in our communal meeting could not be more starkly opposed to the one espoused by the experts. They wanted, above all, that we obliterate the face of the monstrous terrorist; as neighbors, our only hope was to contemplate and be rescued by the faces of community members. Without renouncing the fiction of a single moral community, we were brought face-to-face with the "conquering heart of darkness" of our violent predicament primarily by facing each other. It was essential that alternative descriptions of each other's lives were permitted. But we were far from moral relativism and tolerance toward any disruptive social behavior. We longed for and worked toward a breakthrough that may end the violence, but we did not expect it to come from brandishing "knowledge" or "morality" to dispel our political errors. What we aimed at was establishing a dialogue with our own recent history, one that would have to extend far beyond our community's borders, and thus be able to question, face-to-face, our most sacred forms of believing and acting. In a word, the communal solution was to activate discourse, not to taboo it. If anything, it is the very prohibition of discourse, with its secret commitments, initiatory ordeals, and calls for ineffable self-transcendence, that constitutes the problem. The taboo further contributes to the fetishism of the armed struggle—the assumption that everything in the end depends on, at one and the same time, the irresistibly prohibited and alluringly sacred arms. The timid face and the uncertain voice of the underground activist we had idolized were commanding instruments for transforming the taboo into ordinary behavior. The challenge was how to dissolve the tabooed context, how to find reconciliation in the face of one's political antagonist.

A writer is surely free to argue directly for scientific truth and to preach the principles of universal morality. Yet most influential thinkers of modernity are quite uncertain as to whether art or ethics can ever be "demonstrated" in a scientific manner. Wittgenstein's well-known stance that ethics can only be defined through silence is a case in point. Such an indirect or "maieutic" relationship to ethics was also prominent in Kierkegaard, for whom the question was luring the ethical out of the individual rather than beating it into him (Creegan 1989). In the case of Itziar's town meeting, in which the ethnographer of political violence is asked to face his own informants on a level of intellectual parity, the history of the village provided the ethical and political tension required for the necessary ethnographic distancing. Unmistakable voices in that history spoke simultaneously of a deeply experienced conversion to Catholic sacramentalism, of a sincerely believed Socialist utopia, of an ardently felt promised land of Nationalist freedom, and of the disillusioned skepticism of Modernity.

A subversive displacement concerning "the heroism of terror" was happening in that communal meeting far more poignantly than in any textual interpretation entertained by the writer. It was the disbelief by the former heroes regarding their own heroism that was stunning. The very plenitude of self-transcendent meaning was affirmed as "passé" and "meaningless" by the actors who had themselves constituted us into a community of violence. The result of that spin was unsurpassable irony, an irony built into and then decoded by the community itself.

The fieldwork task consisted for me not in brandishing truth about which the community had to agree, or in devising a strategy to resolve a public policy problem, but rather in listening to dissenting voices and in sketching the borderlines of contrasting representations of the violence. In the town meeting the ethical distance between the "is" and the "ought" was as abysmal as it could be but was not dogmatically imposed by any political or authorial force. The ethical was delimited from *within* the community in the basic idea that meaning is socially constructed. Nor were our standards of the good and the just taken from some transcendent order but were basically forged according to a moral consensus that stated implicitly that whatever was most reasonable for us had to take into account the community's history and long-standing values. The uses of ethnography were ancillary to that goal yet, in my case, decisive. That quintessentially ironic task of indirect communication—of collective representations and rituals neutralized by the very people who gave force to them, of allegories that could suddenly become revelatory of what otherwise could not be said—was, I thought, the task of writing "political terror."

TRAGEDY, FARCE, MELODRAMA:
FROM CLOSED ARGUMENTS TO OPEN COMMUNITIES

An initial problem any writer has to confront with regard to issues of political violence and terrorism concerns the genre in which to plot the events and the arguments. The competition is fierce. Romance, tragedy, comedy, farce, melodrama, warfare, ritual, fantasy—all conjure with their own powers of history and narrative to capture the very essence of terror. The same writer may in fact discover, say, by reading Northrop Frye, that the romance of his central story (the triumph of courage and transcendence) can be made to fit exactly a Homeric tragedy (a crime that is all too human and arouses pity); soon he might note that the story is best cast in the ironic mode as a repetitive farce and will be tempted to distance himself from it all with the burlesque stare of satire (the resolutions expected by human consciousness are always frustrated by failure and death). Finally, his interest may be aroused again, say, by stumbling upon Kenneth Burke's "comic principle of tragedy" (the occasional awareness that the inalterably opposed elements in the world can be comically reconciled in harmony). Whether the story commands the somber resignation of tragedy or the enlightened reconciliation of comedy, whether it searches for the redemption of romance or proclaims the ultimate inadequacy of any representation through satire, the archetypal structure of the plot determines the historian's knowledge and judgment of "what is *really* happening." Such precritical selection is obviously "constitutive of the *concepts* he will use to *identify the objects* that inhabit that domain and *to characterize the kinds of relationships* they can sustain with one another" (White 1973:31). In terrorism discourse, what is termed "the definitional problem" is in fact a problem of narrative style by which the modes of ideological implication are *pre*figured in its specific modes of emplotment and argument.

> This ethnography began on a summer day in 1975 . . . when several Itziar women, who had just witnessed the killing of a villager, assailed me with wide-open eyes and the question "But how can that be?" It was not properly a question but the expression of an unanswerable puzzlement, as when spectators are compelled to witness an epic drama in which men become gods and beasts and are capable of heroic deeds and tragic errors. (Zulaika 1988: xxviii)

That was one of the basic plots in my study of Basque political violence. The events I witnessed in my natal village provided me with the essential dramatic arguments through which to cast the tragic narrative.

The man killed that morning inside a bus filled with rural housewives was Carlos, the bus driver and alleged police informer of the village. After shouting at him "You are a dog!" they shot him to death in front of his brother and sister and the horrified women—my own mother included, whom I found pale and breathless, sitting on the stairs unable to walk to the apartment. His blood, spilled on the public road, remained visible for days. That morning, when I was surrounded by my bewildered neighbors asking "But how can that be?" remains indelibly in my memory. While their eyes were spearing me, pleading for an answer, I remained mute. Paradox and silence became inevitable components of my dramatic argument.

Carlos's political antagonist was Martin. When Carlos became the suspect villain, Martin was the patriotic hero. Both were, however, milk brothers nursed by Carlos's mother after Martin's mother had died. Intimately aware of their past kinship, they were the closest of friends while engaged in various social activities to revitalize the village; when political polarization became unavoidable, each followed a divergent course. Each felt betrayed by the other. But the climax of their relationship for me, both as ethnographer and villager, was in 1980, years after Carlos's killing and a few months before Martin's death from leukemia, when Martin talked to me about Carlos with exceptional passion. He knew that man too well, he kept repeating, better than the Spanish policemen he befriended or the ETA militants who executed him. For Martin, Carlos did not deserve the infamy of such a death, despite his supposed role as an informer. Martin's secrecy (when he decided to take part in underground political activism against Franco's dictatorship) had provoked Carlos's treachery, and when talking to me then, it seemed that Martin was again burdened with a secret about Carlos's humanity that he wished everybody could share. The essence of a man can only be known within his community's boundaries, his dramatic facial expression seemed to imply, and through Martin's eyes, I too felt I knew Carlos differently. Thus propositions about the ultimate boundaries of a symbolic community; about polarization and the construction of the enemy scapegoat; about errors that are not arbitrary crimes but tragic mistakes; about the power of collective representations forcing sacrificial rituals became integral aspects of my Homeric tragedy argument.

A Homeric tragedy! But is this not in itself a literary fashioning of what for all legal purposes is ordinary murder? Tragedy is surely about crime, yet the protagonist commits the fateful error "under conditions so adverse that we watch him with compassion" (Redfield 1975:222); "it is the sort of error a good man would make," even ourselves.

Some Basque intellectuals, both anti-ETA and pro-ETA, took offense at casting the deadly literalness of the battle for national independence into the mold of Greek tragedy, an emplotment that, after all, seeks to persuade us that the hero has fallen into error and forces us to mediate about the relationship between action and its preconditions. The one word that summed up the dangers posed by my ethnography was *ambiguity*—a charge I can hardly dispute on intellectual grounds after having invoked for my actors the Frazerian analogy of "priests and murderers" but which scarcely reflects my personal attitude concerning ETA's violence, since twice during my fieldwork I was in the awkward position of having to write and distribute a pamphlet against ETA in a village in which the majority votes for the pro-ETA political party, Herri Batasuna. While there is risk involved in speaking out openly against an armed organization, I have found that there is as much risk, in moral and intellectual terms, in daring to treat the phenomenon of terrorism ethnographically. One must be ready to be accused of providing "an aesthetic alibi" to terrorists; and even one's personal character may become the subject of strong condemnation by critics "morbidly virtuous," as De Quincey called them, who charge you not only with moral relativism but also with promoting terrorism. One wonders who can be a detached relativist when, as is my case, my family members and closest friends have suffered death threats from both the Spanish Right and ETA.

Any ethnographer of subjects labeled "terrorists" may ipso facto become liable to charges of contamination by merely having transgressed the taboo of never talking to them, even if they are neighbors with whom one has to deal on a daily basis. This explains why, in my case, I have been regularly accused by Basque nationalists of belonging to the CIA, whereas people close to the CIA have suggested, referring to me, that I "may share the expressed grievances of the terrorists" and that "[a] particular conflict can arise if the scholar's methodology relies heavily on personal contact and interviews, for in that circumstance the government may see the scholar as a potential source of information who is withholding critical security information" (Post and Ezekiel 1988:506).

Plots such as those in Homeric tragedy may be useful for the ethnographer who must start by describing how specific institutions and events, murder included, are construed intersubjectively within a community. Itziar villagers, whose electoral votes go mostly for the pro-ETA party, generally view their political activists in the romantic mode, that is, as heroes battling the enemies of their country. Emplotting the historical events in the mode of tragedy was strictly home produced in my own ethnographic harvest, and I warned the reader about it (some Itziar villagers were not likely to agree with it, particularly as I had rescued Carlos from the role of traitor). But when they asked me to give them a talk at the end of my fieldwork, as well as in the presentation of the book, they allowed for my interpretation, which, since it changed the minds of even some prominent former activists, became a dominant one.

Going back to the revelatory town meeting, the central argument had to do with which trope to select for describing our lives. A key question facing us was, should we stick to our values and beliefs in the manner of an ultimate *sacrament* (everlasting and absolute), as we had been taught by Catholic tradition, or should we decide that the trope of *metaphor* (myth, representation) is immensely more adaptive to the religious and political realities of the post-Franco era? The historical exemplars of various former priests and former ETA activists who had given up their sacred callings were invoked to illustrate the dilemma. By questioning the symbolism of such ultimate demands, we were faced with the realization that the basic existential stance depended on which trope (perspective, narrative argument) we elected to live by.

Still, my ethnography stopped short of other competing narrative plots, even if I pointed out that "the irony of the historical sequence could hardly be more striking" (ibid., 95). Reference was made to the fact that a founder of Basque nationalism in the village during the 1930s was kidnapped by a local ETA activist in 1986 on charges of antipatriotism. That was farce, rather than tragedy (according to Marx's characterization of the farcical recurrence of historical personages). In other events too, ETA's language was interpreted by the local people as farce—as when they planted bombs in the village discotheque managed on a nonprofit basis by local youth. In fact, the perception of many Basques seems to be moving in this direction—from tragedy to farce, from sacrament to irony—a change in historical narrative that replaces the meaningfulness of battle with the meaninglessness of the comic reconciliation of opposites.

In the ethnography, the full irony of such meaningless encounters culminates at the cemetery, where the bodies of mortal enemies must literally lie one next to the other and their respective followers must visit and pray over the same piece of ground. These are narratives in which "it becomes impossible to distinguish history from ritual" (Girard 1977:110). The categories of "history" and "ritual" themselves as apt representations of the events become problematic. An ethnographer is likely to insist on the obvious ritual dimension of the entire phenomenon. But it is far from certain that ritual achieves social integration; as Clifford Geertz (1973:167) found in Java, in an equivocal cultural setting, "the rituals themselves become matters of political conflict." In the case of the beleaguered terrorist, one can also observe a process of ritual deterioration; the purposeful tendency is to break down any formal structure and hierarchy for the sake of playing with chance and context, thereby creating the extraordinary dangers of anomaly and taboo. Terrorist acts, in their pure form, can be seen as the result of such a process of ritual aberration in which meaninglessness itself is turned into the ultimate message.

In summer 1992, there was another town meeting that projected a very different picture from the earlier one and that underscores the limits of the community's capacity to deal with its own violence. When I had been asked to speak in the village in 1986 and when the Spanish version of the book was presented in 1990, I had a clear sense that the collective representation about Carlos was definitely being dissolved. In those talks I spoke about the ways we as villagers had constructed and imposed on him the role of scapegoat; my version of the facts was not challenged, and I assumed compliance implied a basic change in the villagers' perception. During my fieldwork period, the village youth had begun to frequent his family's bar and restaurant, which had been boycotted for years. I felt proud of the role of ethnography as a provider of a discursive space in which we could reflect on our collective rituals and neutralize the deadly mechanism of scapegoating. We were forced to reconsider "political responsibility," "innocence of the victim," "patriotic commitment," and so on.

Yet in a 1992 meeting, I realized that those collective representations were still very much in force. The occasion was provoked by the attempt of a Basque television producer to make a documentary on recent events in Itziar based on my book. The protagonists themselves would narrate their own history. With the approval of everyone mentioned in it, as a statement that we took full responsibility for our history, I made a point of not concealing anyone's identity in the book. I expected that, despite the obvious ambivalences, the same attitude would prevail in the town meeting called to discuss the documentary film project. But neither Carlos's nor Martin's families and friends were willing to participate in the project. The motives were various, but what most captured my attention was that, faced with going on camera, the basic arguments for refusal still concerned the victimization of Carlos's family (a charge denied by the rest of the community) and the charge of Carlos's responsibility for his own fate on the part of Martin's family and friends (a charge with which Martin himself disagreed). There were in this meeting all the elements of farce. I felt that Carlos and Martin, now resting side by side in the village cemetery, would have no difficulty respecting and tolerating each other in the present political situation, whereas their families and friends still held to the same representations that produced the tragic results recorded earlier. Among other ironies, I found that the same former priest I had taken as a model of the transition from the symbolism of sacrament to the symbolism of metaphor was the staunchest proponent of the view that all our ills had to be sought in the military defeats of the past. The social intimacy of villagers sitting around a table and talking face-to-face seemed to make the differences in perspective even more insurmountable.

In summary, awareness of the competing narrative plots provides a better understanding of what is going on in political violence. Rather than positing altogether mutually excluding dichotomies between theater and ritual, or congregation and spectacle, or romance and comedy, the local history of violence is both a tragedy and a farce in the experience of Itziar's citizens. Historical representations of myth, ritual, warfare, heroism, and tragedy merge in a single consciousness. Former activists, who fought their own war in the heroic mode, challenge the prevailing modes of romance and heroism as nonsense; what is happening is simultaneously "struggle" for the supporters of the violence, "crime" for its detractors, "stupidity" for those holding a satirical distance. In brief, in both town meetings there were no victorious narratives but rather a growing ironic awareness that the events could be organized according to competing modes of emplotment. But that was precisely the lesson: it is by rescuing history from the violence of a totalizing discourse (whether romance, tragedy, or criminality) that new forms of representation and changes in modes of consciousness are possible. The dialogism between various genres, and the agony produced by competing ideals, marked the new element of rupture at the village meeting, the creative split that turned the single collective representation into a collage of disjointed views. The rhetoric of violence did not deal with empty representations; ethics and politics were truly decided there.

TERRORISM AND THE FACE

Whatever the "terrorist" might be, he or she was not a faceless man or woman in those meetings. It was possible to carry on an I-you conversation with them. When one's birthplace decides that one has friends and neighbors belonging to that category of persons, then the immediate problem becomes simply how to react to their presence. No explanation of the moral and political paradox will provide a definitive answer to the "But how can that be?" of violence and death. Yet seeing literally and figuratively the face of the faceless activist may become, rather than a contaminating taboo proscribed in the name of science, a condition necessary for understanding that inferno of action. In those meetings, the face rescued us from allegory and representation.

But in the background of such reciprocal interaction there emerges also the presence of the impersonal witness, the ethical call to help the other gratuitously, what Emmanuel Levinas (1988*a*:165) characterized as "the asymmetry of the relation of *one* to the *other*" (emphasis in original). This implies, in Jacques Derrida's (1978: 314, n. 37) commentary, "a summoning of the third party, the universal witness, the face of the world." Martin Buber thought that one individual has nothing to say about another; the only authentic relationship, he held, was the living dialogue with another person. The other cannot be thematized; we must speak *to* him, not just about him. Inquisitors and experts should take the example of the seventeenth-century Spanish inquisitor Salazar who spoke to the alleged witches, not just in order to know about them and accuse them of crime, but to convince them of their own tragic self-deception.

Yet am I my brother's keeper? When Cain's desolate interrogation for the absent brother or friend obtains an existential urgency, no response appears to make much sense. Thinkers as diverse as Alasdair MacIntyre and Richard Rorty appeal in the end to the notions of "community" and "solidarity." But dialogue with terrorists? The premise that, whatever they are, they should be perceived as part of one's own community and not as always the evil, disembodied Other projected on a foreign place, that is the lesson I was taught by Itziar villagers when they—as a community—took responsibility for their sons' actions. The villagers could not rely on the representations created by outsiders—the politicians, the news media—as to how to judge their own lives; they could not even trust their own collective representations, as the case of Carlos turned into a demonic scapegoat made painfully obvious. This was a face-to-face interaction that eliminated the privileging of any representation. As concerned neighbors, we were primarily distressed with something prior to criminality, that is, with the ethics that provides a foundation to justice, with contemplation of the face in order not to become dehumanized. Levinas (1988b:175) even calls the face "the opposite of justice." For him, the last word is not justice: "There is a violence in justice." Any historical narrative makes us all too aware of the politics of murder (Foucault 1977). Obviously, we must advocate justice, but this does not rescue authority and morality from their internal paradoxes.

The accusation of terrorism, like that of witchcraft and demonic possession in former times, allows us to deface the accused person and thereby deprive his or her most intimate humanity. The presence of the real face, its commanding proximity, shows itself to be more original that any allegory, ritual, or narrative. Knowledge scorns such immediacy, which it knows time and again to be mediated by various kinds of prejudices. But the goal of knowledge is only more knowledge, and reason becomes its most compelling argument, whereas the kind of puzzlement that forces ultimate questions about the paradoxes of violence demands movement beyond reason: the rational justification for killing, either in warfare or capital punishment, is all too banal for such perplexity. This is where ethical philosophies such as the one proposed by Levinas, in the very exorbitance of their claims, come to the aid of the ethnographer, for they invoke the power to contest knowledge and justice in the name of the other's absolute alterity. The villagers' perplexity while witnessing politically motivated murder in their neighborhood was oblique recognition that everybody was partly responsible for it; the confusion led us to question the intersubjective premises of the community that had orchestrated the killings. The inquiry could only begin by appealing to common sense while contemplating indepth people's faces.

ACKNOWLEDGMENTS

This chapter has benefited enormously from the critical comments and editorial work of Carolyn Nordstrom, Tony Robben, and William Douglass. The fieldwork on which this work is based was supported by grants from the National Science Foundation and the Harry Frank Guggenheim Foundation.

REFERENCES

Creegan, Charles L.
    1989   *Wittgenstein and Kierkegaard: Religion, Individuality, and Philosophical Method.* London: Routledge.
Derrida, Jacques
    1978   *Writing and Difference.* Chicago: The University of Chicago Press.
Foucault, Michel
    1977   *Discipline and Punish: The Birth of the Prison.* New York: Pantheon.
Geertz, Clifford
    1973   *The Interpretation of Cultures.* New York: Basic Books.
    1984   "Anti Anti-Relativism." *American Anthropologist* 86:263–278.
Girard, René
    1977   *Violence and the Sacred.* Baltimore: Johns Hopkins University Press.
Levinas, Emmanuel
    1988*a*   "Useless Suffering." In *The Provocation of Levinas: Rethinking the Other,* ed. Robert Bernascone and David Wood, 156–167. New York: Routledge.
    1988*b*   "The Paradox of Morality: An Interview with Emmanuel Levinas." In *The Provocation of Levinas: Rethinking the Other,* ed. Robert Bernascone and David Wood, 168–180. New York: Routledge.
Post, Jerrold M., and Raphael Ezekiel
    1988   "Worlds in Collision, Worlds in Collusion: The Uneasy Relationship Between the Counterterrorism Policy Community and the Academic Community." *Terrorism* 11 (6):503–509.
Redfield, James
    1975   *Nature and Culture in the Iliad: The Tragedy of Hector.* Chicago: University of Chicago Press.
Rorty, Richard
    1989   *Contingency, Irony, and Solidarity.* Cambridge: Cambridge University Press.
Rose, Clive, Franco Ferracuti, Hans Horchem, Peter Janke, and Jacques Leaute
    1986   *Report of the International Commission on Violence in the Basque Country.* Vitoria: Eusko Jaurlaritza.

Sontag, Susan
    1978   *Against Interpretation and Other Essays.* New York: Octagon Books.
White, Hayden
    1973   *Metahistory: The Historical Imagination in Nineteenth-Century Europe.* Baltimore: Johns Hopkins University Press.
Zulaika, Joseba
    1988   *Basque Violence: Metaphor and Sacrament.* Reno: University of Nevada Press.
    1991   "Terror, Totem, and Taboo: Reporting on a Report." *Terrorism and Political Violence* 3(1):34–49.

EPILOGUE

Warning Sign at Entrance to a
Homeless Person's Shanty in the South Bronx
(Photo: Allen Feldman)

Ethnographic States of Emergency

Allen Feldman

ROOMS WITH A VIEW

In Hitchcock's film *The Birds,* apocalyptic and often incomprehensible scenes of destruction are shown from the familiar vantage point of the film's human protagonists. In one famous scene, we, the viewers, and they, the film's characters, watch a gas station incinerate from behind the protective windows of a diner. Like the witnesses of the avian terror, the cineast experiences the scene of violence from within a closed bounded social space, diner or theater, and through an aperture, the framing device of the window or camera lens. These frames mold an insulating perceptual interior, and the window-lens-aperture promises perceptual transparency and thus comprehension. The aperture and enclosure provide a distancing visual omniscience by which the chaos outside is rendered pictorial, and they anchor a fixed, stable point of view, a temporary shelter from the destruction beyond. These devices establish positions of perception and narration with which the viewer can readily identify. As we momentarily shelter from the outside violence in the midst of this human-centered vision, all coherence, all supports are pulled out from under the perceiver. The camera lens abruptly shifts perspective, swirling upward like a random feather, imposing an aerial view of the burning gas station. In a decentering movement and in a moment of extreme cultural relativism and antirealism, the camera inflicts historical vertigo on the perceiver: we witness the scene of destruction from the formerly unimaginable perspective of the attacking birds themselves. And in Hitchcock's logic, that means we witness the violence from the point of view of a wounded, disordered, and *postnatural* "nature," that is, from the outside. (The "natural" here being the assumed commonsense presumptions of

224

everyday life and the "outside" being the same structure of the everyday now defamiliarized and estranged.) It is a humanly impossible optic, and yet it eloquently unfolds the social implications of the scene of violence without offering a reassuring narration or perspective for the perceiver to lean on. Hitchcock visualizes an inhuman prospect that occupies a perceptual space beyond all social conventions and with which *we* must now come to terms as an intimate, if foreign part, of our own story.

The ethnographer of contemporary political violence stands both inside and outside Hitchcock's gas station as civilizational mise-en-scène, the circumscribed zone of social order, interiority, realism, and perceptual convention. Notions of the inside/outside, of the stable narrative endowing frame, and of the centered perceptual aperture are floundering in contemporary ethnographic experience. The ethnographic witnessing of terror asks of us, with or without our intent or consent, to imagine, however briefly, the position of the birds; to search for legibility and empathy outside the historical conditions and securities in which identification, language, and memory are considered to be possible.

However, in the anthropological canon, the strategy for handling the topic of political violence has been to counterpoise the conjectured disorderly, ephemeral, symptomatic, and anarchic character of the aggressive act with enframing and teleological theories of biological, ecological, and economic determinism. This polarity speaks more to a specific cultural imaginary than it does to concrete inquiry into regional practices and codes and other's points of view. Studies of political violence and conflict, in anthropology and other social sciences, have been particularly implicated by the following metatheoretical premises that authorize the above assumptions:

1. A Cartesian dichotomization of political culture into mentalist ideological discourse and symptomatic-irrational or functional, mechanistic, instrumentalist physical violence;

2. An unexamined paradigm of linear and continuous historical time that frequently coincides with the idea of progress of the political movements under study, which is the temporal structure that underwrites the functionalism and utility of their political violence;

3. The silent premise that there is a one-to-one correlation between units of formal ideological discourse and acts of violence; that there is an inherent descriptive adequacy between official ideological representation and the experience of violence. This assumption underscores the utilitarian model of political violence of political agents and the symptomatic model promoted by social scientists. This taken-for-granted descriptive adequacy of formal ideology in relation to

violence implicitly authorized the reciprocal descriptive adequacy of social science depiction of violence.

There has been little critical distance between the analytic logic of social scientists or policy analysts and the ideological logics that legitimize violent political action in modernity; they share the same metaphysical assumptions concerning the determinism of origins, linear-progressive time, and the functional. Both logics assume that violence as the abode of surface effects can be explained by something outside itself, that something being a beginning, which thereby implies an ending. In the social sciences one diagnoses violence-as-symptom to find causes and cures. The discourse on violence is mainly prescriptive discourse. No one asks to what extent prescriptive teleological frameworks are adequate to the description of violence and to what extent they skew any depiction of political aggression. Further, the Cartesian influence is never more apparent than when one "writes" violence, because that act of writing itself supposedly lifts physical violence to a symbolic, nonmaterial level, bringing it to an equally symbolic end that coincides with the conclusive termination of prescriptive discourse.

However, in the last decade, in cultural studies, the subject of violence has loosened its moorings as a result of the destabilization of an inherited Cartesian mind/body dualism, in the aftermath of theories of symbolic efficacy, with the challenge to traditional ethnographic narrative, and as a result of notorious historical experiences of ritualized and chronically irrational instrumental reason. The thematic and theorization of violence now floats like a rumor through unexpected corridors of ethnographic practice and cultural studies, no longer bound to clear-cut origins and causation and therefore detoured from final definitions and prescribed ends. Theory building in the discipline can no longer lay explanatory claim to the stable ground of determinism or static material and ideological structure, while, in turn, acts of social violence increasingly disclose a self-generating organization and internal propulsion that marks the most disruptive and murky practices of destruction with the architecture of cultural construction.

Ethnographers, working in diverse zones of political emergency, have been tackling violence, terror, and death through methods of somatic, sensory, affective, semiotic, symbolic, phenomenological, linguistic, performative, and social historical reconstruction. While duly recognizing the historical and economic frames within which acts of violence and death unfold, many contemporary workers in political emergency zones have rejected reductionist theory and have granted social violence and the meaning and nonmeaning it issues an autopoetic drive, which entails recognizing that violence possesses structuring and enframing effects of its own.

Stanley Diamond's dictum of the late sixties, that the discipline needed to develop a "sociology of horror," has returned with full ironic and predictive force.

This contemporary ethnography of violence constitutes a field site that requires exploration, one that is in transit, in-the-making, an on-the-way reality that has not yet arrived and may already have slipped past, a casualty of a global struggle for memory and meaning against violence and terror. The very existence of a "new ethnography of violence" marks profound shifts in post–cold war and postcolonial historical experience as much as it may refract new epistemological insights. Because of the contingent historical positioning present in this body of work, it is not the task of this ethnography to progress to theoretical closure, to introduce finality or the definitive to its methods or motives. For teleology (willingly or unwillingly) is the province of the agents and victims of violence encountered in the field and/or portrayed in these ethnographies of violence. Nor is it the present task of ethnographic insight to uncover conclusive exits from the world-historical labyrinth of political terror; rather it is to explore the "middle passage" of oppression and to possibly assemble counterlabyrinths and countermemories against the forgetting of terror.

In the spaces of death, and even in low-intensity terror zones, the lenses of analytic and perceptual certitude are irrevocably torn. No person or method at this stage in history can remove the Andalusian dog's razor from the pierced eye of the historical witness. In post-Holocaust modernity, older and customary perceptual edifices undergoing trauma, shock, and disordering penetration issue forth new things to be perceived and new ways of sensing. The loss of older perceptual sureties does not necessarily lead to blindness but can make new things visible. The violent, the dead, the disappeared, the tortured, the dismembered, and the disfigured entering into ethnographic writing force open numerous cracks, rips, and gaps in the graphics that record their entry. It is from the historically necessary descriptive *inadequacy* of conceptual footholds and the historical excess of terror-ridden experience that ethnographic exploration must begin, and we can expect no linearity or continuous paths through the ethnographic state of emergency.

This journey through the labyrinth of violence is also an exploration of the possibility of witnessing and memory in the zone of violence and terror. In the emergency zone, the ethnographer bears witness to the collective struggle of peoples bearing witness to violence and creating novel vehicles of historical memory, an effort that can wander through many cul-de-sacs and circles in which memory, perception, and narrative are self-consumed like an ourobouros, the mythic snake that devoured itself in an unending cycle of destruction and regeneration. Yet I suggest that this is an unavoidable passage for the ethnographer of violence, one that can be made with the communities where fieldwork unfolds. In the state of political emergency, the ethnographic process is a travail through layers of sensory and narrative distortion, white noise, and surrealistic particularities that not only are the internal product of the space of terror and death but that also arise from the contradictory abutment of the ethnographers' own social contexts and disciplinary dispositions with local situations and knowledge. Making culture in the zone of political emergency is for both the ethnographer and the informants a matter of making contradictions, of mixing knowledge with nonknowledge, narratives with silence, experience with the unacceptable. This is a crucial labor that in some way speaks to the formation of witnessing as a historical process, to historical being as a state-of-witness.

Blunt confrontation with both the perceptual and the narratological structure and antistructure of the political emergency zone will serve to move anthropological theory away from the clichéd posture that states "we" cannot really write violence—that all such attempts to write violence are illegitimate cultural and ideological intrusions and superimposition. This half-truth treats violence, its participants and victims, as passive objects and reciprocally endows our representational drives with exclusive agency that is fated to be foiled by murky death and terror. We return again to a neo-Cartesian dualism. In the very moment that it suggests an equation between ethnographic depiction and violence, this edict against writing bars violence from the ethnographer's social interiority by inferring that violence stands in a relation of pure externality to his or her consciousness and historical being. The dialectical formation of consciousness through apparatuses of esoteric and exoteric violence and coercion is ignored by the iconoclastic imperative. The polarization of writing and violence also ignores the extent to which ethnographic depictions of modern, colonial, and postcolonial violence are invariably confronted by other political apparatuses of writing that organize the violence of the field site, such as juridical, penal, military, economic, and ideological institutions. Modern political violence is born in the midst of organized writing, it can be a continuation of institutional inscription by other means, and it never fails to be legitimized or sanctioned by writing. Contrary to the insulating conceits of numerous academics, writing is not simply a distantiating or aestheticizing practice external to violence, and violence is rarely on the nether side of the political aesthetics of institutional technical rationality, statistical, legal, and penological record keeping, and the material instruments of ideological discourse.

The stricture against writing violence begs another question: what does chronic political violence do to systems of representation, and how are depictive practices and genres altered by the impact of concerted terror and material destruction? This question, which firmly situates epistemology in history, exposes pseudodeconstructionist qualms about the representation of the other as clandestine attempts to preserve residual depictive traditions from the wreckage and ravages of novel historical experience. If writing violence means that we will ultimately reach the ends of writing, then the response is not to cease writing but to explore what lies beyond writing's margins, and whatever that is, it is not solely certain silence.

RUMOR AND INDIGENE HISTORIOGRAPHY

Since the Enlightenment, the writing of history has been conceived as a process by which res gestae (acts) became res factae (facts). Through source-material criticism, this progression supposedly bypassed the fictive "res fictae"; invention was seen to violate the writing of history (Kosseleck 1985). "He who invents violates the writing of history; he who does not violates poetic art" (ibid., 213). However, as the writing of history itself became historicized and infused with the distortions of temporal perspective, the factual limits of representation moved to the fore. The historical text as a creature of time demonstrated the secret life of invention within the factual. Historical perspectivism broke ground for a poetics of history, what Reinhart Kosseleck terms the "fiction of its facticity" (ibid., 215). It was also conceded that the denial of invention frequently excludes the inner probability, the connections that poetics and imagining uncover between events. And Paul Ricoeur (1973) has pointed out that res gestae could not attain historicity without the imaginary both at the time of enactment and at the time of written depiction.

Ethnography stands at the crux of such conflicts over depiction, because quite frequently the ethnographer's immersion in everyday life structures exposes the descriptive limits of official ideology and institutional discourse. Ethnographic recuperation can pluralize and expand what narrative genres and voices are admissible. This is particularly so when ethnography is practiced against monophonic, stratified information cultures and cultures of the state. Such multiplication of historical voice is not merely a matter of textual representation, for whenever the stratification of discourse in a society is interrupted by a previously canceled voice, we are witnessing the active and creative emergence of novel political subjects.

In both academic and spontaneous popular historiographic practices, historical reality is never simulated in totality but only reproduced through encryptment and abbreviation. In states of emergency, practices of abbreviation condense the sensibility and processual components of crisis and not only are molded around particular content but also incorporate, as indispensable to the codifying act, the enabling fictions of facticity and truth.

The appearance of rumor, mythmaking, and other narratives of mystification in many of these chapters speaks to shifts in the social organization of
truth claiming which demand ethnographic attention.

Rumor as a type of collective wide-awake dreaming intermingles fact and
fiction in such a manner that can only be termed ethnographic. This is so
because as popular historiography, rumor addresses not only what has
happened but what could happen within the given configurations of disorder. Rumor is prognostic, not in terms of actual prediction, but in terms of
a culturally mediated sense of possibility, structural predilection, political
tendency, and symbolic projection. It provides a preview of how historical events will be culturally and ideologically negotiated, distorted, transformed, recollected, and rendered into allegory.

The chapters in this volume compel one to consider rumor as a narratological form and practice independent of the specificity of its changing
contents. The specific content of individual rumor may appear and disappear, but the emotional and cognitive investment in rumor as narration or
historicization permeates these studies. Informed by the terror of rumor,
the rumor of terror, the rumor of the ethnographer's end, the informant's
death, and society's death, many of these contributions are part-rumor
themselves. They are ethnographies *of* rumor, ethnographies *from* rumor,
and ethnographies *toward* new rumor (see Marcus 1991 on corridor talk
in anthropology). The intractable wall of violence, death, and victimization witnessed, in one form or another, by the authors is attested to by the
intrinsic inability of both the authors and the people they met with and
write about to fully portray what has occurred. This means that significant
segments and depths of experience will drift from and toward fogs of
rumor, dream, hallucination, and other arbitrary imagery. Yes, there are
unavoidable facts, deaths, and acts of violence here, but the social crises
examined in this volume are also crises of facticity.

Fluctuation, randomness, and variability as narrative can be analyzed as
the central formal effect of rumor dissemination. Rumor is twinned with
violence because the flux of both exhibits an autopoetic structure. Is this
to reify rumor as narrative production? I think not. Rumor is not the object of a reifying sensibility, it is its very infrastructure. Rumor reproduces
through the defacement of authorship, of agency; while participation in
its substance can transfer a kind of historical agency to those removed from
a sense of social authorship. In Hegelian/Marxian thought, reification's
prerequisite is agency voided and its terminus is human agency fabricated
from an external nonhuman source. Reification, despite its association
with the rigidity of things, with deathlike states, does not mean an absence
of flux or movement. The term was applied to nomadic structures of substitution and surrogation, religious myths, value equivalencies, circulating
commodity forms, and sexual desire. Fetishization of the production of

the new was considered by Walter Benjamin and Theodore W. Adorno as reification. As formulaic novelty, as practices of mobile and flexible content substitution, rumor and reification are each other's condition of possibility.

Carolyn Nordstrom writes in this volume,

> If people are defined by the world they inhabit, and the world is culturally constructed by the people who consider themselves a part of it, people ultimately control the production of reality and their place in it. They produce themselves. But they are dependent on these productions. (136)

I suggest that it is only in anticipation of violence, or during and after violence and terror, that a sensibility of concerted and at-risk social reproduction comes to haunt everyday life, which is at precisely the moment when replication, getting-on-with-it, becomes impossible. In turn, a public culture of rumors reveals the extent to which the sense of control over reality is finite, and the extent to which control has to be reasserted through exaggeration and imaginative supplementation. But this imaginary intervention does not simply denature what was once experienced as pregiven. Rather it reveals the extent to which this compensation of the imaginary is simply an intensification of an imaginative infrastructure that formerly upheld the existing state of things now fading or decentered (see Castoriadis 1989). Rumor attacks social solidities and appropriates them as further but earlier aspects of the rumor apparatus. Under the regime of rumor everything becomes patchwork; an infrastructure of hidden bricolage floats to social consciousness like a submerged stitched-together body. The causal crudity of rumor is a self-conscious central literary attribute. In emphasizing the constructed, assembled nature of social narrative, rumor draws attention to the fabricated character of all other social narratives whose seams and welding once did not show so clearly.

By turning apparently once-stable social structure into provisional and contingent narrative, rumor becomes the production of a countersociety. The social production of rumor is the social production of collective experience in the absence of wide-scale social credibility. Rumor emerges from, and accelerates, the collapse of official organs of institutional depiction, memory, and information dissemination. Rumor mills ironically counterconstruct society as a discrete and objectifiable entity through the process of documenting its fracturing. As discourse it trails and traces the inability of official social institutions to replicate themselves in time and space. Thus in Somalia, China, and Guatemala, as Anna Simons, Frank Pieke, and Linda Green observe, the state is quick and eager to piggyback on the popular culture of rumor, to recolonize public culture so as to manage and control the collective and spontaneous modalities of depiction.

The in situ spontaneous historiography of social crisis comprehended as *rumor* is a sudden and necessary infusion of mass aesthetics, an extempore poetics of experience, and an aperture-apparatus through which res gestae attain presence and normative visibility. The sequential superimposition of each oral myth on the other is an acoustic effect that responds to and simulates the experience of accelerated waves and floods of historical time itself.

The acceleration of disjunctive temporal experiences, the intrusion of situations bearing multiple, nonsynchronous, and concentrated temporalities accentuates the perspectivist determination of historical perception and truth claiming (Bloch 1988; Feldman 1994; Seremetakis 1994). The appearance, presentation, and apprehension of past and present shifts with each impinging event or with rumor-as-event. Rumor, with its inherent discontinuity, lapses, jerry-rigged compensations, and unstoppable flow, reverberates with incompatible chronic polyphony.

With the proliferation of rumor, multiplicity and discontinuity that were previously unobserved, invisible, or tamed by the official narrative unification of everyday life enter as autonomous historical forces. Retrospective interpretation feeds off the pastness, the absence, of accomplished events and emancipates language from the event, which reciprocally emancipates the poeticized event from the past as a self-contained zone of finished acts. It is frequently from such displacements that postnarrative, postrumor historical action originates. Rumor, as in situ depiction, is a crucial structural element of historicity that expands the gauge of what is admitted as event and thus expands and complicates the presumptions and horizons of historical action.

Rumors are ideologies in search of new techniques of event authentication; thus they fabricate and encompass causality and consequence within the same narrative form as Simons, ethnographer and relief worker in Somalia, concludes of rumors, in this volume:

> In short they stitch together what may well be correct facts but in doing so omit gaps, as if correlations must always be linked by causal arrows, with the strength of detail then proving causality. (50)

Can this not also describe ethnographic analysis in certain circumstances? Can we insist on rigid barriers between ethnographic inference and vernacular structures of inference that become all the more virulent in the political emergency zone? History is frequently made and written with and from rumor to the extent that historical action may be mediated by "illegitimate," informal, provisional, and improvised on-the-ground systems of knowledge. The concept of history itself is a culturally specific form of rumor, particularly when it is positioned by class, gender, and cultural inequities and discontinuities.

Nordstrom describes the conditions that give rise to ad hoc historiographic inferential practice and narrative.

> With the onslaught of excessive violence, the boundaries defining the family, community, and cosmos slip, grow indistinct, reconfigure in new and painful ways. And through the breached boundaries, the substance of each spills out across the landscapes of life in a way that is unstructured, highly charged, and immediate. (135)

She speaks of the local Mozambican concept of *dislocado*, which overtly refers to persons, communities, and population uprooted by the public terror. But the notion of dislocado must also infer the displacement of social knowledge and language and the destruction of systems of reference to which rumor responds. Nordstrom recollects,

> I am reminded of a conversation I had with a young teenage soldier in the bush of north-central Mozambique. I asked him why he was fighting and he looked at me and in all seriousness replied, "*I forgot.*" (137)

Green, writing of her fieldwork in Guatemala, also observes,

> Fear thrives on ambiguities. Rumors of death lists and denunciations, gossip, and innuendos create a climate of suspicion. No one can be sure who is who. (105)

In Mogadishu, Simons notes how rumor as graffiti appears on the built environment, recoding the material surround with counterproposals of the social. There is a transitive movement and a tension between the residual meanings of the older edifices and the graffiti commentary that has been montaged on these social surfaces. This montage encapsulates the unfolding of new forms out of defunct old ones whose still-visible remains anchor the sense of chronological progression. Through the graffiti rumor, public space becomes less solid; official utility is subverted and displaced by unpredictable prospects. Public space is no longer serviceable in accustomed ways; it is now announced and advertised as a zone of accentuated risk taking.

Rumor also renames the field site for the ethnographer. Its whispers enter into field experience like a boundary demarcating murmuring that announces the passage into the state of emergency. The ethnographer is first made aware of wider social disturbance when the usual sources of facts, the channels and flows of information on which his or her work is dependent, are interrupted and broken up by political white noise. Here is Frank Pieke, an anthropologist of Chinese social organization, thrown into the midst of Tian'anmen Square and asking the participants of one of the first demonstrations for their substantive demands.

> Obviously the people here are extremely reluctant to talk to a foreigner. Even a colleague whom I happened to run into treats me like somebody with a contagious disease. (62)

To find out what is happening after the first outbreak of violence in Mogadishu, Somalia, Simons is forced to rely on a Euro-American walkie-talkie
network:

> [A]s most people [Western relief workers and diplomats] were located within
> largely elite neighborhoods, it was never entirely clear what was happening
> throughout the city. (45)

> [M]ost of the Somalis I knew were extremely reticent about discussing
> what they thought had occurred and why they thought violence had finally
> erupted. (46)

Rumor for the ethnographer, and perhaps for the informant, emerges
first as silence. It is as if the first wound of violence, the initial and simultaneous damaging of individual bodies and the corporate body, effaces the
social capacity for description. Things are thought but not said, and when
a speech emerges it is not from that aborted thought but from the inter-
vening gap of the not-said. Rumor begins at this border of silence around
the kernel of the absent event, the disappeared body, the silenced name.
Terror and pain is all the more effective when it is experienced as an effect with no cause, with no definable place of its own except the locale of
one's own body.

MATERIAL DREAMS OF THE STATE

Rumor, as the language of risk, is a lens that identifies possible targets and
accesses emerging social and personal needs, a calculus that organizes
new relations between chance and necessity. In zones of violence, the terror of everyday life is risk and rumor felt on the body. Rumor somaticized
is the dream of the executioner borne within the imputed victim's body.
Through rumor and risk perception, embodiment is doubled: expected
victimizer and potential victim are intermingled in the same form. The
body becomes transitive and historicized by the conjuncture of chance
and finality. Torture and assassination frequently are rumor materially enacted on other people's bodies (see Feldman 1991), which are then, in
turn, transmuted into rumor as victims are first subtracted by violence as
living entities and then frequently made to vanish altogether as both persons and corpses by state silence and/or popular incomprehension.

How do we access the microlanguage of terror that is conveyed by gesture and expression from body to body in the everyday "silent" apprehension that occurs within the rumor of surface normalcy? This is intertextual
terror wherein each body is both itself and the other who promises the
body's negation. When the state is the primary agency of violence, this
haunted and possessed body becomes an artifact of the state. Rumor-

terror is sunk into the person as the embodied rationality of the state. Ted Swedenburg, recently returned from the experience of the Palestinian intifada and Israeli counterinsurgency, emerges under the clear sunshine of a suburban Californian neighborhood to hallucinate a local gardener holding a rake as an Israeli soldier with an Uzi. His vision recaptures the dynamic of inversion and irony in the emergency zone, where normalcy is rendered temporary cover for the turbulent currents of overturning terror. But his perception is also revealed here as being haunted and possessed by the afterimages and aftereffects of the counterinsurgency apparatus.

Rumor aggravates and accelerates the process by which history is consumed by its effects and reemerges as myth, folk knowledge, illness, dreams, ideology, theory, confusion, nerves, and nonmeaning. These forms, in turn, multiply the efficacy of events. Green follows the incarnations of rumor.

> [L]ow-intensity panic remains in the shadow of waking consciousness . . . and so the chaos one feels becomes infused throughout the body. It surfaces frequently in dreams and chronic illness. (109)

Through systematic disappearances, terror transforms the state of personhood into rumor, into dream. As rumor becomes the substance of the social, it derealizes and surrealizes the materiel of experience, which becomes increasingly oneiric. Rumor is the narrative daydream of the social unconscious that has reworked or even jettisoned societal master narratives. Rumor transforms the life-world into a sonar-ridden echo chamber in which sensory signals emitted by the subject's body and voice rebound in distorted and cryptic forms, registering indirect contact with randomness and death.

LOST AUTHORSHIP/FAILED REFERENTS

What happens when the "informant" can no longer narrate or author because all reference has been removed? Nordstrom, commenting on the war in Mozambique, correlates this phenomenon with the disappearance of everyday life itself and the overtaking of ideological rationale by the action of violence (see also Feldman 1991). Loss of reference can also be the abutment of more than one frame of mutually exclusive referentiality. There is a disassociation between "the normal" and the zone of terror and alterity, when each, in its turn, becomes routine and exceptional. People exist in both places simultaneously, and frequently with an anomalous comprehension of their dual existence on either side of the border between the ordinary and the extraordinary. These two territories of the self repeatedly exchange position, each sphere reciprocally becoming exotic for the person who is divided between them. Nordstrom recalls a torturer who glues photographs of his mutilated victims into an album alongside biographical snapshots of a personal prewar normalcy that no longer exists. Is this his attempt to render his violence understandable to himself and to others by resituating them in older contexts of fact and normalcy?

When we write, we construct a center, an author. But in the rationalized randomness of terror, all authorial functions are put into question and authorial sites are subject to drift. The popular emergence of rumor as public culture and social discourse is the collective, and unvoiced, recognition that even the most generic authorial functions of social actors—their capacity to muster and mobilize resources of the self, relationships, community and institutional roles, and everyday life—have evaporated. Rumor attempts to reinscribe authorship to exert the privilege of narration and the narrator against the burdens of excess experience, surplus meanings, and untellable tales.

Silence is also rumor; it can be the state's production and dissemination of indifference in public culture, but this indifference is not only formalist, rationalized, and procedural, as Michael Herzfeld (1992) claims, but violating, material, and an-archic. It removes the capacity of individuals, kin groups, and communities to name themselves through their historical experience. Thus Antonius Robben, interviewing military officers of the Argentine junta, is shocked by the installed lived rumor-of-normality that is maintained in the aftermath of the state's disappearance of political opponents. Green relates the official denial of the Guatemalan security forces when asked about the fate and whereabouts of the disappeared. Here the feigned ignorance, the incarceration of the state's victims in a zone of indifference, is itself a depoliticizing rumor bureaucratized as official (non-)knowledge.

In the zone of terror, normalcy-as-rumor takes on a trompe l'oeil effect; as a better imitation of itself, it is inserted into the seas of violence as an administrative support, life raft, and temporary shelter, and normalcy persists in this fashion long after. The state uses silence, indifference, public denial, and self-censorship imposed on the masses to fabricate a superimposed normalcy: this is the simulacrum of the routine that is reworked and hastily shoved into place after violence and that becomes increasingly pregnant with the potential of further terror. This is why at certain junctures in the narratives presented, particularly Green's and Nordstrom's, highly naturalistic, Hemingwayesque writing suddenly burst forth in a schizoid and ambiguous attempt by the ethnographer to grasp and author the real, to detail all the more minutely because the apparent solidity and exhaustiveness of the realist description will be betrayed through the eruption of violence, nausea, and weightlessness, as terror rushes in from behind the curtain of the conventional.

THE VICTIM BEYOND

The state of emergency puts forth existentials that exceed, evade, and will not be contained by formulaic techniques and norms of fact setting. Consider how post-Holocaust quantification, no matter how necessary, contributes to the stratification and hierarchical objectification of victims by number and abbreviates and numbs the material-spiritual cosmos of the event. A variant of this is related by Maria Olujic, a "native" ethnographer writing of Croatia. She was told in reference to the killing of five European Community observers by Serbian irregulars, "the deaths of these five observers will mean more to Europe and the whole world, more than all of the deaths of the thousands of Croatians thus far." Facticity is hierarchical, preferential, and culture-bound. Cathy Winkler describes how legal facticity rebifurcates her body as a rape victim, partitioning the objective from the subjective and the sensorial, the jural-medical from the autobiographical. It alienates the material record of rape trauma, rationalizing the automatic recording capacities of the body's nerves and surfaces and fetishizes the genitalia as the axes of the legal personality of the victim.

Centers of historical or factual record like "Europe" or the courtroom are grounded on a partial facticity that attains the holistic. Yet there are facts that elude culturally mediated notions of the factual. This excess is transmitted as violent force on the certitude of both the anthropologist and the "informant" in the emergency zone. There are facts that will not be admitted into existing albums of facticity. Thus Ted Swedenburg, remembering his friend, the assassinated Nabil, is forced to confront, like Joseba Zulaika, the pre-, post-, or extraideological dimensions of political violence. Victims like Nabil exceed the totalizing project of ideology. They encapsulate historical excess by resisting final codification, for they are its casualties. These ideological ghosts consequently embody contradictory historical and cultural messages for the ethnographer. They are the boundaries that the ethnographer of violence (reluctantly) crosses that can place one beyond ideology and public culture. Zulaika, who ruminates on the impact of Basque insurgency on his natal village, meditates on two deceased friends, an ETA activist and an ETA victim. However, these factual assignations can never exhaust the reality of these friends for him. Now deposited in the village cemetery, their full mnemonic is uncontainable by the limits of sociopolitical categorization. Death, memory, and emotional pain render them irredeemably other. One friend was killed by ETA as a rumored informer. However, to die by rumor and then to be definitively named informer by that act is to die twice, by bullet and by political mythmaking; both acts introduce irrevocable closure for personhood. For Zulaika, in the death of this rumored informer who was also his friend, the imputed political fact is to the person what the tombstone and its few perfunctory remarks are to the well of the grave and the unending process of physical dispersion (see Seremetakis 1991). Here arbitrary political classification materialized in an act of violence assaults deeper social memories and more profound, if personal, facts, turning these materialities into ghostly rumor and illusive recollection.

The victim of violence is, in part, an unrecoverable depth that cannot and should not be definitively represented by ideology and its ordinance of facticity. The victim is an irreconcilable absence. The political victim, deceased or alive, is always partially the disappeared. Something has been subtracted even from those who survive and return, something that can only accommodate symbolic mediation, emotions, and memory. New social networks, microcommunities of pain, are formed around the particularity of the removed, the subtracted, and the returned. These missing parts of community and family and their own missing or disfigured body parts are concentrated vessels of history. It is through this fecund "lack" that remembrance takes place. In public demonstrations, such as those that occurred in Central America and Argentina, the photographs of disappeared children are borne by their parents like totemic, ancestral figures, for it is their absence that introduces qualitatively new time into the survivor's lives, new origins and new ends.

To identify the victim as lack, as beyond final representation, is not to say that victims are negligible or should remain silent. When the victim does speak, this recollection and signifying holds the possibility of subverting public memory and discourse from without by imposing the inadmissible from spaces and experiential strata that public culture cannot occupy or claim to know. However, as Robben points out through his theory of seduction, far too frequently when the victim speaks it is with the very instruments of objectification, fact setting, truth claiming, and other alluring cultural logics that state terror arrayed against the victim in the first place. Something has to dramatically alter within these channels of communication for the victim to emit and hear his or her own voice in its full discordance and difference. The mute victim is both the other side of rumor and a rumor personified. Rumor and victimage occupy the nexus of the crisis in communicative capacity. Rumor and victimage form a couple.

FAILED TOTALITIES: FROM AUTHOR TO WITNESS

By totality, I mean the mythic concept of an inert whole called society in which the parts occupy a fixed position in an unchanging closure. Totalizations are acts, agendas, programs, and political instruments, like terror and violence, that attempt to install the holistic myth onto the dispersion of historical and material experience. Many of the authors here write within the aftershocks and afterimages of the violent attempt to calibrate ideological agendas on the backs of arbitrary victims. To what extent does ethnography follow through with the composition of totality? Are we complicit in its restoration through textual effects and encompassing analytic reductions?

In the zones of terror there is a risky back-and-forth passage between the dispersal of everyday life and the unifying space of totalization. This is concentrated in Zulaika's gravitation to the metaphor of the priest who quits the Church and the everyday existentials of the former ETA terrorist. Does the ethnographer of violence make similar passages and at what risk? The act of totalization, the summing up of history and society, is a contingent act, only occurring at specific moments and spaces that can evaporate, leaving this finalizing act out of context. Does the ethnographer experience ethnography in that manner? The embarrassment of the book, the finished volume, is the face of the persistence and transformation of social experience after the book. The book totalizes, functions as a ludicrous dam attempting to stop the flow of experience only to be washed away by it, leaving the ethnographer standing on nothing, or everything if that nothing is considered as sheer historicity itself.

Though Zulaika wants to focus on how the "community" defines acts of violence, that act of definition, like the ethnography itself, can be washed away and deflated by the material force of other interpretations—of the state, the media, and the political organization. These forces may make it impossible to define community, which is what his Basque village attempts to do when it exerts moral frames against acts of violence. The autonomy of that act of self-definition is contested by more efficient technologies of totalization. Civil war, counterinsurgency, and terrorism remove the community's capacity for self-definition. For each killing, arrest, assassination, or torture is established as an ever more finalizing act of redefinition and renaming.

The ethnographer writing autobiographical terror must write from the outside in, from the edge of ethnographic coherence, dissolving the center of the ethnographic narrative-optic to the same extent that the edges, the limit experiences of violence and terror, dissolve and disassemble all social centers, anchorages, and agents of final definition. In many of these essays, ethnographic perception, like rumor, moves past itself, beyond the scope of past ethnographic glances, eyes falling out of eyes, as theoretical perception trips from one analytic plane of dissolving social order to another—from economy to social structure to culture to ritual to language— each once, enabling plane of theoretical perception collapsing inward like a house of cards. Within this collapse, each site of social anchorage is revealed as artifice and as rumor to which we have become habituated. During the rebellion in Tian'anmen Square, Pieke witnesses social order literally sliding out from under itself. It trips from a rhetorical edifice in which the political agent is framed by a preexisting posture in the division of labor and social stratification to a situation in which social actors actively solidify a provisional social structure. In Pieke's contribution, the Chinese work unit attempts totalization by ceasing to be a passive recipient of structure and becoming self-constructing. At Tian'anmen Square, public performances by the work unit's representatives carve out an emerging and novel space of imagined community. This is a shift from the performative—the replication of preexisting, mandated, and prescribed codes—to performance—the active construction of novel social narratives, acts, and spaces without obedient or mimetic reference to preinstituted codes. This sequence can also be found in recent mutations of social theory from structure-centered models to action-, agency-, and performance-centered models of social and political constitution in which society is a project and not a reified predeterminant.

In a number of the chapters, Nordstrom's, Simon's, Green's, and Swedenburg's, the ethnographer conducts fieldwork and writes in the violent aftermath of failed totalization. In Swedenburg's, the intifada passes from totalizing status to the fragmentation and exhaustion of everyday life.

> [T]hey will say that the struggle has entered a new stage. Many people were weary, worn down, introspective, pessimistic about the outcome of "peace" negotiations, preoccupied by the dull grind of economic hardships, alarmed by the growing constraints on the activities of women. The heroic days of intifada on the march are over. (25)

The intimacy between violence, writing, and totalization is quite evident in Jean Genet's depiction of his sojourn with the Palestinian insurgents as cited by Swedenburg. For Genet's descriptions draw on an Enlightenment anthropological tradition that can be traced to a Rousseau essay on theater, the spectacle, and the festival in the letter to d'Alembert. Against the atomization, alienation, and distantiation of eighteenth-century experience, Rousseau reimagined a people's festival where all social relations would become immediate, transparent, and dis-alienated. It would be a festival where, unlike theater, no artifice of representation would mediate meaning and communication, where there would be no division of labor between performers and audience. The Rousseauian festival banishes representation in its political and semiotic sense. It represents nothing outside of itself. It is the utopia of totalization where an enlightenment transparency of social relations unfolds, building on premodern traditions of carnival and world-upside-down. For Genet, the Palestinian revolution is a Rousseauian festival. Genet invokes this imagery when he uses phrases like "idiotic delight" and "happy smiles" and where exhaustion and fatigue and ennui can set in, as in any party that has gone on too long: "It was for *fun* as much as anything." The Palestinians are seen by

Genet through a lens of Durkheimian collective effervescence, which moves between the inversions of festival and "funeral procession." Though Genet also fabricates a doubled totalization. He is a tourist of another culture's festival of totalization. It never engaged "the whole" of himself. Genet holds his self in reserve, as if wary of the same seductiveness that troubles Robben in this volume, and even though Genet extracts enjoyment from the Palestinian festival, he ultimately experiences it from an anti-Rousseauian position "as if from a window or a box in a theatre, and as if through pearl-handled opera glasses."

Genet never seems to experience the fragmentation, the dispersal of identity, the existential death in the field that is part and parcel of the ethnographic breakdown experience and that is aggravated in the spaces of terror. Instead Genet undergoes a loss of particularity in his vocabulary of analysis. In representing the Palestinian cause, he accedes to the universalizing iconography of nineteenth-century nationalist ideology. Sartre and Foucault were also known for this particular habit of abandoning the micrological detail of their customary analysis for the clichés, blandness, and clumsiness of totalizing political generalities. It is this seduction that ethnography cannot afford and must abstain from. Which is why Swedenburg immerses himself in popular memory and there encounters, as I did in Northern Ireland, the chasms between everyday life experience and the aesthetics of official ideological formulations.

In the state of ethnographic emergency, the body and perception of the ethnographer overtake themselves, reaching a societal edge and the far limits of ethnography itself. Recently, anthropologists have become fascinated with borders and border crossings, but at the undomesticated borders bumped against in these chapters there is little fortuitous mixing of styles, little fecund heterogeneity and hybridity, for there is little social glue left at those border crossings-to-the-abject. At these borders history and experience have outstripped society and all its arts and artifices. Ethnographic vertigo conjoins historical vertigo in which all those positioned at the social edge perform and survive through a spontaneous folklore of disappearing everyday life and society. In the zone of ethnographic emergency, where mental maps go akilter, where all things are askew, the ethnographer, like any rumormonger, labors to connect confusions in the absence of totality, conclusion, and closure. Rumor-from-crisis, no matter how eschatological, moves against any sense of an ending through unstoppable regurgitation. The narrative absence of ending refracts the absence of social closure, of sealed social totality that guarantees all narrative terminations, emplotments, and endings in advance. Ethnography, here, links experiences, meanings, and narrative with no transparent sense of their origins, ends, and kinship; the ethnographer lacks a storyboard guaranteed in advance. In these chapters, and in the situations of violence and terror they abut, to what extent is ethnography rumor stabilized? To what extent is rumor itself a social knowledge that has yet to institutionalize itself, to put forth and legitimize its own pasteboard cutout of the social, its own trompe l'oeil? To what extent is narratable history an accumulation of rumors that have settled into durable form and the tombstone of institutional memory? What are the relations between a social reconstitution that takes place through writing or through institutional practices of public reordering?

Can we deny the anxiety of influence in those analyses ignited by experiences of infiltrating apprehension and societal vagueness? When the ethnographer writes himself or herself out of terror, this writing will issue distortion effects, the white historical noise of the writer's own residual historical situation. These views are layered over the flow of jumbled indigenous events. Simons's description of the walkie-talkie network in Somalia illustrates this. The network attempted, through the electronic centralization of rumor, to restore a Western metanarrative on the events unfolding in Somalia. The walkie-talkie network was the restoration of a solidifying discourse that allowed the Western visitors to firm up their subject positions in relation to the violence unfolding from obscure corners and crevices of the third world. This was cultural self-seduction through technological intimacy and cultural intertextuality.

Swedenburg speaks of being seduced by the fun of resistance, Robben of the language and memory of seduction. But what renders seduction almost efficacious here is the extent to which Robben shares a devolved cultural inheritance with the agents of terror in Argentina: they have committed violence in the name of Eurocentric civilizational values. Both Right and Left turn to European history as the totalizing allegorical frame from which they describe the Argentine fragments of terror, violence, and political reordering. The concentration camp is paradigmatic for the Left, as are rationalized penological detention centers for the Right. The mutual Eurocentric inheritance extends to the analytic vocabulary Robben shares with the leftists he interviewed, which makes the possibility of a Benjaminian barbaric inversion of the civilizational doubly unsettling. Do we witness one such inversion when Robben asks his right-wing informants about the possibility of "more *humane* counterinsurgency methods" (emphasis added)?

This myth of objectivism that animates Western historical inquiry also animates Western policymaking, including the policy of terror and the planning and administration of a "detention center and torture center." Terror silently transformed into culture (instrumental rationality is a cultural form) is the worst terror of them all for it compels the question (implicitly asked above), to what extent is culture terror provisionally stabilized and integrated with everyday life?

Robben argues "that seduction is a dimension of fieldwork that is especially prominent in high-conflict research because the informants and interlocutors have great personal and political stakes in making the ethnographer adopt their interpretations." In Argentina, according to Robben, the foreign (i.e., Western) social scientist is seen as a politically neutral juridical courtroom recorder—an extremely naive and politically mediated image through which the ethnographer is invested as an imaginary object, which is crucial to any act of seduction. His informants position Robben between a mythical conceptualization of Western memory—neutral, objectifying, terminal, and above the fray—and their own seductive and emotional acts of recollection. Here Cartesian dichotomies (discussed earlier) that must have surely animated the in situ enactment and conceptualization of violence now organize the act of constructing the public memory of violence.

What about the self-referentiality of remembering and telling in Robben's interviews? The narrator is not simply outside the performance of oral history, of memory, but is actively constructed and reconstructed in and through that action of recalling, relating, and seducing. This would imply that positioning Robben as the imaginary arbiter of final truth involves wish images, desire, and the dynamics of self-seduction as the machinery of memory. A finality of truth is extracted from the sheer presence of Robben as "European" witness, who symbolically returns its possibility to his informants merely by listening and by supposedly being "seduced." Seduction here is a search for an external guarantee for a totalizing fixation of violence and history. It is the viewpoint that there is no internal structure in Argentina on which to fix the truth of the past, whether that is the truth of the Right or the Left. This seduction of self and other becomes a mode of memorialization drawing on emotional complicity. Seduction and emotion may be the modalities through which people recall the sensorium of violence. Robben implies that seduction comes after the narration, as its effect, that ideological intent is already in place prior to the story. But seduction may also be the vehicle of narration. Is this seduction of a resonant other impression management as Robben claims, or is it memory management? Here Robben is not manipulated and diverted by informants away from cultural depth to flash surface (a temporary state of affairs as evidenced by the penetrating analysis of his chapter) but thrown into the deep end of another historical pool.

Seduction should be located not only in the fieldwork process but after it has been halted as well. When the ethnographer emerges from ethnographic zones of emergency, field notes and personal memory are woven

back into the reassuring seductive murmuring of the discipline. The intertextual environment that the report of terror comes to reside in is akin to
the intertexuality of the Euro-American walkie-talkie network in Somalia.
Such intertextual reinforcements are also evident within scholarly treatments of violence, in the form of received models and paradigms, gate-
keeping-peer-reader bureaucracies, the honorifics of acknowledgment (in
articles and books), and the rest of the paraphernalia that attests to the
ethnographer's written return to the Same after the discontinuity of the
field site.

The thrust of disciplinary form and methods compels one to reduce
the particular and novel to that which is already known and considered
universal. Consider how recently in anthropology the totalizing categories
or fetishes of nationalism, religion, and ethnicity have been too rapidly and
too easily deployed as reductive covering concepts in reference to Eastern
Europe and elsewhere. However, these very same categories are also indispensable weapons for agents of violence and domination. In contrast,
what theoretical language did anthropologists develop for those social
movements and activists seeking to create antiessentialist civil societies?
For the most part these groups were off the analytic map; anthropology
and other discourses, fore-armed with the seductive language and theories
of cultural essentialism did not seem willing to distinguish between ethnicity as inheritance, resource and partial habitus from ethnicity as a
managed instrument of state policy, as state rationality by other means.
Resurgent ethnicity—the Rip Van Winkle return-of-the-repressed and the
authentic—was certainly a rumor promoted in the West in reference to the
violence in the former Yugoslavia. In this manner emergent violence in
this area was theoretically managed through a facile "tribalization" of an-
tagonists without fully considering the role of the modern *culture* of the
state in the production and militarization of ethnicity and tribes. Here the
explanations and language of the social scientist and the butchers frequently coincided.

Rumor settles on the Other as classification, text, or violence, leaving finished
ideological objects, the dead and the depicted, in its wake.

The tendency for rapid totalization is an assertion of the authorial position, whether that position is individual, disciplinary, or cultural. It reveals
our historical implication in the culture of the state by ignoring the fact
that totalization is never encompassing and exhaustive but always reductive, distorting, and exclusionary. Totalization can only occur through the
mutilation of the open-endedness, the horizon, of historical experience; it
shuts down history as that which is persistently indicated. Political violence
and terror appear from within the crevices of failed totalities, from the
gaps between political closure and lived experience. Instrumental violence
is the glue by which the totalizing political project and the open-ended

rupture of social experience are to be reconciled. As material practice, violence makes the dispersed parts fit which have been chosen to form the mythic whole. Agencies of violence select those parts by what they do not destroy.

WRITING THE IN-HUMAN

Robben, after considerable conversation with the key figures of the Argentine military junta, asks, how can we establish intersubjective understanding with a person who has violated the very humanity we are trying to understand? The same question can be asked in reference to those who have been subjected to the extremities of violation. How can they be understood and depicted if they dwell on the other side of the border of conventional or known bodily sensory and moral experience? "After Auschwitz" (see Adorno 1973) the chronic violence of the state has introduced a new cultural archipelago of difference and otherness in its efforts to replicate or salvage the state.

The question Robben poses infers another: can we assume that humanity and intersubjectivity are already completed historical projects that promise us a firm ground for such transindividual understanding? History ultimately "dehumanizes" by expanding the scope and gauge of the anthropological. In turn, terror and violence expand the definition of the anthropological by engaging the *in-human*, which is beyond yet intrinsic. This is why ethnographers and others who write about violence from within particularity, who explore the coherence of its non-sense, are frequently accused of dehumanizing their subjects (Zulaika, pers. comm.; Nordstrom, pers. comm.). It is suggested we generate a form of pornography (E. Valentine Daniel, pers. comm.), practice sensationalism, or are simply amoral and perhaps morbid (Seremetakis, pers. comm.). Such charges are not uncommon in the oral culture and review practices of the social sciences. These insinuations frequently culminate in high-minded appeals to the anchor of a commonsensical universal humanity.

The anthropology of violence, the cultural analysis of terror, call up limit experiences that speak to the end(s) of "Man," the historical erasure of residual, circumscribed, and culturally binding definitions of humanity. The "humanist" reaction is to reabsorb death's particularity back into the confines of a global and ahistorical ethical anthropology—an anthropology of continuity. Earlier I suggested that a crucial ethnographic stance salvages the particularity of the victim while systematizing the violence arrayed against the subject: that to do otherwise is to be complicit with other in situ modes of ideological totalization. The victim is at the intersection of multiple forces that form and deform the recipient of violence. But this very violence produces excess historical experience, which I can only term historicity: historical substance that is beyond existing ideological appropriations; experiences that, no matter how negative, speak to the possibility of postideological countermemory, sensory alterities, and emerging historical horizons. The ethnographic reconstruction of violence must write from and toward a ground that few existing moralities can account for. Writing violence becomes the exploration of moralities that have not yet arrived but that are busy being born from amoral acts.

The appeal to an ahistorical global humanism, the often-hysterical calls for overt precultural moral judgment, interdicts the cultural depth of the victim. This posture serves many utilities but not that of historical possibility. As a deculturalizing reaction it is equivalent to the "Kill-the-Indian-save-the-man" policy once applied to Native Americans concentrated on government reservations. This was the watchword of the educational, linguistic, and religious evisceration of offending Native American culture that took place in the name of global humanistic values, which presumed a universal anthropological substratum of continuity beneath the deviance of "the native."

Violence and terror install their own indigene processes that render presumed a priori humanity unrecognizable. The effects of violence and terror cannot be scratched off the surface of body consciousness, and the resilience and life affirmations of those who experience political abjection are not indicative of the survival of universal and pregiven human essences or commonalities. Rather *identities-of-the-aftermath* are transmuted protean selves, the resymbolized consequences of unerasable terror.

I would propose that it is through an ethnography of sensory particularity, of regional modes-of-being, of disjunctive life-worlds that these postviolence identities can best be comprehended and depicted (see also Seremetakis 1994). An ethics of ethnographic witnessing would acknowledge that no experience of violation can be reduced to another, and yet these acts and events cohere into a chain of the irreducible, a patchwork structure of polyphonic particularity and historicity. To witness and to write the in-human is to encounter boundary-bending situations and impossible anthropologies that are horrific, moving, and abiding. It is to encounter what is left over and discarded when all humanisms and other strategies of homogenization (among which we must include systemic terror) have exhausted their material efforts at ideological distillation.

In Greek, the concept of *antifonisi* (antiphony) possesses a social and juridical sense in addition to its aesthetic, musical, and dramaturgical uses. Antiphony can refer to the construction of contractual agreement, the creation of a symphony by opposing voices. It also implies echo, response, and guarantee. *In Greek, the prefix anti- does not only refer to opposition and antagonism but also equivalence, "in place of," reciprocity, face-to-face.* These meanings are embedded in the vocabulary of laments. Mourners in their laments claim to "come out as representative" (*na vghó antiprosopos*) of the dead (*prosopo* means face or person, and antiprosopos means representative). A related and emotionally laden phrase is "to witness, suffer for, and reveal the truth about" the dead (*na tíne martirísoume*). The concept embodied here does not necessarily evoke Christian liturgical belief. . . . The term itself has pre-Christian usages that possess antiphonic and dyadic inflections. The term *marturion* (witness) appears in Herodotus and is associated with the oracles of the dead (*nekromanteion*). . . . The *marturion* was also a coded message composed of two incomplete halves, one each in the possession of sender and recipient. Completion and decipherment of the message required joining the two parts. (Seremetakis 1991:102)

Linda Green, writing of fieldwork in Guatemala and looking to the work of Michael Taussig, speaks of the ethnographic need to give terror sentience. But here we can ask, whose sentience?

Anthropologist as scribe, who faithfully documents what the people themselves narrate as their own histories, that which they have seen, smelled, touched, felt, interpreted, and thought. (108)

But can we assume a common sensorium that would enable such a transference? The mere mention of a division of the senses here is a translation mechanism by which a commonality is constructed, but this is obviously culturally mediated and biased. We concentrate *their* experience into *our compartments* to endow their sensorium with coherence. But what if this historically created sentience challenges the very conditions of sensory experience as the ethnographic witness knows it? What has happened to the senses and perception in the spaces of terror? Do these sensory divisions Green notes still hold true, if they were ever there? In many zones of political stasis and terror, it is clear that violence and terror is directed not only against a political subject or community but also against the structure of everyday life; that is to say, it interdicts that which enables material experience to be reproduced over time and in space. Systemic violence wipes out the material supports of experience, conservation, and memory; it can eradicate the possibility of its recipients recording its effects. There is no coincidence that Nordstrom, writing of the war in Mozambique, speaks of Renamo, whose tactics include severing the noses, lips, and ears of civilians. These symbolic mutilations are acts against the organs of social witnessing, attacks on the individual body that affect the corporate body and its capacity to construct memory. What are the equivalents in the corporate body of mutilated organs of evidence and perception; organs that are transformed by violence into ruins and by social memory into allegorical emblems? Violence that is historically, legally, and politically self-conscious erases its tracks in its own actions by canceling the cultural sense organs of its victims and reciprocally the social capacity to witness—each mutilated body a message of what is to be forgotten and silenced.

But this is not the only trajectory that representation can take. In the zones of sensory subtraction or fragmentation, the ethnographer can be literally *incorporated* as a witness and organ donor. The ethnographer's vision, audition, tactility, and speech may be asked to complete the incomplete bodies and selves of the dead, the missing, and their survivors. A crucial component of the enculturation process in the spaces of death and the zones of terror is that the ethnographer-witness relinquishes ownership over personal organs of perception that must be reinhabited, expanded, and intermingled to accommodate the material metaphors of a new sensorium. During fieldwork in Belfast, my perception was no longer my own when I ceased to have telephone conversations that lasted more than thirty seconds, when I never used people's names over the telephone, when the back of my scalp itched as I felt the patrolling British soldiers tracking my movements with the barrels of their automatic rifles, when I leaped off the front parlor couch along with my hosts at a car backfiring in the night, when I abruptly terminated conversations because police vehicles were circling the neighborhood streets with more frequency since I had arrived, when I left notes documenting my whereabouts and appointments before going into the night to be picked up by paramilitaries for drinking sessions in obscure private pubs, and when I was able to "tell" who was Protestant and who was Catholic by reading frequently imaginary, microscopic signs.

Sensory acculturation often occurs in small details and everyday events, even in dreams, illnesses, and waking hallucinations, as Swedenburg found out far from the field site. Nordstrom, sitting with a group of women in a war zone of Mozambique, describes one such deceptively mundane moment.

> We were sitting on the ground chewing on the stalk of a weed (I was chewing on the weed because the women had handed it to me; the women did so out of a habit they had developed to appease their appetites when food was scarce). (146)

Through the inedible the women communicate where the history of their suffering is encoded—in everyday material experience—and make a statement concerning at what level of being their experience should be stored by the witness-other.

In Winkler's account of rape, the act is announced in the displacement of the sureties of her everyday life and domestic space. The rape is first chronicled in the minute perceptual disjointedness of her household arrangements, socks set out to dry and the basement window interfered with. In hindsight, these molested objects become sensorial harbingers of, and inanimate witnesses to, the rendering of her own body as object. Inadmissible shifts in one's social situation are frequently invisible and subtle, and they are first registered in the obscurities of the everyday, in the crevices of unexamined micrological life-worlds such as the domain of objects and everyday speech acts. As Nordstrom confides, "The most silenced stories at war's epicenters are generally the most authentic." This is also to say that the real story of the war, the violence and the terror, is always elsewhere and thus contingent on ever-shifting historical, perceptual, and biographical perspectives that move through silence or screams.

There is also the eerie image captured by Maria Olujic in Croatia, which synthesizes both the bodily passion and the pain of estrangement that can be inscribed on the landscape as material culture and that can eventually organize both the infliction and the reception of violence. Here a returning Croatian awakens his senses and his sense of place through self-inflicted pain-as-sustenance and memory.

> In the warm glow of the sunset on a scorching summer day, I was picking blackberries by a dusty road adjacent to my father's house. From a distance, I could see a white car piled high with suitcases on its roof. Moving at a snail's pace, the car pulled up and stopped next to me. An elderly passenger, clearly a returning emigrant, stepped out of the car, a suit jacket thrown over his forearm. Without speaking, he approached and wrenched a footlong branch from the blackberry bush and began chewing on it, including thorns and unripe berries. I looked at him in bewilderment, thinking that he would choke on the sharp thorns. In a quick sweeping glance, I looked at the other three people in the car. No one said anything. The man slowly walked back to the car and got in. As the car left, all I could see was the cloud of dust particles shimmering in the afternoon sun. . . . The blackberry symbolized the sweet return, the reuniting, and the thorns conveyed the feeling of suffering, the anguish of a foreign place. (188)

These stories, which locate the structure of events in the structure of things, recount the materiality of witnessing where historically layered experience can be invested in a resonant artifact or substance and the common gesture takes on major cross-cultural and transpersonal significance (see Seremetakis 1994). Sometimes the storage site of historical excess is not a thing or a substance but a person. Nordstrom describes how, in the war zones of Mozambique, certain people become overburdened with the experience and memory of violence. They carry magnitudes of violence within them. Attempts are made to heal them and to expel the stored violence. However, at the same time these repositories of violence personified are themselves, the walking social memory of the collective and empathic storage sites of mass corporeal experience. These figures are sacrificial emissaries, their perceived dis-ease and their subsequent curing, like the expulsion and rehabilitation of Oedipus, allow the reconstituting community to encapsulate and handle miasma to both codify and dispel it. This healing process, the societal-laying-on-of-hands, is as cathartic for the community as it is for the healed individual. Each rumor of healing is socially therapeutic. These tales anticipate collective reconciliation. Both the conditions of contamination by violence and of intervention by healing are crucial to historicizing a social memory of terror and installing this memory with a sense of ending.

Stories, experiences, and sentience that are relayed to the anthropologist are another and further sacrificial strategy that establishes the witness-emissary as storage site precisely because this figure does not stay but takes the symbolic excess of violence away and outside. If full witnessing across cultures, histories, fears, and pains is a matter of altered sentience, then it is most likely an involuntary process, an experience that moves beyond explicit rationalities of coeval dialogue as they are theorized by the volunteerism of the new ethnography. Green recalls how she was shown the hidden burial sites of the disappeared in Guatemala.

> In Xe'caj, people would point out such sites to me. On several occasions when I would be walking with them in the mountains, women would take me to the places where they knew their husbands were buried and say, "Mira, el está allí" (Look, he is over there). (119–120)

How do we understand this *command* to "look"? At this juncture the ethnographer's moral and perceptual position is radically altered and clarified both through and beyond fieldwork transactions. For this command is not a moment of dialogue or a formal interview; though its punctuation may have gestated there. It is an imperative, one that offers little choice other than to turn away, to not look. This call-to-witness captures in one breath the force of history itself. It encapsulates and replicates a *history of sensory shock,* a history of the lack of perceptual choice. Perceptual choice is the privileged position, and certainly a power of the state that transmutes this power into silence over the disappearance of its victims. The absence of perceptual choice becomes the struggle for memory as an alternate sensory organ—and in Guatemala forgetfulness and remembrance are intermingled in the landscape itself through these secret burials.

The command interpellates the ethnographer and seems to infer, *you are here, you have or should accumulate enough experience to see what is pointed out, and you are now morally and historically responsible for what you see and learn. It is a responsibility for those who live with this knowledge because it can kill us, it has killed us—it can now kill you. Look and experience not only the finitude of those who are buried here but experience your own mortality that is unfolded by the limits of your vision, which no longer distances, objectifies, or empowers but im-*

plicates you through its finitude. This place of absent bodies, of the remembered dead with no names, is also the place of the death of your vision.

By naming and commanding our vision, our perception, this imperative is the act by which the survivors embody the ethnographic witness as a sense organ of *their memory. They* assign *their* senses to the ethnographer without guarantee of reception, recall, or permanence. The same assignment occurs when Nordstrom is handed the root to be chewed in Mozambique. We will never plumb the historical, emotional, and interpersonal depths that reside in this command to look. Why are we finally the recipients of it? For the vision directed by this command must be qualitatively differentiated from any media-inspired voyeurism and from Western photocentrism. How, in the context of our own public culture(s), do we translate the dead, the dying, the terrorized, the disappeared from media-constructed phantasms; rumors, to a condition of historical actuality? For this is a command to be accountable for both full sensory depth and experiential limits. How do we fulfill this account? What is our debt? What organs of cultural intelligence do we owe, what organs of transplant shall we receive, in order to keep faith with the unwritten body of the other?

REFERENCES

Adorno, Theodore W.
    1973   *Negative Dialectics.* New York: Continuum.
Bloch, Ernst
    1988   *The Heritage of Our Time.* Cambridge: MIT Press.
Castoriadis, Cornelius
    1989   *The Imaginary Institution of Society.* New York: Columbia University Press.
Derrida, Jacques
    1981   *Disseminations.* Translated by Barbara Johnson. Chicago: University of Chicago Press.
Feldman, Allen
    1991   *Formations of Violence: The Narrative of the Body and Political Terror in Northern Ireland.* Chicago: University of Chicago Press.
    1994   "On Cultural Anesthesia: From Desert Storm to Rodney King." *American Ethnologist* 21(2):404–418.
Foucault, Michel
    1972   *The Archeology of Knowledge.* New York: Pantheon.
Herzfeld, Michael
    1992   *The Social Production of Indifference: Exploring the Symbolic Roots of Western Bureaucracy.* Chicago: University of Chicago Press.
Kosseleck, Reinhart
    1985   *Futures Past: The Semantics of Historical Time.* Cambridge: MIT Press.
Marcus, George
    1991   "A Broad(er)side to the Canon." *Cultural Anthropology* 6(3): 385–405.

Ricoeur, Paul
   1973   "The Model of the Text: Meaningful Action as Text." *New Literary History* 5:91–120.
Seremetakis, C. Nadia
   1991   *The Last Word: Women, Death and Divination in Inner Mani.* Chicago: University of Chicago Press.
   1994   "The Memory of the Senses." Pts. 1 and 2. In *The Senses Still: Perception and Memory as Material Culture in Modernity,* ed. C. Nadia Seremetakis, 1–43. Boulder: Westview Press.

THE DOING OF ANTHROPOLOGY

Myrna Mack

Myrna Mack

Elizabeth Oglesby

The last time I saw Myrna was at 5:00 A.M. on June 30, 1990, when she dropped me off at the airport in Guatemala City. I was leaving the country after four years, en route to a job in New York. When the call came from Guatemala on September 12, I felt like I had stepped out my front door only to turn and see my house explode. "They killed Myrna last night." The familiar, chilling Guatemalan grammar. Not "Myrna was killed." They killed her. In Guatemala, the word "they" is as unambiguous as can be.

Myrna Mack was a Guatemalan anthropologist: talented, spirited, and audacious. Her research in Guatemala's rural areas was pioneering, and I had the privilege of working with her. Early in the evening of September 11, Myrna was stabbed twenty-seven times as she left her office in downtown Guatemala City. The brutality of the attack and the state of Guatemalan politics made government security forces immediately suspect, and this was confirmed months later when a military intelligence officer was identified as Myrna's killer.

Who was Myrna Mack, and why was she killed? Myrna's life was an example of a profound commitment by a social scientist to her society. As a founding member of AVANCSO (the Association for the Advancement of the Social Sciences, a leading research institute in Guatemala City), Myrna believed that social science has an ethical imperative to address the issues most relevant to society, particularly those that affect the poorest strata of society. With enormous energy, Myrna dedicated the last three years of her life to documenting the rural displacement caused by the Guatemalan army's "scorched earth" counterinsurgency sweeps of the early 1980s. While it might seem impossible to hide the existence of 1.3 million displaced peasants in a country of 9 million, in fact many Guatemalans knew virtually nothing about the displaced. Myrna's studies helped break the silence.

Her vocation for fieldwork and talent for communicating earned her the trust and affection of indigenous communities in many parts of Guatemala; however, her deep identification with these populations ultimately proved threatening to the military.

I remember Myrna's optimism, her ability to make the impossible seem possible. She told me how she had returned to Guatemala in 1982, after receiving her master's degree in England. "To be in Guatemala in 1982 was like walking on the moon," she said. "Absolutely nothing moved." Social science research had effectively come to a halt with the bitter civil war and military repression after 1980. More than one hundred university professors and researchers were murdered; a similar number went into exile. Still, Myrna returned with optimism.

Myrna had an electric wit that could alternately override or underscore the black side of her country. "The difference between a U.S. scholar and a Guatemalan scholar," she told visiting researchers, "is that in the United States, you say 'publish or perish.' Here, we say 'if we publish, we perish.'" A burst of laughter followed, even as the irony lingered.

That irony shaped Myrna's life. For decades, Guatemala has been a haven for U.S. scholars studying the country's Indian cultures and, more recently, documenting the effects of social upheaval on those cultures. While foreign academics can count on relatively unimpinged and risk-free access to even the remotest regions, few Guatemalan social scientists dare venture far outside the capital city. For Myrna, this double standard was infuriating, and she was determined to break the barrier.

In early 1987, when Myrna and I began to travel together, much of rural Guatemala was in shambles. The counterinsurgency campaign had left more than four hundred villages destroyed, two hundred thousand refugees in Mexico, and several times that number displaced within the country. Military control was pervasive throughout the countryside, and our first trips into the rural areas were tentative and exploratory. What sort of research was possible in Guatemala?

The next four years brought incredible advances. We joked that we had destroyed an entire fleet of Suzuki jeeps from the Budget Rent-A-Car office in Guatemala City by taking them into places not meant for even four-wheel-drive vehicles. In all these regions, Myrna carefully documented the experiences of the displaced: the massacres that drove thousands into hiding in the mountains and the slow return of villagers to their former lands. She became widely respected as one of the few people in Guatemala City who could accurately describe conditions in the highlands, and she was a key resource for nongovernmental organizations (NGOs) and the Catholic Church as these sectors confronted the urgent yet politically delicate issue of refugee resettlement.

When Myrna was killed, few colleagues inside or outside the country

expected the case to become anything more than just another statistic in
Guatemala's long trajectory of state violence. But Myrna's sister, Helen
Mack, was determined to investigate the crime and prosecute those responsible. An unassuming woman with no prior political involvement, Helen
faced threats and institutional intransigence in her tenacious search to uncover evidence of the army's role in Myrna's murder. After a prolonged
trial in which a key witness was gunned down and eleven judges withdrew
from the case, in February 1993, Noel de Jesús Beteta, a former army
sergeant, was convicted of stabbing Myrna Mack to death—the first time
that the Guatemalan state had ever been held accountable for a political
crime. In 1992, Helen Mack won Sweden's Right Livelihood Award (also
known as the "Alternative Nobel Peace Prize"), and she created the Myrna
Mack Foundation to help other Guatemalans pursue human rights cases.
She continues to press for charges against the military superiors who ordered her sister's murder.

Myrna Mack's assassination produced results that were in many ways
the opposite of what her killers intended. Helen Mack's battle against military impunity attracted the attention of Guatemalan society, and as Guatemalans learned more about Myrna and her research, public concern for
the victims of the war grew. Ironically, Myrna's death led to more concrete
assistance for the displaced communities, a goal that had frustrated her
during her fieldwork.

Included here are brief excerpts from letters Myrna Mack wrote to a
friend between May 1988 and December 1989. The letters were never intended to be read by anyone other than the addressee, and their language
is direct, unpretentious. They mark distinct moments of Myrna's last two
field research projects. Originally printed in 1992 as an epilogue to Myrna's final study on the displaced (which her colleagues at AVANCSO completed and published posthumously), these letters convey more than just
the difficult conditions under which Myrna conducted her research; they
reveal the inner conflict of a scholar torn between the demand for "objectivity" as evidence of theoretical and methodological rigor and the human
response that her research evoked. They are the private testimonies of a
Guatemalan anthropologist who died at the age of forty because she insisted on carrying out a type of fieldwork that was at once engaging and
engaged.

May 29, 1988

What troubles me is that all I do is talk to people. I draw out their sad histories, and that's it. I feel my role reduced to one of extraction.

June 24, 1988

These research trips have been enriching in so many ways. I'm thankful
for the opportunity to travel, but I still wonder how to give something worth-

while back to the communities. I feel so comfortable with people in the countryside. It makes me feel—I don't know how to describe it exactly—but it feels very positive to be with them, to listen to them and accompany them with a little conversation. Although it's painful to witness their pain, their sadness, frustration, impotence. . . . Can there ever be any hope for them?

But interesting things always surface in those areas. I spent one day at the army base interviewing the local military personnel, and I had a chance to meet a young Indian woman who works for the army's Civilian Affairs office. It started to rain in the middle of our interview, and so we waited out the storm together, talking about all sorts of things. She started to tell me about her life, and it was obvious that she has suffered like the rest of her people. She fell in love with a *ladino* from the town, and she was crushed when his father insulted her for being an "*india*" and accused her of chasing after the boy for the family's money. "But I love him," she insisted to me, "he has green eyes and looks like a gringo." She has also felt the lash of violence, with the death of her father and two brothers, but she says she joined the army out of a desire to help her people. It's all very complex, and it makes me realize that no matter what side you're on in all this, people, especially the people in this region, have an overwhelming need to speak, to tell about their lives, to confide in a sympathetic listener. The next day, the same young woman ran up and hugged me on the street, saying she had forgotten to tell me that she needs toys for the children and something to get rid of lice. . . . How to process all this? I have some idea, but I don't know if it's enough.

November 1, 1988

The truth is that I never imagined how much work was involved in putting everything in order for the final report. You barely have a breathing space before sitting down to write, although I think that through the writing process we have begun to construct a deeper analysis. This whole experience has been enormously important, and I feel very satisfied with what I've learned. The problem, though, is the space limitation they've imposed on us; we can hardly include the richness of all the testimonies we've compiled. . . .

We had considered doing a follow-up report next year, but once we began to design the project it turned into something much larger than the original study. We'll be taking on not only internally displaced populations, but repatriating refugees, which means that we'll also have to visit the refugee camps. We are planning to do fieldwork in several regions of Guatemala (Alta Verapaz, the Ixil Triangle, Ixcán and Huehuetenango), as well as in the refugee camps in southern Mexico, and possibly Mexico City. The good news is that funding for the project appears assured. Hopefully, that is, because the budget is rather high, although the project this time is for 15 months and includes the publication of two preliminary "progress reports." The truth is that I'm very uneasy about this second project, because I am not at all sure where we are going to find researchers. We want a four-person research team, but the problem is, who's willing to do it?

Until recently, I had decided to abandon this line of research. . . . I was planning to start something in the Cakchiquel area looking at the changes in the peasant economy caused by the introduction of nontraditional export crops (why peasants have switched from corn to endives, okra, brussel sprouts, celery, etc.). But the attraction of the other project kept pulling me in, and so here I am, getting ready for next year.

April 7, 1989

Moving on to other things. Two weeks ago, I visited a number of villages in Alta Verapaz, in an area so remote that a hammer and nails would seem to be the cutting edge of technology. I had been invited to accompany the local priest, and at the same time I found the trip useful for the study. It was unbelievably strenuous, not only because of the hike into the area (up and down mountains), but because of the rhythm we kept up; we visited something like nine villages in five days. There were days when the priest said mass in two different villages. It was an exciting trip from the point of view of the research, but at the same time you find yourself inundated with sadness at the misery that abounds everywhere. Add to that the impotence of not being able to do anything. We witnessed a tragic case in one village. There was a little boy (three years old, although he looked no more than a year old) who had been sick for three months. He started with diarrhea and never recovered. We estimated he would die within a day or two of our visit, and all the priest did was perform some rites. . . . The parents, out of desperation, had tried to lower the boy's fever by applying a compress of boiled leaves, or so we imagined, and the leaves were so hot that they left burn marks all over the poor thing's neck. He must have received third degree burns. What to do? If we tried to take him to a hospital he would almost certainly die en route, so we decided if he's going to die, he should die with his family . . . but the cries of the mother, grandmother, etc., you can imagine what that does to you. That was just one of the depressing scenes we have around here.

I've traveled a lot this year, to Mexico, Central America, and, of course, to the interior of the country. You're right; those forays into the interior are a source of strength for me. I feel close to the people there, and those moments make me forget other hurtful things in my life. I have seen new places where beauty and sorrow are intertwined, where there is a silent struggle to rise above pain and despair, to not surrender. But the minuscule changes occur at such a "low intensity" rate, while the social costs are inordinately high.

July 4, 1989

I love to feel the mountains alive in my veins, complete with their rivers, their coolness, their torridity. And I am inspired by their people who survive amid such poverty and grief. Of course, all this is only part of the picture; there is still the frustration of not knowing what to do.

December 16, 1989

My last trip was to a village in Chajul, in late November and early December. We stayed eight days, and again it was a very rich experience. By the time we left, the people in the community appeared to be growing attached to us (we had been there once before), seeking us out and inviting us to visit them in their houses. They have such an enormous need for someone to listen to them. I can't stop feeling frustrated at my inability to offer more concrete help.

ACKNOWLEDGMENTS

I am grateful to the Association for the Advancement of the Social Sciences (AVANCSO) in Guatemala for permission to translate and reprint these passages from Myrna Mack's letters, originally published in *¿Dónde está el futuro? Procesos de reintegración en comunidades de retornados* (AVANCSO 1992).

Ricardo Falla and Beatriz Manz in Berkeley
(Photo: Mariela Shaiken)

Reflections on an
Antropología Comprometida

Conversations with Ricardo Falla

Beatriz Manz

The Spanish term *comprometida* is not easy to translate. The dictionary uses the English words "commit" or "involve." In Latin America it means to participate in a committed way; to opt for and to side with. For me, the term brings to mind the extraordinary personal life and professional commitment of Ricardo Falla, a Guatemalan anthropologist. Falla, a slight, modest man in his early sixties, has an engaging smile and a warm demeanor. He is also a Jesuit priest. He has written extensively and perceptively on Guatemala, from his *Quiche rebelde* (1979) to his most recent publication, the moving and deeply disturbing *Massacres in the Jungle* (1994).

In this latest book, Falla chronicles the destruction and death the Guatemalan military unleashed on tens of thousands of Mayan peasants in the early 1980s. Several thousand Mayas who escaped these massacres formed communities hidden deep in the Ixcan rain forest, calling themselves "Communities of Population in Resistance" (CPRs). During a November 1992 Guatemalan army offensive in a remote area of the Ixcan near the Mexican border, soldiers discovered that Ricardo Falla had been living with the CPRs for nearly six years. The army found Falla's field notes, book manuscript, religious articles, and baptism records and then widely publicized his involvement with these communities. Instead of seeing the work of an extraordinary anthropologist and priest, the high command declared Falla to be a guerrilla commander, the equivalent of a death sentence in Guatemala.

I had known of Ricardo Falla's life among the CPRs and corresponded with him occasionally during this period. When he came to Berkeley to discuss the publication of *Masacres de la Selva* (for which he had asked me to write the foreword and the epilogue), it occurred to me to tape one of our conversations. I saw him again in Santa Tecla, El Salvador, where I once

more placed the mini tape recorder in front of him. As usual he grudg-
ingly complied, complaining in his typically modest manner that he could
not figure out why anyone would want to know what he thought!

In speaking with Falla, I was fascinated to learn that he was originally
inspired to study anthropology and conduct fieldwork among the Yaruros
in Venezuela as a result of the work of Claude Lévi-Strauss. In the often
cited *Tristes tropiques*, Lévi-Strauss begins by stating bluntly, "Travel and trav-
ellers are two things I loathe—and yet here I am all set to tell the story of
my expeditions." The anthropological "expeditions" and attitude of Falla
and Lévi-Strauss, however, are quite different, underscoring broader differences in the field itself. The conversations below grapple with some of these
differences concerning anthropological agendas, approaches, alliances, and
commitments to the communities of study. One of the most important issues is the relationship of the anthropologist and the community. Clifford
Geertz writes in *Works and Lives* (1988:132), "One of the major assumptions upon which anthropological writing rested until only yesterday, that
its subjects and its audience were not only separable but morally discon-
nected, that the first were to be described but not addressed, the second
informed but not implicated, has fairly well dissolved. The world has its
compartments still, but the passages between them are much more numerous and much less well secured."

If there is an anthropologist who has informed as well as implicated the
audience, that individual is Falla. Involved in the lives of Mayan Indians
since the 1960s, his most recent *compromiso* with the Communities of Population in Resistance has added a new dimension to his work. His participation in these communities and the scholarly work he has produced have
both strengthened the communities and brought new understanding to
their plight, informing and implicating the audience. Moreover, Falla's
writings and intervention in international forums are all aspects of his
unique approach, which encompasses full participation, acute observation,
deep commitment, and witnessing. Under these circumstances, choosing a
research theme or committing to a project within a community demands
new levels of seriousness and responsibility.

Writing about and involving an audience beyond the community has
become a concern of a new generation of scholars. Nancy Scheper-Hughes
writes in *Death without Weeping* about her personal engagement in recording human conditions based on observation and testimony: "The act of
witnessing is what lends our work its moral (at times its almost theologi-
cal) character." She goes on to state something that deeply resonates with
many of us involved in the Guatemala experience. "So-called participant
observation has a way of drawing the ethnographer into spaces of human
life where she or he might really prefer not to go at all and once there
doesn't know how to go about getting out except through writing, which

draws others there as well, making them party to the act of witnessing" (1992:xii). Thus Ricardo Falla has made us party to the act of witnessing the conditions and injustices imposed on the CPRs through his book *Massacres in the Jungle.*

What follows is one of the conversations I had with Falla concerning the role of anthropologists. I began by asking him to tell me something about his work with the Communities of Population in Resistance. Specifically, I was curious about how his role as an anthropologist was different from his role as a priest.

RF: My role as a priest involves saying mass, performing baptisms, and conducting catechism classes, everything a priest normally does. Then there is the pastoral work, which has a more social component, a more organizational or practical slant, as opposed to pure research work. Through the pastoral work we promoted projects like experiments with new types of crops, such as soybeans. Another project was to bring national and international events to the attention of the CPRs, because the population in resistance needs to know what's happening outside its immediate vicinity.

BM: Why would people so isolated need to have this broader vision? [I couldn't resist playing the devil's advocate and pressing Falla on this point.]

RF: Otherwise, people lose perspective; the CPRs become an island, isolated from Guatemala and the rest of the world. People lose their sense of purpose, because all they're struggling for is that island. We tried to counter that insulation with education and analysis, not a heavy structural analysis, but a lighter analysis of current events: illegal logging in the Petén jungle, the awarding of the Nobel Peace Prize to Rigoberta Menchú, the defeat of the Sandinistas in Nicaragua, or the fall of communism in the Soviet Union. We used news events as a way to encourage people to creatively analyze their own lives. What does the decline of socialism have to do with the CPRs? Mainly, it highlights that popular participation is essential to a process of social change. Or how does logging in the Petén affect us? The CPRs live in what could be called an ecological sanctuary, where the jungle is valued because it provides shelter from the army. But even so, there is a temptation to clear away the old-growth forest in order to plant crops. What will happen later when the CPRs open up to the outside world and find there is a market in Mexico for mahogany? What kind of resource management strategies will the communities adopt?

These are some of the aspects of my work that are not explicitly religious but are part of a pastoral plan. Then there is the research itself, although, naturally, even in my capacity as a priest or pastoral agent, I take notes on everything: the meetings, people's problems, my own problems, the creative "sparks" that I see might turn into fruitful projects. These personal notebooks were stolen by the army during a raid last year. They were not research notes per se but diaries that recorded my impressions of the dynamics within the communities. This is the advantage that someone who has spent years in a community has over an anthropologist who arrives for a year of research; you notice how the community is changing even though on the surface things appear the same. Village life might appear static, but every so often an innovation occurs. A village festival that buys and roasts a calf might become an incentive to introduce cattle into the local economy, for example.

BM: In other words, this is quite a different method than one used by traditional anthropology, wouldn't you say?

RF: It is the method I use because of my involvement with the communities, but anyone who's really immersed in a community could use the same method. You just need to be disciplined about taking notes. But it's not just a matter of writing things down, because when you're gathering data you become like a sponge; that is, anything counts.

BM: Is that advantageous or disadvantageous?

RF: It has both advantages and disadvantages.

BM: Such as?

RF: The advantage is that you can obtain a lot of information in a short time. And it also helps when you want to know in a systematic way what people really think about something. For example, I might want to know how people view the resistance. One way to find out might be to take a simple poll, but another way would be to classify the arguments. What type of arguments correspond to what type of person? Without a serious effort at investigation and reflection, I could overlook a lot of the significance of those arguments. It's like learning a language. A person can live somewhere for years and they will never master the language unless they make an effort to learn the underlying grammatical rules. Research is making the effort to reflect on the information being absorbed.

Of course, all this takes place alongside the danger of army attack. It's not simply a question of researching peasant economy but of accompanying people during emergency evacuations, observing community meetings—what is the decision-making process?—and reconstructing all this as the basis of a more complete study. You live with the people and accompany them, although this can also be detrimental to the research.

BM: How so?

RF: It can be detrimental in the sense that as you immerse yourself, you begin to participate in the myths that exist in every community, and you might lose some of your critical perspective. But it's also valuable because you gain insights based on adaptation, on trial and error. You know what will work and what won't, and you have a sense of whether or not your hypotheses and conclusions are well-founded. Someone coming in completely cold, however, runs the risk of formulating conclusions that really have no basis.

BM: Some would say that your work as an anthropologist in these communities isn't valid because you lack objectivity.

RF: No doubt there are those who would say that, including the army. One colonel, for instance, tried to convince a foreign delegation that *Massacres in the Jungle* was based on—how did he phrase it?—prepared interviews, or coerced interviews; that is, the interviews were not completely fabricated but channeled in such a way so as to get people to say what I wanted to hear. Obviously, in such a conflictive situation people choose sides, and everything gets filtered through one lens or another. Researchers will also get their data filtered through that same lens. The way I respond to that type of accusation is to point to my sources. How good are the sources? If the army disagrees, let them carry out their own investigation, with their own sources, so that they can then shed their own light on events. That's what I propose in the book. Hopefully, the army will show the other side of the massacres, but in an accurate way. How did the soldiers feel when they went in to kill people? What was it that provoked them? What kind of master plan did the army have that directed soldiers to carry out a massacre in one village but not in the next one? Did the plans change on the ground? Those kinds of questions have intellectual relevance, but they are also important from the standpoint of social justice, in order to uncover the chain of command that led to the massacres.

BM: When you addressed a group of students recently, you said something that impressed them very much. You spoke of the need to understand the army's actions from a theoretical point of view, but then you paused a moment and said, "But it isn't right." In addition to trying to understand a phenomenon, you are proffering a judgment. You stated, "This is unjust." Isn't it rare for an anthropologist to say that?

RF: Well, I don't know if it's rare or not. What I'm saying is that you have to treat the army as a social agent, with its own rules of behavior. We have to try to understand those rules as if we ourselves were subject to them. At the same time, we can't remain at that level, because then why have we done this study?

BM: Just to do it. For many scholars in the West, and for that matter in the third world, research is often done for its own sake.

RF: Just to do it? To earn money? Or prestige? Or power? That's where I think it's essential to have certain parameters; that is, there are some things that are just deplorable. We can't fall into a cultural relativism trap by saying, Well, that's the way the army is, it's a military culture, and so they do all of those things, and we must understand it, and the others have a culture of fatalism and we must understand that, too, and that's the end of it. We need a set of criteria that says there are some things that are simply unconscionable. Now, I am not an expert in human rights law, but I believe that anthropology has the potential to enrich human rights work.

BM: But why mix anthropology with human rights?

RF: It is mixing anthropology with a certain sense of justice. Justice means human rights. We have to judge, especially in a context of such terrible oppression like we have in Guatemala, with the bloodbath that has taken place. We can't just remain passive and study the massacres as the product of a military culture. We can't fall into that. We're striving to give strength to the voice of the people. We have to choose sides. You either choose to understand the army, and its judgment of events, or you choose the judgment of the people. Or you can opt for your own opinion, because you're also looking for the truth in all of this, and perhaps you're not in complete agreement with the popular view. The "people" can be wrong.

BM: Guatemala must be the country most studied by anthropologists. You are an anthropologist. Right now, and during the whole time you were with the CPRs, there are dozens and dozens of anthropologists doing research. Why investigate massacres instead of researching kinship systems or folklore?

RF: I consider anthropology to be all-encompassing; that's what gives it its richness. I've always defended anthropology, like Joaquín Noval did. We always defended the value of anthropology, although sometimes it was criticized as the "science of the magnifying glass." So you want to find out what's happening in that household? Well, kinship is certainly important; it forms the backbone of some societies. But I think that if we are going to construct a science to serve people, that is, the dispossessed and persecuted, then we have to look for the topics that are most relevant to their suffering.

BM: Do you think that anthropology should strive to serve people?

RF: Well, if not, then why are we doing research?

BM: So that academics in Europe and the United States can read what we write.

RF: I hope academics in Europe and the United States *will* read it. But their reading should give something back to the people, because if not, then we are just stuck in this great paradox of E-mail and faxes. How is it possible that such an incredible technological advancement has not led to an improvement in the welfare of the world? On the contrary, it seems to have made things worse.

Something similar is occurring within anthropology. I think it's fabulous that there have been scientific and methodological advances. Some people have a calling to study kinship systems or alcoholism, or mythology, or whatever, and that should not be disparaged. Still, there should be something returned to the people who are the objects of all this research. It should not just be a subjective intention but an objective relation. The benefit to the world—to the third world with such poverty and so much injustice.

BM: With all the professional options that you have, how did you decide what type of research to engage in? How did you end up living with the CPRs? Your approach is obviously very atypical for an anthropologist. A typical anthropologist in the United States, for example, chooses a research topic based on what he or she reads in the library, often without any connection to the community that is going to be the object of that research. How does this approach strike you; that is, what kind of a relationship do you think an anthropologist should have with a community? Should the community have input into the choice of a research topic?

RF: The community—or your own world, your country, your roots— should influence you, although not necessarily in the sense that there has to be a vote or an assembly to decide what to study.

BM: But should there be an accordance, an exchange of ideas?

RF: Absolutely. The research agenda should arise from and be in harmony with the needs of the people. The impression I have of anthropology, and perhaps I am completely outmoded, is that traditional anthropology was a type of science of submersion; it led aspiring anthropologists to submerge themselves in "primitive" or "marginal" cultures, like Lévi-Strauss with the Bororos. His book *Tristes tropiques* motivated me to go and live with the Yaruros (in Venezuela), where I experienced the worst hunger pains of my life. The same thing with Malinowski. Now, the problem is that many of these researchers returned from the field feeling like they'd earned their anthropologist badge, and thus the excuse to withdraw into other less engaged arenas. Maybe it's also a question of age. But the point is the intention of the work. What is the purpose? and what permanent commitments does this demand of you?

In my case, the motivation to work with the CPRs originated when I was in Nicaragua and went to visit the refugees. This was when I first began to hear tales of the horrible massacres. I was very moved by this; it was like a calling, the kind of calling you feel in your veins that makes you forsake your own interests, your own problems or emotional crises. Of course, there may also be an element of adventure, or curiosity. Or in my case, a religious motivation. I was moved by the story of a friend of mine, another priest named Fernando Hoyos, who joined the guerrillas in 1980 or 1981. His decision left me feeling ashamed; it made me reevaluate my own commitment. If he was willing to join the guerrillas and sacrifice his life, which is what happened, why wasn't I also willing to make a supreme sacrifice?

Even though I was working in Nicaragua during a critical time, I felt there was still something else I should be doing to defend the [Catholic] Church. The Church has been criticized for selling out to the rich and so on, and I felt that by going into the CPRs I had an opportunity to clear its reputation a bit, to justify the presence of God in history and vindicate what is vital about the Church. When I was accompanying the CPRs, it wasn't just me who was there; it was the Church.

BM: There is an analogy in this. Fernando made you feel guilty and motivated you to do something. Your commitment now underscores the shortcomings the rest of us have, and serves as an example, especially to a generation of younger anthropologists. Perhaps you will be a model for some of those students, despite the fact that the prevailing trend—sanctioned by many professors—is for students to choose a thesis topic merely because it interests them intellectually, without taking into account whether or not their research can contribute to the welfare of the populations they are studying. In other words, they are channeled into doing research that is completely divorced from reality or needs. It might be that we are entering an era when new anthropologists won't be able to do what you did.

RF: Well, they might go even farther.

BM: I wonder. Here we have the precedent of you and Myrna Mack, two Guatemalan anthropologists committed to social justice, one now dead and the other in exile. As Myrna used to say, in the United States "you publish or you perish, for us here in Guatemala it's the other way around." It makes me wonder about third world anthropologists in general, whose numbers are unfortunately too few; that is, I wonder whether third world anthropologists can possibly allow themselves the luxury of indifference, like so many northern colleagues seem to be able to do.

RF: I think it's unfair to generalize. I'm telling you what happened to me. I consider myself to be a man of faith, and a man of faith is someone who follows a calling. It could be someone who doesn't believe in God, but is following some intangible spark that leads that person toward a greater commitment. I have obeyed a calling (in spite of some disobedience). That calling has been very strong, and it has led to some moments of light, such as now. That's why I came to the United States, because it was an opportune moment to expose that light. Not so people will praise me, but so they will understand the force of the calling. Perhaps it can be an example for anthropologists, and for the religious community as well. I'm sure there are many priests or seminary students who will observe my case and think, this man is sixty years old and look what he's doing. What are we doing? It's an example. Words inspire, but examples lead. Eventually, the light will fade, and new lights will emerge, and we hope that as generations replace one another a process of renovation will occur.

BM: You say you're a man of faith. I am not a woman of faith. Do you mean to say that only an anthropologist who is also a priest, or a nun, can attain that calling?

RF: I'm talking about faith as a force, not necessarily as a religious conviction. Faith is the response to that intangible interior motivation.

BM: You mean ideals?

RF: Ideals, yes, but ideals that have a material base, that lead you into risky situations, into sacrificing your life. You are not necessarily going to be killed for those ideals, but you are giving your life, your inner self. It's something that pushes you, something that won't let you rest.

BM: But, look, between faculty meetings and classes and publishing and everything else that occupies us here, you know there are probably a lot of people who don't understand what you're referring to. That was my point about the difference between a third world anthropologist and a first world anthropologist. At least in the third world, that indifference weighs on our conscience. But I don't think that many anthropologists here can relate to what you're saying.

RF: Maybe it doesn't translate very well, but I still maintain that this is a human experience; this belongs to the human construct of anthropology, or philosophy. It's something human that we all feel, though we may express it in different ways. It could be a song, or a sense of longing.

BM: Perhaps all someone wants is to advance his or her career.

RF: Well, if that's all they want to do, then they are not hearing that song. But the song is there. This is something I analyzed in a short book that's probably not very well known; it's called *Esa muerte que nos hace vivir.*

BM: If I were asked to come up with one word to describe experiences with fieldwork in conflictive areas, the word I would choose would be *indifference*. The inconsistency between the experience of a researcher in the field and life in the academy, the disconnection as far as security—not just personal safety but material security—is so great for so many anthropologists, especially those of us involved in disenfranchised, militarily oppressed communities. When the research is finished, there is often a comfortable university job back home. You, however, maintain a commitment to the populations you are researching. Perhaps your religious convictions help you uphold that commitment.

RF: But you are not indifferent.

BM: Let me put it sarcastically. One could say that if I were really committed, I would be in Guatemala, not in Berkeley.

RF: There are many kinds of commitments. You and I are committed in different ways, just like I am not committed in the same way as the guerrillas in Guatemala. Or perhaps I am not committed any more because I left Guatemala?

BM: That's different. You left because you had to. You had no choice.

RF: True.

BM: In the final analysis, you choose what's best for the people, while many of us don't. Maybe I could do more valuable work in Guatemala than as a professor at Berkeley. Right?

RF: I wonder if that's really true. I used to be criticized for the opposite reason, for wasting my time in the field when I could have accepted a university position. In turn, I was critical of other Jesuits who I felt weren't "immersed" enough with the poor. However, my attitude changed with the death of the Jesuits in El Salvador. Those Jesuits were academics, one was rector of the Central American University, but they experienced the ultimate immersion: they died for the poor. In other words, I think we risk being overly romantic: you don't have to live with the poor to be working on their behalf; the point is to bring about a structure change, albeit gradually, and it can be more effective to work at a different level. There are many types of commitment. You're interviewing me now because I left Guatemala; if I had stayed with the CPRs, none of this would have been publicized.

BM: Why did you choose to live with the CPRs instead of opting for a university position?

RF: In hindsight, I could list a number of factors that influenced my decision, but at the time it was intuition. I was moved by the stories of the massacres, pulled into that history, like when you fall in love and as you learn more you can no longer resist the attraction of the relationship. That's what happened to me, although the first survivors I interviewed were not from Ixcan but San Francisco Nentón.[1] That first exposure was not as thorough, because I wasn't familiar with the prior history of the area, and the informants were clearly uneasy about telling me certain things.

BM: So, you did not choose a research topic rather arbitrarily, as is often done?

RF: Yes, but I was constrained by the fact that I couldn't return openly to Guatemala. My name had appeared on a death squad list while I was in Nicaragua. This was a period when priests were being killed in Guatemala and a lot of Church people had to flee the country.[2] My meetings with the Guatemalan refugees in Nicaragua therefore became a substitute for going back to Guatemala, and as I listened to their stories, I began to imagine ways that I could reenter the country through the conflict zones, combining pastoral work with an effort to investigate the cause of the refugees' flight. The experience of documenting the San Francisco massacre convinced me that work of this type could have an international impact; there was an audience of influential people who wanted to know what was happening in Guatemala. The violence struck me as something terrible, but also something unprecedented, something significant in the country's history. I hoped information about the massacres would eventually resonate within Guatemala as well.

Once all the material is gathered, you need a theoretical apparatus. The point is not to use theory in isolation, but as a tool of analysis to help you understand what you have just witnessed. If as a result of this process of analysis you can make a contribution to social science, so much the better. But it should not be just an abstract exercise. The first volume of my study on Ixcan, which has not yet been published, looks at the experience of popular organizing in the 1970s. From about 1975 on, we were very interested in peasant organizing. I turned to the theories of peasant movements: What are the determining factors? What are the limitations? Cabarrus wrote a book about the peasant struggles in El Salvador that helped me to formulate some hypotheses about the situation in Guatemala.[3] The last chapter of that volume took a long time to write and is the most theoretical.

BM: Why haven't you published this volume?

RF: Because it's very detailed. It reveals things that if made public right now might be harmful to the people themselves.

BM: When do you intend to publish it?

RF: Who knows? Perish then publish!

BM: As an anthropologist, why were you interested in peasant organizing?

RF: Well, I don't know if it was as an anthropologist or as a member of a Catholic Action group. We saw the potential for peasants to play a role in a process of social change in Guatemala. I say "we" because while I was involved in research, others were working more on the level of social action. We produced a number of studies that are still just typewritten manuscripts. In 1975, I did a short piece that looked at Indian labor on the agro-export plantations. Other colleagues then tried to come up with ways to link the highland populations with the seasonal workers who migrated to the coast. In 1978, we did a study in Nicaragua with the same question: What made people organize? We looked at the ins and outs of the failed 1978 insurrection.

BM: Many of the foreign anthropologists who had worked in Guatemala left the country during the worst years of violence. When you realized you couldn't do research openly in Guatemala, why didn't you choose to work in some other country?

RF: Other anthropologists didn't necessarily have the same roots in Guatemala, and they had to continue working. I was also outside the country, in Nicaragua, during the most violent years of 1980 and 1981, but fortunately I found a way to return to work within the country. Your comment about the two Guatemalan anthropologists—one dead and the other in exile—is not exactly true. I am exiled now, but I was inside Guatemala for nearly six years. Anyway, there are lots of people who are not in Guatemala but who are *with* Guatemala.

BM: Do you feel a commitment to the people you are researching, a responsibility to contribute to their welfare in some way, to produce something that will be of concrete benefit?

RF: Well, yes. For instance, in *Massacres in the Jungle* I knew I had to be meticulous in recording the names of those killed, because their relatives, their children, might someday read the book. Each name in the book corresponds to a real person. But we shouldn't assume that the villagers are going to read what we write. They are not readers. If the material can be translated into a more popular format, OK, but in general the work is not going to have a direct impact on the people themselves. Ideally, the researcher should provide a chance for the people to see how their voice is reflected in the work. However, many things will seem obtuse to them, although the work can still be very useful to another audience that can then give something back to the community.

BM: It's obvious that people cooperated enormously with your research. Do you think it would have been possible to gain the same level of cooperation if you had been investigating a more abstract topic that the people cared less about?

RF: Maybe not, and I think this is essential. The research agenda should reflect the priorities of the people; if not, then you practically have to dynamite the information out of them, inventing questions so they will talk to you. There has to be a certain interest on their part in what you are doing. This was a problem I had during my dissertation research. I went to the field to investigate the impact of population growth, but all people wanted to discuss were the new religious movements in the communities. It was much more difficult to get data on the original subject, and it would have meant wasting the opportunity to hear what people really had to say. It was the same with the massacres; people wanted to tell me about the massacres.

BM: What does it mean to live in resistance? How is unarmed resistance defined by the CPRs?

RF: Resistance in that context means not being killed and not leaving the country. The difference between the CPRs and the refugees is that the CPRs are resisting from within Guatemala.

BM: But are people identifying with the country as a whole or with a particular region? Do they think of themselves as Guatemalans?

RF: Yes, I believe so, but they are also defending their own land, which makes their determination to resist that much stronger. The entire social organization of the CPRs—collective production, self-defense, even education, health, and pastoral work—revolves around the resistance; this means not only eluding the army but finding ways to meet material needs and keep morale high. If your boots are too tight and you can't work because of blisters, then you might lose your will altogether and decide to surrender. But how can boots, or machetes, be obtained in the jungle? The CPRs, then, are not just sitting still hoping the army won't detect them; they have created a whole social system in order to survive. And they are aware in some way that their resistance is linked to a broader struggle within Guatemala. That link is being strengthened now, as the CPRs take a new direction toward recognition as a civilian population, a political step to ensure their survival. Instead of hiding under the canopy of the jungle, the CPRs are putting themselves under the protection of public recognition. They are well aware that they will not gain this alone but must count on national and international solidarity. They are contributing toward a larger struggle, and that larger struggle is reciprocating toward them.

BM: How do people manage the danger in their lives, in terms of life-affirming ceremonies and interpersonal support?

RF: There is a great deal of solidarity within the CPRs, a willingness to divide up scarce resources, among relatives first and then among other villagers or between villages. The question of ceremonies is more complicated because the persecution tends to disrupt the recognized customs; the communities cannot count on being able to perform certain rituals regularly. However, the traditional ceremonies are very important. If the goal of the repression is to break the bonds that exist between people, these rites help preserve social unity. Celebrating mass in a moment of flight may not seem wise, but it helps to draw people together. Or, for example, a baptism has enormous importance for the people in the CPRs. They want their children baptized in the normal way and the "normality" of the ritual becomes a reaffirmation of their own humanity. We are not animals or outcasts, we are human beings, Christians, and Guatemalans. Of course, original elements do appear. In wedding ceremonies, instead of the traditional coins exchanged between men and women, we use corn. The man gives the corn husk to the woman, and she returns it to him in the form of a tortilla, symbolizing the commitment of each to their life-sustaining labors. But these are minor adaptations.

BM: How has the war changed their sense of community identity?

RF: The war determines the social structure of the CPRs. Children, orphans, become everyone's responsibility. Churches lose their walls, and the environment becomes more ecumenical. Production is collective; everything in the village revolves around production. How long can this be sustained? There is collective production because of the war and the need to defend people working in the fields.

These conversations with Ricardo Falla point to a view of anthropology as offering a unique perspective and methodology in the social sciences for understanding the human condition. Research in conflict zones brings the anthropologist even closer to the community, and the suffering and fear one is witnessing is likely to lead to a special closeness and commitment. It is complementing anthropology with a certain sense of justice.

ACKNOWLEDGMENTS

I would like to thank Elizabeth Oglesby for translating these conversations from Spanish.

NOTES

1. An estimated 352 people were killed in the village-farm of San Francisco Nentón, Huehuetenango, on July 17, 1982. See Ricardo Falla, "We Charge Genocide," in *Guatemala: Tyranny on Trial, Testimony of the Permanent People's Tribunal* (San Francisco: Synthesis Publications, 1984), 112–119.

2. The Catholic church suffered severe persecution in the 1970s and 1980s. Sixteen priests were killed, and the bishop of the diocese of El Quiché left the country, along with most of the priests and nuns of that region. These exiles settled in nearby countries such as Mexico and Nicaragua where they formed the Guatemala Church in Exile.

3. Carlos Rafael Cabarrus, *Genesis de una revolución: Análisis del surgimiento y desarrollo de la organización compesina en El Salvador* (Mexico, D.F.: Centro de Investigaciones y Estudios Superiores en Antropologia Social, 1983).

REFERENCES

Falla, Ricardo

1979   *Quiche rebelde*. Guatemala: Editorial Universitaria.

1983   Masacre de la Finca San Francisco, Huehuetenango. Copenhagen: IWGIA. Also published in English as "Voices of the Survivors: Massacre at the Finca San Francisco," Cambridge, Mass.: Cultural Survival.

1984   "We Charge Genocide." In *Guatemala: Tyranny on Trial, Testimony of the Permanent People's Tribunal*. San Francisco: Synthesis Publications, 112–119.

1992   *Masacres de la Selva: Ixcan, Guatemala (1975–1982)*.

1994   *Massacres in the Jungle: Ixcan, Guatemala, 1975–1982*. Boulder: Westview Press.

Geertz, Clifford

1988   *Works and Lives*. Stanford: Stanford University Press.

Lévi-Strauss, Claude

1974   *Tristes tropiques*. Translated from the French by John and Doreen Weightman. [1st American ed.] New York: Atheneum.

Scheper-Hughes, Nancy

1992   *Death without Weeping: The Violence of Everyday Life in Brazil*. Berkeley: University of California Press.

Jeff Sluka and Companions in Divis Flats

Reflections on Managing Danger in Fieldwork

Dangerous Anthropology in Belfast

Jeffrey A. Sluka

In many areas of the world, anthropological fieldwork is more dangerous today than it was in the past.[1] There are approximately 120 "armed conflicts" (euphemism for wars) in the world today (Nietschmann 1987), and given that about one-third of the world's countries are currently involved in warfare and about two-thirds of countries routinely resort to human rights abuses as normal aspects of their political process to control their populations, it is clear that few anthropologists will be able to avoid conflict situations and instances of sociopolitical violence in the course of their professional lives (Nordstrom and Martin 1992:15). While it has long been recognized that danger is probably inherent in anthropological fieldwork, it is only recently that the methodological and subjective issue of danger has been addressed directly and systematically. In 1986, Nancy Howell first called attention to the need to discuss the issue of danger in fieldwork in an unpublished paper, "Occupational Safety and Health in Anthropology." She noted that the personal dangers involved in doing fieldwork had largely been ignored, denied, or taken for granted and argued that this issue should be a major concern of anthropological fieldworkers. She also suggested that one of the professional associations should conduct a comprehensive survey of occupational safety and health in the discipline, and this idea was adopted by the American Anthropological Association (AAA). In 1990, the first publications directly dealing with danger in fieldwork emerged—an AAA special report titled *Surviving Fieldwork* (Howell 1990) and an article titled "Participant Observation in Violent Social Contexts" (Sluka 1990). This chapter presents an updated and revised version of my earlier article on managing danger, incorporating reflections on new fieldwork. I begin with a brief description of the research setting during my two periods of fieldwork in the Catholic-nationalist ghettos of Belfast, Northern Ireland, in 1981–1982 and 1991 and then make some general comments and recommendations concerning the conduct of ethnographic research in dangerous or violent social contexts, deriving from these experiences and similar ones by other anthropologists.

While special ethnographic, methodological, theoretical, and ethical sensitivities are required when working on, and in, dangerous areas, to a substantial degree the dangers faced by anthropologists in their fieldwork can be mediated through foresight, planning, and skillful maneuver. While this chapter deals specifically with participant observation in countries characterized by political instability, conflict, and insurgency, much that is said is broadly applicable to generalized situations in which field-workers may be in physical danger from human sources (i.e., research partici-pants, authorities, and others).[2]

SETTING

In 1981–1982, I conducted research in Divis Flats, a Catholic-nationalist ghetto on the lower Falls Road in Belfast. This research was based on par-ticipant observation and interviews with seventy-six families, and the mono-graph emerging from this was a study of the social dynamics of popular support for the Irish Republican Army (IRA) and Irish National Libera-tion Army (INLA) (Sluka 1989).[3] After nearly a decade, in July 1991, I re-turned to the Catholic-nationalist ghettos of Belfast for six months of field-work on "aspects of political culture in Northern Ireland." These "urban village" ghetto communities represent the major battlegrounds or "killing fields" of the war in Northern Ireland. For over twenty-three years, the res-idents of the Catholic-nationalist ghettos have been caught between the urban guerrilla warfare of the IRA and INLA and the counterinsurgency operations of the Security Forces. Since the beginning of the war in 1969, the British authorities have sought to contain repression and resistance within the Catholic ghettos of Belfast, Derry, Newry, and other towns and cities and in the rural border areas where Catholics are the majority popu-lation (e.g., the so-called bandit country of south Armagh around Cross-maglen) (Rolston 1991). Counterinsurgency operations and the "dirty war" apparatus (Dillon 1990; Faligot 1983), coupled with the activities of pro-government death squads and sectarian attacks by Loyalist extremists, have created an unpredictable deployment of terror concentrated in these communities, with the result that every family or household can tell you about a relative, neighbor, or friend in jail or killed by the Security Forces or Loyalists. The Catholic ghettos are "killing fields" in the sense that they represent the major sites of violence, the battlegrounds where domination and resistance in general and the war in particular are concentrated, con-tained, and isolated. They are spaces of violence, death, and transformation that continually generate both recruits to the Republican paramilitaries and enough popular support and sympathy among the rest of the people to maintain the current struggle.

When I returned to Belfast in 1991, two things had occurred in the interim that directly affected this research. First, in 1986, a bloody internal feud split the INLA and led to the formation of a new, breakaway paramilitary organization calling itself the Irish Peoples Liberation Organization (IPLO). Second, in 1989, my book on popular support for the IRA and INLA in Divis Flats was published. I sent a copy of the book to friends in Belfast, who subsequently lent it to a number of people to read, including senior Republican activists. Because of the close association of the INLA, and now IPLO, with Divis Flats, I had contacts who advised me that if I ever returned to Belfast and wanted to meet the "High Command" of the IPLO, this could be arranged. Because this research was based on sabbatical leave, I was able to pursue an attempt at participatory research. I wanted to return to Belfast before I decided exactly what research I would engage in, and I wanted to find a subject that offered to be of mutual advantage to me and to the local community. I hoped local people in Belfast might suggest such a research topic.

When I arrived in Belfast I was introduced by friends, in a local pub, to, first, Martin "Rook" O'Prey, the local Belfast commander of the IPLO, and a few days later, the overall commander, Jimmy Brown. (I name these people here because they are now deceased and are publicly recognized as having held these positions in the IPLO at the time of their deaths.)[4] Brown told me that he had read my book and thought it was very good. He then shocked me by asking if I would be interested in writing a book about the IPLO. I said that might be possible, if we could agree on the precise conditions and expectations involved, and we arranged to meet a week later to talk about it. A few days before this meeting could take place, Rook O'Prey, who I had only just met, was assassinated by a Loyalist death squad in his home, one of the new houses built as part of redevelopment, at the bottom of Divis Tower and in plain sight of the army observation post on top. The meeting was postponed a week, and then I met with Brown and the new commander for Belfast.

These IPLO leaders told me that if I was interested in writing a book "like the first one" about their organization, they would "open all the doors" I needed to gather the information. The first thing I discussed with them was, did they know what an anthropologist was and understand what I would be doing? I said that as a social scientist I was committed to objectivity—that is, letting the evidence lead to the conclusions—and the politics of truth. I was willing to write an ethnography of the IPLO if I was allowed academic independence and freedom to write the truth as I saw it, as a result of my own research. The IPLO leaders agreed to this. They knew what an anthropologist was and wanted me to act as one because they believed that an independent academic study would carry more authority and could not be easily dismissed as propaganda. They said they would like to see a book that presented an inside or participant's view of the IPLO. They admitted that they hoped the book would do two things for them. First, because the IPLO lacked effective means of publicizing their perspective—for example, nothing like the weekly paper, *An Phoblact/Republican News,* which presents the perspective of the Provisional Republican movement (Sinn Fein and the IRA)—the book would be a chance to present their perspective to the world and describe who they were, what they were doing, and why they were doing it. Second, the book would humanize the people in the IPLO, which might serve as a partial antidote to the concerted propaganda campaign by the British authorities aimed at vilifying and dehumanizing them as an aspect of their counterinsurgency or "psychological warfare" operations.

The conditions we agreed on were that I would be allowed to talk to or interview any member I wished, and I could ask questions freely. The interviews would be completely open, and I was not required to submit a list of the questions or subjected to any other apparent monitoring or control practice. During the course of the research, I was never refused an answer to any question. (As with my previous research, I voluntarily chose not to ask about some things such as weapons, finance, and planned military operations, which I felt were unnecessary and potentially dangerous both to me and to other research participants.) I was free to do my anthropological "thing," with only two conditions. I promised that I would allow the IPLO to review the manuscript of the book before it was published. They would not have editorial control, but I agreed to two things. First, I would alter anything in the manuscript necessary to ensure the immediate security of any living member of the IPLO, for example, to protect anonymity of the research participants. Second, if there was anything else in the manuscript that we disagreed on, I would give them a right of response. That is, while I would not modify or delete my own independent conclusions and interpretations, I would include IPLO statements expressing their disagreement with my views wherever they felt it necessary. I thought this was fair, since it would leave readers of the book to judge for themselves whose view they gave more credence to. This struck me as an equitable and reciprocal research "bargain," in which both the researcher and participants stood to benefit, and believed that it did not compromise my professional ethics. It also represented, to the best of my knowledge, the most direct, open, and unimpeded access any researcher has yet been granted to a paramilitary organization in Northern Ireland. I decided to accept the IPLO's offer and approach the research as an experiment in liberation anthropology.

Over the next six months I researched and did fieldwork with the IPLO. This was based on interviews, library and archival research, and participant observation—as far as I thought this was practicable in the circumstances. I conducted formal interviews with fifteen members of the IPLO, selected to provide a representative cross-sample; I conducted interviews in Catholic-nationalist ghettos in Belfast, Derry, Newry, and Dublin, with men and women of all ranks and including both founding and new members. I spent considerable time "hanging out," traveling with, and talking informally with about two dozen other IPLO members and attended a number of IPLO-related social and political functions, such as the funeral and other events surrounding the death of Rook O'Prey.

With regard to the dangers inherent in such fieldwork, I handled or "managed" these much as I had during my first period of research in Belfast (see Sluka 1990). But this new research involved much more direct and intense interaction with guerrilla fighters than I had had in 1981–1982, and it presented new problems and dangers. Because members of the IPLO are actively involved in a war, their lives are dangerous, and it is dangerous simply being with them. As with the IRA and INLA in my previous research, I never felt that I was in any danger from the IPLO. As before, my major concern was the authorities—particularly the army and police—and Loyalist paramilitaries, both of whom I believed represented more of a threat now than before because now I was directly researching a guerrilla organization. In particular, the fieldwork period was marked by a major increase in Loyalist violence, from which academics were not immune. In September 1991, Adrian Guelke, a lecturer in politics at the Queen's University of Belfast, was shot by a Loyalist death squad from the Ulster Freedom Fighters (UFF, generally acknowledged as a nom de guerre or front for the Ulster Defense Association). In the early hours of the morning, two or three masked gunmen entered his house and he was shot in the back at close range with a pistol as he lay sleeping with his wife. His life was saved when the automatic pistol used in the attack jammed. Guelke is a South African-born opponent of apartheid who has lived in Northern Ireland since 1974. A distinguished academic, he had no connections with any paramilitary or political groups and was working on a book comparing political violence in South Africa, Israel, and Northern Ireland. The motives for the attack are not clear, and the Security Forces claim it was a case of mistaken identity, but Guelke believes that South African elements, who have links with the Loyalist paramilitaries, may have set him up.[5]

I tried to ameliorate these dangers in two ways. First, I tried to camouflage my research with the IPLO as best I could so that only they and a couple of close and trusted friends knew that I was doing it. I did research on two other projects at the same time (one on Republican martyrs and the other on the cultures of terror and resistance in Northern Ireland),

and when asked about my research, I talked about these instead. Second, I tried to control and limit my contact with IPLO members. They were not the only people I spent my time with. In fact, most of my time was not spent with IPLO members, particularly in the first few months of the fieldwork, when I worked on other projects and did library and archival research on the history of the IPLO. Restricting interaction with research participants is not ideal in participant observation, but I believed it necessary for security reasons. As the research progressed, I spent increasingly more time with IPLO members, and the most intense period of interviewing and participant observation occurred during the last two months.

In the end, during the course of this fieldwork, I was not directly threatened in any way. While I was stopped by Security Forces patrols for identity checks twice while in the company of IPLO leaders, I was not approached by the army or police, and they never indicated to me that they were aware that I was conducting research with the IPLO. When asked by soldiers and police about my research, I told them I was studying political culture and did not mention the IPLO. On one occasion I crossed the border illegally with Jimmy Brown on a trip to Dublin. When I told him I was driving to Dublin with Jimmy, a trusted friend warned me that under no circumstances should I use the back roads to avoid the border checkpoints. He warned that if I ran into a Security Forces patrol or SAS unit (the elite commando forces of the British army) on a deserted back road while alone in a car with the commander of the IPLO, I was likely to be shot dead. When Jimmy and I reached the border, I followed his directions and we used back roads to cross and avoid the checkpoint. I did so because I believed that he was in the best position to decide on the route we should take. I only did this once, and I probably would not do it again.

On one occasion I was participant observer during an IPLO operation, a propaganda exercise. This was a photo-shoot for publicity purposes, and an IPLO photographer was present. I was invited along because they figured I could take some photos of my own for the book. Six armed IPLO members in military uniform and wearing masks, dark glasses, and IPLO armbands emerged in Poleglass (a Catholic-nationalist ghetto on the outskirts of West Belfast) to set up a vehicle checkpoint. They stopped about half a dozen cars and then disappeared. The operation lasted only a few minutes but was probably the most dangerous thing I have ever done as an anthropologist. Armed guerrillas are usually shot on sight in Northern Ireland. For the IPLO to emerge in public in this way is to enter a combat situation. Because of the constant surveillance and patrolling of these districts by the Security Forces, such operations have to be planned very carefully, and there is always a distinct danger of encountering an army patrol or undercover unit or being observed by the surveillance helicopters constantly hovering overhead.

Another new problem I faced resulted from the fact that I taped the fifteen formal interviews. In my previous research I had not taped interviews, so the necessity of protecting tapes was a new experience. I tried to protect these in two ways. First, I tried to ensure there was nothing on them that would directly identify any individual, particularly the interviewee. Second, I hid them away from the house where I lived, so there was never more than one there at a time. Of course, these were not foolproof protections. I felt justified in making the tapes because I had formal agreements with the IPLO as an organization and the individuals interviewed that I would try to use IPLO members' own words to present their views in the book. Because they were willing to accept the risk, and I believed I could protect the tapes and minimize that risk, I taped the interviews.

REFLECTIONS AND RECOMMENDATIONS

What then are my recommendations to anthropologists considering fieldwork in dangerous or violent social contexts? Before you go to the field, try to evaluate as realistically as possible the degree of danger, and try to identify potential sources of danger. Decide if you are prepared to accept the risks involved, and if you are, consider both what sorts of actions you might take to ameliorate or manage them and what sorts of actions might exacerbate them. Give some thought to what an "acceptable level" of danger might be. I assume that most researchers are not prepared to give their lives for their research and would retreat to safer ground if a direct threat to life or limb arose. Recognize as well that you may have to terminate your research on your own initiative, or that the authorities or other "powers that be" may compel you to do so. Always have a plan of escape, a means of extricating yourself from the situation as quickly as possible, should the need arise.

Discuss the potential dangers with advisers and colleagues, and seek out people with direct experience in the area where you intend to do your research. If at all possible, try to go to the proposed field location for an exploratory visit before you commit yourself to doing research there. I was able to visit Belfast for two weeks during the summer prior to my arrival there for fieldwork.

Investigate your sources of funding. For example, Myron Glazer (1972: 137), a sociologist who studied student politics in Chile, learned only after his return from the field that his funding came from a U.S. Army-sponsored research group. Today, governments, militaries, and intelligence agencies are funding research both directly and indirectly through front organizations (e.g., right-wing think tanks). Ethical considerations aside, it can be dangerous to accept funding from agencies that one's research participants consider objectionable. Certainly, the danger of being defined as a spy is greatly exaggerated if one is funded by the military or the CIA. Know the origins of your funding, consider how people in your research area might view those origins, and be open with them about it.

Given that the people among whom anthropologists do their research have usually never had an anthropologist working in their midst, it should be kept in mind that they are naturally going to try to figure out what you are doing there. Usually, at least at first, they will define the anthropologist with reference to preexisting categories derived from experience with other strangers who have appeared in the community. Spy, journalist, policeman, tax collector, and missionary are common categories often mistakenly applied to anthropologists in the field. It is essential that researchers in the field make a substantial effort to counter these public definitions of themselves, a process entailing a conscious effort at impression management (Berreman 1962; Goffman 1959). It can be done by recognizing how people are likely to define you, avoiding acting in ways that might reinforce these suspicions, and being as honest and straightforward as possible about who you really are and what you are really doing.

Because the most common suspicion that research participants have about anthropologists is that they are spies, and it is difficult to find an anthropologist who has done fieldwork who has not encountered this suspicion, this danger deserves special mention. Being defined as a spy is inherently dangerous, and the link between anthropology and war-related research has exacerbated this danger (see Sluka 1990). Anthropologists have been involved in war-related, particularly counterinsurgency, research, others have had their research used or "applied" by governments, militaries, and intelligence agencies to help plan military operations, and spies or intelligence agents of various sorts have used the cover that they were anthropologists. As a result, people in many parts of the world have come increasingly to believe that anthropologists, even those engaged in "innocent" (or in Boas's [1973] terms "honest") research, are actually or potentially dangerous to them. Many nations and peoples are therefore justifiably suspicious of anthropologists and will not allow them to do research, and fieldwork has become more dangerous today than it was in the past.

If you do not want to be defined as a spy, then do not be one or act like one. (See Glazer 1970 for a good account of dealing with research participants' suspicions that the researcher is a spy.) At first, I avoided asking questions about sensitive political topics. In a similar manner, anthropologists seeking to counter suspicions that they are missionaries would at first avoid asking questions about religion. The sociologist Ned Polsky (1967: 126–127) suggests that a good rule of fieldwork in sensitive contexts is to "initially, keep your eyes and ears open but keep your mouth shut. At first try to ask no questions whatsoever. Before you can ask questions . . . you should get the 'feel' of their world by extensive and attentive listening."

When you consider how your research participants are likely to define you, consider ways of not only countering these definitions but of also promoting one that will enhance your safety and your research. It is not enough to not be a threat to your research participants; act in such a way as to *be seen* not to be a threat. In my case, my association with the priest and the former IRA man was fortunate in this respect because once they accepted my explanations of what I was doing in Belfast, others found it easier to do so as well. Polsky (ibid., 129) refers to this cumulative effect as "snowballing"; "get an introduction to one [informant] who will vouch for you with others, who in turn will vouch for you with still others." He suggests that it is best to start at the top, with the most prestigious person in the group you are studying. He also suggests that answering research participants' questions frankly will help in this regard (ibid., 131). I suggest that it is important to give people as honest and complete a description of what you are doing as you can, particularly when they specifically ask for such an explanation.

However, people will develop their own explanations of what researchers are doing, and these are often much-simplified versions of the explanations given by the researchers themselves. It is very common for research participants to reduce the sometimes quite involved explanations given by researchers simply to the explanation that they are "writing a book" about the community or some aspect of it. For example, this was both William Foote Whyte's (1943:300) and my own experience. It is important to bear in mind that people may reduce your best and most complete explanations to much simpler, less accurate, and perhaps inaccurate ones. It can also be dangerous to give simplified explanations of what you are doing. For example, if you simply tell people that you are writing a book about them, when they learn specific details of what you are writing about, they may believe that you have misled them. They will naturally wonder why you would want to do so and wonder if you have some ulterior motive. Be honest and give as complete and accurate a description of what you are doing as you can, but recognize that people are going to interpret and possibly misinterpret this. Continuously monitor their definitions of you, as these may change over time, and view your efforts at impression management as an ongoing process.

That you should approach this as a conscious effort at impression management is not to suggest that this should be some sort of cold-blooded Machiavellian manipulative strategy. Like Polsky, I argue that it is important to be honest with people. This is imperative both ethically and with reference to managing danger. Being dishonest is more dangerous than being honest, because it creates the possibility of being caught out in a lie. By extension, acting ethically is also safer than acting unethically.[6] Be as honest and ethical as possible, bearing in mind that it is your research participants' definition of these things that you should seek to conform to rather than your own. Of course, this may raise other dangers, for example, when the definitions of what is ethical differ between the group studied and other groups in society, particularly between the group studied and the authorities.

Being honest is relatively simple as long as you have nothing to hide. This was not a problem during my first period of fieldwork, but it became one during the second period because I needed to camouflage my research with the IPLO. I told the authorities vaguely that I was studying aspects of political culture; the IPLO and a few trusted friends knew I was working with the IPLO; and I told everyone else I was doing research on Republican martyrs and the cultures of terror and resistance. In most fieldwork situations today, marked as they are by conflict, it will probably prove to be impossible to be completely truthful with everyone. Nonetheless, it is a good danger management strategy to be as truthful as possible.

Along with honesty, flexibility can be important in danger management. Consider how far you are prepared to modify your interests, methods, and goals to adapt to dangerous contingencies that may arise. Doing research in a dangerous environment may produce situations in which researchers must consider modifying or perhaps even compromising their work. These are difficult decisions to make, and they may be fateful both for the research and for the researcher. Polsky discusses flexibility, summing it up in the comment that "a final rule is to have few unbreakable rules." He points out that you should revise your plans "according to the requirements of any particular situation" and recognize that you will probably encounter "unanticipated and ambiguous situations for which one has no clear behavioral plan at all" (1967:133).

While in the field, take precautions to secure your field notes and recordings. To do so is, of course, required to protect your research participants, but it may also be necessary to protect yourself. This issue is discussed by Jenkins (1984), who suggests that one should be selective in information gathering. He points out that some information should not be used at all and recommends that information of this sort should not be recorded. Some information is best kept only in one's head. When sensitive information is recorded, it is imperative to protect research participants' anonymity. Jenkins (ibid., 156) suggests that one carry around only the current day's notes, and it is probably advisable in some cases that you never have more than a few weeks' notes in your possession at any time while in the field. Your notes can be kept under lock and key, and arrangements can be made to periodically remove them from the field (perhaps by mailing them off or by depositing them in a safe deposit box).

Consider the possibility that some dangers may not end once you return from the field. There may be those at home who object to your research, and they may threaten you as well. (For example, I have been threatened by Loyalists since I left Belfast.) Also, consider the possibility that ethical and other considerations may mean that you will not be able to publish your findings.

If you intend to do research on political topics, particularly if you intend to do "partisan anthropology" or participate in political activities, it goes without saying that the dangers are correspondingly greater.[7] In reference to "partisan anthropology," the Association of Social Anthropologists' book on ethnographic research notes that "siding with a guerrilla movement . . . can be dangerous to oneself as well as to one's objectivity" (Ellen 1984:80). It is interesting to note that the usual concern is not that such involvement may be dangerous but rather that it may not be "objective." It should be kept in mind that one does not actually have to be a member or supporter of a political organization to be at risk from their enemies. Association, even if purely "objective," can be dangerous in itself. In some cases the status of an outsider or "objective scientific observer" provides a degree of protection, but do not count on it. And if you are actually a participant, your status as a social scientist will probably offer you no protection at all.

One might think that neutrality is a good danger management strategy, but this is not always the case. For example, June Nash, in what is perhaps the best account by an anthropologist of managing dangers encountered while conducting fieldwork in a politically sensitive environment, notes,

> In Bolivia it was not possible to choose the role of an impartial observer and still work in the tin mining community of Oruro, where I had gone to study ideology and social change. . . . The polarisation of the class struggle made it necessary to take sides or to be cast by them on one side or the other. In a revolutionary situation, no neutrals are allowed. (1976:150)

By contrast, Frances Henry (1966) discusses research in a situation of conflict between the government and trade unions in Trinidad. She notes,

> Commitment to the unions . . . could conceivably have led to loss of freedom, detention, or, at the very least, deportation. . . . On the other hand, commitment to the government could have resulted in loss of rapport with union officials. Identification with either faction can lead to serious personal difficulties and it obviously limits one's research freedom. (Ibid., 553)

Henry was able to establish rapport with both sides and discusses how she got around attempts to get her to abandon her neutrality. Basically, she did so by expressing "sympathy or agreement with persons on both sides" (ibid.). In face-to-face interactions with her research participants, she expressed sympathy with them, even though they had conflicting points of view. While Henry maintains that in fact she was "neutral," this was not the image she presented to her research participants. Rather, she misled her informants by presenting an image of being on their side when she knew that she was not. Besides the ethical questions this raises, Henry admits that this was dangerous, and I would not recommend it.

In some cases, professing neutrality may be a good danger management strategy; in others, it may not be. In some cases, you may want to tell some people that you are neutral and others that you are not. It may sound like a case of "situational ethics," but I had no qualms about telling British soldiers on the streets of Belfast who inquired as to my personal politics that I was a "neutral social scientist" while at the same time letting my research participants in the ghettos know that I sympathized with their situation.

When conducting research based on participant observation in communities involved in political conflicts, it is generally the case that, as Nash, myself, and many others have found, "no neutrals are allowed." As Glazer (1970:314) notes, "In times of heightened group antagonism there is little room for neutrality." This does not necessarily mean that you have to become a partisan. In my case, it was sufficient to communicate in various ways to people where my "sympathies" lay; that is, with them. Whether or not you take sides, those actively involved in the situation are going to define whose side they think you are on. They will act toward you on the basis of this definition, regardless of your professions of neutrality.

Gerrit Huizer (1973), a social psychologist who has done fieldwork in several Latin American countries, including El Salvador and Chile, provides illumination here. When he worked in a village in El Salvador, government officials often warned him of the "dangers" of living among the peasants. Despite these warnings, he chose not to carry a pistol like government officials did. Instead, he "relied mostly on the common human sympathy" he felt for the villagers. Basically, Huizer's approach to handling danger is to gain people's confidence by convincing them that you are "on their side." This is done by sincerely identifying with their interests, understanding and sympathizing with their problems and grievances, and showing them that you are willing to act accordingly (ibid., 21, 28). I think that this is quite the most common approach taken by anthropologists today, and it can be very effective as a danger-ameliorating approach to fieldwork.

When working in a community in which guerrilla organizations are present, you must learn to walk softly. Be sensitive to what sorts of questions may be asked and what sorts are taboo. For example, I found that it was all right to ask people what they thought of the IRA and INLA, if they did or did not support them and why, about the role the guerrillas played in the community, and about criticisms they had concerning them. But I did not ask questions about things like arms and explosives, or about who might be a guerrilla or actively involved with them. If you want to make direct contact with guerrillas, it is best to make it known that you are interested in this and then wait until they come (or do not come) to you. If you do make contact (which is illegal in most cases), you must be flexible and honest with them.

In situations in which insurgencies are going on, field-workers may have to deal with both the insurgents and the authorities combating them at the same time and this can be a very difficult task. Often, if you become associated with one, this alienates you from the other. In many field situations the authorities represent a significant source of danger. This warning is particularly true if you are studying or involved with political organizations. For example, Arnold Ap, an anthropologist in West Papua, was tortured and killed by the Indonesian army in 1984, as a result of his association with the Free Papua Movement (OPM). The army claimed that he was "a known OPM helper" (Osborne 1985:xiv). And in 1980, Miriam Daly, a lecturer at the Queen's University of Belfast, was assassinated, probably by intelligence agents, as a result of her involvement with the Irish Republican Socialist party (Faligot 1983:98).

Just as I found in my research, Polsky found that most of the risk in his fieldwork came from the authorities rather than from his research participants. He notes that "most of the danger for the field worker comes not from the cannibals and head-hunters but from the colonial officials" (1967: 145). In his particular case, he found that most of the risk came from the police rather than from the "career criminals" that were his research participants.

> The criminologist studying uncaught criminals in the open finds sooner or later that law enforcers try to put him on the spot—because, unless he is a complete fool, he uncovers information that law enforcers would like to know, and, even if he is very skillful, he cannot always keep law enforcers from suspecting that he has such information. (Ibid.)

The dangers emanating from the authorities include the risks of intimidation, physical assaults, arrest, interrogation, torture, prosecution, imprisonment, and even execution or assassination. Other dangers include being defined as a guerrilla "sympathizer" or being accused of "giving aid and comfort to the enemy," as a result of which the authorities may revoke their permission for the research. These dangers should be recognized, and efforts should be made to reduce them. (See Carey 1972 for a good

discussion of the legal risks faced by researchers in situations in which illegal activities occur.)

An associated phenomenon that can also generate danger is the fact
that "people tend to associate the research that a researcher is conducting
with the researcher himself" (Henslin 1972:55). As Henslin points out, if
you do research on drug users or homosexuality, you may fall under suspicion of being a drug user or homosexual yourself. If you do research on a
political movement, some, particularly those opposed to that movement,
may believe that you are a partisan. The more political or controversial a
subject one researches, the more likely one is to be suspected of bias or
partisanship.

While you are in the field, do not grow complacent about the dangers
you face, and do not treat the situation as a game or adventure. Do not
ignore potential threats when they arise: they rarely just "go away" if you
ignore them. For example, dangerous rumors may emerge at almost any
time while in the field. Whether these rumors are true or false, they should
be dealt with. If they are false, they should be publicly denied rather than
ignored. If there is some truth to the rumors, work to convince people
that you are not a threat, and if you are a direct threat, get out. James T.
Carey (1972:86–87) discusses "handling damaging rumors" in fieldwork
and makes some useful suggestions. Try to anticipate the circumstances
under which dangerous or damaging rumors are likely to arise, and then
limit your actual observations of activities and situations (e.g., illegal ones)
that might lead to these circumstances. If and when such rumors do arise,
try to get people who have vouched for you in the past to do so again.

Make a continuing effort to define and redefine risks and dangers in
light of actual experiences, and work to reduce such dangers by improving
old methods and developing new ones as your network of contacts and degree of experience expand over time. Managing the dangers inherent in
fieldwork in a context like that of Belfast is not something that can be gotten out of the way in the first few weeks in the field and then dismissed as
taken care of. On the last day of my first period of research in Belfast, I
was returning home to pack and found the street cordoned off by the
army. They would not allow me to go down the street to my house because
of the presence of a "suspect device." I argued with a sergeant about it,
and he finally said in disgust that I could go to the house if I was prepared
to take responsibility for the risk. It turned out that local children had
taped some wire to a can of paint and rolled it under an army Land Rover
as a prank.

With time, you may be able to successfully allay suspicions and reduce
some of the dangers, but new ones will continue to arise. One need not be
paranoid about the dangers involved in doing research in violent social

contexts, but a good dose of realistic appreciation goes a long way. And, all in all, it is no doubt better to be a bit paranoid about such things than it is to be a bit complacent about them.

Finally, remember that while most dangers can be mediated at least to some degree by skillful maneuver, some dangers may be beyond management. For example, despite your best efforts at danger management, simple bad luck can sometimes result in the termination of the research, or worse yet the termination of the researcher. Researchers working in dangerous environments should, like professional gamblers, recognize that their enterprise is inherently a combination of both skill and luck (Ellen 1984:97). Good luck can sometimes help overcome a lack of skill, and well-developed skills can go far to help overcome the effects of bad luck. But sometimes no amount of skill will save one from a gross portion of bad luck. What distinguishes the professional from the amateur, in both gambling and anthropology, is the concerted effort always to maximize skillful handling of the situation, while recognizing that skill alone is no guarantee of success. Danger is not a purely "technical" problem and is never totally manageable.

It might seem that most of these recommendations amount to little more than common sense. They are by no means exhaustive, but I hope that they are thought provoking or "consciousness raising" and indicative of some of the problems involved in managing danger. They are intended to be a starting point from which those considering research in dangerous contexts can map out their own strategies for conducting fieldwork safely. It should go without saying that counting on people to rely on common sense is a wholly inadequate approach to almost anything. Certainly, it is not adequate for advisers to tell their students that they should use "common sense" while they are in the field, and leave it at that. The example of the anthropologist shot in Belfast is a case in point. Some might say that his mistake was simply that he did not use common sense. My point has been that such an analysis of these cases is an inadequate response.

CONCLUSION

These observations were made in reference to my experience in Northern Ireland, where a guerrilla war has been going on now for more than twenty-three years. As I said at the beginning, there are about 120 armed conflicts in the world today. There is an urgent need for research in all of the places where these conflicts are occurring, and many other violent or dangerous locations as well.

Fieldwork is possible even in the most dangerous contexts. Anthropologists should not select themselves out of research in such contexts on the basis of stereotypes, media images, or inadequate information concerning the dangers involved. And they should not select themselves out of such research because training in managing such dangers is not provided in anthropology. Many more anthropologists could and should do fieldwork in these areas. The dangers are often exaggerated, and in most cases they are not insurmountable.

The world is not becoming a safer place for the pursuit of anthropological fieldwork, but, perhaps for that very reason, there is more need now for such research than there has ever been before. We can meet this challenge, but we should do so rationally by considering the dangers as methodological issues in their own right. The intention of this chapter has been to further our consideration of danger as a methodological issue and contribute to developing ways of minimizing risks and protecting anthropologists while they are in the field. It is not an exaggeration to say that this is, in fact, a matter of life and death.

NOTES

1. At least sixty anthropologists have died of "fieldwork mishaps" in the past decade (Howell 1990), and at least three have been killed "on the job" as a result of political violence. In 1982, Ruth First, a South African-born anthropologist and professor, was killed by a mail bomb in her office at Maputo University in Mozambique. "It is suspected that the bomb was sent by the South African secret service to end her effective political protests against apartheid" (ibid., 100). In 1984, the Melanesian anthropologist Arnold Ap was tortured and killed by the Indonesian army in West Papua, allegedly because of his association with the Free Papua Movement (OPM). In 1990, Myrna Mack, a Guatemalan anthropologist, was brutally assassinated as she was leaving the research center where she worked in that country. She had been studying the effects of the civil war on indigenous peoples. In February 1993, a former Guatemalan soldier was sentenced to twenty-five years in prison for her murder.

2. It should also be noted that Nancy Howell's *Surviving Fieldwork* is the first comprehensive study of "the risks that are taken, and the prices that are paid for doing fieldwork in the ways we do" (1990:1). It is intended to help field-workers anticipate the dangers they will face and prepare for preventing and responding to them. She shows that anthropology can be dangerous and that hundreds of anthropologists have failed to protect themselves from dangers and have been victims of fieldwork. She devotes a chapter specifically to human hazards of fieldwork, which includes descriptions and discussion of incidents involving arrest, military attack, suspicion of spying, living through political turmoil, factional conflict, and the taking of anthropologists as hostages in the field.

3. The risks and dangers of participant observation-based research in Belfast are described in detail in my article on managing danger in fieldwork (Sluka 1990).

4. Seven months after completing this research, in August 1992, Jimmy Brown was shot dead in a feud within the IPLO. This feud ultimately led to the dissolution of the organization by the IRA in November of that year.

5. In 1989, three members of Ulster Resistance—a quasi-paramilitary loyalist group set up in 1985—were charged in Paris with arms trafficking, receiving stolen goods, and conspiracy for the purpose of terrorism. They had been found in a hotel room with a mock-up of a Blowpipe shoulder-fired missile launcher, built by Protestant workers at the Shorts factory in East Belfast. With them were an American arms dealer with CIA links and a South African diplomat. Later, South Africa issued a statement rejecting allegations of links with Loyalist paramilitaries and denying they had supplied them with weapons. However, it is thought South Africans supplied Loyalists with their biggest-ever arms shipment in January 1988.

6. Conducting fieldwork in dangerous contexts raises very important ethical issues. I have struggled with these issues both personally and professionally for many years. I have chosen not to discuss the ethics of conducting research in dangerous contexts here because, in my opinion, that issue is more important than the issue of managing danger in fieldwork and therefore deserves a paper (or better yet, a book) devoted exclusively to it. Others may be of the opinion that it is inappropriate to discuss managing danger without discussing the larger issue of the ethics of conducting research in dangerous contexts. However, for the reason stated above, I have chosen to stick specifically to the topic of managing danger. The question, therefore, is, what is the relationship between ethics and managing danger?

7. The best contemporary example of drastic partisan anthropology is the case of the Dutch anthropologist Klaas de Jonge, who was involved in smuggling weapons and explosives for guerrillas of the African National Congress. To avoid arrest, he sought asylum in a Dutch embassy office in Pretoria, where he spent two years before being allowed to leave South Africa as part of a prisoner exchange in September 1987.

REFERENCES

Berreman, Gerald D.
    1962   "Behind Many Masks: Ethnography and Impression Management." In *Hindus of the Himalayas,* by G. Berreman, xvii–lvii. Berkeley and Los Angeles: University of California Press.

Boas, Franz
    1973   "Scientists as Spies." In *To See Ourselves: Anthropology and Modern Social Issues,* ed. Thomas Weaver, 51–52. Glencoe, Ill.: Scott, Foresman.

Carey, James T.
    1972   "Problems of Access and Risk in Observing Drug Scenes." In *Research on Deviance,* ed. Jack Douglas, 71–92. New York: Random House.

Dillon, Martin
    1990   *The Dirty War.* London: Arrow Books.

Ellen, Roy F., ed.
    1984   *Ethnographic Research: A Guide to General Conduct.* London: Academic Press.

Faligot, Roger
    1983   *Britain's Military Strategy in Northern Ireland: The Kitson Experiment.* London: Zed Press.

Glazer, Myron

1970   "Field Work in a Hostile Environment: A Chapter in the Sociology of
          Social Research in Chile." In *Student Politics in Chile,* ed. Frank Bonilla
          and Myron Glazer, 313–333. New York: Basic Books.

1972   *The Research Adventure: Promise and Problems of Fieldwork.* New York:
          Random House.

Goffman, Erving

1959   *The Presentation of Self in Everyday Life.* New York: Anchor.

Henry, Frances

1966   "The Role of the Field Worker in an Explosive Political Situation."
          Current Anthropology 7, no. 5 (December): 552–559.

Henslin, James M.

1972   "Studying Deviance in Four Settings: Research Experiences with Cab-
          bies, Suicides, Drug Users, and Abortionees." In *Research on Deviance,*
          ed. Jack Douglas, 35–70. New York: Random House.

Howell, Nancy

1986   "Occupational Safety and Health in Anthropology." Paper presented
          at the annual meetings of the American Association of Practicing An-
          thropologists, 10 April, Albuquerque, New Mexico.

1990   *Surviving Fieldwork.* Washington, D.C.: American Anthropological
          Association.

Huizer, Gerrit

1973   *Peasant Rebellion in Latin America.* Harmondsworth: Penguin. [Chapter
          2, "A Field Experience in Central America," and chapter 3, "A Field
          Experience in Chile."]

Jenkins, Richard

1984   "Bringing It All Back Home: An Anthropologist in Belfast." In *Social
          Researching: Politics, Problems, Practice,* ed. Colin Bell and Helen Roberts,
          147–163. London: Routledge and Kegan Paul.

Nash, June

1976   "Ethnology in a Revolutionary Setting." In *Ethics and Anthropology:
          Dilemmas in Fieldwork,* ed. Michael Rynkiewich and James Spradley,
          148–166. New York: Wiley and Sons.

Nietschmann, Bernard

1987   "The Third World War." *Cultural Survival Quarterly* 11 (3): 1–16.

Nordstrom, Carolyn, and JoAnn Martin

1992   "The Culture of Conflict: Field Reality and Theory." In *The Paths to
          Domination, Resistance, and Terror,* ed. Carolyn Nordstrom and JoAnn
          Martin. Berkeley, Los Angeles, and Oxford: University of California
          Press.

Osborne, Robin

1985   *Indonesia's Secret War: The Guerrilla Struggle in Irian Jaya.* Sydney: Allen
          & Unwin.

Polsky, Ned

1967   *Hustlers, Beats and Others.* Harmondsworth: Penguin.

Rolston, Bill
1991 "Containment and Its Failure: The British State and the Control of Conflict in Northern Ireland." In *Western State Terrorism,* ed. Alexander George. Cambridge: Polity Press.
Sluka, Jeffrey A.
1989 *Hearts and Minds, Water and Fish: Popular Support for the IRA and INLA in a Northern Irish Ghetto.* Greenwich, Conn.: JAI Press.
1990 "Participant Observation in Violent Social Contexts." *Human Organization* 49 (2): 114–126.
Whyte, William Foote
1943 *Street Corner Society.* Chicago: University of Chicago Press.

CONTRIBUTORS

Allen Feldman is presently conducting policy research and fieldwork and training ethnographers on the cultural construction of risk and harm reduction at the National Development and Research Institutes in New York City. He is the author of *Formations of Violence: The Narrative of the Body and Political Terror in Northern Ireland* (Chicago: University of Chicago Press, 1991), *The Northern Fiddler* (Belfast: Blackstaff Press, 1980), and the forthcoming *Towards a Political Anthropology of the Body: A Theoretical and Cultural History* (Boulder: Westview Press).

Linda Green is Assistant Professor in the Department of Anthropology and the School of International and Public Affairs at Columbia University. Her forthcoming book, *Fear as a Way of Life: Mayan Widows in Rural Guatemala*, will be published by Columbia University Press.

Beatriz Manz is Associate Professor in the Department of Geography and the Department of Ethnic Studies at the University of California, Berkeley. She is also Chair of the Center for Latin American Studies at UC Berkeley. She has written, among other books, *Refugees of a Hidden War: The Aftermath of Counterinsurgency in Guatemala* (Albany: State University of New York Press, 1988).

Carolyn Nordstrom teaches Peace and Conflict Studies and Women's Studies at the University of California, Berkeley. Her previous book, *The Paths to Domination, Resistance, and Terror,* co-edited by JoAnn Martin, is a companion to this volume. She is currently completing a book on frontline warfare in Mozambique.

Elizabeth Oglesby is a doctoral student in geography at the University of California, Berkeley. She lived in Guatemala from 1986 to 1990, where she was a researcher at the Association for the Advancement of the Social Sciences (AVANCSO).

Maria B. Olujic served as the Deputy Minister of Science, Republic of Croatia, from 1991 to 1993. She is Assistant Professor at the Institute for Applied Social Research, University of Zagreb. Currently, she is an H. F. Guggenheim Fellow conducting research on sexual coercion and war in the former Yugoslavia.

Frank N. Pieke is Lecturer in the Department of Sinology at Leiden University, the Netherlands. He has carried out extensive fieldwork in the People's Republic of China, and his forthcoming book is titled *The Ordinary and the Extraordinary: An Anthropological Study of Chinese Reform and the 1989 People's Movement in Beijing* (Kegan Paul).

Antonius C. G. M. Robben is Professor of Anthropology in the Department of Cultural Anthropology at Utrecht University, the Netherlands. He is the author of *Sons of the Sea Goddess: Economic Practice and Discursive Conflict in Brazil* (New York: Columbia University Press, 1989). He is currently writing a book on political violence in Argentina during the 1970s.

Anna Simons is Assistant Professor of Anthropology at the University of California, Los Angeles. Her book *Networks of Dissolution: Mogadishu* is forthcoming (Boulder: Westview Press). She is currently at work on a book about the U.S. Army Special Forces.

Jeffrey A. Sluka is Senior Lecturer in Social Anthropology at Massey University, Palmerston North, New Zealand. He has extensive research experience in Belfast, Northern Ireland. He is the author of *Hearts and Minds, Water and Fish: Popular Support for the IRA and INLA in a Northern Irish Ghetto* (Greenwich, Conn.: JAI Press, 1989).

Ted Swedenburg is Assistant Professor of Anthropology at the American University in Cairo. He is the author of *Memories of Revolt,* on the 1936–1939 rebellion in Palestine (Minneapolis: University of Minnesota Press, in press), and co-editor of *Displacement, Diaspora, and Geographies of Identity* (Durham: Duke University Press, in press).

Cathy Winkler is Associate Professor in the Department of Sociology and Anthropology at Tuskegee University, Alabama. She has written extensively on rape and sexual violence and her book, *Raped Once, Raped Twice, and Raped a Third Time,* is forthcoming. She has also researched gendered authority in Mexico.

Joseba Zulaika teaches Anthropology and Basque Studies at the University of Nevada, Reno. He is author of *Basque Violence: Metaphor and Sacrament.* He has also written ethnographies on fishermen, hunters, soldiers, and artists.

INDEX

Absurdity, 131, 142–143
Africa Confidential, 59–60 n. 2
Ambiguity, 216, 233; in rape, 165, 176–177, 178–179
Amnesty International, 7
Anthropologist (ethnographer): dehumanizes subject, 86, 245; interprets, 36; objectifies subject, 158; as participant-collaborator, 16–17, 26, 29, 72, 76, 77, 78, 84, 206–222; as participant-observer, 31, 262–263, 264, 278–282, 286–287; personalizes subject, 33–34, 36; rapport with subject of, 31–32, 84, 85, 86, 95–96, 216, 262; role of, 263–274; seduced, 16–17, 83–84, 85–99; subject's view of, 283–284; as voice for others, 11, 12, 76, 108; as witness, 31, 248, 249, 250–251, 262, 263
Anthropology: accidental, 16, 65, 76–77; ambiguity in, 216; conflict over depiction in, 229; covert, 87; danger in, 20, 276–294; partisan, 286, 289; of violence, 3, 4–10, 12, 13–20, 106–108, 139–140, 226–229
Antiphony, 246–247
Anyanwa, K. C., 136, 142, 144
Ap, Arnold, 288, 291 n. 1
Arendt, Hanna, 120
Argentina, 81–103; dirty war in, 16–17, 81–82; the disappeared in, 81, 83, 92–93, 99; historical reconstruction in, 82–83
Artaud, Antonin, 144
Astiz, Alfredo, 91

Baker, James, 190–191
Balkans, violence in, 2. *See also* Croatia
Barry, Kathleen, 157–158
Basque violence, 206–222; by ETA, 19, 206, 207, 208, 209, 215, 216, 217, 237; in Itziar, 206, 207, 213, 216, 218
Baudrillard, Jean, 85, 88, 138
Belfast, Northern Ireland, 277–282
Benjamin, Walter, 34, 37
Berbera, 58
Berreman, Gerald D., 87
Borges, Sandra S., 158
Bourdieu, Pierre, 7, 146
Boutras-Ghali, Boutras, 59
Brown, Jimmy, 278, 281
Buber, Martin, 219
Burke, Kenneth, 214
Bush, George, 58, 59, 190

Cabarrus, Carlos Rafael, 271
Camus, Albert, 106, 131, 137
Canetti, Elias, 8
Carey, James T., 289
Carpio, Ramiro de León, 120
China: intellectuals flee, 66; fieldwork in, 65–80; protest movements in (*see* Tian'anmen Square protest); work units in, 64, 65, 66
Chinese People's Movement, 16. *See also* Tian'anmen Square protest
Cixous, Helene, 9
Clausewitz, Carl von, 90, 91, 97

Designer:	UC Press Staff
Compositor:	Prestige Typography
Text:	10/12 Baskerville
Display:	Baskerville
Printer:	Bookcrafters, Inc.
Binder:	Bookcrafters, Inc.